CRIMINAL LAW

The University of Law

CRIMINAL LAW
THIRD EDITION

Amanda Powell

The University of Law
2 Bunhill Row
London EC1Y 8HQ

British Library Cataloguing in Publication Data

A catalogue record for this book is available from the British Library

ISBN 978 1 80502 214 5

Preface

This book is part of the 'Foundations of Law' series of textbooks, designed to support postgraduates in their study of the core subjects of English law.

It is anticipated that the reader can then move on to studies for their professional examinations (eg the SQE and BSB assessments) comfortable that they have an understanding of foundational legal principles.

Each textbook aims to provide the reader with a solid knowledge and understanding of fundamental legal principles and rules. The series aims to give the reader the opportunity to identify and explore areas of critical interest whilst also identifying practice-based context.

For those readers who are students at The University of Law, the textbooks are used alongside other learning resources to best prepare students to meet outcomes of the Postgraduate Diploma in Law and related programmes.

We wish you every success as you learn about English Law and in your future career.

The legal principles and rules contained within this textbook are stated as at 1 May 2025.

Contents

Table of Cases

Table of Legislation

1 Introduction to Criminal Law and the Criminal Justice System

LEARNING OUTCOMES

When you have completed this chapter, you should be able to:

- appreciate the social and practical context and technical nature of criminal law;
- explain how the criminal justice system operates.

1.1 Introduction

Crimes, and those who commit them, make the news headlines on a daily basis. Many of you will already be aware of certain offences and will have an understanding of how the criminal justice system of England and Wales works, from your reading of press reports and viewing of media programmes, both real and fictional. However, the public perception of crime and the reality may be very different, and most people will not appreciate that the total of all reported crime has fallen significantly since its peak in 1995. Despite this, there are certain groups who are more at risk, for example, students are the most statistically likely group to become a victim of crime against property, and a male aged between 16 and 25 is most at risk of becoming a victim of violent crime.

The criminal justice system covers criminal procedure, the law of evidence, the law relating to sentencing and the substantive criminal law. However, this textbook will deal mainly with the last of these aspects, including analysing the elements that must be present to convict a person of a particular crime and any possible defences that may be pleaded to avoid conviction. For example, the offence of murder raises (amongst others) the following questions: What does a person have to do to commit murder? What state of mind is needed before they can be convicted of murder? Could that person avoid a murder conviction by claiming that they were drunk at the time they killed someone? What if they claim the victim 'provoked' them in some way – would that make a difference?

These issues will be considered in relation to every offence covered so you have a clear understanding of when a person is guilty of a crime as well as those situations where they may escape liability.

A large part of substantive criminal law is based on decisions made by the appeal courts, and we will therefore look briefly at the criminal appeal system to enable you to understand the importance of the decisions of these courts to the substantive law. However, this textbook does not analyse the law of evidence in any detail, and you do not need to concern yourselves with whether a defendant's story will be believed. You will simply be deciding whether, on the facts given, the elements of an offence are present and whether a defence may be available.

As well as studying the current law, at times you will also be referred to proposals for change and encouraged to evaluate your views on whether you regard it as satisfactory or not. For example:

- Do you believe there should be criminal liability if a person fails to act to rescue someone in need?
- How do you think the 'mercy killing' of a terminally ill person should be treated by the criminal courts? Should the mercy killer be treated in the same way as a mass murderer, and receive a mandatory life sentence?

Criminal law is an interesting and stimulating area of law and we hope you will enjoy studying it. As you do so, you will also be acquiring and practising some vital skills necessary for any lawyer, in whatever area of law you choose to practise in the future. These will include statutory interpretation, the critical reading of cases, an ability to state and explain your opinion and, very importantly, solving legal problems.

1.2 What is a crime?

There are some forms of behaviour that most people would instantly recognise as a crime deserving of punishment, such as deliberately killing someone without excuse (murder) or having sexual intercourse with a woman who does not consent (rape). But what if they just shouted at the victim? This scenario could give rise to an assault charge if the victim thought that the defendant might use violence against them; if not, this is unlikely to be classed as criminal behaviour. What if the defendant drops a pint glass onto the floor whilst drinking at the pub? This could be a pure accident, in which case the behaviour is not blameworthy. Alternatively, the defendant may have broken the glass deliberately or recklessly, thereby satisfying the requirements of an offence of criminal damage.

Although there has been considerable discussion over the years as to what the definition of a crime should be, the consensus is that a crime is committed against society: a public wrong deserving of punishment rather than an act which could be compensated with money under the civil law. Sometimes there can be an overlap between those situations that amount to a criminal offence and those which are dealt with by the civil courts. For example, a person could face criminal prosecution for assault, but the victim could also bring a civil claim for compensation for the injuries suffered and an order that the defendant keeps away in the future.

Criminal proceedings are usually brought by a public official, often the Crown Prosecution Service (CPS). Once charges have been laid, the case can proceed to trial even if the victim does not want the matter to be taken any further. If the defendant does not plead guilty, there will be a trial and a final verdict. A criminal sanction will be imposed, and these are designed to meet a number of different requirements: to punish offenders, to reduce crime (including by deterrence), to reform and rehabilitate offenders, to protect the public and to enable offenders to make reparation to persons affected by their offences. Imprisonment, community sentences such as completing unpaid work, and fines (paid to the court) can all be imposed.

1.3 Why criminalise certain behaviour?

The main 'goal' of criminalisation is often said to be the protection of society, namely that people will be deterred from behaving in a way that is unacceptable or potentially dangerous to others if they know they will be punished for it. Another important reason for imposing criminal liability is to punish those who have caused harm or loss either to people or to property. Both of these could be used to explain, for example, the existence of the crimes of murder and theft.

However, many criminal offences have been created as a reaction to public opinion, such as increased legislation on the possession of knives, and a strengthening of the law of corporate manslaughter. Furthermore, conduct may be decriminalised as a result of more enlightened public attitudes, for example, the lowering of the age of consent for homosexual persons. Thus, the law reflects the opinions and beliefs of society generally as to what should and should not be classed as criminal behaviour at that moment in time. A person found guilty of such a criminal offence can be punished by removal from society (imprisonment) or by other, lesser, forms of punishment or rehabilitation/education, for example, unpaid community work or attending drugs rehabilitation programmes.

However, there are some offences that do not seem to achieve any of the goals of criminalisation, such as the driver who commits a speeding offence by exceeding the 30 mph speed limit by driving at 34 mph. The punishment is often minor (a small fine and three penalty points on a driving licence are the norm), it is arguable whether the driver is rehabilitated or educated in the dangers of speeding, and it does not prevent similar offences as a significant number of drivers regularly break the speed limit without worrying that this is a crime. Of course there are differing views: these offences are justified as they exist to protect society, specifically other road users and pedestrians.

Attitudes on the criminalisation of certain forms of behaviour will often be influenced by our own experiences and by our moral (and sometimes religious) views, but there are two main schools of thought on the reasons for criminalisation.

1.3.1 The moralist approach

This approach seeks to criminalise conduct that is regarded as morally blameworthy even if no harm has been caused. For example, the moralist approach approves of the criminal liability that attaches to being found drunk and disorderly contrary to s 91(1) of the Criminal Justice Act 1967, and of the offence contrary to s 9 of the Sexual Offences Act 2003 committed when a boy (aged just 18) has sexual intercourse with his consenting girlfriend aged 15 years and 11 months.

The approach may be criticised as an invasion of privacy. Indeed, in a leading report on the criminalisation of homosexual activity, the Wolfenden Committee on Homosexual Offences and Prostitution of 1957 commented that:

> It is not ... the function of the law to intervene in the private lives of citizens, or to seek to enforce any particular pattern of behaviour, further than is necessary.

1.3.2 The utilitarian approach

The Wolfenden Committee also highlighted that the purpose of the criminal law was:

> ... to preserve public order and decency, to protect the citizen from what is offensive or injurious, and to provide sufficient safeguards against exploitation and corruption of others, particularly those who are particularly vulnerable.

This statement appears to support the second school of thought, namely the utilitarian approach which criminalises conduct that, in addition to being blameworthy, also causes identifiable harm. Into this category would fall offences such as rape, murder, assault, theft and criminal damage, as all involve harm being inflicted against a person or property.

In reality, criminal behaviour will usually be both blameworthy and potentially harmful, but it is important to be aware that, if the moralist approach is followed, there is no need for specific harm to be identified.

Later in this textbook, you will see the operation of these two schools of thought in the judgments of the House of Lords in *R v Brown* [1994] 1 AC 212 which concerns the defence of consent to assault. The majority of the judges, represented by the judgment of Lord Templeman, adopt a moralist stance; whilst the minority view as expressed by Lord Mustill reflects the utilitarian approach.

1.4 The Rule of Law

The Rule of Law is a fundamental aspect of the criminal law. There should be no criminal liability except for conduct specifically prescribed by law; and the law should be clear, with any ambiguity being interpreted in favour of the defendant. A defendant must not be punished for being wicked or acting wickedly unless their behaviour falls within the definition of a criminal offence. For this reason, offences should not be created to have retrospective effect; if you smoke a cigarette today and this becomes a crime tomorrow, you should not be guilty of that offence on the basis of today's smoking. Furthermore, there can be no criminal liability unless the defendant is convicted following a proper trial according to the law, and the penalty on conviction must be within the limits prescribed by law.

1.5 The classification of offences

Although this textbook does not cover criminal procedure in any detail, you may encounter certain terms that relate to the classification of different offences, and these are explained here.

Some criminal trials are listed before a judge and jury in the Crown Court and others take place in the magistrates' court. Although all criminal cases begin in the magistrates' court, the final trial venue will depend upon the type of crime with which the defendant is charged (and possibly on where the defendant wants to be tried).

All criminal cases are classified as summary only, either-way or indictable only offences and this is primarily governed by s 17 of the Magistrates' Courts Act 1980.

1.5.1 Summary only offences

Summary only offences are those which are regarded as less serious crimes. Such offences must be tried in the magistrates' court and not in the Crown Court. (There are exceptions to this rule but they fall outside the scope of this textbook.) Although many of these are motoring offences, such as driving without due care and attention, threatening to inflict violence on another individual (assault) is a summary only offence, as is causing criminal damage to property where the cost of the damage is no higher than £5,000.

In the magistrates' court, cases are usually heard by three lay magistrates who are not required to have any legal qualifications. They rely on their legal adviser to advise them on points of law. Alternatively, the matter could be dealt with by a district judge (magistrates' court) who is a qualified solicitor or barrister.

Although summary only offences are generally regarded as less serious crimes, in recent years there has been increased pressure to push more cases to be tried in the magistrates' courts as it is quicker and less expensive than a Crown Court trial.

1.5.2 Either-way offences

Either-way offences are the middle range of offences which could be tried in the magistrates' court or in the Crown Court. These offences include theft (other than low-value shoplifting), dangerous driving, burglary and certain types of assault.

The final venue for the trial of either-way offences is laid down by ss 18–22 of the Magistrates' Court Act 1980 (as amended). At present, assuming the defendant is pleading not guilty, the venue for trial will depend initially on whether the magistrates' court is prepared to deal with the case. The magistrates will take account of whether they believe they can cope with the legal and factual complexities of the case and specifically whether, given the seriousness of the case, their sentencing powers would be adequate if the defendant were to be found guilty.

If the magistrates decide they are not able to deal with the matter, the defendant will be told that the trial must take place in the Crown Court. This will usually happen if the magistrates conclude that the offence would merit a higher sentence than they could impose if the defendant was found guilty. The maximum sentence that a magistrate can impose is six months' imprisonment for any one offence. Thus, if a person is charged with an offence of burglary (for example) and the magistrates decide that a prison sentence of say 12 months would be an appropriate punishment, they must decline jurisdiction (refuse to conduct the trial) and send the case to be dealt with in the Crown Court.

If the magistrates are prepared to keep the matter, believing their powers of sentencing are adequate to deal with the case, the final decision as to where the trial is held will rest with the defendant, who can decide whether they want to be tried by the magistrates or in the Crown Court. Some defendants opt for a Crown Court trial in this situation as there is a widely held belief that members of a jury, who are drawn from the public, will be more sympathetic to a defendant's case than the magistrates would be.

In the Crown Court, the judge will decide all issues of law, for example whether certain evidence can be referred to in court. However, it is the jury who decide the facts of a case; whether, on the evidence that they hear, the defendant should be found guilty or acquitted. This system is different to that in the magistrates' court where the magistrates decide all issues of law and fact.

1.5.3 Indictable only offences

The final group of offences, those which are classified as indictable only, are the most serious crimes such as murder, rape and robbery. These must be tried in the Crown Court before a judge and jury.

1.6 Burden and standard of proof

The defendant's guilt is determined by the magistrates or a jury who assess the evidence put before them. Before convicting the accused of an offence, there must be proof that the accused committed the criminal behaviour with the required guilty state of mind.

1.6.1 Legal burden of proof

In a criminal case, the burden of proving that a defendant is guilty of an offence usually rests with the prosecution. This burden extends to proving the guilty conduct and necessary state of mind required to establish the criminal offence, and also to disproving any potential defences that might be available to the defendant.

The main authority on this point is *Woolmington v DPP* [1935] AC 462, a case in which the defendant was charged with murder, having killed his wife by shooting her. The House of Lords stated that it was for the prosecution to prove that the defendant had intended to kill his wife (or at least that he intended to cause her really serious harm); it was not for the defendant to prove that it had been an accident. In his judgment, Viscount Sankey LC said:

> Throughout the web of the English criminal law one golden thread is always to be seen, that is the duty of the prosecution to prove the prisoner's guilt.

There are some situations, however, where the defendant does have to prove a defence. At common law, the defendant must prove the defence of insanity if they wish to rely upon this defence to evade criminal liability. There are also some statutory defences where the burden is on the defendant to prove the defence exists, for example, if the defendant wants to rely on the defence of diminished responsibility to the offence of murder.

Despite these exceptional cases, the prosecution always has to adduce evidence of the defendant's guilty conduct and (usually) their guilty state of mind.

1.6.2 Standard of proof

Where the burden of proof falls on the prosecution, the court must be satisfied beyond reasonable doubt that the defendant should be convicted of the offence charged. This is a very high standard and, if the court is in any reasonable doubt after hearing all the evidence of the case, the defendant must be acquitted as the prosecution has not discharged its burden.

Even if the defendant does have a burden of proof to discharge, the standard of proof is lower than that which has to be met by the prosecution. If the defendant is required to prove a defence, they need only do so on a balance of probabilities, so that it is more likely than not that the defence exists.

1.6.3 Evidential burden

Although the defence rarely has a burden of proof to discharge, the defendant will often have an evidential burden imposed on them. This simply means that the defence must raise some evidence of a fact in issue (usually by the defendant and/or someone else giving evidence in the witness box) so as to convince the court that the matter deserves consideration. Thereafter, the prosecution must disprove the issue beyond reasonable doubt.

The evidential burden often arises when the defendant is raising a specific defence such as using reasonable force in self-defence.

Example

The Crown has evidence that Ellen hit Oksana causing Oksana to suffer a black eye, and has decided to charge Ellen under s 47 of the Offences Against the Person Act 1861 (assault occasioning actual bodily harm). The prosecution must prove the following elements beyond reasonable doubt:

(a) That Ellen hit Oksana.

(b) That Oksana suffered an injury.

(c) That Ellen had the necessary state of mind to be guilty of the offence (for example, that she intended to hit Oksana or was reckless in hitting her).

In the witness box, Ellen claims that she only hit Oksana because Oksana had threatened Ellen and was about to slap her. Ellen is raising the issue of self-defence. By saying this in evidence, Ellen has satisfied the evidential burden placed upon her, so now it is up to the prosecution to show, beyond reasonable doubt, that the self-defence argument is not valid.

1.7 Criminal appeals

Because many of the principles considered in this textbook were established by judges sitting in the criminal appeal courts, it is important to understand the main routes of appeal that are available in a criminal case. These differ depending on whether the appeal is by the prosecution or defence, and also where the original trial took place.

A basic awareness of the options available to the appeal courts will assist in understanding the cases that appear in this book:

(a) If (on appeal against a conviction by a jury) the Court of Appeal holds that the judge's direction contained an error of law, the appeal must normally be allowed and the conviction quashed.

(b) However, the appeal can be dismissed and the conviction upheld if the Court of Appeal is certain that the conviction is safe because the only possible verdict that a properly directed reasonable jury could have reached would have been one of 'guilty'. In other words, even if there has been an error, the conviction can still be upheld if the Court of Appeal applies what is known as the 'proviso'.

(c) If a conviction is quashed there is a general power to order a retrial in such circumstances.

(d) The Crown cannot appeal against a jury's verdict of not guilty, but the Attorney-General can make a reference to the Court of Appeal to settle (clarify) a point of law for the future. These cases are cited as *Attorney-General's Reference (No 1 of 1999)*, for example. However, whatever happens on such a reference, the defendant remains acquitted.

(e) Either side can appeal to the High Court (King's Bench Division) on a point of law against a decision by magistrates. It is important to note here that if the magistrates acquit the defendant and the prosecution refers the matter on a point of law to the High Court, it can result in the reversal of the magistrates' decision (unlike Crown Court acquittals).

(f) A defendant can appeal against their sentence. If the sentence is imposed by a magistrates' court, the appeal lies to the Crown Court; but if the sentence is imposed following a jury trial (Crown Court), the appeal is to the Court of Appeal. Unlike a defendant's appeal to the Crown Court against sentence, if the defendant appeals to the Court of Appeal against sentence, the sentence will either be confirmed or reduced; it cannot be increased.

(g) Following a Crown Court trial, the prosecution has no right of appeal against sentence but can ask the Attorney-General to refer the sentence to the Court of Appeal if it is considered that the sentence is 'unduly lenient'.

1.8 Criminal Cases Review Commission

The Criminal Cases Review Commission (CCRC) is an independent body established by s 11 of the Criminal Appeals Act 1995. Its role is to enquire into a case and possibly refer it to the Appeal Courts, usually once all normal avenues have been exhausted.

If an accused was convicted following a Crown Court trial and all appeals were subsequently refused, the defendant could now ask the CCRC to investigate their case. If the CCRC decides the conviction may be unsafe, it can refer the matter back to the Court of Appeal for re-consideration, and that Court has exactly the same powers as it would have on appeal by the defendant (see above).

The CCRC can perform a similar function following a conviction by a magistrates' court but here the matter would be referred to the Crown Court.

The CCRC is involved in miscarriage of justice cases. Previously, the Home Secretary performed this role and dealt with cases such as the Guildford Four, Birmingham Six and Bridgwater Four. When new evidence came to light casting doubt on the safety of the convictions, these cases were referred back to the Court of Appeal long after the defendants had exhausted their rights of appeal.

Since its creation, the CCRC has been instrumental in the quashing of many convictions including that of Derek Bentley, hanged in 1953 for the murder of PC Sidney Miles; Ryan James, convicted in 1995 of murdering his wife; and Sally Clarke, convicted of murdering her sons, primarily on the basis of expert evidence relating to sudden infant death syndrome. This evidence was eventually found by the Court of Appeal to be unreliable and led to the quashing of Ms Clarke's conviction and a review of many other cases involving sudden infant deaths.

1.9 Proposals for reform

When studying the various aspects of criminal law, it will become apparent that some decisions of the Appeal Courts are widely regarded by academics and others as badly flawed because the decision is incoherent, illogical, unclear, or contradicts previous authorities. Some decisions can be explained only as having been decided on grounds of public policy. When reading articles and books, you will find academic commentary on these cases, and also on what the author thinks the law should be.

On occasion, references will be made to proposals for change. Most of these have come from the Law Commission – a body which endeavours to reform aspects of the criminal law to redress the problems outlined above. Examples are the report by the Commission in 2002 on issues relating to fraud, and in 1995 on the proposed changes to the law relating to corporate liability for manslaughter. These reports contributed to the implementation of the Fraud Act 2006 and the Corporate Manslaughter and Corporate Homicide Act 2007, considered later in this textbook. A further major topic for the Law Commission was the law relating to homicide (murder and manslaughter), and we will also study the resulting reforms to the law in this area.

Law Commission Reports are often helpful to explain the current law and its problems as well as, of course, outlining proposals for change. Remember, though, that many of these proposals have not yet been enacted.

2 General Principles: Actus Reus

LEARNING OUTCOMES

When you have completed this chapter, you should be able to:

- analyse the definition of a crime and understand the concept of actus reus, including the rules of legal and factual causation;
- explain the law relating to acts, omissions and states of affairs.

2.1 Introduction

In this chapter, you will begin your focus on the substantive criminal law, including the elements that must be proved by the prosecution to secure a conviction for a criminal offence. There is a Latin phrase that is fundamental to establishing criminal liability, namely *actus non facit reum nisi mens sit rea.* According to Lord Hailsham, as stated in the case of *Haughton v Smith* [1975] AC 476, this means 'an act does not make a man guilty of a crime, unless his mind be also guilty'. Consequently, there are usually three key components required for a conviction:

(a) guilty conduct by the defendant (actus reus);

(b) guilty state of mind of the defendant (mens rea); and

(c) absence of any valid defence.

Thus, if a person deliberately shoots their neighbour in a dispute over a property boundary, and the neighbour dies, for the offence of murder, the prosecution must prove that the accused killed a person (the actus reus), that they had the necessary mens rea (an intention to kill or cause really serious harm) and there was no valid defence (for example self-defence if it was submitted that the neighbour was about to assault the accused).

Later on in this textbook it will become apparent that sometimes a defendant can be convicted of a crime even though they have no guilty state of mind (for example, strict liability offences), but proving the actus reus of a crime is always essential to securing a conviction.

2.2 General principles of actus reus

The actus reus of every offence is different and may be found either in statute or in case law. The actus reus is essentially anything referred to in the definition of an offence other than the state of mind required of the defendant or reference to a possible defence.

Examples

(1) *The offence of criminal damage is established under s 1(1) of the Criminal Damage Act 1971:*

A person who without lawful excuse destroys or damages any property belonging to another intending to destroy or damage any such property or being reckless as to whether any such property would be destroyed or damaged shall be guilty of an offence.

The actus reus of the offence of criminal damage is therefore:

(a) *the destruction or damage of property;*

(b) *which belongs to someone other than the defendant.*

The references in the definition to 'intention' and 'recklessness' relate to the defendant's state of mind at the time of the offence and are not therefore part of the actus reus; instead they are the mens rea (state of mind) requirements which are discussed in the next chapter. The statute also includes the phrase 'without lawful excuse' and this is a reference to a defence to the crime of criminal damage.

(2) *The offence of murder is established at common law. The modern definition is as follows:*

The unlawful killing of a human being with malice aforethought [the intention to kill or to cause really serious bodily harm].

The actus reus of the crime of murder is the killing of a human being. The reference to 'malice aforethought' is concerned with the defendant's state of mind at the time of the killing and is therefore the mens rea. In addition, the use of the word 'unlawful' within the definition means essentially 'without a defence'.

2.3 Types of crimes

In most instances, the defendant must *do* something before they can be said to have committed a criminal offence; in other words, criminal liability requires a positive act by the defendant. However, although this is usually the case, it is not always so. In some cases, the actus reus of an offence may be established by proving that the defendant failed to take action, or even just by proving that a state of affairs (certain circumstances) existed. As a consequence, although the concept of actus reus is commonly referred to as the 'guilty act', this is misleading as it may be satisfied in a number of ways.

Furthermore, the actus reus of the offence may require additional circumstances to exist and/or consequences to follow from the defendant's actions before it is established. For example, for the offence of criminal damage, the defendant must not only do something (destroy or damage property) but also the circumstance must exist that the property belongs to another.

The actus reus of an offence will therefore consist of one or more of the following components:

(a) an act (or sometimes a failure to act) by the defendant;

(b) the existence of certain circumstances at the time of the defendant's conduct;

(c) certain consequences flowing from the defendant's conduct.

To identify which of the three elements listed above are needed to establish the actus reus of a particular crime, the relevant legislation should be consulted for statutory offences plus any case law which has interpreted that provision; for common law offences (established by case law), judgments of the court will assist.

2.3.1 Conduct crimes

A conduct crime usually involves an act (although it may also include an omission to act in certain situations, as will be seen later in this chapter). For most offences, the actus reus is defined so that it requires conduct on the part of the accused. To be criminally liable, the defendant must act in a particular way and an example of such an offence is perjury under s 1 of the Perjury Act 1911. The offence is satisfied if the defendant willfully makes a statement under oath that they know to be untrue. This may be regarded as a 'pure' conduct crime because it is the defendant's behaviour rather than the result itself that is criminalised, so it would make no difference whether the false evidence had any impact on the outcome of the trial or not.

2.3.2 Result crimes

Where an offence is described as a result crime, it is not enough that the defendant acts in a specific way; certain consequences must follow from that behaviour before the actus reus of the offence is established. Thus, for the offence of criminal damage, the property must be damaged or destroyed; and for murder, the defendant must have caused the deceased's death. If this element of causation cannot be established, the actus reus of the result crime is not proved. Causation issues will be considered in more detail later in this chapter.

Although offences may be labelled as 'conduct crimes' or 'result crimes', this is not always helpful as there is often an overlap. For example, an assault occasioning actual bodily harm requires conduct (such as a punch) but also a 'result', namely some harm to the victim. Furthermore, an offence may be described as a conduct crime, because the defendant must behave in a certain way, but also certain circumstances need to exist before the actus reus of the offence is established. An example is the offence of rape. The defendant's conduct is penile penetration of the vagina, anus or mouth, but the actus reus is only established if it is also proved that, at the time, the other person did not consent. The circumstances of the lack of consent must be proved as well as the penetration.

2.3.4 States of affairs crimes

Some offences do not require any conduct at all. They are defined so that the actus reus is satisfied simply by the existence of a state of affairs, or a particular set of circumstances. The effect is that the defendant may be liable even though they had no control over the situation.

For example, in *R v Larsonneur* (1933) 97 JP 206 a French citizen was deported from Ireland to England against her will. She was convicted of an offence of being found illegally in the United Kingdom despite the fact she had no choice in the matter. The actus reus of the offence in this case was established by the defendant being 'found' in the United Kingdom after leave to enter the country had been refused. The defendant of course had no control over her presence here: she had been delivered to the port of Holyhead by the Irish police and handed over to the authorities whereupon she was charged with this offence! It would be difficult to sustain an argument that the defendant's conduct in this case was voluntary in the usual sense of the word.

This case demonstrates that, in rare instances, the defendant does not actually have to do anything to be convicted. If they are found to be in a particular situation and that is enough to satisfy the actus reus requirements of an offence, the defendant will be liable even though they were not responsible.

> **_Example_**
>
> *Naomi is at a local bar, celebrating the start of the weekend. Because she is driving home, she only drinks orange juice but, unknown to Naomi, one of her colleagues adds vodka to her drink. At the end of the evening, Naomi gets into her car, which is parked on the road outside, but is so affected by the alcohol that she cannot even get the key into the ignition. She is approached by a police officer, breathalysed and found to be above the legal limit for driving.*
>
> *Although Naomi has done nothing except sit in her car, she is guilty of an offence under s 4(2) of the Road Traffic Act 1988, which makes it a crime to be in charge of a motor vehicle on a road or other public place while unfit to drive through drink or drugs. This is because the actus reus is complete as soon as Naomi gets into the car, as s 4(2) is a state of affairs offence.*

The justification for such offences is public policy; it is regarded as more important to prevent drunken or drugged motorists from driving than being concerned with unfairness to a particular individual. Such offences are, however, the exception rather than the rule. They are known as offences of absolute liability and are very unusual.

In summary, therefore, it is essential to check the definition of an offence to identify all the elements of the actus reus. These could include conduct by the defendant, the existence of certain circumstances and/or certain results occurring, or even in rare cases that a state of affairs existed at the time of the offence.

2.4 Liability for omissions

In most cases, a defendant in a criminal case will have taken positive steps in relation to a particular crime; for example, a person who uses a key to scratch the side of a car commits the actus reus of criminal damage. Similarly, in most murder cases, a defendant has stabbed, shot or beaten the victim to death.

However, as mentioned earlier, it is sometimes possible to establish the actus reus of a criminal offence where the defendant has failed to do something: in other words, they are criminally liable for a failure or omission to act. There are many statutory offences which incur liability in these circumstances, for example in road traffic situations, including failing to stop at a red light or after an accident.

There are also offences that cannot be committed by omission, such as burglary, theft, robbery and rape. This is because all these crimes require a positive act by the defendant: for example, it would be impossible to accuse a man of rape without his active participation in sexual intercourse as this is an essential element of the offence.

2.4.1 General rule

In England and Wales there is no general duty recognised by the criminal law upon a person to intervene and help someone in trouble. The effect of this is that, for example, a stranger is under no obligation to save a child drowning in a puddle even though they could easily have done so, without any risk to themselves.

Example

Patricia is walking along a pavement one cold snowy evening when she sees a young woman slip on some ice and fall into the road, knocking herself unconscious. Patricia decides to do nothing to help, despite realising the danger from any passing traffic. The woman is run over by a car and dies from her injuries. Although Patricia certainly has a moral responsibility to try to help the woman, she does not incur any criminal liability by her failure to do so.

The recent case of *R v Gallen* [2024] EWCA Crim 1096 revisited the issue of liability for omissions in relation to the common law offence of preventing the lawful and decent burial of a dead body. It was held that 'preventing' does require some positive action such as covering the body to conceal it. The judge commented that merely failing to report a death may be regarded as reprehensible, but it did not justify a departure from the principle that the law does not generally criminalise mere omissions or failures to act. Thus, seeing a body and leaving it where it lies is not enough to render a person guilty of unlawfully preventing the decent and lawful burial of the body.

To counter the harshness of the general rule, various exceptions to this principle have developed which allow the defendant to be found criminally liable for their omission.

2.4.2 Exceptions to the general rule

Traditionally, there are four recognised types of situation under the common law in which a person can commit the actus reus of a crime by failing to act.

2.4.2.1 Special relationships

Where there is a special relationship between the defendant and the victim, the defendant could incur criminal liability for failing to act.

In the case of *R v Gibbins and Proctor* (1918) 13 Cr App R 134, the defendants were convicted of murdering a 7-year-old child who died of starvation. The first defendant, Gibbins, was the child's father. The court held that, as a parent, he had a duty to care for his child. He had failed to do so and was therefore said to have committed the actus reus of murder - he had killed a human being by his omission to feed the child.

The second defendant, Proctor, was not the mother of the child but, nevertheless, she was convicted of murder due to her failure to provide food. The court said that she had assumed a duty towards the child by choosing to live with the father and by receiving house-keeping money from him. There was therefore a close relationship with the child which placed a duty on Proctor to act to care for them. Her failure to do so established the actus reus of murder.

What would have happened if Proctor had simply cohabited with Gibbins but had not received house-keeping money: would she still have a special relationship with the child? The answer to this question is not clear, but a look at some other cases suggests that the answer may be yes, although much would presumably depend on the particular facts of a case.

2.4.2.2 Voluntary assumption of care

Although it is unsurprising that the existence of a close relationship may give rise to a duty to act between parents and children, or between spouses, this principle extends further than might, perhaps, be expected. It includes those situations where a person voluntarily undertakes to care for another who cannot care for themselves, whether due to infancy, mental illness or physical disability.

In *R v Stone and Dobinson* [1977] 1 QB 354, the two defendants took in Mr Stone's sister, Fanny, to live with them. Fanny was an eccentric who suffered from anorexia. Her physical condition deteriorated and she became bed-ridden. The two defendants had physical and mental difficulties of their own and did little to assist Fanny, who eventually died of blood poisoning caused by infected bed sores. The defendants were charged with her manslaughter (causing her death), the prosecution arguing that they had failed to take proper steps to care for Fanny when they were under a duty to help her.

Both defendants were convicted. The reasoning given by the court was that a duty applied because Fanny was a blood relation to Stone, as she was his sister. Furthermore, both defendants had assumed a duty to act because Fanny was living in Stone's house and they took (limited) steps to try to care for her. The court accepted that they had made occasional but ineffectual attempts to help Fanny, for example by leaving her food and trying to get medical help. However, their failure to properly care for Fanny meant they had caused her death and were therefore liable for manslaughter.

This decision has been heavily criticised as the potential implications are wide ranging. For instance, does it mean there is a duty to care for all blood relations such as elderly parents, adult siblings and so forth? We may be under a moral duty to do so, but most people would be surprised to discover that they could face criminal charges for causing the death of a relative if, for instance, there was a family rift and they totally ignored a parent in need of care. Does the court's decision mean a duty to act applies in relation to anyone who stays in our home? What about short-term visitors? In the case of Dobinson, she seems to have been punished for her ineffectual attempts to care for Fanny: would she have been better off if she had totally ignored her and done nothing?

The full reasoning of the court is to be found in the judgment of Lane LJ:

> At the close of the Crown's case, submissions were made to the judge that there was no, or no sufficient, evidence that the appellants, or either of them, had chosen to undertake the care of Fanny.
>
> That contention was advanced by counsel for the appellant before this court as his first ground of appeal. He amplified the ground somewhat by submitting that the evidence which the judge had suggested to the jury might support the assumption of a duty by the appellants did not, when examined, succeed in doing so. He suggested that the situation here was unlike any reported case. Fanny came to this house as a lodger. Largely, if not entirely due to her own eccentricity and failure to look after herself or feed herself properly, she became increasingly infirm and immobile and eventually unable to look after herself. Is it to be said, asks counsel for the appellants rhetorically, that by the mere fact of becoming infirm and helpless in these circumstances, she casts a duty on her brother and Mrs Dobinson to take steps to have her looked after or taken to hospital? The suggestion is that, heartless though it may seem, this is one of those situations where the appellants were entitled to do nothing; where no duty was cast on them to help, any more than it is cast on a man to rescue a stranger from drowning, however easy such a rescue might be.
>
> This court rejects that proposition. Whether Fanny was a lodger or not she was a blood relation of the appellant Stone; she was occupying a room in his house; Mrs Dobinson had undertaken the duty of trying to wash her, of taking such food to her as she required.
>
> There was ample evidence that each appellant was aware of the poor condition she was in by mid-July. It was not disputed that no effort was made to summon an ambulance or the social services or the police despite the entreaties of Mrs Wilson and Mrs West.
>
> A social worker used to visit Cyril. No word was spoken to him. All these were matters which the jury were entitled to take into account when considering whether the necessary assumption of a duty to care for Fanny had been proved.

> This was not a situation analogous to the drowning stranger. They did make efforts to care. They tried to get a doctor; they tried to discover the previous doctor. Mrs Dobinson helped with the washing and the provision of food. All these matters were put before the jury in terms which we find it impossible to fault. The jury were entitled to find that the duty had been assumed. They were entitled to conclude that once Fanny became helplessly infirm, as she had by 19 July, the appellants were, in the circumstances, obliged either to summon help or else to care for Fanny themselves.

The judgment of Lane LJ suggests that the defendants in *Stone and Dobinson* might have escaped liability if they had done nothing at all to help Fanny. There appears to be no general liability towards one's relatives or persons staying at your home: it was the assumption of a duty towards Fanny by both defendants arising out of their ineffectual attempts to care for her that led to criminal liability. It is apparent from this case that the role of caring for others should not be undertaken lightly because, if done badly enough, criminal liability may result if death or injury occurs. However, an individual is not required to do a great deal to comply with their duty and absolve themselves of such responsibility. All that Stone and Dobinson needed to do in the situation in which they found themselves was to summon help, such as an ambulance or social services.

2.4.2.3 Cross-over between special relationship and voluntary assumption of care

The category of persons who may be held to have a special relationship with a victim, so as to be liable for failing to act, is still unclear. The only point which can be made with any certainty is that a parent has a special relationship with their minor child and is under a duty to act. As far as other relationships are concerned, a sensible conclusion would seem to be that a special relationship is formed if one assumes a duty to care for the victim, for example, by accepting payment or accommodation in return for caring for an individual, or perhaps where one invites a person, unable to care for themselves, to permanently live as part of one's family.

It may seem unjust that liability arises simply because the victim is a blood relative or because the defendant has offered limited hospitality to them, and the law is by no means clear in this area. Indeed, in the case of *R v Ruffell* [2003] 2 Cr App R (S) 330, it was held that a defendant who assumed a duty of trying to revive a friend who took drugs was correctly convicted of manslaughter of that friend when he failed to care for him properly.

There is one area of special relationships that causes particular difficulties. Imagine that you have assumed a duty of care towards a family member who is terminally ill and who tells you that they do not want you to take steps to help them as they wish to be left to die. If you follow your relative's instructions, could you face criminal liability for their death because you failed to act?

This situation occurred in the case of *R v Smith* [1979] Crim LR 251. Here, the defendant was charged with the manslaughter of his wife, who died after giving birth to a still-born child. There was evidence that the wife had told her husband not to seek medical attention and he had respected her wishes. By the time the wife changed her mind and the defendant called the doctor, it was too late to save her life.

The trial judge instructed the jury that, in deciding whether the defendant had been released from his duty to act to help his wife by her specific directions, they should consider her state of health. If she was capable of making rational decisions, it might be reasonable for the defendant to respect her wishes (so as not to be liable). If, however, the wife was so ill that she had lost the ability to make such decisions, it might be reasonable to override her wishes, whatever she said. In this case the jury were unable to reach a decision and so the defendant walked free, but the words of the trial judge suggest that, if the victim is capable of deciding their own fate, the defendant could be released from any duty to act established by the common law.

Another interesting point to come from the case of *Smith* is the apparent acceptance that there is a special relationship between husband and wife, and this category can therefore possibly be added to the list above. Note, however, that *Smith* is only a first instance decision and the higher courts have not ruled on this issue.

The other case that assists in determining when a defendant is released from a duty to act is that of *Airedale NHS Trust v Bland* [1993] 1 All ER 821. Tony Bland was one of the victims of the Hillsborough football stadium disaster and he suffered catastrophic injuries after being crushed in the stadium. He was diagnosed as being in a persistent vegetative state, meaning that the part of his brain which governed conscious thought had been destroyed. He had been in this condition for over three years when his doctors, with the support of his parents, applied to the court for permission to discontinue medical treatment and artificial feeding.

Doctors and medical staff are under a duty to care for their patients, either under the special relationship criteria or more likely under a contractual duty (see below), but the doctors argued that this duty should cease if it was felt not to be in the best interests of the patient. Tony Bland was assessed as having no quality of life or any prospect of improvement, so that both the doctors and Tony's parents considered it was not in his best interests to continue to sustain his life artificially.

In this case, the court accepted the medical evidence that the injuries suffered by Tony meant there was no prospect of any further conscious existence and granted permission to discontinue treatment and feeding. Tony died shortly afterwards.

The decision of the court is important for many reasons:

(a) The House of Lords (now the Supreme Court) confirmed that doctors should seek court permission before withdrawal of life-sustaining treatment such as artificial feeding, although in *Frenchay Healthcare NHS Trust v S* [1994] 2 All ER 403, the Court of Appeal accepted that there may be emergency situations where prior approval is impracticable.

(b) The judges in *Bland* also confirmed that if a patient has refused life-saving treatment, for example for religious reasons, not only is a doctor released from their duty to act but they would be committing a criminal offence of assault if they did. This view would seem to endorse that of the trial judge in *R v Smith* above.

(c) Lastly, it is clear from *Bland* that the court was only concerned with omissions to act; there is still no legal right for a doctor to take positive steps for the purpose of ending a patient's life, for example by deliberately administering an overdose of medication to a terminally ill person.

In addition to there being criminal liability for failing to act if there is a special relationship between the defendant and the victim, there are other situations where liability may arise and these are discussed next.

2.4.2.4 A contractual duty to act

If a contract of employment specifies certain obligations to act, a failure to comply with these can lead to criminal liability. Such a duty to act arises, for example, in the contracts of medical staff (to care for their patients), of the emergency services (to take all reasonable steps to maintain the safety of the public) and people such as lifeguards at local swimming pools (to act to ensure the safety of those who use the pool).

Liability for failure to act in accordance with contractual obligations was considered in *R v Pittwood* (1902) 19 TLR 37. In this case, the defendant was a railway worker who was employed to guard the gate at a level crossing. One of his contractual duties was to open and close the gate so people could pass safely. He failed to close the gate on one occasion and a person was killed by a train. The defendant was convicted of manslaughter. He was contractually obliged to act to protect members of the public and was therefore liable in criminal law for his failure to act (or more accurately, in this case, for the *consequences* of his failure to act, as he was prosecuted and convicted for causing the death which followed).

In modern society, people employed as carers or healthcare professionals are contractually bound to act and could be liable for a homicide offence if they fail to take steps to prevent those in their care from suffering harm.

> ***Example***
>
> *Sandra is a care worker who is employed by Great Care Ltd. She is responsible for visiting a number of elderly patients during the day. However, Sandra is rather lazy and often misses out those who are suffering from dementia as she knows they will not be able to inform on her. Muriel is 86 years of age and is scheduled to receive two visits a day to ensure that she eats and drinks properly. However, Sandra fails to attend many of these appointments and, as a consequence, Muriel dies of dehydration. Because Sandra is under a contractual duty to care for Muriel, she is liable under the criminal law for her omission.*

2.4.2.5 Creation of a dangerous situation

Thus far, we have identified three situations where the criminal law can prosecute someone for their omission. A more recent development is the duty that arises if a person creates a dangerous situation. If the defendant does something that endangers the victim and they are aware of it, they are under a duty to take reasonable steps to prevent the harm from occurring.

> ***Example***
>
> *Dhruv parks his car on a hill but forgets to put on the handbrake. As he walks away, he realises his omission but, because he is in a hurry, he does not return to the car. He walks past two children playing outside their house a little further down the hill. A few minutes later the car rolls down the hill and hits one of the children, killing them. Dhruv caused the child's death by failing to put on the handbrake, but only if Dhruv is under a duty to act can he be held criminally liable.*

In this situation, because Dhruv has created a dangerous situation by failing to apply the handbrake, the law imposes a duty on him to take steps to remove the danger. However, Dhruv is only required to return to the vehicle and pull the handbrake on; it is his failure to do this that leads to criminal liability.

In *R v Miller* [1983] 1 All ER 978, the defendant was a squatter who lay on a mattress in his squat, began to smoke a cigarette and fell asleep. He awoke to find that the lighted cigarette had fallen onto the mattress causing it to smoulder. Instead of taking steps to remedy the situation, Miller simply got up, moved to another room and went back to sleep! The house caught fire but fortunately the defendant was able to escape. He was subsequently charged with causing criminal damage to the property.

Miller argued that he could not be convicted as he had not actually done anything. He conceded that he had failed to act but submitted that there was no criminal liability for such an omission. The House of Lords disagreed. Upholding his conviction for criminal damage, the judges stated that the defendant had created a dangerous situation by smoking in bed and, having realised this, he was then under a duty to take steps reasonably available to him to prevent further damage.

What steps will be reasonable will obviously depend on the circumstances in which the defendant finds themselves. Awaking to a small fire, Miller might have been expected to tackle the problem himself (if such action posed no danger to him), but if he had woken to find the house already ablaze, he may only be required to telephone the fire service after escaping.

It is important to note that the criminal law does not expect people to be heroes in these types of situation, simply to take reasonable steps to remedy the dangerous situation that they have created.

2.5 A statutory duty to act

In addition to the common law exceptions to the general rule that a defendant is not liable for an omission, there are various situations where a legislative provision imposes a duty on individuals to act in a certain way in a given set of circumstances. Parents must care for their children under the Children Act 1989; and car drivers must stop after being involved in an accident (Road Traffic Act 1988, s 170). The statute also provides that a failure to act in accordance with these provisions will result in criminal liability.

2.6 Differences between statutory and other duties to act

There are a number of differences between failing to comply with a statutory duty to act and failing to comply with other duties to act, for example, contractual duties and special relationships. In particular, the penalties imposed by the courts are often quite different.

Failing to act when required to do so under a statutory provision will usually lead to prosecution for the omission itself, for example, failing to stop at a red light. The penalties often consist of a fine and possible endorsements on one's licence if it relates to a driving offence. Failing to act when there is a duty to do so imposed by contract or by a special relationship will usually result in criminal prosecution for the *consequences* of that omission. If the consequence is the death of a person, as in the cases of *Pittwood* and *Stone and Dobinson* referred to above, a conviction of murder or manslaughter can lead to a lengthy term of imprisonment being imposed.

There are those who consider that the way in which breaches of contractual obligations are prosecuted is unfair. Although it may be correct to hold someone criminally liable in these circumstances, they should (perhaps) be charged with an offence of 'failing to comply with a contractual duty' rather than with an offence which reflects the consequences of that failure. For example, Pittwood should have faced a charge of failing to close the crossing gate rather than a charge of manslaughter for causing the death of the victim. If this had been done, so that he had been prosecuted for the omission to act (as happens with most cases of failing to comply with a statutory duty) rather than for an offence which reflected the consequences of his failure to act (a charge of manslaughter), the sentence imposed by the court following his conviction would have been considerably lower and he would have avoided the criminal label of being a 'killer'.

2.7 Voluntary acts

Generally, where the actus reus of an offence requires conduct on the part of the defendant, whether an act or omission, liability will only accrue where the conduct is willed. All this means is that the defendant's movements must be voluntary rather than a reflex action or an act over which they have no control. It would be illogical if a person who, for example, fainted on a crowded train and fell onto someone while unconscious was prosecuted for an assault.

In the case of *Hill v Baxter* [1958] 1 QB 277, the court gave the example of a person being attacked by a swarm of bees whilst driving and said that they would not commit the actus reus of the offence of careless driving if they lost control of their vehicle as their actions would not be voluntary. Similarly, if when cutting a piece of birthday cake, the defendant's hand is grabbed by one of the party guests and the knife, while still in the hand of the defendant, is then plunged into the chest of the victim, there will be no voluntary act and no liability for assault.

Where the defendant alleges that their conduct was involuntary, they may be advised to plead the defence of automatism. Automatism can be successfully argued only if the defendant is blameless. So, for example, if the defendant, when driving home from work, suffers an attack of cramp resulting in them losing control of their vehicle and colliding with another car, the defendant will not have committed the actus reus of careless driving because their actions were involuntary and they were not to blame. But what if the defendant was driving home after completing a night shift at work and they lose control of their vehicle as a result of falling asleep? Would they be guilty of a driving offence as a result of the subsequent collision? Here the defendant's actions may still be involuntary, but in this example it can be argued that the defendant was partly to blame – upon feeling tired they should have stopped their vehicle and rested – and so the defendant could be guilty of careless driving.

2.8 Causation

In this section, the concept of causation will be discussed. Causation applies to result crimes because, as part of establishing actus reus, the prosecution must also demonstrate that the accused's act or omission actually caused the prohibited consequence.

Examples

(1) *Daria stabbed Vera (conduct) leading to Vera's death (result).*

(2) *Deshi failed to seek medical help for his daughter (omission) so that the child died (result).*

In both these examples, the act or omission led directly to the victim's death so that, in legal terms, the defendants caused the deaths. Indeed, in most cases, it will be easy for the prosecution to demonstrate that the defendant caused a consequence so as to incur criminal liability. However, there are occasions when the issue is less clear and the courts have spent some time analysing problems of causation in criminal cases. Two tests have been developed to determine causation, and both must be established before the actus reus of a result crime can be made out. It is important to emphasise that causation is an element of the actus reus and should be dealt with as such, rather than as a separate entity or as part of the mens rea.

In this chapter, the issue of causation is discussed in the context of homicide, but note that it may arise in any result crime as the general rule is that a defendant is criminally liable only if they can be shown to have caused, both in fact and law, harm to the victim.

2.8.1 Factual causation

Factual causation is the principle that the defendant cannot be considered to be the cause of an event if the event would have occurred in precisely the same way without the defendant's act or omission.

Thus, the first test to be satisfied is whether the defendant, as a matter of *fact*, caused the victim's death (or other prohibited consequence). The question to be asked here is: '*But for* the defendant's conduct, would the victim's death have occurred in the way that it did?' If the answer is 'no', factual causation will be established. If the answer is 'yes' or 'maybe', for example, if there was more than one cause of death, other matters will need to be considered before causation can be proved.

Example

Dan shoots Jimmy, a healthy 25-year-old, at point blank range and kills him instantly. Dan has caused Jimmy's death as a matter of fact and the 'but for' test is easily satisfied: but for Dan's act, Jimmy would not have died as and when he did.

In the case of *R v White* [1910] 2 KB 124, the defendant poisoned his mother's drink intending to kill her. Although she suffered a fatal heart attack after drinking a small amount of the liquid, medical evidence confirmed that her death occurred from heart failure unconnected to the poisoned drink. The defendant's actions did not contribute to his mother's death, and so he was not liable for causing it.

Clearly, everyone must die at some time; however, for factual causation to be established, the defendant's act (or omission) must accelerate the death. The courts have held that the acceleration of death must be 'significant'. In *R v Cheshire* [1991] 3 All ER 670, the Court of Appeal confirmed that 'significant' here simply meant 'more than negligible'. This is for the jury to decide as a question of fact, but a day or two can be sufficient to establish factual causation.

Example

Harriet suffocates her mother who is terminally ill with only a few days left to live. Although the success of applying the 'but for' test may be less obvious here, because Harriet's mother had 'days' to live when she was killed, it is likely that factual causation would be satisfied.

Smith and Hogan (*Criminal Law*, 14th edn) provide an example of what would be 'negligible' acceleration:

> D and V are roped together mountaineers. V has fallen over a one thousand foot precipice and is dragging D slowly after him. D cuts the rope and V falls to his death five seconds quicker than both V and D would have fallen. Any acceleration of death is killing but factors that produce a very trivial acceleration may be ignored. D's act is not a sufficiently substantive cause of V's death.

However, although this test provides some assistance in deciding whether the defendant is guilty, it is of limited value. If all the prosecution has to demonstrate is factual causation, because the test is so wide, it could catch people who in reality have only a very tenuous connection with the victim's fate.

Example

Lilian arranges to go shopping with her friend, Mimi. As Mimi is walking down the high street to meet Lilian, she is knifed by a stranger and subsequently dies.

Although it would be unfair to say that Lilian caused Mimi's death, if the factual causation question is applied (but for Lilian's action would Mimi have been killed?) the answer would be that she did cause the death. If Lilian had not invited Mimi to go shopping, she would not have been in the high street and been stabbed. Therefore, but for Lilian's actions, Mimi would not have died.

Figure 2.1 Factual causation

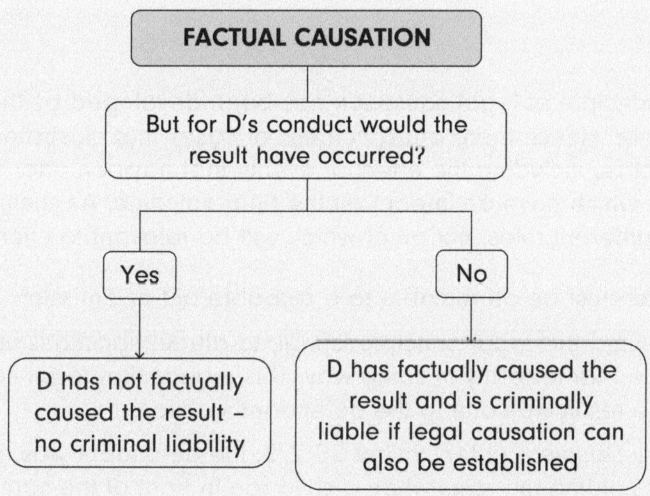

Clearly, it is wrong for a person to be held responsible for all consequences of their conduct on a never-ending basis. The law has to draw the line somewhere, and it is for this purpose that the principle of legal causation was introduced.

2.8.2 Legal causation

Satisfying the test of factual causation is only the first hurdle. To establish causation in criminal law, the prosecution must also prove that the defendant was the legal cause of death. Specifically, the defendant's conduct must be a substantial and operating cause of the consequence.

Figure 2.2 Legal causation

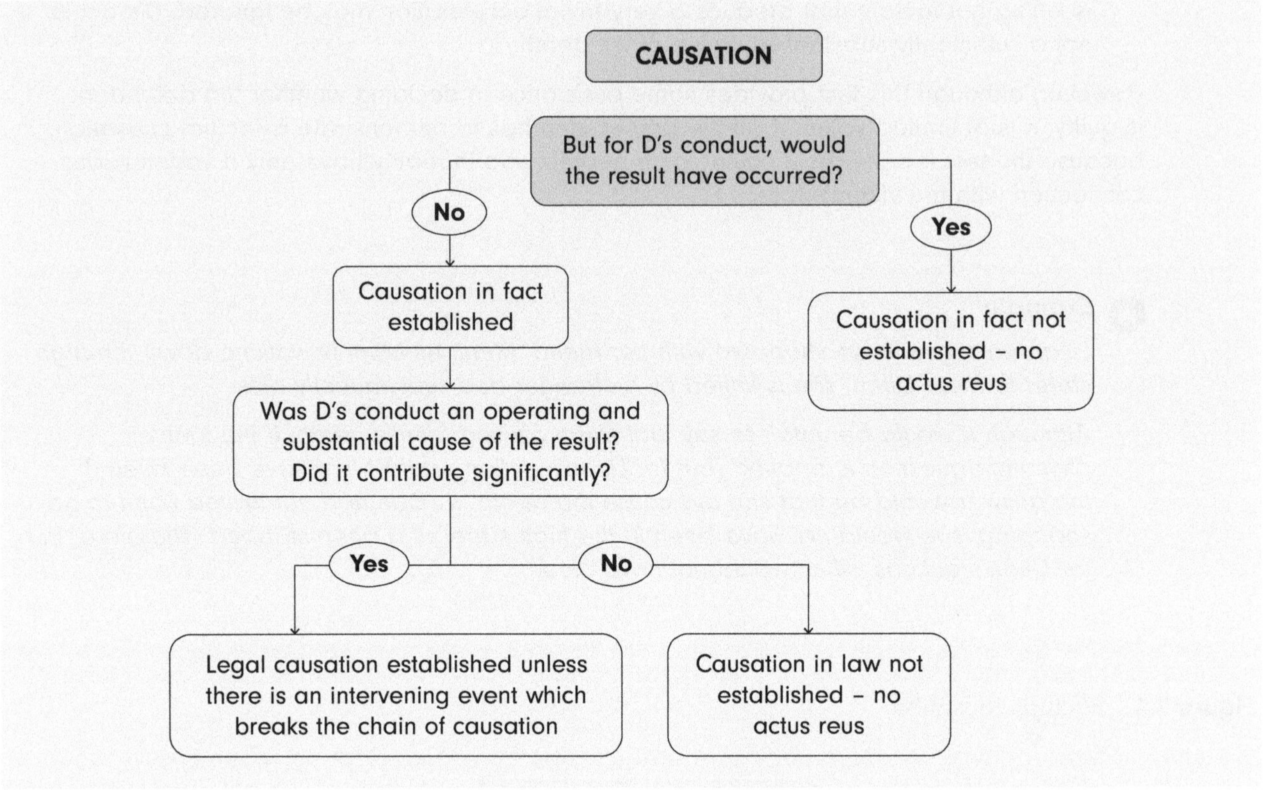

Over time, the principle of legal causation has been developed by the judges in a somewhat piecemeal manner. Hence there are a number of cases that illustrate how legal causation operates in practice, including the effect of events that happen after the defendant's involvement, but which have an impact on the final outcome. As such, legal causation is a combination of different rules, not all of which will be relevant to every situation.

2.8.2.1 The consequence must be attributable to a culpable act or omission

The rationale behind this legal principle is that, to attract sanctions under the criminal law, a person must be blameworthy in some way. This means that legal causation will only be established if the result was due to the defendant's action.

In the case of *R v Dalloway* (1847) 2 Cox CC 273, the defendant was negligently driving a horse and cart without holding the reins when a child ran in front of the cart and was killed. The jury was directed to convict for manslaughter only if they were satisfied that holding the reins would have saved the child. The jury acquitted, presumably being of the view that even though there was a culpable act, it did not cause the child's death which could not have been avoided.

2.8.2.2 The culpable act must be a more than minimal cause of the consequence

The prosecution must prove that the accused's contribution to the death of the victim is more than trivial or minimal. A defendant will be the legal cause of the consequence only if their conduct was the 'operating and substantial cause' of that result – *R v Smith* [1959] 2 QB 35 (which is considered later in this chapter) and *R v Malcherek and Steel* [1981] 2 All ER 422. Lord Lane gave judgment in the *Malcherek* case as follows:

> There is no evidence in the present case that at the time of conventional death, after the life support machinery was disconnected, the original wound or injury was other than a continuing, operating and indeed substantial cause of the death of the victim ... There may be occasions, although they will be rare, when the original injury has ceased to operate as a cause at all, but in the ordinary case if the treatment is given bona fide by competent and careful medical practitioners, then evidence will not be admissible to show that the treatment would not have been administered in the same way by other medical practitioners. In other words, the fact that the victim has died, despite or because of medical treatment for the initial injury given by careful and skilled medical practitioners, will not exonerate the original assailant from responsibility for the death.

The defendant's appeal was refused on the basis that their actions continued to be an operating cause of the victim's death.

2.8.2.3 The culpable act need not be the sole cause

There may be multiple causes of the particular result and it does not matter that the defendant's act was just one of these. This is a principle that has long been established in case law. In *R v Benge* (1865) 4 F & F 504, the defendant was a foreman of a track-laying crew and, as a result of misreading the train timetable, the track was up at a time when a train was due. The resulting accident caused death. Although the signalman and train driver were also at fault, the defendant could not rely on this to avoid liability.

More recently, in the case of *R v Pagett* (1983) 76 Cr App R 279, the defendant held his girlfriend hostage and then used her as a human shield when the police fired back at him. He was found guilty of manslaughter and the Court of Appeal commented that:

> ... in law, the defendant's act need not be the sole cause, or even the main cause, of the victim's death, it being enough that his act (or omission) contributed significantly to that result.

The effect of these principles is demonstrated in the next example.

Example

Ibrahim and Rayyan stab Nabeel who dies of his injuries.

(1) The medical evidence establishes that both inflicted fatal wounds. In this instance, legal causation is clear and both defendants are guilty of murder.

(2) The medical evidence indicates that no single stab wound caused Nabeel's death, but it is proved that both defendants hurt Nabeel causing him serious injury. Although neither the the injury inflicted by Ibrahim nor that inflicted by Rayyan would, on its own, have caused Nabeel to die, the combination of injuries inflicted in the two attacks does kill him. In this instance, both defendants have caused death as the injuries inflicted by each of them contributed significantly (meaning 'more than negligibly') to the death of Nabeel.

In summary, the effect of this rule is that, just because there are multiple causes of a particular result, liability is not precluded; more than one person may be liable for homicide or other result crimes.

2.8.2.4 Taking the victim as the defendant finds them

On occasion, the victim will have an unusual physical or mental state or belief which contributes to their death. The judges have adopted a robust approach to these cases, and defendants take their victims as they find them. If the victim is suffering, for example, from a serious heart condition or refuses medical treatment because of religious beliefs where such treatment could have saved them, the defendant has to answer for the consequences that follow, even if these are completely unforeseeable. If a defendant happens to choose a frail victim, or one with firm beliefs on medical treatment which lead to the refusal of such treatment, that is their bad luck.

The authority for this proposition is *R v Blaue* [1975] 1 WLR 1411. In this case, the defendant stabbed a woman who refused a blood transfusion because of her religious beliefs. The victim died of the injuries inflicted by the defendant, although medical evidence suggested that a blood transfusion would have saved her life. The defendant was said to have caused the woman's death and was convicted of manslaughter. On appeal against conviction, Lawton LJ said:

> ... those who use violence on other people must take their victims as they find them. This in our judgment means the whole man, not just the physical man ...
>
> ... The question for decision is what caused her death. The answer is the stab wound. The fact that the victim refused to stop this end coming about did not break the causal connection between the act and death.

This issue was also considered in *R v Watson* [1989] 2 All ER 865. The defendants had thrown a brick through the window of the home of an 87-year-old man who suffered from a serious heart condition. When the man awoke to find the defendants in his home, they verbally abused him and he died 90 minutes later of a heart attack. The defendants were convicted of manslaughter. On appeal, the Court of Appeal (although allowing the appeal on a different ground) confirmed that, if the jury were properly directed, it was open to them to decide that the defendants had caused the victim's death.

This principle is sometimes referred to as the 'eggshell skull rule' on the basis that if the accused taps the victim on the head with a ruler using force that would normally only lightly bruise, but in this case break's the victim's skull because it is particularly soft, the defendant should not escape the consequences of their act.

2.8.3 The chain of causation must not be broken

Defendants have sometimes tried to argue that the link between their act and the result (usually death) has been broken by an intervening act or event. This may be referred to by its Latin name of *novus actus interveniens*, which translates to 'a new and intervening act'. The effect of an intervening act that breaks the chain of causation is that the defendant will not be the cause of the result and will be absolved of liability for it. Often you will see this referred to as an argument that the chain of causation has been broken.

This aspect of legal causation is left to the jury to decide as a matter of common sense but, to assist them in their deliberations, various guidelines have emerged from Appeal Court decisions. These are likely to be of relevance in three situations:

(a) where the *victim* acts in a particular way;

(b) where an act by some *other person* intervenes between the defendant's conduct and the end result; and

(c) where some *event* occurs between the defendant's conduct and the end result.

Each of these will be considered in turn. However, in general terms, the argument that the chain of causation has been broken will not succeed if the court decides:

(a) that, despite there being an intervening event, the injuries inflicted by the defendant were still an operating and substantial cause of death; or

(b) if there was an intervening act or event, this was foreseen or foreseeable. Here, the court must decide whether it was foreseen by the defendant or foreseeable by the reasonable person that such an event was likely to occur in the normal course of events.

2.8.3.1 Victim's acts

The general rule is that if the victim does something *after* the initial act or omission of the accused but *before* the consequence occurs, and that intervention is 'free, deliberate and informed' (voluntary), then legal causation will not be established. However, although this principle remains valid, it will rarely apply in practice. For example, if a victim decided not to get medical help and died of their injuries, the defendant would almost certainly remain liable as their conduct contributed significantly to the victim's demise. Alternatively, the court may find that the victim suffered from a mental condition which influenced their decision, in which case the 'thin skull' rule would apply.

There are two important potential exceptions to the general rule, these being where the victim tries to escape and where they commit suicide.

'Escape' cases

When determining the impact of the victim's escape, the court will consider how foreseeable the victim's response was. In *R v Roberts* (1971) 56 Cr App R 95, the victim jumped out of a moving car as a result of the defendant's unwanted sexual advances. The defendant was held liable for an assault occasioning actual bodily harm despite the injuries having been caused in part by the victim's own conduct.

This is an example of what are referred to as 'fright and flight' cases. The chain of causation is not broken here because the victim's act is not free, deliberate and informed; effectively, they have been forced into the situation.

However, a defendant will not always be liable for the consequences of a victim's escape. In the case of *Roberts*, Stephenson LJ stated that if the victim's act was 'so daft as to make it [the victim's] own voluntary act' then the chain of causation would be broken.

Example

Junaid has accepted a lift home from Yonis whom he met at a pub. On the way, Yonis threatens Junaid that if he does not pay £10 towards the petrol, he will slap him. Junaid is afraid of Yonis, so he opens the car door while they are travelling at 50 miles per hour along a busy road and jumps out. Junaid is hit by a vehicle that is following Yonis' car and dies of head injuries which he sustained during the escape. This response would not be regarded as reasonably foreseeable in the circumstances as it is an excessive reaction to the threat.

In summary, when determining the issue of causation, the court will take into account:

(a) whether the escape is within the range of reasonable responses to be expected of a victim in that situation;

(b) if the victim's response is proportionate to the threat; or

(c) whether it is so 'daft' as to be a voluntary act; and

(d) the fact that the victim is acting in 'the agony of the moment' without time for thought or deliberation.

Suicide

In some cases, the impact of the victim's suicide may be covered by the principle that the defendant must take their victim as they find them, as discussed earlier in the chapter. However, this issue was revisited in a recent case.

In *R v Wallace* [2018] EWCA Crim 690, the defendant threw sulphuric acid upon her partner, Mark van Dongen, whilst he was asleep. His injuries were horrific, including full thickness burns to 25% of his body. He was in a coma for four months, lost the sight in one eye and most of the sight in the other, his lower left leg had to be amputated and he was paralysed - at one point, only being able to move his tongue. After developing further complications, the victim applied for euthanasia, which is legal in Belgium, and his wish was granted.

The Court of Appeal rejected the defence argument that the actions of the doctors broke the chain of causation and that the act of voluntary euthanasia was a free, deliberate and informed decision sufficient to count as an intervening event. The judges stated that the question was whether it was reasonably foreseeable that the victim would commit suicide as a result of his injuries. All the circumstances should be taken into account to determine whether voluntary euthanasia fell within the range of reasonable responses that might have been expected from a victim in his situation. Although in this particular case the jury found the defendant not guilty of murder, in principle, voluntary euthanasia does not necessarily break the chain of causation.

2.8.3.2 Third party intervention

An act by a third party may qualify as an intervening event sufficient to break the chain of causation if it is a voluntary one that contributes to the result. If successfully pleaded, the original defendant is not liable for the death at all.

This may cover a variety of situations where someone other than the accused or the victim acts. An example would be an ambulance driver who crashes their vehicle while driving the victim of a stabbing to hospital, resulting in the victim's death.

This is an area where the law has developed over time, but the general principle can be summarised thus:

- A defendant will not be liable if a third party's intervening act is either free, deliberate and informed, or is not reasonably foreseeable.

In the case of *Pagett* (see above), the victim's death was caused by the action of the police officer in firing at the defendant. Here, the officer's response was not free, deliberate and informed as he was acting instinctively in self-defence; and it was reasonably foreseeable in the circumstances because the defendant was shooting at the officer at the time. As a consequence, the police officer who shot the victim was absolved of all criminal liability. Furthermore, because his action did not break the chain of causation, the defendant, who used his girlfriend as a human shield, was found guilty of causing her death.

2.8.3.3 Intervening events

Thus far we have considered the effect of an intervening act by the victim or a third party, but what if a natural event intervened to become the immediate cause of a victim's death. For example, a defendant shoots their victim in the legs and runs out of the building, just before it is demolished by an earthquake. The victim dies of crush injuries from the collapsing building. In this situation, the defendant would have a much better chance of arguing that the chain of causation between their act and the death of the victim had been broken, because it is not reasonably foreseeable that an earthquake would occur. There is no direct binding authority on this point, presumably because such things rarely happen, but the general view is that the same 'reasonable foreseeability' test would apply.

Examples

(1) *Charis argues with Bonnie and strikes her, leaving her unconscious by the side of a stream. The injury is not sufficiently serious to cause death. Although it is a sunny afternoon, there is a sudden thunderstorm and the stream becomes swollen with flood water. Bonnie drowns. Charis is not liable for Bonnie's death because the flooding is (objectively) not foreseeable. Consequently, it will break the chain of causation.*

(2) *Charis argues with Bonnie and strikes her, leaving her unconscious on the beach. The tide comes in and Bonnie drowns. Charis would be liable for Bonnie's death by drowning as the tide coming in is a natural event that is reasonably foreseeable.*

The chain of events may also be broken by events other than natural ones, for example, where the victim is left in a house that is subsequently blown up in a gas explosion.

2.8.3.4 Causation in cases of medical negligence

One particular area where the law has developed in relation to causation is that of medical negligence. There have been several cases in which defendants have argued that a victim has died not because of their actions, but because of negligent treatment by the medical profession. Effectively, the defendant is arguing that it was the poor medical treatment (intervention by a third party) that caused death and broke the chain of causation and thus the defendant should be absolved from liability.

Example

Josephina attacks Kirit who suffers an injury to his leg as a result of the attack. He is taken to hospital where a junior doctor wrongly gives Kirit a dose of antibiotics to which he is allergic. Kirit's medical notes clearly indicate that he suffers from this allergy, but the doctor fails to spot this. Kirit dies as a result of an allergic reaction to the medication.

It is clear that Josephina satisfies the 'but for' test of factual causation: if she had not injured Kirit, he would not have been a patient at the hospital and would not have suffered the negligent medical treatment.

Turning to legal causation, the question to consider is whether the chain of causation has been broken. Josephina will argue that the injury inflicted by her to Kirit's leg was not an operating and substantial cause of death. Furthermore, that it was not foreseen by her, nor reasonably foreseeable, that Kirit would receive negligent or bad medical treatment. She would therefore submit that the chain of causation between her initial act and the subsequent death of Kirit has been broken by the intervening event of the poor medical treatment. It is fair to say that, although some jurors might be persuaded by such an argument, equally, others would still want to hold Josephina criminally liable for Kirit's death.

In order to avoid an easy escape by a defendant who is, after all, responsible for putting the victim in the hospital in the first place, the courts have developed a line of authorities to deal with such situations.

In *R v Jordan* (1956) 40 Cr App R 152, the victim died in hospital eight days after being stabbed by the defendant who was convicted of murder on the ground that he had caused the victim's death. There was, however, evidence that the victim had been given poor medical treatment in hospital and that, at the time of his death, the initial wound inflicted by the defendant had largely healed.

On appeal, the defendant's conviction was quashed. The Court of Appeal held that the medical treatment received by the victim was 'palpably wrong'. Indeed, he actually died of broncho-pneumonia as his lungs became waterlogged due to the large quantities of liquid which was given intravenously. The view of the Court was that where death followed from normal medical treatment used to deal with an injury inflicted by the defendant (presumably, for example, where death occurred from complications following surgery necessitated by the original injury), death could be regarded as having been caused by the defendant; but where the treatment was 'not normal', the same inference could not be drawn.

The decision in *Jordan* was clearly generous to the defendant and is an extreme example limited to its facts. Later cases, although not overruling *Jordan*, have been anxious to stress that it was 'an exceptional case' and have developed tests which are much more likely to secure the conviction of the defendant who caused the initial injuries.

In *R v Smith* [1959] 2 QB 35, the victim died at an army medical centre shortly after being stabbed by the defendant. There was evidence that the medical treatment the victim received had been 'thoroughly bad' and might have affected the victim's chances of recovery. On appeal against a conviction for murder, the defendant argued that the trial court had not properly addressed the question of causation, specifically the defendant's claim that the medical treatment given had acted as an intervening event to break the chain of causation between the defendant's act and the subsequent death of the victim.

The appeal was dismissed by the Courts-Martial Appeal Court (broadly speaking, the military equivalent of the Court of Appeal). In his judgment, Lord Parker CJ set out the following guidance in determining whether the defendant could be said to have caused the victim's death:

> ... if, at the time of death, the original wound is still an operating cause and a substantial cause, then the death can properly be said to be the result of the wound, albeit that some other cause of death is also operating. Only if it can be said that the original wounding is merely the setting in which another cause operates can it be said that the death did not result from the wound. Putting it another way, only if the second cause is so overwhelming as to make the original wound merely part of the history can it be said that the death does not flow from the wound.

It is established law that the defendant's conduct need not be the sole or main cause of death as long as it is a substantial cause, with 'substantial' simply meaning 'more than minimal'. Lord Parker CJ, in *Smith*, was clearly following this line of reasoning.

In medical treatment cases, following *Smith*, the defendant will find it difficult to argue a break in the chain of causation if the injury they inflicted is still operating at the time of death. As a result, even cases of quite serious medical negligence may not be enough to enable the defendant who inflicted the initial injury to escape liability.

This point was demonstrated in the leading authority on this topic, namely *R v Cheshire* [1991] 1 WLR 844. In this case the defendant shot a man who underwent surgery, including a tracheotomy, as a result of the gunshot wounds. The victim died two months later due to scar tissue at the tracheotomy site obstructing his breathing. The defendant argued that he should not be responsible for the victim's death, as the negligent medical treatment broke the chain of causation. This issue was considered by the Court of Appeal and Beldam LJ gave the judgment, extracts of which are set out below:

> When the victim of a criminal attack is treated for wounds or injuries by doctors or other medical staff attempting to repair the harm done, it will only be in the most extraordinary and unusual case that such treatment can be said to be so independent of the acts of the defendant that it could be regarded in law as the cause of the victim's death to the exclusion of the defendant's acts ...
>
> ... In a case in which the jury have to consider whether negligence in the treatment of injuries inflicted by the defendant was the cause of death ... the defendant's acts need not be the sole cause or even the main cause of death it being sufficient that his acts contributed significantly to that result. Even though negligence in the treatment of the victim was the immediate cause of his death, the jury should not regard it as excluding the responsibility of the defendant unless the negligent treatment was so independent of his acts, and in itself so potent in causing death, that they regard the contribution made by his acts as insignificant.

It is clear from the words of Beldam LJ that the Court of Appeal would be extremely reluctant to allow a defendant to escape liability because of poor medical treatment received by the victim except in the most exceptional cases. This applies whether the victim's death is due to positive (and wrong) action by doctors or by their inaction. The only point that can be made with certainty, therefore, is that the test established in *Cheshire* will be applied by the court where a question of causation falls to be determined in a medical case, and that the court will decide cases on the particular facts.

Example

Continuing with the example (above), Josephina would escape liability for causing Kirit's death only if the court found that the poor medical treatment he received was so independent of Josephina's acts and, in itself, so potent in causing death that Josephina's contribution to Kirit's death was regarded by the court as insignificant. The court would require evidence on matters such as how serious was the initial injury inflicted by Josephina, how long Kirit had been in hospital when the negligent treatment was administered and how near he was to a full recovery in deciding, according to Cheshire*, whether Josephina caused his death. However, it seems unlikely that Josephina would be successful in arguing a break in the chain of causation.*

Finally, how do the rules of causation apply where the defendant attacks a victim who then cannot receive medical treatment for a pre-existing condition because of the injuries inflicted by the defendant?

This situation was considered by the Court of Appeal in *R v McKechnie* [1992] Crim LR 194. In this case, the defendant attacked his victim causing them to suffer severe head injuries. On admission to hospital, doctors discovered that the victim suffered from a duodenal ulcer. A medical decision was made that, because of the head injuries, it would not be possible to operate on the ulcer. The victim died five weeks later when the ulcer burst. The defendant was found to have caused the victim's death and was convicted of manslaughter, a decision upheld by the Court of Appeal. The defendant had argued that he was not responsible for the ulcer and, as that had killed the victim, he could have no liability for the death. The Court of Appeal confirmed that the chain of causation between the defendant's attack and the victim's death was intact because the assault had prevented an operation on the ulcer which would have saved the victim's life. The decision not to operate had been reasonable and it was not 'so independent of the acts of the accused that it could be regarded in law as the cause of the victim's death'. This decision is consistent with the principle that a defendant must 'take their victim as they find them', considered at **2.8.2.4** above.

It appears therefore that in cases of medical treatment, the courts are inclined to place great emphasis on the 'but for' test to hold the defendant liable. Only in very extreme cases will poor treatment break the chain of causation between the defendant's act and the victim's death.

2.8.4 Overview

It is clear that, in order to establish the actus reus of murder, the prosecution must be able to prove both factual and legal causation. Set out below is a diagram which provides an overview of the principles that apply to legal causation and the acts and events that may break the chain of causation, so the defendant is no longer criminally liable for the result.

Figure 2.3 Legal causation and intervening acts

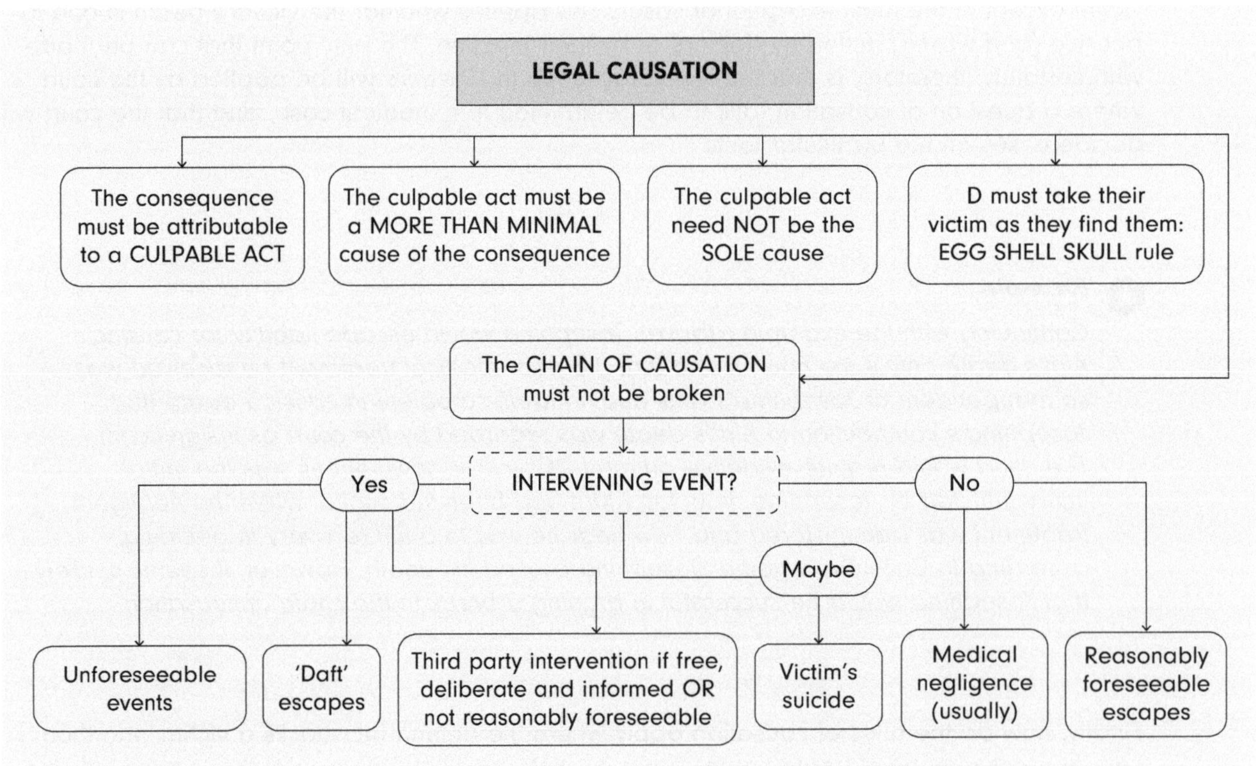

2.9 Summary

This concludes our examination of the basic principles relating to the actus reus of an offence. The specific actus reus requirements of individual crimes will be covered as they arise, but remember that, usually, the actus reus is only part of the definition of the offence that has to be proved against a defendant. In most instances, the prosecution must also establish that the defendant had a guilty mind at the time they committed the actus reus.

(a) To be criminally liable, the defendant must satisfy all the elements of the actus reus for the particular crime.

(b) The actus reus of an offence may involve an act or an omission (conduct crimes); certain consequences being caused (result crimes); or the existence of surrounding circumstances (state of affairs crimes).

(c) The general rule is that there is no criminal liability for an omission to act, but there are exceptions, namely statutory duty, contractual duty, special relationship, voluntary assumption of care and duty to avert a danger created.

(d) Causation must be proved as part of the actus reus for result crimes. For factual causation, it must be established that 'but for' the defendant's conduct, the result would not have occurred as and when it did. Legal causation requires the defendant's conduct to be a more than minimal cause of the result, so that it is an operating and substantial cause of the outcome.

(e) If the chain of causation is broken by an intervening event, the actus reus will not be established. Such events include: an unforeseeable escape; a voluntary act by a third party; negligent medical treatment that was 'so independent of the defendant's act' and 'so potent in causing death' that the contribution made by the defendant was rendered insignificant; and events that are not reasonably foreseeable.

(f) The eggshell or thin skull rule states that the defendant must 'take their victim as they find them'.

Next, you should attempt the activity to test your understanding of the legal principles that apply to actus reus.

ACTIVITY

Timothy pushes Elizabeth who falls backwards and hits her head on a stone fireplace at her home. Elizabeth is knocked unconscious and Timothy decides to leave her lying on the floor. Later, a fire breaks out and Elizabeth is burnt to death.

PART 1

Could Timothy be said to have caused Elizabeth's death? In considering your answer, first apply the 'but for' test to determine factual causation. If you decide that Timothy did, as a matter of fact, cause Elizabeth's death, would you expect him to be prosecuted for an offence relating to homicide; in other words, it is just for him to face criminal liability for Elizabeth's death? Note that even if causation is satisfied, Timothy is unlikely to be guilty of murder as he lacks the relevant criminal state of mind and the appropriate charge would be manslaughter.

COMMENT

Factually, applying the 'but for' test, Timothy could be said to have caused Elizabeth's death. Even if there is no evidence that the injuries he inflicted would have been sufficient to cause death or that Timothy was in any way responsible for the fire, if he had not knocked Elizabeth unconscious, she would have been able to escape. Hence, 'but for' Timothy's act, Elizabeth would not have died as and when she did.

PART 2

There is no direct link between Timothy's act and Elizabeth's death, so could he try to escape liability by submitting that the test for legal causation has not been satisfied, thus absolving him of responsibility?

COMMENT

If the principles established in *Malcherek and Steel* are applied, the injury Timothy inflicted on Elizabeth does not appear to have been a substantial and operating cause of her death which was brought about by burning. However, he will remain liable if the intervening event, the fire, does not break the chain of causation.

PART 3

Whether the outbreak of the fire breaks the chain of causation will depend upon whether it is a foreseeable event. In what circumstances would it be more likely that this test would be satisfied?

COMMENT

In the absence of any further information, it does not appear that Timothy foresaw, or that a reasonable person would have foreseen, that a fire would break out at Elizabeth's home, and therefore the test of legal causation would not be satisfied. As a consequence, Timothy could not be convicted of any charge relating to the causation of Elizabeth's death.

He is more likely to be found to have caused Elizabeth's death if, for example, as he left the house, Timothy saw a cigarette burning a hole in the sofa near to where Elizabeth was lying. Such information would suggest that it was foreseeable, at least to a reasonable person, that a fire would break out.

3 General Principles: Mens Rea

LEARNING OUTCOMES

When you have completed this chapter, you should be able to:

- identify the mens rea elements of a criminal offence;
- explain and apply the law relating to intention, recklessness, negligence and strict liability;
- understand the principles of transferred malice and the co-incidence of actus reus and mens rea.

3.1 Introduction

As discussed previously, three components are required to establish liability for a criminal offence, namely, guilty conduct by the defendant (actus reus), a guilty state of mind (mens rea), and absence of any valid defence. In this chapter, the second element will be analysed.

In most criminal offences, the prosecution must prove that the defendant committed the actus reus of the offence with, at the appropriate time, the relevant guilty mind. Mens rea is the term used to refer to this mental or fault element. In the majority of offences, the defendant must be shown either to have *intended* something to happen, or to have been *reckless* as to whether certain circumstances would exist or whether certain consequences would follow from their conduct. However, this is not always the case: sometimes the defendant can be convicted not because of what their state of mind *was* at the time of their guilty conduct but what it *should* have been.

The mens rea requirements of particular crimes can usually be gleaned from the formal definition of an offence. For example, the statutory definition of criminal damage makes it clear that the prosecution must prove the defendant had the criminal state of mind of intention or of recklessness (as regards damaging or destroying property belonging to another) before they can be convicted of the offence. Unfortunately, the mens rea requirements are not always so obvious; for example, the definition of murder requires the unlawful killing of a human being 'with malice aforethought'. As will become apparent, it took a considerable amount of judicial debate before the House of Lords decided what this phrase meant!

3.2 Intention

Intention is the most culpable type of mens rea. The word itself is used commonly in the English language, but, surprisingly, its interpretation has caused some difficulty in the context of criminal law as will be discussed below.

Intention should not be confused with motive as the two concepts are quite different. The defendant who kills the victim because they raped a relative, or the mercy killer who genuinely wants to end the pain of a loved one and to allow them to die with dignity, will be guilty of murder. Their motive may be admired or understood by many, but this is irrelevant when determining criminal liability. As long as the defendant killed someone and intended to do so, or intended to cause really serious injury, they have the actus reus and mens rea of murder regardless of their reasons for acting in this way. In such a case, the defendant will be guilty of murder unless they have a defence.

3.2.1 Direct intention

The ordinary definition of intention would include wanting something, setting out to achieve something or having something as an aim. The *Oxford English Dictionary* lists the following: 'intended or purposed; a purpose or design; ultimate purpose; the aim of an action'. Applying this definition suggests that a defendant intended something to happen (or intended a particular circumstance to exist) if they wanted to bring it about, so that it was their aim, purpose, goal or desire.

The courts would describe such a situation as a case of direct intent.

Example

Tobias deliberately shoots a gun at Sid from a distance of two metres. He kills Sid and is charged with murder. Tobias says he did not intend to kill Sid or to cause him serious harm (the mens rea for murder). Can the prosecution prove intent in these circumstances?

(1) Tobias says he lacked mens rea because, although he wanted Sid to die, he did not think it would happen as Tobias is a terrible shot and he believed the bullet would miss Sid.

Here, Tobias could be said to have the mens rea for murder as he wanted to kill Sid; it was his aim, purpose or desire to do so. In such a situation, the court would find it easy to conclude that Tobias had the required direct intent. The fact that Tobias thought he would probably miss is irrelevant: if events turned out the way he hoped they would, Sid would be killed. In cases of direct intent such as this, the fact there is a possibility or even a probability that the defendant will not achieve their goal is disregarded.

(2) Tobias says he lacked mens rea because he and Sid were just fooling about: Tobias did not realise the gun was loaded.

In this scenario, Tobias does not have the necessary mens rea for murder. It was not his aim or wish to kill Sid and, as he thought the gun was not loaded, he cannot be guilty of murder. He lacks the required intention to be guilty of this offence.

Where there is a direct attack on the victim by the defendant, the issue of intention is clear, and the jury will be given no direction as to the meaning of intention. In such cases, as Lord Bridge stated in the case of *R v Moloney* [1985] 1 AC 905 (HL), the judge should avoid any elaboration or paraphrase what is meant by intent and should leave the matter to 'the jury's good sense'. The judge will simply tell the jury, on a charge of murder for example, that the defendant must have intended to kill or to cause really serious harm to have the necessary mens rea.

It is clear that a defendant has the direct intent to commit an offence if the consequence, whether it be death, criminal damage or assault, is their aim or purpose. But what if the defendant argues that they did not set out to achieve something – that it was not their aim or purpose to bring about a particular outcome.

3.2.2 Indirect intention

Although defining intention should be straightforward, in practice the courts and legislators have sometimes struggled to achieve this. Indeed, case law has broadened the law of intent beyond the everyday meaning so that it also recognises indirect or oblique intention (the terms are interchangeable). This is a concept that has been developed by the courts to cover cases where the defendant argues that the outcome was not their main aim but an unfortunate by-product of what they did set out to achieve.

Example

Talia plants a bomb on a plane which is timed to explode when the plane is in the air over the Atlantic. She does this because the plane is carrying Talia's valuable antiques which are well insured. She hopes that the antiques will be destroyed so that she can claim the insurance money. The plane explodes, killing the crew and Talia is charged with murder. She submits that she did not intend to kill the crew – she hoped that by some miracle they would be saved. The question for the court is whether Talia intended to kill them.

Although, morally, intention should be made out so that Talia can be convicted of murder, it would be difficult to argue that she had direct intent because her primary purpose was not to kill; her aim or her desire was to destroy the antiques and to claim the insurance money. However, Talia must have known it was almost certain that people would die. In cases such as these, where it may be difficult to establish direct intent, the courts will rely upon 'indirect' or 'oblique' intent.

Cases on indirect intent occur most frequently in the context of murder, because this offence cannot be committed recklessly. Precisely what the accused must foresee, and with what degree of certainty in order to have intended the consequences, arose in a number of cases and was the subject of frequent disagreement. Ultimately, the direction of indirect or oblique intent was settled after a series of Court of Appeal and House of Lords cases.

The first of these was *R v Moloney* in which the defendant shot his stepfather dead after a drunken competition to see who could load a gun the fastest. The defendant said he had no idea in firing the gun that he would injure his stepfather: he had no direct intent to kill or cause really serious harm. The jury was required to decide whether the defendant had an indirect intent. The House of Lords confirmed that there would be some situations where the jury would need guidance on whether they could conclude that the defendant had the mens rea of intention, although they were at pains to point out that such occasions would be rare.

In cases where assistance was required, the judges in *Moloney* suggested that the jury should be told to ask themselves whether they (the jury) believed that death or really serious injury was a *natural* consequence of the defendant's act; and if so, were they satisfied that the defendant had foreseen this. If the answer to both was yes, the jury should be instructed that they had evidence from which intention *could* be inferred (although they did not have to so infer).

The *Moloney* guidelines soon came under scrutiny in the next case to consider indirect intent, *R v Hancock and Shankland* [1986] 1 AC 455 (HL). In this case two striking miners dropped a concrete block from a bridge onto a taxi that was taking a miner to work, killing the taxi driver. When charged with murder, the defendants said they only intended to block the road and scare the working miners into stopping work. The trial judge in *Hancock and Shankland* dutifully followed the guidelines issued by the House of Lords in *Moloney* and the defendants were convicted. However, on appeal, the House of Lords decided that their own guidelines were unsafe and misleading, and suggested instead that the jury questions should include a reference to probability.

The decisions in *Moloney* and in *Hancock and Shankland* led to difficulties in those cases where the defendant did not set out to achieve the death or serious injury of the victim and, thus, direct intention did not apply. There was confusion about the meaning of the words 'natural' and 'probable' – does 'natural' mean all consequences following from the defendant's conduct? Does 'probable' mean there is a more than 50% chance of the consequence occurring, or must it be a higher percentage?

These questions were answered by the Court of Appeal in *R v Nedrick* [1986] 1 WLR 1025 (CA) and necessitated a change in the wording of the guidance developed by the earlier authorities. It was held that if, in a murder case, the judge felt that the jury would benefit from some guidance on the meaning of indirect intent, the following should be put to them:

(a) Did the jury consider that death or serious injury was virtually certain to occur as a consequence of the defendant's actions?

(b) If so, did the jury believe that the defendant foresaw death or serious injury as a virtual certainty?

The jury should be told they could not infer intention unless they answered 'yes' to both these questions, and even if they did answer in the affirmative, they did not have to infer intent: they then simply had evidence from which intention could be inferred.

The use of the words 'virtually certain' does appear less ambiguous than 'natural' or 'natural and probable', and it seems to convey more clearly that the jury must be almost sure that death or serious injury would follow and that the defendant foresaw this as a consequence. Applied and considered properly, therefore, the use of the 'virtual certainty' test makes it less likely that indirect intention will be inferred.

The final important case on this area, and the leading authority, is *R v Woollin* [1999] 1 AC 82 (HL). The defendant in this case killed his three-month-old son by throwing him against a hard surface. It was clear on the facts that the defendant had no desire (direct intent) to kill or seriously injure his son, but the question remained as to whether, nevertheless, he could be said to have an indirect intent to do so. In giving his judgment, Lord Steyn approved the test set out in *Nedrick*, stating that it 'provided valuable assistance to trial judges'. However, he did agree with academic criticism that the word 'infer' may detract from the clarity of the direction and should be replaced with the word 'find'. Thus, a judge giving such a direction today should explain that the jury may 'find' the defendant had an intent to kill or do serious injury if they are satisfied:

(a) that death or serious bodily harm was a virtually certain consequence of the defendant's voluntary act; and

(b) that the defendant appreciated that fact.

Lord Steyn considered that the trial judge would be best placed to decide whether there was a need to give the guidance in any particular case and confirmed that this would not occur in all cases, but only those 'in which the defendant may not have desired the result of his act'. In the *Woollin* case itself, Lord Steyn felt that the murder conviction was unsafe due to a material misdirection by the trial judge to the jury and so he substituted a conviction of manslaughter.

Example (continued)

Continuing with the scenario above in which Talia planted a bomb on a plane, the jury would be told to consider two issues, namely:

(a) Was the consequence virtually certain to occur from the defendant's act (or omission)? In this case, by planting a bomb in the plane timed to go off when the plane was in the air, it was virtually certain that crew members would either be killed or seriously injured.

(b) If so, did the defendant foresee the consequences as virtually certain to occur? Given the drastic nature of Talia's act, it is likely that the jury would conclude that Talia herself foresaw the demise of the crew members as virtually certain to occur.

Having reached these conclusions, the jury have evidence from which they can find that the defendant intended the consequences of their act (or omission); thus, that Talia did intend to kill or cause really serious harm to the crew.

It is extremely unlikely that if anyone was asked to define intention, they would come up with the two-stage test from *Woollin*. Effectively, it is an artificial definition to prevent some (undeserving) defendants literally getting away with murder. The fact that the result must be a virtual certainty means that it will catch only a few defendants who would not otherwise be convicted anyway on the basis of their direct intent.

3.2.3 Criminal Justice Act 1967, s 8

In cases involving indirect intent, jurors will have to consider what the defendant foresaw at the time of their act (or omission); but in the absence of a clear confession, how can the jury ascertain this?

Section 8 of the Criminal Justice Act 1967 provides some assistance. When determining whether a person has committed an offence, the court:

(a) shall not be bound in law to infer that he intended or foresaw a result of his actions by reason only of its being a natural and probable consequence of those actions; but

(b) shall decide whether he did intend or foresee that result by reference to all the evidence, drawing such inferences from the evidence as appear proper in the circumstances.

In other words, the test is what the defendant *themselves* foresaw, not what a reasonable person would have foreseen; but what a reasonable person would have foreseen is a good indication, which a jury can take into account, in deciding what this particular defendant *did* foresee.

Example (continued)

Continuing with the example (above), Talia gives evidence in court that it never crossed her mind that the crew would be killed. The effect of s 8 is that the jury does not have to simply accept whatever she says. In this instance, it would be obvious to a reasonable person that the crew would die if a plane exploded over the ocean. This would help the jury decide whether Talia is telling the truth when she says she did not foresee death as a virtually certain outcome. As Talia's story is so unlikely, the jury would not believe her. However, they must not conclude that simply because a reasonable person would foresee something as virtually certain, it is automatically the case that Talia foresaw it as such.

3.2.4 Summary of intention

The present law on intention may be summarised as follows:

(a) Most crimes may be committed either intentionally or recklessly, but there are some (such as murder) where the prosecution must prove the defendant intended the result.

(b) Where intention is considered by the jury, they will usually rely on their common-sense to assess the evidence and to decide whether the defendant intended the prohibited result.

(c) If the defendant's primary purpose was to bring about a particular consequence, they intended that consequence no matter how unlikely they were to succeed. This is direct intent.

(d) In cases where the trial judge believes the jury would benefit from further guidance on determining the issue of intention (in cases of indirect intent), they should be told they can only find intention on the part of the defendant if satisfied that:

(i) the consequence was virtually certain to occur; and

(ii) the defendant foresaw that consequence as being virtually certain to occur.

(e) In cases involving proof of intention, the motive of the defendant is usually irrelevant.

The following flowchart summarises the approach the courts will take when deciding whether the defendant has the intention to commit a certain result.

Figure 3.1 Intention

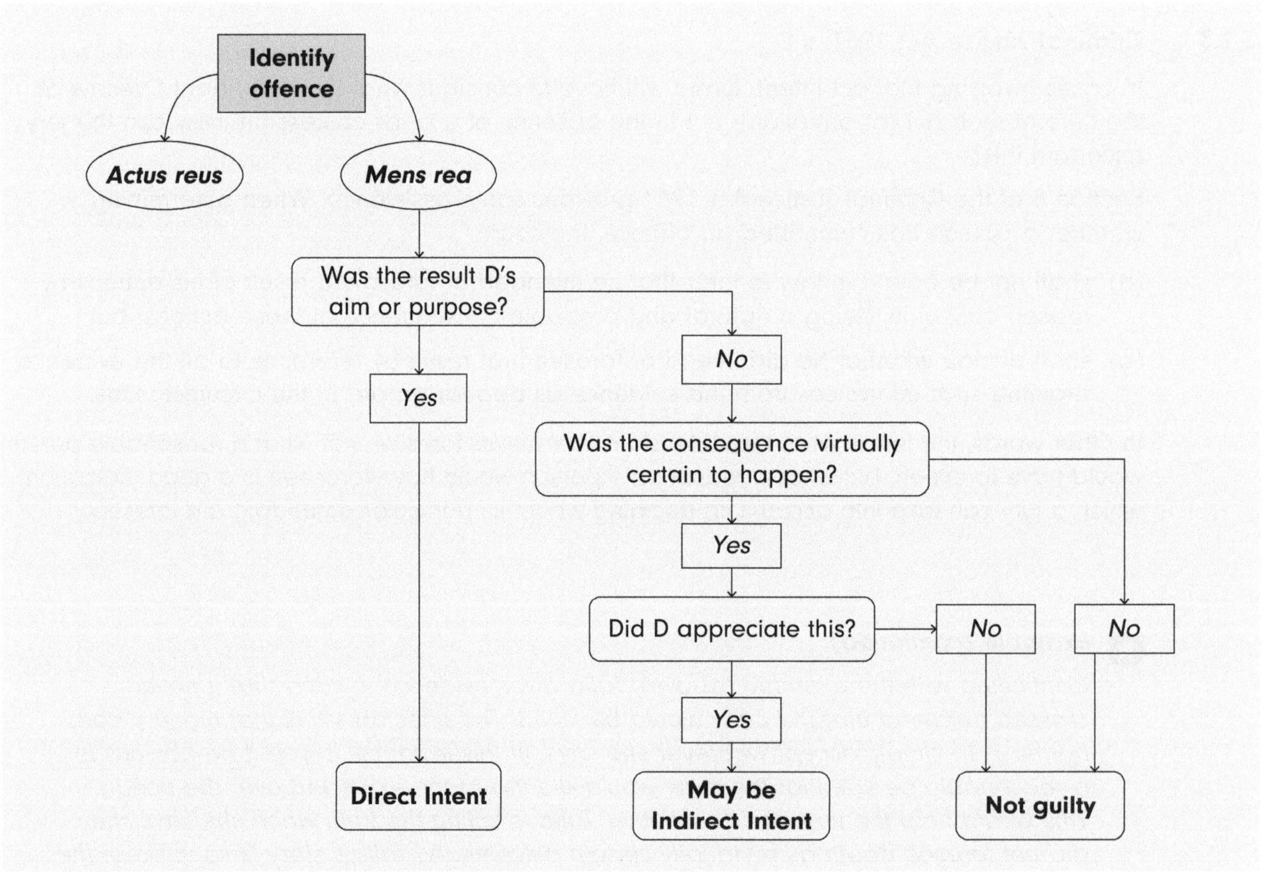

3.3 Recklessness

Whilst there are crimes that can only be committed intentionally, for the majority of the substantive offences, it is not necessary to establish an intention to do something on the part of the defendant: establishing that they intended *or* were reckless as to whether a consequence could occur or as to whether a circumstance might exist is sufficient to establish mens rea.

Unfortunately, although recklessness is a critically important term in criminal law, Parliament has not created a statutory definition. As with intention, it is the judges who have been left to interpret the meaning of recklessness and, again, this has caused confusion to those involved in the criminal justice system. To a lay person, the term 'reckless' conjures up words such as 'careless', 'without thinking', 'dangerous' or 'wild' when talking about reckless behaviour. However, in criminal law, 'reckless' has a specific meaning, the definition of which has been considered and formulated by case law. In brief, it involves an examination of the risks involved in the defendant's behaviour and the state of mind of the defendant when they took that risk.

3.3.1 Justification of risk

A requirement for recklessness is that the defendant takes an unjustified risk so it follows that if they take a risk that is justified, they cannot be reckless.

Assessing justification of risk in the abstract is impossible because much will depend on the facts of the case, including why the defendant decided to take that risk, what the risk was, what consequences occurred and so on. What is clear is that justification of risk will be assessed according to the standards of the reasonable person - an objective test. The courts will consider the social utility or benefit involved in taking the risk when deciding whether it was justified. Prosecutors, members of the jury or magistrates, as reasonable people, will therefore apply their own standards. In simple terms, they will ask themselves whether they would have considered there to be any merit in taking the risk if they had been in the defendant's position.

In most situations, the taking of a risk that an illegal circumstance will exist or that an illegal consequence will follow from the defendant's actions will be unjustified. As a result, in the criminal courts, very little time is taken up by considering whether the taking of a risk was justified, with that assessment having usually been made by the prosecution in deciding whether to proceed with a criminal charge. Indeed, the vast majority of cases will involve people who have been involved in an obviously unjustified activity.

Although an essential ingredient of recklessness, the taking of an unjustified risk is not enough in itself to satisfy this type of mens rea, and the prosecution must also prove that the defendant had a particular state of mind when they took that risk. It is this aspect that will be considered next.

3.3.2 Recklessness - subjective or objective?

Traditionally, the courts took the view that a defendant was reckless if they foresaw a risk that something might happen as a result of their behaviour and, with that foresight, they went on, without justification, to take that risk.

In the case of *R v Cunningham* [1957] 2 QB 396, Byrne J gave the leading judgment agreeing with the definition of 'malice' first expounded by Professor Kenny in 1902:

> Malice must be taken not in the old vague sense of wickedness in general but as requiring either (1) an actual intention to do the particular kind of harm that in fact

was done; or (2) recklessness as to whether such harm should occur or not (ie the accused has foreseen that the particular kind of harm might be done and yet has gone on to take the risk of it).

Following the case of *Cunningham*, therefore, recklessness was regarded as requiring proof that the particular defendant foresaw the risk and went on to take it: the fact that the court felt that they should have foreseen it was not enough to establish recklessness.

The meaning of recklessness was well settled until the early 1980s when the decision of the House of Lords in *Metropolitan Police Commissioner v Caldwell* [1982] AC 341 threw the area into turmoil and resulted for some 20 years in two different tests for recklessness. The judges decided that an objective standard should be imposed when assessing whether a defendant had behaved recklessly in the context of criminal damage. As a consequence, defendants who failed to give any thought to a risk which would have been obvious to the reasonable person would be judged as reckless under the criminal law in this context. The decision in *Caldwell* was the subject of much academic commentary and debate, and it was heavily criticised, not least because the test that applied depended on the offence with which a defendant was charged, leading to great confusion.

3.3.3 The current position

Following a reconsideration of these issues in the case of *R v G* [2004] 1 AC 1034, the meaning of recklessness was clarified, with the House of Lords overruling the decision in *Caldwell* and returning to the 'traditional' interpretation.

In the judgment given by Lord Bingham in *R v G* [2004] 1 AC 1034, he argued that Parliament intended 'reckless' to have the same meaning as put forward by the Law Commission in its Report on Offences of Damage to Property (Law Com No 29) published in July 1970 and in Working Paper No 23 which pre-dated the Criminal Damage Act 1971. In his view, the Report revealed a very plain intention to replace the old-fashioned expression 'maliciously' with the more familiar expression 'reckless' and to give 'reckless' the same meaning afforded to it by *Cunningham* [1957] 2 QB 396.

Lord Bingham set out four reasons for overruling the objective test of recklessness as set out in *Caldwell*:

(a) It is a basic principle that conviction of serious crime should depend on proof not only of the actus reus of the offence but also that the offender's state of mind whilst doing the act (or omission) was culpable. It is not blameworthy to do something involving a risk of injury to another if the defendant genuinely does not perceive the risk.

(b) The decision in *Caldwell* was capable of leading to obvious unfairness as it was neither moral nor just to convict a defendant on the strength of what someone else would have apprehended if the defendant had no such apprehension.

(c) Criticism of *Caldwell* expressed by academics, judges and practitioners should not be ignored.

(d) In *Caldwell,* the majority's interpretation of s 1 of the Criminal Damage Act 1971 was a misinterpretation which was offensive to principle (of criminal law which requires subjective recklessness) and apt to cause injustice. Hence, the need to correct it was compelling.

The effect is that there is now one test for recklessness, and this is subjective. A defendant is reckless if they foresee a risk that something may happen as a result of their behaviour (or a particular set of circumstances might exist) and, with that foresight, go on without justification to take that risk. An awareness of any level of risk, however small, is sufficient.

Example

Ryan punches Sydney once in the face during an argument over money. Sydney falls backwards, hits his head on the edge of a nearby table and suffers a fractured skull.

The risk of causing injury would be considered unjustified by the standards of reasonable people as there is no social utility in punching someone due to a disagreement over money. However, given the circumstances (only one punch and no weapon used), it would be difficult to establish that Ryan intended to cause serious harm. The prosecution is far more likely to be able to prove that Ryan was reckless as to causing such harm, specifically that he foresaw there was such a risk but went on to take it anyway. This would satisfy the mens rea for a lesser assault.

3.3.4 Summary of recklessness

The present law on recklessness can be summarised as follows:

(a) The test for recklessness is subjective or *Cunningham* recklessness. This applies to any criminal offence in which recklessness forms part of the necessary mens rea.

(b) The test is whether this defendant foresaw a risk (subjective) of whatever is required by the specific offence and went on to take it, and the risk is unjustified (objective).

Set out below is an overview to assist your understanding.

Figure 3.2 Recklessness

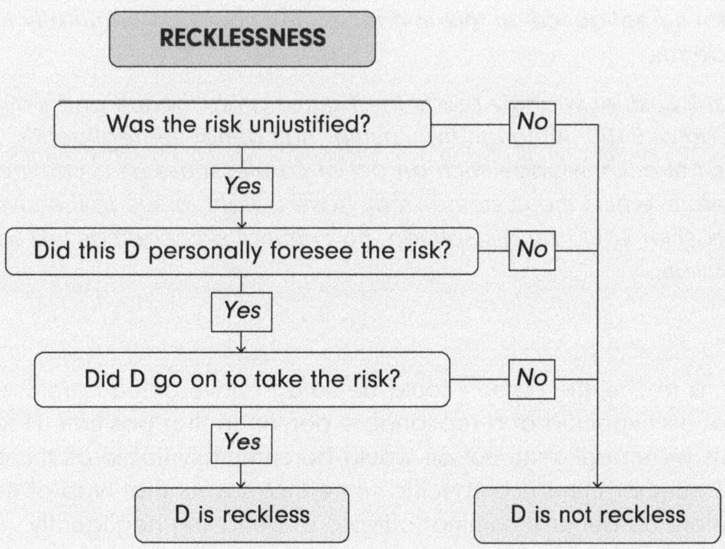

3.4 Negligence

Some offences may be committed without proof of intention or recklessness by the defendant. Where the mens rea only requires negligence, the defendant is judged on an objective standard that can be satisfied even if the defendant is unaware of the risk, provided it is an obvious one. Because the defendant is punished for failing to measure up to the standards of the reasonable person, this may operate harshly as the accused may not understand or even be capable of recognising the risk.

The term 'negligence' is used extensively in the law of tort, as well as being a word in everyday language. It is generally understood to mean 'carelessness' and most incidents of negligence give rise to civil rather than criminal liability. For example, if a surgeon removed a patient's healthy left kidney instead of the diseased right one, the doctor or the hospital could be sued for compensation. There are, however, some situations where, in addition to or instead of any civil claim, the negligent person could be prosecuted for a criminal offence.

Examples

(1) A motorist drives from a side road onto a main road without giving way to oncoming traffic. Here, the driver could be charged with the criminal offence of driving without due care and attention as they have fallen below the standard of the competent motorist (who would have given way). This form of negligence is specifically punished under an offence created by s 3 of the Road Traffic Act 1988.

(2) A doctor prescribes medication to a patient whose records clearly show they have an intolerance to the drug prescribed. The error is spotted and no harm is suffered by the patient. Because of this, there is no criminal liability, despite the fact it was only good luck that saved the patient from taking the medication and suffering potentially dangerous consequences.

(3) As in (2) above, but the patient dies from an allergic reaction to the prescribed medication. Logically, as the doctor's behaviour was identical, the outcome should be the same. However, because the patient died as a result of the doctor's negligence, in this instance, they could be criminally liable for the death.

(4) A bank cashier wrongly reads the figures on a cheque and pays a customer £10 instead of £100. Although the cashier has behaved negligently, the criminal law does not acknowledge such an act of carelessness as a criminal offence. Again, therefore, whilst the customer may have a right to sue in the civil courts and/or the cashier could be disciplined, no criminal proceedings will follow from such behaviour.

In the situations above, the person could be said to have acted carelessly and in a way that would not be expected of a reasonable person in that position. However, although all the individuals were negligent, not all would be criminally liable as this depends upon the outcome and whether there is a specific crime that covers that type of negligent behaviour. There is therefore no general criminal offence of behaving negligently.

3.4.1 Negligence and common law offences

Only rarely does negligence give to rise criminal liability in the common law, but an offence where negligence satisfies the mens rea is gross negligence manslaughter.

Example

Mrs McVey has warned the school attended by her son, Cameron, that Cameron has a severe, life-threatening, allergy to nuts. The information has been passed on to all the catering staff. Despite this, one lunchtime, Cameron is given a sandwich by Donna that has traces of nuts in it. This fact is clearly highlighted on the label, which also states that the sandwich should not be eaten by anyone with a nut allergy. Cameron takes a bite of the sandwich, suffers an extreme allergic reaction and dies. The catering assistant, Donna, may be liable for the offence of gross negligence manslaughter. This is because her actions may be judged as having fallen so far below the standard of the reasonable employee (the objective standard) as to be criminally liable.

3.4.2 Negligence and statutory offences

Negligence appears far more often in the definitions of statutory offences. One such example is driving without due care and attention contrary to s 3 of the Road Traffic Act 1988, which provides:

> If a person drives a mechanically propelled vehicle on a road or other public place without due care and attention, or without reasonable consideration for other persons using the road or place, he is guilty of an offence.

As this is a crime of negligence, the prosecution need not prove that the defendant intended to drive in this way, nor that they behaved recklessly. To be guilty of this offence, all that is required is that the defendant did drive without due care and attention (or without reasonable consideration for other road users) – their state of mind at the time is irrelevant. The court will simply assess whether the standard of the defendant's driving measured up to that of a reasonable driver and any deviation from this, no matter how slight, can lead to criminal liability.

Examples

(1) Daisy drove at 30 miles per hour in the outside lane of a motorway to get a better view of an accident that had just occurred on the opposite carriageway.

(2) Krishnan failed to give way when entering a major road. He passed his driving test the day before this incident occurred.

(3) Gwyn drove through a red traffic light because he was anxious to get his pregnant wife to hospital.

All these drivers fell below the standard of the reasonable motorist and would be convicted of driving without due care and attention. This is because no account is taken of the person's experience or the reason why they drove in this way, so it is irrelevant that Krishnan had only just passed his test and Gwyn was trying to help his wife.

Although it might be submitted that those who are inexperienced at driving should be assessed against the standards of the reasonable newly qualified driver, this argument would fail. In *McCrone v Riding* [1938] 1 All ER 157, the test to be applied in assessing whether an individual would be guilty of an offence of careless driving was discussed by Lord Hewart CJ:

> [The] standard is an objective standard, impersonal and universal, fixed in relation to the safety of other users of the highway. It is in no way related to the degree of proficiency or degree of experience attained by the individual driver.

Hence, even if a driver has a very good excuse for acting as they did, this will be disregarded.

In the examples (above), any information about what happened as a result of the careless driving has deliberately been omitted. There are no references to accidents, damage to property or personal injury to any individuals, and this is because such matters are not taken into account in deciding liability under s 3. It is the manner of the driving that is important, not the consequences of it.

Serious incompetence on the part of a motorist can lead to a more serious charge under s 2 of the Road Traffic Act 1988, namely the offence of dangerous driving. In order to secure a conviction, the prosecution would have to establish that the defendant drove 'a mechanically propelled vehicle dangerously on a road or other public place'. Under s 2A(1), the defendant must have driven in a manner which fell *far* below what would be expected of a careful and competent driver, and it would be obvious to the careful and competent driver that driving in such a way would be dangerous. Alternatively, under s 2A(2), the defendant will be driving dangerously if the condition of their vehicle is such that it would be obvious to a careful and competent driver that driving it in that condition would be dangerous.

In all cases under s 2A, therefore, the defendant is being assessed by the standards of the reasonable person (the careful and competent driver). They will only be guilty of an offence under s 2, however, if their behaviour has fallen far below what would reasonably be expected of a such a driver. Something more than the simple negligence required for careless driving is necessary.

3.4.3 Summary of negligence

For crimes where the mens rea may be satisfied by negligence:

(a) A person is punished simply for failing to measure up to the standards of the reasonable person.

(b) Although both recklessness and negligence involve the taking of an unjustifiable risk, there is a key difference:

  (i) recklessness is the conscious taking of an unjustifiable risk;

  (ii) negligence is the inadvertent taking of an unjustifiable risk.

  In other words, negligence can be proved simply by showing that the defendant's conduct fell short of an objective standard.

(c) Although the defendant may also have acted intentionally or recklessly, this is not required to establish criminal liability; it is what the defendant did that is relevant.

(d) Because the test is objective, individual considerations are not taken into account.

Set out below is an overview of negligence to assist your understanding.

Figure 3.3 Negligence

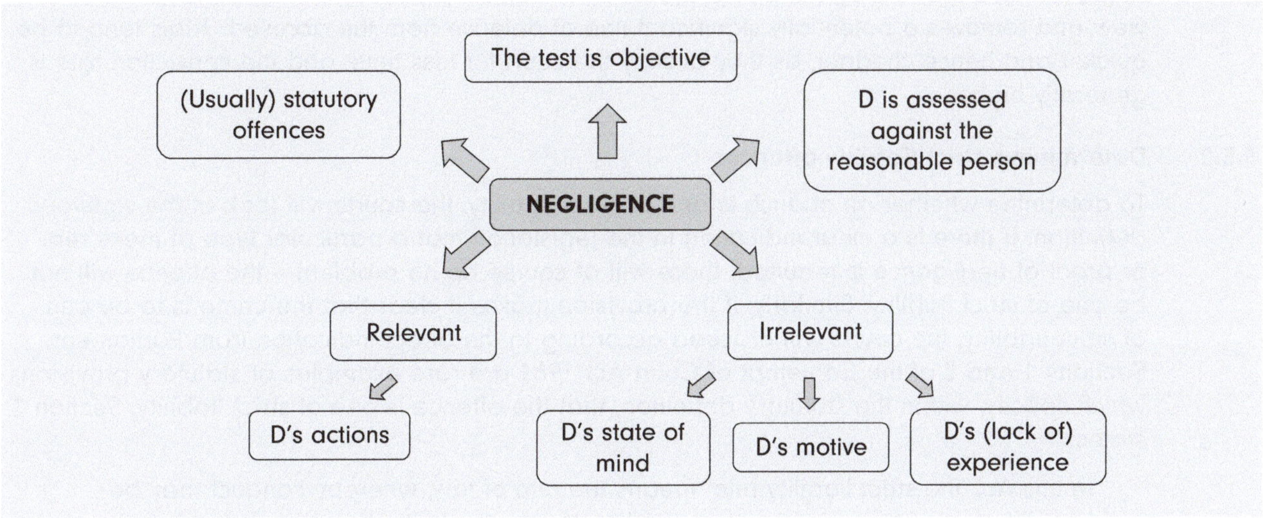

3.5 Strict liability offences

Another situation when a defendant may be convicted of a crime without having mens rea is where the offence is one of strict liability. Such an offence is one where, in relation to some element of the actus reus, neither mens rea nor negligence is needed for a conviction.

3.5.1 Type of offences

The vast majority of strict liability offences have been created by statute. They are designed to regulate certain types of behaviour with the aim of discouraging incompetence and unsafe actions, whilst encouraging greater vigilance and safety. Most do not apply to the population at large but rather to those people who are engaged in particular forms of conduct. For example, health and safety provisions often create offences of strict liability, as does legislation relating to the environment or the misuse of drugs. Similarly, there are numerous road traffic offences (such as driving without insurance) and licensing laws (serving alcohol 'after hours') which are strict liability offences.

At times, the strict liability rule may operate harshly, for example, in *Smedleys Ltd v Breed* [1974] AC 839, a small caterpillar was found in one of millions of tins of peas sold by the defendant. The company was found guilty under the Food and Drugs Act 1955 despite the difficulties of preventing such an event and the fact they had taken all reasonably practical steps to do so. The justification for the offence being strictly liable was the importance of consumer protection - a matter of social concern. Strict liability may also result in injustice where the defendant inadvertently commits the actus reus without any criminal intent. In *Pharmaceutical Society of Great Britain v Storkwain Ltd* [1986] 2 All ER 635, a pharmacist supplied prescription drugs after being presented with a fraudulent prescription. The pharmacist was not involved in the fraud, had no knowledge that the doctor's signature was forged and believed the prescription was genuine. However, despite being entirely blameless in the situation, because the offence under s 58(2) of the Medicines Act 1968 is one of strict liability, the pharmacist was convicted.

There are various public policy reasons as to why these offences are strictly liable. Not having to prove mens rea makes criminal prosecutions much simpler from an evidential point of view and removes a potentially significant line of defence from the accused. Trials tend to be quicker and hence cheaper, as they occupy the court for less time, and the conviction rate is generally higher.

3.5.2 Determining strict liability offences

To determine whether an offence is one of strict liability, the courts will look at the statutory definition. If there is a clear indication in the legislation that a particular type of mens rea or proof of negligence is required, there will of course be no problem – the offence will not be one of strict liability. Similarly, if the provision makes it clear that the crime is to be one of strict liability, the courts will proceed according to the direct indication from Parliament. Sections 1 and 2 of the Contempt of Court Act 1981 are rare examples of statutory provisions which specify, within the statutory definition, that the offence is one of strict liability. Section 1 states:

> In this Act 'the strict liability rule' means the rule of law, whereby conduct may be treated as a contempt of court as tending to interfere with the course of justice in particular legal proceedings regardless of intent to do so.

Section 2(1) provides that the strict liability rule applies only in relation to publications.

In some statutes, however, Parliament has omitted any reference to whether mens rea or negligence is required.

Example

Section 5 of the Road Traffic Act 1988 states:

(1) If a person–

(a) drives ... a motor vehicle on a road or other public place ... after consuming so much alcohol that the proportion of it in his breath, blood or urine exceeds the prescribed limit he is guilty of an offence.

The actus reus elements of the crime are: driving (1); a motor vehicle (2); on a road or other public place (3); and with an excess amount of alcohol (above the prescribed limit) in the driver's blood, breath or urine (4). However, there is nothing in the definition that suggests any mens rea or negligence requirements; for example, there is no mention of words such as 'with intent', 'recklessly' or 'without due care'. This could mean that the offence is one of strict liability, but absence of a reference to mens rea or negligence in the definition is not conclusive proof to that effect.

In fact, this offence is a crime of strict liability: under s 5 of the Road Traffic Act 1988, a person who drives after consuming excess alcohol is guilty even if they did not know or foresee the risk that the amount of alcohol they had consumed would exceed the prescribed limit, or indeed if they were unaware they had been drinking alcohol at all (for example, if their drinks had been spiked). Thus, the defendant can be convicted even though they lacked mens rea for the crucial element of the offence, namely, that their alcohol level exceeded the prescribed limit.

To assist in determining whether a crime is one of strict liability, the House of Lords provided guidance in the case of *Sweet v Parsley* [1970] AC 132. In his judgment, Lord Reid made the following important points:

(a) If the words of the statute make it clear either that the offence is one of strict liability, or that mens rea is required, that is the end of the matter: the court will proceed accordingly.

(b) If there is no indication, there is a presumption that 'Parliament did not intend to make criminals of persons who were in no way blameworthy in what they did': and so there is a presumption that the courts should 'read in words appropriate to require mens rea' in order to give effect to the will of Parliament.

(c) However, this presumption can be overturned if 'some reason can be found for holding that (mens rea) is not necessary'.

(d) The fact that other sections of a statute do require mens rea is not conclusive proof that a section which is silent on mens rea is intended to impose strict liability.

(e) Where a section is silent as to mens rea, the courts will need to go outside the wording of the Act to establish the intention of Parliament, specifically, to decide if the crime is one of strict liability.

(f) Lord Reid felt that a distinction should be drawn between 'quasi-criminal acts' and 'truly criminal acts'. In the former, the courts may easily decide to infer strict liability where the statute is silent. However, in the latter type, the court should be more reluctant to do so having regard to the stigma attached to a criminal conviction and the potential undermining of confidence in the judicial system if 'manifestly unjust' convictions are publicised.

In *R v Brown (Richard)* [2013] UKSC 43, the Supreme Court emphasised the importance of the presumption of mens rea, stating that it was a 'constitutional principle' that should only be displaced where the statutory wording was either very clear or it was an 'unmistakably necessary implication'. Lord Kerr went on to say that this presumption was even stronger where the offence was one that could be described as 'truly criminal and carries a heavy penalty or substantial social stigma'.

3.5.3 Summary of strict liability

(a) Offences of strict liability are exceptions to the general rule that mens rea is required for criminal offences.

(b) A person may be convicted of an offence even though they lack the mens rea for one or more elements of the actus reus.

(c) In some instances, the statute expressly states that the offence created is one of strict liability or uses words, such as 'intentionally', that make it clear it is not.

(d) In the absence of anything express, a rebuttable presumption applies that the offence is not strictly liable.

(e) Usually the higher the social stigma and the greater the penalty on conviction, the more likely that mens rea will be required.

Set out below is an overview of strict liability to assist your understanding.

Figure 3.4 Strict liability

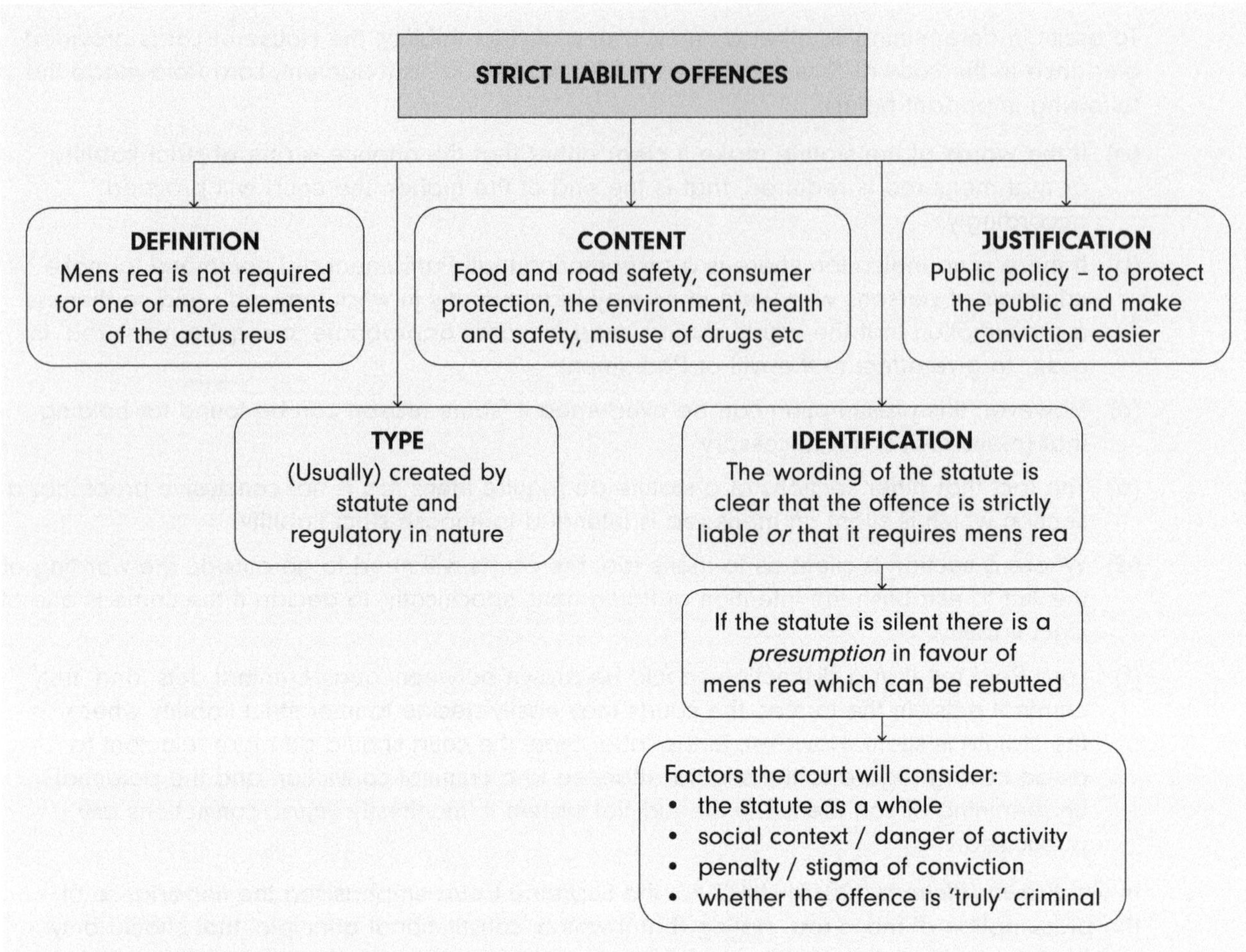

Having analysed the mens rea of intention and recklessness, and identified the exceptions to the general rule that mens rea is required for criminal offences (negligence and strict liability offences), the remainder of this chapter covers other relevant legal principles.

3.6 Transferred malice

On occasion, the defendant may attack the wrong person, or steal the wrong property, and this is where the doctrine of transferred malice comes into play.

Example

Terianne hates Jane and wants to kill her. She points a gun at Jane's bedroom window planning to shoot and kill her. She sees Jane at the window, fires the gun and runs off into the night, believing she has killed Jane. In fact, her shot missed Jane and hit Sally, Jane's flatmate. Sally dies from her injuries and Terianne is charged with murder.

Terianne has the actus reus of murder as she has killed a human being (Sally). But does she also have the mens rea of murder, in other words, did she intend to kill or cause really serious harm? With regard to her actual victim, Sally, the answer is, of course, 'no': she did not intend to kill Sally or cause her serious injury – in fact, Sally was her best friend and she is devastated by her death. However, Terianne intended to kill someone (Jane), and this is sufficient to justify a conviction for murder. This is logical as it would be unjust for Terianne to avoid liability just because she shot a different victim to that intended.

The outcome is achieved through the doctrine of transferred malice. This confirms that if a defendant has the 'malice' (intention or recklessness) to commit a crime against one victim (or one particular piece of property), the malice is transferred so that the mens rea they had in relation to their original victim is transferred to the actus reus they commit against another, unintended victim.

This is demonstrated by the diagram below which illustrates how Terianne's mens rea for murder in relation to Jane (she wanted to kill her), is transferred and coupled with the actus reus she commits of killing Sally to make her guilty of this offence.

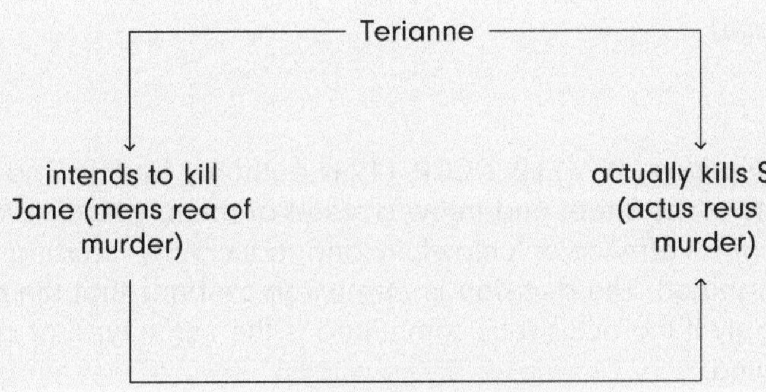

In the same way, if the defendant plans to scratch his ex-wife's car, thus causing criminal damage, and by mistake scratches the (very similar) car belonging to her husband instead, he is still guilty of criminal damage. The mens rea of criminal damage that he had in respect of his ex-wife's car is transferred and combines with the actus reus of damaging her husband's car.

The doctrine makes sense as, in both the cases above, the defendant has the mens rea for the type of crime they commit. It is right, therefore, that they should be held responsible for their actions and should not escape criminal liability simply because their plan failed. The authority for the doctrine of transferred malice is *R v Latimer* (1886) 17 QBD 359. In this case, the defendant was quarrelling with a man referred to as C in a public house. The defendant aimed a blow at C with his belt, but the belt glanced off C and struck another person (R) who was badly injured. The defendant was charged with an offence of unlawfully and maliciously wounding R contrary to s 20 of the Offences Against the Person Act 1861. He argued that the blow to R had been an accident and he therefore lacked the mens rea necessary to secure a conviction for assault. In dismissing the defendant's appeal against conviction for assaulting R, Lord Coleridge CJ said:

> We are of the opinion that this conviction must be sustained. It is common knowledge that a man who has an unlawful and malicious intent against another, and in attempting to carry it out, injures a third person, is guilty of what the law deems malice against the person injured, because the offender is doing an unlawful act, and has that which the judges call general malice, and that is enough.

However, the law would be too onerous if a defendant were to be held criminally liable for every unintended consequence, and so a limitation is placed on the doctrine of transferred malice.

Example

Isabella intends to hit Sunita on the head by throwing a stone at her but the stone misses, bounces off a nearby tree and breaks a window. The issue is whether Isabella may be charged with criminal damage (to the window) on the basis that she showed 'malice' towards Sunita (she intended to hit her).

In this instance, her malice for assault cannot be transferred to give Isabella the mens rea required for criminal damage. Although it may seem logical that, as Isabella had some form of criminal intent, that intent could be transferred to whatever crime she did in fact commit, this is not what the law says. The reason is that the crime actually committed (criminal damage) was of a wholly different nature from that which she had planned (assault).

The case of *R v Pembliton* (1874) LR 2 CCR 119 is authority for this. The defendant had been fighting with people in the street and threw a stone at them, which struck and broke a window. He was convicted of an offence of 'unlawfully and maliciously' causing damage to property, but successfully appealed. The decision in *Pembliton* confirms that the doctrine of transferred malice will only apply if the actus reus committed is the same type of crime as the defendant originally had in mind.

Transferred malice is a useful vehicle by which (apparently deserving) defendants can be convicted of the appropriate offence. However, most offences may be committed recklessly and, in such circumstances, the doctrine is unlikely to be required at all.

Example

Edward throws a vase at William intending to strike him, but he misses and hits William's friend, Dido, who is standing next to him. This would be sufficient for the actus reus of the offence of physical assault. Although the prosecution could rely upon the doctrine of transferred malice, there is another basis upon which Edward could be convicted.

Most offences (murder being an obvious exception) can be committed recklessly. Although Edward does not intend to hit Dido, he may be reckless as to doing so. If the prosecution can prove that Edward foresaw even the smallest risk of hitting Dido, and he went on to take that risk, he is guilty of physical assault. Given that Dido is standing so close to William, it is likely that the court will find that he satisfies the mens rea of recklessness.

3.6.1 Summary of transferred malice

To conclude:

(a) Under the doctrine of transferred malice, the defendant's intention towards A may be transferred to B where they commit the actus reus of the same offence in relation to B.

(b) Malice may be transferred from person to person, or from object to object.

(c) There is a limit to the scope of this doctrine; where the actus reus and mens rea relate to different types of offences, transferred malice does not operate.

(d) If the mens rea of the offence includes recklessness, it may not be necessary to consider the doctrine of transferred malice at all.

3.7 Coincidence of actus reus and mens rea

Although actus reus and mens rea are discussed in two different chapters, the concepts are inextricably linked. For there to be criminal liability, it is essential that the actus reus and mens rea coincide in time; in other words, the accused must have the required mens rea at the same moment they commit the actus reus.

Example

Silas has been involved in a dispute with his neighbour (Howard) for months over a planning issue. He is furious when Howard is granted the planning permission he applied for, and Silas decides that he will kill Howard. However, Silas does not take any action and so, because there is no actus reus, he is not criminally liable.

After speaking to his wife, Silas calms down and decides to continue painting the outside of his house. As he is doing so, his neighbour walks past and, just at that moment, Silas accidentally drops a tin of paint. The tin lands on Howard's head, killing him. At this point, Silas has the actus reus for murder but not the mens rea, so again no criminal liability.

3.7.1 Continuing act

To ensure that the actus reus and mens rea do coincide in time, so the defendant may be convicted of the relevant offence, the courts have been willing to stretch the concept of an act. In *Fagan v Metropolitan Police Commissioner* [1969] 1 QB 439, the defendant was sitting in his car when he was approached by a police officer who told him to move the vehicle. Fagan accidentally reversed the car onto the officer's foot. At this point, Fagan lacked the mens rea for an offence as his action was inadvertent. However, when he realised what had happened, he refused to move the car and turned the engine off. He was found guilty of assault on the basis that the actus reus was a continuing act that coincided at some point with the required mens rea.

It is apparent from this case that, where an actus reus may be brought about by a continuing act, it is sufficient that the defendant had mens rea during its continuance despite not having the mens rea at its commencement.

3.7.2 Single transaction

In the case of a continuing act, there is one act to which the mens rea is linked. However, the issue has also arisen where a combination of events has led to the unlawful outcome. In such circumstances, the courts have been similarly imaginative in circumventing the principle of coincidence of actus reus and mens rea. They have achieved this by the interpretation of a number of consecutive events as a 'single transaction'. This overcomes the complexes of determining criminal liability if it is not possible to identify when a result occurred or what caused it.

Example

Jim, as part of his plan to kill Kaydian, hits him over the head with a bottle. Believing that Kaydian is dead, Jim decides to dispose of the body by throwing it over a cliff to make the incident look like an accident. Kaydian, however, did not die when he was hit with the bottle but died of exposure some time later.

The actus reus of the offence of murder is the killing of a human being and clearly, as a result of Jim's actions, Kaydian is dead. The mens rea of murder is an intention to kill or cause really serious harm. When Jim hit Kaydian over the head with the bottle, his motive was to kill him and therefore he had direct intent to kill. However, as Kaydian survived the attack, the actus reus was not present. When Kaydian actually died (the actus reus of murder), Jim thought he was disposing of the corpse, and, therefore, he did not have the necessary mens rea.

The facts of the above example are similar to the case of *Thabo-Meli v R* [1954] 1 All ER 373. The Privy Council rejected the defendant's argument that the actus reus and the mens rea did not coincide, with Lord Reid stating that 'it was impossible to divide up what was really one series of acts'. Rolling the body over the cliff was part of a preconceived plan and just one of a number of acts which essentially amounted to a single transaction. It was held that the defendant had the mens rea when he set out and should not avoid liability just because he thought (at the time of the victim's death) that his plan had already been achieved.

Later cases have confirmed the decision in *Thabo-Meli* and have also extended it to situations where there is no pre-arranged plan but there is a continuous series of events.

In the case of *R v Le Brun* [1991] 4 All ER 673 the defendant assaulted his wife and then tried to move her. His wife slipped from his grip and banged her head on the pavement, thereby suffering a fractured skull from which she died. The defendant was charged with manslaughter but argued that the cause of death was an accident. He stated that he had the mens rea (of assault) when he hit his wife but that had not caused her death, so there was no actus reus at that stage. Death was a genuine accident and he therefore did not have the mens rea of any offence at the time when death was caused. The defendant's conviction was upheld by the Court of Appeal. Lord Lane said that where the unlawful application of force (hitting his wife) and the eventual act causing death (dropping her) were part of the same sequence of events, the fact there was a lapse in time between the two did not enable the defendant to escape liability.

3.7.3 Summary of coincidence of actus reus and mens rea

(a) The general position is that before there can be criminal liability, the actus reus and mens rea must coincide in time.

(b) There are two exceptions to this rule:

  (i) The continuing act principle applies where the defendant's act satisfies the actus reus of an offence and, at some point, they also have the necessary mens rea for that offence.

(ii) The single transaction principle is likely to arise where there is an implied series of events and from the outset the defendant seems to be involved in criminal activity. Provided the eventual act that causes death is part of the same sequence of events as the initial act, it does not matter that there is a time lapse between the two.

3.8 Basic, specific and ulterior intent

Earlier in this chapter, the mens rea elements of direct intent and indirect intent were discussed. However, the word 'intent' is also used in a different context in the criminal law, namely, to classify offences. An appreciation of what is meant by basic, specific and ulterior intent is vital to understanding, for example, the defence of intoxication.

Most offences are crimes of 'basic intent'. These are traditionally defined as those offences where a lesser form of mens rea is required than intention. Thus, criminal damage and most assaults will fall within this category as either intention or recklessness will satisfy the mens rea.

In contrast, 'specific intent' offences are those where the only mens rea that will suffice to convict a person of the crime is that of intention. Examples are murder, assault under s 18 of the Offences Against the Person Act 1861 and theft.

Reference to ulterior intent also appears in relation to some criminal offences, for example, burglary. When this term is used it means that the prosecution must prove an 'extra' element of mens rea against the defendant before it can secure a conviction. Essentially, in addition to establishing that the defendant committed the actus reus of an offence with the appropriate mens rea, in offences of ulterior intent, the prosecution must also prove that the defendant had an additional mens rea, namely, that they intended to produce some consequence which went beyond the actus reus of the crime (even though they might not have actually succeeded).

Although this sounds complicated, the concept is straightforward when applied to a concrete example such as burglary. Under s 9(1)(a) of the Theft Act 1968, a person is guilty of burglary if: 'he enters any building or part of a building as a trespasser and with intent to commit theft or inflict grievous bodily harm or criminal damage'. The actus reus of the offence is entering a building or part of a building as a trespasser. The basic mens rea is that, on entry, the defendant must either know they are entering as a trespasser or foresee the risk that they may be trespassing. However, proving these two elements will not be enough to convict a defendant of burglary under s 9(1)(a). In addition, the defendant must be shown to have an ulterior intent to steal, to inflict grievous bodily harm, or to cause criminal damage once they are in the building. They do not actually have to do any of these but the extra state of mind (an intention to do so) must be established if the defendant is to be convicted of burglary under s 9(1)(a).

3.9 Ignorance of the law

Although for most serious crimes the defendant must intentionally or recklessly commit the actus reus of the offence, there is no requirement for the defendant to appreciate that what they are doing is criminal. Ignorance of the criminal law is never a defence, even where it was impossible for the defendant to have known the law.

3.10 Mistake of fact

On occasion, the defendant makes a mistake of fact which causes them to believe their conduct is innocent. In this instance, the defendant lacks some knowledge which is needed for the mens rea. An example will illustrate.

Example

After his exams, Ted picks up a textbook wrongly believing that it is his and rips it up, before throwing it in the bin. Unfortunately, it is his friend's textbook. For the offence of criminal damage, the defendant must realise that the property destroyed or damaged does or might belong to another. If the defendant wrongly believes that they own the property, they will lack the necessary mens rea of the offence and will therefore not be liable. If believed, Ted would not be guilty of criminal damage.

Alternatively, a defendant may consider a risk and, as a result of a mistake, wrongly conclude that there is none. Here the defendant would escape liability if the crime in question required the mens rea of either intention or recklessness.

It is important to note that there is no separate defence of mistake. It is simply that the mistake may prevent the prosecution from proving the necessary mens rea for the offence or provide the basis of a defence, for example that of self-defence.

A genuine, albeit unreasonable mistake may be sufficient to negate the mens rea requirement of an offence, as mens rea depends on what this particular defendant thought. Inevitably, however, the more unreasonable the defendant's mistake is, the less likely the court is to believe that it was an honest one (see s 8 of the Criminal Justice Act 1967 considered earlier).

3.11 Summary of actus reus and mens rea

It is important to understand the concepts of both actus reus and mens rea as they provide the underlying structure to the criminal law; effectively, they are the 'coat-hanger' upon which hang all the various elements of the different offences.

Figure 3.5 Actus reus and mens rea

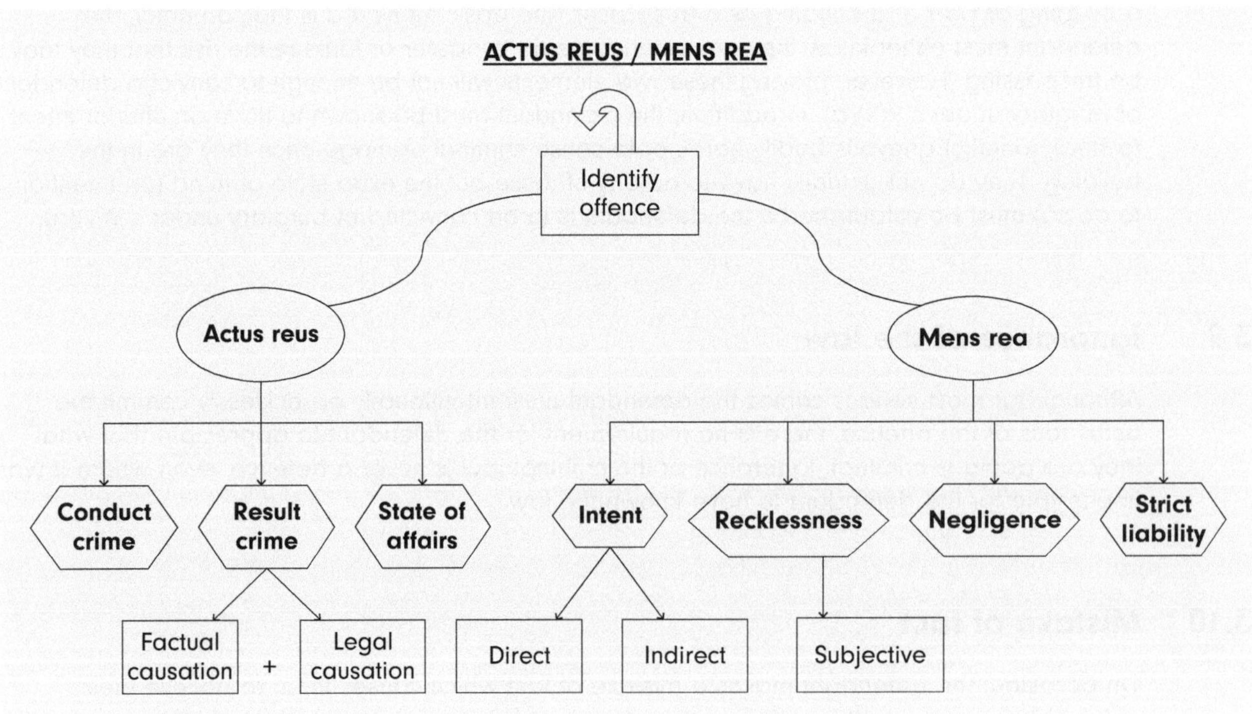

That concludes our consideration of the basic principles of criminal law. To assist your understanding of these concepts, you should attempt the activity below.

ACTIVITY

Barry, a man of low intelligence, sets fire to his council property to try and force the local authority to rehouse him and his family. The fire quickly takes hold and within minutes the house is burning ferociously, destroying the stairs so that, although Barry and his wife manage to escape, their two young children are trapped in the bedroom. They are overcome by the smoke and die before they can be rescued. Barry is devastated by the deaths as he genuinely loves his children. To convict Barry of murder, the prosecution must prove that the defendant intended to kill or cause grievous bodily harm.

(1) Does Barry have direct intent for murder?

(2) If not, is the test for indirect intent satisfied?

(3) If Barry denies the mens rea, what provision may help the jury in assessing his evidence?

COMMENT

(1) Barry is adamant that it was not his intention to kill his children or to cause them grievous bodily harm. Furthermore, doing so would defeat his aim or purpose as the family would not be rehoused in these circumstances.

(2) Indirect intent: If the jury is not satisfied that Barry had direct intent to kill or cause grievous bodily harm, they will be directed as follows:

   (a) Was the consequence - the death of the children - virtually certain to occur as a result of Barry's act? Given that he set fire to a house at night, knowing there were young children asleep upstairs, the jury is likely to conclude that the objective test is satisfied.

   (b) Did Barry appreciate that the deaths were virtually certain (subjective)? This is more problematic and would depend upon his evidence. Barry may have been confident that he and his partner would be able to get the children out of the house before the fire took hold. However, although Barry is of low intelligence, the risks and consequences of a house fire are well known and may be found to be within his contemplation.

(3) To assist, under s 8 of the CJA 1967, the jury may take into account what a reasonable person would have foreseen when deciding what this particular defendant foresaw. Even so, given the evidence that Barry loved his children, it is unlikely the jury would find such intent.

4 Assaults

LEARNING OUTCOMES

When you have completed this chapter, you should be able to:

- explain the legal elements of selected statutory and common law non-fatal offences against the person and analyse how these apply to factual scenarios;
- understand how the defence of consent operates to absolve a defendant from liability for assault in certain situations;
- appreciate how some areas of the criminal law remain controversial.

4.1 Introduction

Assault has been on the statute books for over 160 years and for considerably longer as a common law offence, making it one of the more established of crimes. Assaults may take place in a range of situations, from brawls in nightclubs, to fights between rival teams at football matches, amongst gangs establishing territory or imposing control, and in the context of domestic violence. According to government statistics, just under 2% of the adult population are assaulted each year, and although the percentage is lower than the high of nearly 5% in 1995, for each person this is a significant event. It should also be borne in mind that this represents the national average so the figure would be much higher or lower in some areas. Dealing with such behaviour is important from a social policy perspective to ensure that people may go about their daily lives without fear.

This chapter will explore the main non-fatal offences against the person. There are a number of such offences ranging in severity from the infliction of really serious injuries to causing mental harm to simply instilling fear. Indeed, assault is best understood as a generic term referring to a category of related offences rather than a single crime.

4.2 Hierarchy of assaults

In this chapter you will discover that the law recognises various different assault offences and distinguishes between a defendant who so severely attacks someone that they nearly die, and one who merely pushes a person causing no injury at all. In other words, there is a sliding scale of offences dependent upon the degree of harm caused to the victim and, to a more limited extent, the mens rea of the defendant.

In order of severity, beginning with the least serious, the offences are:

(a) simple and physical assault;

(b) assault occasioning actual bodily harm;

(c) maliciously wounding or inflicting grievous bodily harm;

(d) wounding or causing grievous bodily harm with intent.

The classification and maximum sentences reflect this hierarchy with the penalty ranging from a fine to life imprisonment.

4.3 Common law assaults

There are two assaults that derive from the common law, namely simple assault and physical assault. These two offences are collectively known as common assault and the main difference between them is that, for the offence of simple assault, the accused need not make any physical contact with the victim at all. However, in practice, simple and physical assault normally occur together so that, for example, the defendant may raise their fist as a threat, before actually hitting the victim.

Although these offences are referred to in statute, s 39 of the Criminal Justice Act (CJA) 1988 merely confirms that they are summary only offences triable in the magistrates' court, and the maximum sentence is 6 months' imprisonment and/or a fine; no definition is included.

4.4 Simple assault

'Assault' is a word that is often used in everyday circumstances and in the media, but it has a specific interpretation in the criminal law context.

The classic definition of simple assault is any act that intentionally or recklessly causes another person to apprehend immediate and unlawful personal force (*Fagan v Metropolitan Police Commissioner* [1969] 1 QB 439). We shall refer to this type of assault as 'simple assault', but other writers and lawyers use different terms, for example 'common' or 'technical' assault. In this context they all have the same meaning.

4.4.1 Actus reus

To determine whether the accused has satisfied the actus reus of simple assault, namely causing the victim to apprehend immediate and unlawful personal force, the offence must be broken down into its constituent parts.

First, the assault must be unlawful, and it is important to bear in mind that not all assaults are. A police officer may use reasonable force to make an arrest, perhaps to apprehend someone running away from a crime scene; and an individual may use reasonable force to defend themselves, or others, or indeed their property.

The actus reus requires the victim to apprehend unlawful force or violence. An assault may be committed in a variety of ways and those set out below are just some suggestions.

Examples

Biko is an aggressive man. He:

(1) chases after Anthony, threatening to beat him up;

(2) pulls out a gun and points it at Sanjay;

(3) raises his arm as if to strike his partner;

(4) sends a text message to Oliver stating: 'u r dead'.

In all these situations, Biko has committed the actus reus of assault as it is the apprehension of the unlawful force that is important. The fact that there is no violence or touching is irrelevant as this is not a requirement. As a consequence, for simple assault, no injury or harm needs to be caused.

What if Biko:

(5) threatens to punch Pip, a martial arts expert who is not afraid of Biko; and

(6) creeps up behind Juliette unnoticed and jumps on her back.

In example (5), the actus reus of assault is satisfied. This is because the victim is only required to apprehend the force, in other words, be aware of it. They do not have to fear it in the sense of being frightened. As long as Pip believes he is about to be unlawfully touched, that is sufficient. With regards to Juliette, because Biko approached unnoticed, Juliette did not apprehend any unlawful force at all, so Biko is not guilty of simple assault (although he may be liable for physical assault as discussed later in this chapter).

For the actus reus of simple assault to be satisfied, the threat must be of *immediate* unlawful personal force. It is not enough that the victim immediately apprehends that the unlawful personal force may occur; the victim must anticipate that the force will actually occur immediately. As a consequence, realising straightaway that someone might hit or make physical contact at some stage in the future will not be enough. So if the defendant says, 'I will be around next week with the boys to give you a good kicking', they will not be guilty of simple assault because the victim on hearing the threat realises that force might follow, but in several days' time.

However, it will be sufficient if the victim fears that force could occur immediately. This applies particularly where modern technology is used, such as a mobile telephone, as the defendant may in fact be very close to the victim when making the threat of violence. In the case of *R v Burstow* [1997] 4 All ER 225, the defendant stalked his victim over several years, sending her photographs and letters, telephoning her and visiting her home. The victim suffered psychiatric injury as a result. The court held that if the victim feared that the defendant could strike at any time, this would satisfy the actus reus of assault.

4.4.1.1 Assaults by words or silence

In the past, there was some dispute as to whether words alone could amount to an assault without any other gesture. However, the House of Lords in *R v Ireland* [1997] 3 WLR 534 indicated that they could; indeed, words can be far more intimidating than actions. If someone says aggressively, 'I'm going to beat you up to such an extent that even your own mother won't recognise you', there is no reason why they should not be liable for an assault even though they make no other physical gesture.

Another controversial area that the House of Lords addressed in the case of *R v Ireland* was whether silent telephone calls could amount to an assault. Lord Steyn confirmed that they could, 'depending on the facts'. A silent caller intends by their silence to cause fear, and the victim may fear the possibility of immediate unlawful personal force as they do not know where the caller is. Whether or not a defendant is liable in these circumstances depends 'in particular on the impact of the caller's potentially menacing call or calls on the victim'. The justification for the decision was the psychological impact of the repeated calls on the victims; hence one silent call is unlikely to be enough, but a pattern of silent calls may be.

4.4.1.2 Conditional threats

One final point on the actus reus of simple assault is that of conditional threats. If the defendant says to the victim, 'If you do not shut up, I will slap you', is that an assault? Although, to some extent, whether the victim gets hit or not is in their own hands, the law takes the view that the unjustified restriction on their personal liberty is unwarranted and the defendant should still be liable for assault (see *Read v Coker* (1853) 13 CB 850). This assumes that the conditional threat also satisfies the 'immediate' force requirement.

4.4.2 Mens rea

The mens rea for simple assault is that the defendant must intend to cause the victim to apprehend immediate unlawful personal force, or be reckless as to whether such apprehension is caused (*R v Venna* [1976] QB 421).

> ***Example***
>
> *Simranjit is having a quiet drink in a cocktail bar with some friends. She is at the bar waiting to be served when Ziliang comes in and tries to jump the queue. When Simranjit politely asks Ziliang to wait his turn, he looks at her, raises his fist and says: 'Don't hassle me or I'll smash your face in'. Ziliang, however, does not touch Simranjit.*
>
> *In this instance, he has committed an assault because he:*
>
> *(1) raised his fist;*
>
> *(2) threatened Simranjit; and*
>
> *(3) both appear to be intentional acts.*
>
> *The first two points would therefore constitute the actus reus and the third point the mens rea. It is irrelevant that there was no physical contact.*

The test for recklessness is subjective (*R v Spratt* [1991] 2 All ER 210); thus, the defendant must foresee the risk that the victim will apprehend immediate unlawful personal force and go on to take that risk. It does not matter that others would have foreseen the risk; if the defendant did not, they are entitled to an acquittal.

> ***Example***
>
> *Felix is at his local park watching a football match. He is standing very close to the pitch shouting encouragement and cheering. His team's wing player, who has not been playing very well, notices Felix standing close by with both arms raised and with his fists clenched. He can also see that Felix is shouting and fears that Felix is about to hit him.*
>
> *Although the actus reus of simple assault is present (because the wing player feared he was about to be hit), the mens rea is not. Felix was only shouting encouragement and therefore clearly did not intend to cause an apprehension of immediate force. Furthermore, he is not reckless as Felix himself did not realise there was a risk that his conduct would be so regarded – he was just supporting the game.*

4.4.3 Summary of simple assault

This flowchart gives an overview of the offence of simple assault.

Figure 4.1 Simple assault

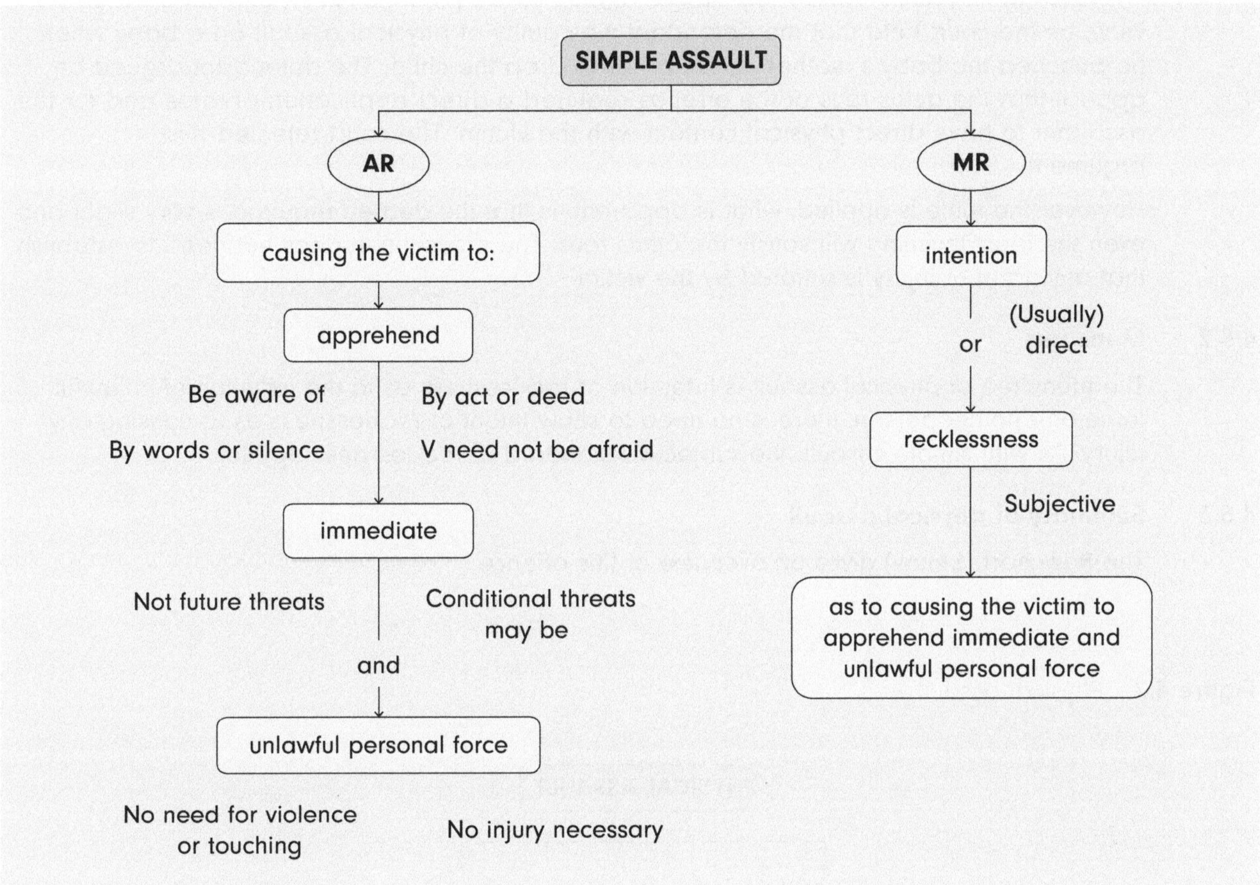

4.5 Physical assault

If simple assault is causing an apprehension of immediate, unlawful personal force, physical assault is the infliction of that force. It does not have to be a serious attack; indeed, any unlawful touching (with the appropriate mens rea) will suffice. Another term used for a 'physical assault' is a 'battery'. Although simple and physical assault normally go together (so the victim thinks they are going to be hit and then they are), they do not have to. There can be a physical assault without a simple assault, for example, where the defendant approaches the victim from behind, unheard, and hits them over the head. The victim did not apprehend the force as they did not hear the defendant - thus there is no simple assault - but there clearly is a physical assault.

4.5.1 Actus reus

The actus reus of physical assault requires the infliction of unlawful personal force on the victim, and this may be applied in a variety of ways:

(a) By direct physical contact between two people including pushing, prodding or hitting. This may involve the use of a weapon (for example a cosh, knife or gun).

(b) The application of force may not necessarily be direct. It may include throwing an object or spitting at someone or even deliberately cycling over the victim's foot.

(c) Most academic criminal lawyers would argue that the application of force can be indirect, for example deliberately placing an obstacle behind a door so the victim trips over it (see *DPP v K* [1990] 1 WLR 1067), or a defendant setting their dog on the victim.

The case of *Haystead v Chief Constable of Derbyshire* [2000] 3 All ER 890 supports this view, as the court held that the defendant was guilty of physical assault on a baby when he punched the baby's mother, causing her to drop the child. The defendant argued on appeal that the actus reus of the offence required a direct application of force and for the assailant to have direct physical contact with the victim. The court rejected this argument.

However the force is applied, what is apparent, is that the degree required is very slight and even the least touching will satisfy the actus reus. The prosecution does not need to establish that any harm or injury is suffered by the victim.

4.5.2 Mens rea

The mens rea of physical assault is intention or recklessness as to the infliction of unlawful force on another person; there is no need to show intent or recklessness as to causing any injury. As with simple assault, the subjective standard of recklessness applies.

4.5.3 Summary of physical assault

The flowchart (below) gives an overview of this offence.

Figure 4.2 Physical assault

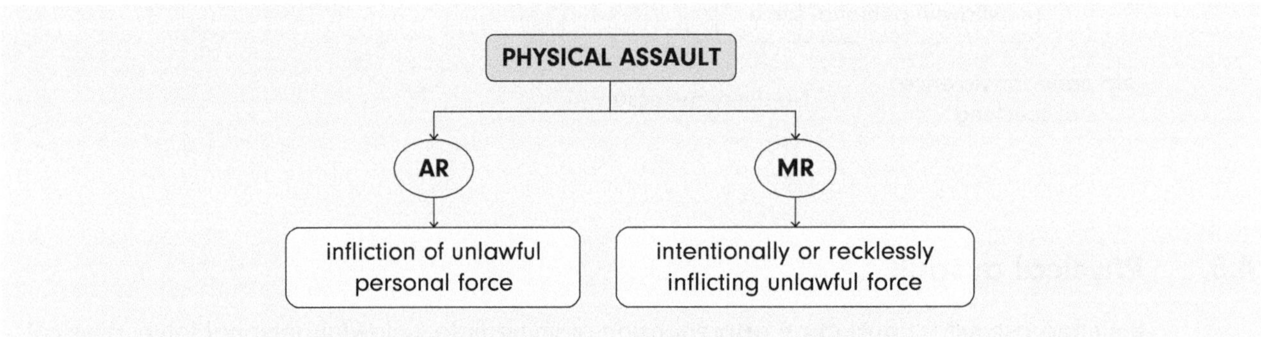

4.5.3 Practical application of simple and physical assault

Although there is no doubt that simple and physical assault are separate offences, the term 'assault' is commonly used by lay people and lawyers to mean either or both. Indeed, this is the meaning that will be adopted in this textbook, and if it is necessary to distinguish the offences, the terms 'simple assault' and 'physical assault' will be used.

To assist your understanding, set out below are examples of how the two offences interact in a practical context.

Example

(a) *Craig tells his teenage daughter, Fay, that if she continues to see her girlfriend, Tilly, he will break every bone in Tilly's body. In this instance, Craig has not committed simple assault. Although there is a clear threat, Fay does not apprehend any violence against her as the threat is directed against her girlfriend; and neither does Tilly as she was not present when the words were spoken.*

(b) *If Craig speaks these words to Tilly, it will not be simple assault because his threat is a conditional one - he will only attack Tilly if she continues to see Fay. In these circumstances, Tilly does not apprehend immediate unlawful force and so Craig is not guilty of simple assault. This is an unusual example and most common law assaults are much more straightforward, with a clear threat by the defendant to the victim causing them to fear immediate violence.*

(c) *Fay ignores her father. In anger, Craig seeks out Tilly and punches her in the face. Now Craig has committed an offence - that of physical assault - because he has actually inflicted unlawful force on Tilly.*

It is clear that whether one or both of these common law assaults have been committed will depend upon the particular facts.

4.6 Statutory assaults

For the remainder of this chapter, the statutory offences will be explored. All these offences may be found in the Offences Against the Person Act (OAPA) 1861. Because of this, some of the original language is rather old-fashioned but, fortunately, the terms have been given modern meanings.

4.7 Assault occasioning actual bodily harm (OAPA 1861, s 47)

The first of the more serious assault offences is found in s 47 of the OAPA 1861. This offence carries a maximum sentence of five years' imprisonment and is triable either way - either in the magistrates' court or the Crown Court. Section 47 states:

> Whosoever shall be convicted upon an indictment of any assault occasioning actual bodily harm shall be liable ... to be imprisoned for any term not exceeding five years.

4.7.1 Actus reus

The actus reus of s 47 consists of three elements and these are:

(a) an assault;

(b) which occasions (causes);

(c) actual bodily harm.

The first requirement is that there must be an assault, and either a simple or physical assault will suffice. However, because a s 47 assault is essentially an aggravated form of common assault, the wording in the statute makes it clear that harm must be caused, although there is no further guidance on how significant the injury must be to satisfy this offence. Fortunately, case law provides some assistance. According to *R v Miller* [1954] 2 QB 282, actual bodily harm means any hurt or injury calculated to interfere with the health or comfort of the victim. The harm does not have to be serious or permanent, but it must be more than 'transient or trifling'.

Examples of actual bodily harm would include where the victim suffers a split lip, significant bruising, a temporary loss of consciousness or even where the defendant cut a substantial piece of the victim's hair. However, if the victim only suffers a very small bruise, a minor scratch or a red mark on the skin, from a slap, which quickly fades, this would not satisfy the definition. In practice, the Crown Prosecution Service follows a Charging Standard Code in order to decide what offence to charge. Examples in the Code of actual bodily harm that would lead to a s 47 charge include those where there has been significant medical intervention and/or permanent effects have resulted. This would include cases where there is the need for several stitches (but not the superficial application of steri-strips) or a hospital procedure under anaesthetic.

More recently, there has been an increase in cases where the harm that the victim suffers is mental rather than physical, for example, depression and anxiety. In the case of *R v Ireland* [1997] 3 WLR 534 (above), Lord Steyn confirmed that actual bodily harm is capable of including psychiatric injury. However, it needs to be a recognisable clinical condition, for example, anxiety neurosis or reactive depression. Strong emotions such as rage, extreme fear or panic do not suffice. Medical evidence would need to be called by the prosecution to establish the psychiatric injury, if the issue is not admitted by the defence, and the severity of the psychological harm will determine the level of statutory assault for which the defendant is liable.

4.7.2 Mens rea

For many years, determining what amounted to the mens rea of s 47 caused confusion. It was generally agreed that the mens rea was intention or recklessness - but as to what? Was it sufficient that the defendant intended or was reckless as to the assault, or did they have to intend or be reckless as to the causing of the harm as well?

The question was finally answered by the House of Lords in *R v Savage; R v Parmenter* [1991] 4 All ER 698. In this case, the defendant intended to throw a pint of beer over the victim, but the glass also left her hand. It broke and a piece of glass cut the victim's wrist. The judges decided the mens rea was intention or recklessness as to the assault only, and so the defendant was convicted despite her lack of desire to cause harm. The effect of this ruling is that all the prosecution has to prove is that the accused (for example) hit the victim deliberately, and provided injury is caused of sufficient gravity, they are guilty of a s 47 assault. In summary, the element of causing actual bodily harm is relevant only to the actus reus of this offence and not the mens rea; there is strict liability as to this aspect.

Example

Vijay hits Blake and injures him by giving him a black eye. In his police interview, he states: 'I admit I intended to hit Blake, but I never meant to injure or harm him and the thought never entered my head that I might.' Vijay has satisfied the requirements of an assault under s 47 of the OAPA 1861 because:

- *Actus reus: Vijay hit Blake (the assault) which caused (occasioned) a black eye (the actual bodily harm).*
- *Mens rea: The mens rea is to intend or be reckless as to the assault. Vijay admits that he intended to assault Blake. The fact he did not intend or foresee the risk of any harm or injury is irrelevant as this is not required.*

4.7.3 Summary of s 47 assault

To conclude, there is no difference between the mens rea for simple/physical assault and the mens rea for an assault under s 47 of the OAPA 1861. The only difference between the offences is that for s 47 there must be some bodily harm caused, but this is an actus reus issue.

Set out below is an overview of assault occasioning actual bodily harm.

Figure 4.3 Assault occasioning actual bodily harm

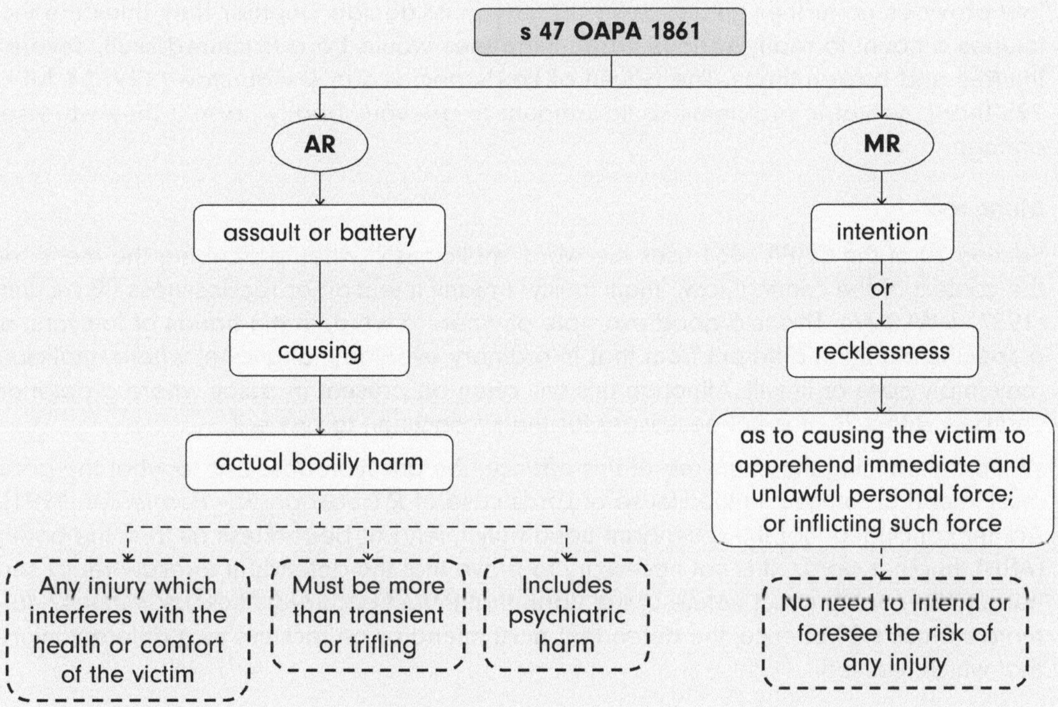

4.8 Wounding or inflicting grievous bodily harm (OAPA 1861, s 20)

The next offence up the scale of seriousness is s 20 of the OAPA 1861, which states:

> Whoever shall unlawfully and maliciously wound or inflict any grievous bodily harm upon any other person ... shall be liable ... to imprisonment for a term not exceeding five years.

As with the s 47 assault, this offence is triable either way. It is interesting to note that s 20 carries the same maximum sentence as s 47 even though it is a more serious offence, as wounding or grievous bodily harm must be established rather than just actual bodily harm. In practice, however, sentences are usually heavier under s 20 than for s 47.

4.8.1 Actus reus

The actus reus of s 20 is to unlawfully wound *or* inflict grievous bodily harm. Unlawfully simply means that the act of wounding or inflicting grievous bodily harm was not done with any lawful justification, such as acting in self-defence or in defence of another, as confirmed in *R v Horwood* [2012] EWCA Crim 253.

A wound requires both layers of the skin to be broken (*Moriarty v Brookes* (1834) 6 C & P 684); effectively, the prosecution is literally looking for blood. Cuts of any size or severity or lacerations are the most common examples, but because, rather oddly, there is no reference to the wound being serious, a scratch that draws blood will suffice. Although this may be an important point academically, in practice, according to the Crown Prosecution Service's Charging Standard Code, wounding will only generally be charged when the cut is significant. Note that bruising or internal bleeding are not wounds no matter how serious the bleeding, as the skin has not been broken (*JJC (a Minor) v Eisenhower* [1984] QB 331), although severe internal bleeding could amount to grievous bodily harm.

Grievous bodily harm means 'really serious harm' (*DPP v Smith* [1961] AC 290), but case law provides no further guidance so the jury must decide whether they think the victim's injuries amount to really serious harm. Examples would be a fractured skull, severe internal injuries and broken limbs. The House of Lords decided in *R v Burstow* [1997] 4 All ER 225 that psychiatric problems could amount to grievous bodily harm if they were severe enough.

4.8.2 Mens rea

Section 20 of the OAPA 1861 uses the word 'maliciously' when describing the mens rea. In the context of the criminal law, 'maliciously' means intention or recklessness (*R v Cunningham* [1957] 3 WLR 76). This is a good example of where a word, in the hands of lawyers, acquires a specific meaning different from that in ordinary everyday language, where 'maliciously' may imply spite or ill will. Although this will often be present in cases where a defendant is charged with s 20, it is not necessary for the prosecution to prove it.

When determining the mens rea of this offence, the question arises as to what the accused must intend or foresee. In the House of Lords case of *R v Savage; R v Parmenter* [1991], Lord Ackner concluded that the defendant need only intend or be reckless as to some bodily harm (ABH). In other words, it is not necessary to prove that the defendant foresaw really serious harm (GBH) or the exact nature of the harm that in fact occurred. Thus, as with s 47, for the more serious s 20 offence, the defendant must intend or be reckless to a different injury than that which resulted.

Example

Clint is involved in a fight with Bill and punches him in the face. Bill stumbles backwards, falls over and hits his head on the corner of the table fracturing his skull. Clint is charged under s 20 of the OAPA 1861. When questioned, Clint came up with the following responses - are these sufficient to establish the mens rea for s 20?

(1) *'Bill was asking for it, I hit him really hard and wanted him to really suffer.'*

This is clearly adequate mens rea for s 20 as it appears that Clint wanted to inflict really serious harm. Clint has a higher level of intent than required for a s 20 assault, so he would satisfy the mens rea for this offence.

(2) *'OK I hit him really hard. I thought I would break his jaw, but I never intended he should fracture his skull. I'm really sorry about that.'*

Clint is liable for s 20 because, again, he intended grievous bodily harm. The fact that he envisaged a broken jaw and not a fractured skull is irrelevant. It is not necessary for the defendant to intend the precise injury that actually occurred.

(Note: in the two examples above, although Clint satisfies the mens rea for s 20, because he intended really serious harm, he would also be liable for the more serious offence under s 18 of the OAPA 1861.)

(3) *'Look, I never meant to really harm Bill. I suppose I realised I might, but I didn't want it to happen.'*

This is different from the previous examples as Clint did not intend grievous bodily harm. However, by saying that he realised he might really harm Bill, Clint is admitting that he foresaw the risk and went on to take it. His words indicate that he is reckless as to grievous bodily harm and provide adequate evidence of the mens rea for s 20. This is because Clint need only be reckless as to some bodily harm for a s 20 assault.

(4) *'I suppose when I think about it now I ought to have realised the risk of really hurting Bill, but it never crossed my mind at the time. I thought the worst thing I would do is give him a black eye.'*

The first sentence establishes that Clint did not intend, nor was he reckless as to causing, grievous bodily harm. The fact that others might think the risk was entirely obvious is irrelevant as it is subjective recklessness - Clint must foresee the risk. However, the second sentence clearly shows he was at least reckless (if not intending) to cause some harm, and this is an adequate mens rea for s 20. Remember the defendant does not have to foresee grievous bodily harm or the actual injury that occurred, only some harm.

(5) *'OK, I intended to hit him, but it honestly never entered my head that there was any chance of causing him any injury.'*

What Clint is saying here is that he intended the assault but did not foresee the risk of any harm. Therefore, in this example, there is no mens rea for s 20 as it is a crucial element that the accused foresees the risk of some harm or injury. (However, this mens rea - an intention to assault - is enough to charge him under s 47.)

4.8.3 Summary of s 20 assault

Set out below is an overview of the elements required for an assault under s 20 of the OAPA 1861. The offence appears inconsistent in that the smallest cut will satisfy the actus reus as it will count as a wound; however, if the injury does not draw blood, only really serious harm will suffice. Furthermore, for the mens rea, the level of harm anticipated by the accused may be lower than that caused - actual rather than grievous bodily harm.

Figure 4.4 Malicious wounding or inflicting grievous bodily harm

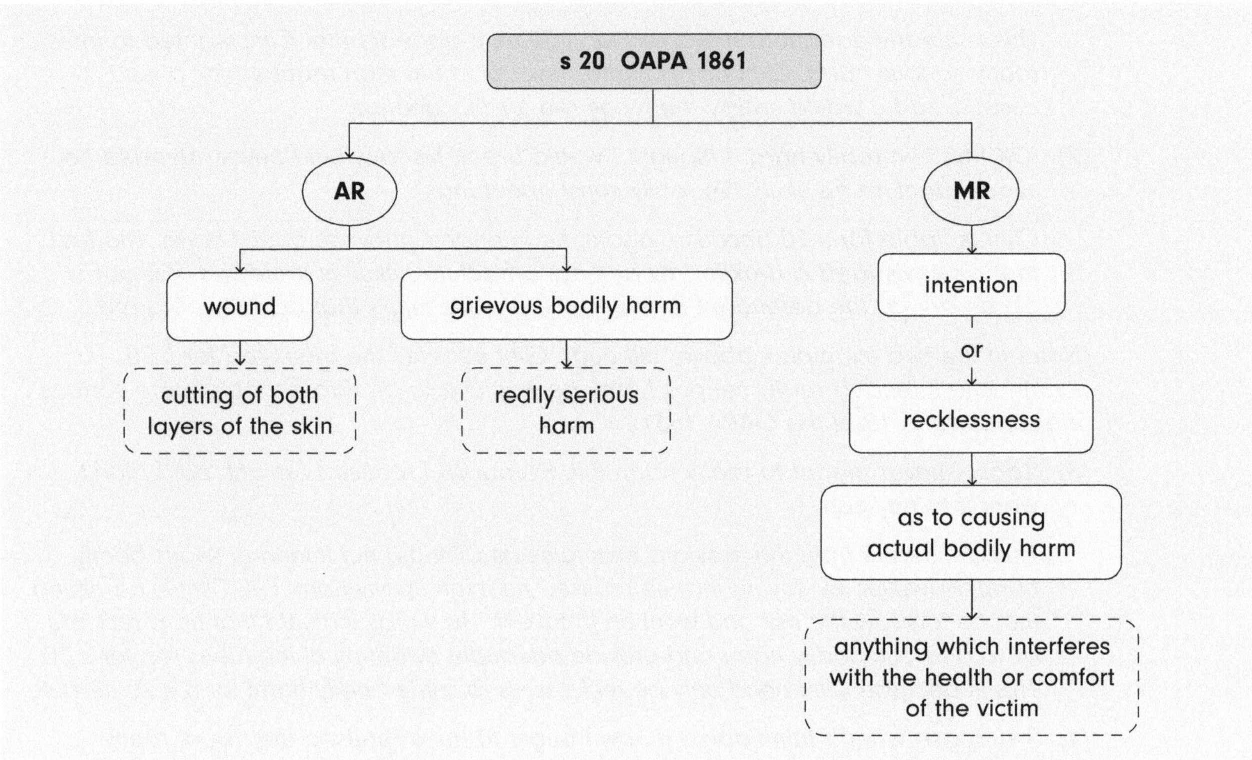

4.9 Wounding or causing grievous bodily harm with intent (OAPA 1861, s 18)

Section 18 is the most serious non-fatal offence against the person, as reflected in the maximum sentence of life imprisonment. It is an indictable offence, so that it can only be tried in the Crown Court before a judge and jury. Note how, as the offences have become more serious, first the injuries have got more severe (actual bodily harm for s 47 and grievous bodily harm or wounding for ss 20 and 18); and then the requirements for the mens rea have increased as s 18 can only be committed intentionally. Section 18 states:

> Whosoever shall unlawfully and maliciously by any means whatsoever wound or cause any grievous bodily harm to any person ... with intent ... to do some ... grievous bodily harm to any person, or with intent to resist or prevent the lawful apprehension or detainer of any person, shall be guilty of an offence, ... [and shall be liable] to imprisonment for life.

Understanding the non-fatal offences is not easy given that they tend to overlap, as demonstrated by s 47 where the definition of the assault includes the common law offences within it. This issue is also apparent with s 18 where the actus reus is the same as for s 20, namely, wounding or causing grievous bodily harm. However, once the mens rea is taken into account, s 18 is even more confusing as it creates multiple offences – four variations in total.

The ways of committing a s 18 offence are:

(1) unlawfully and maliciously causing grievous bodily harm with intent to cause grievous bodily harm;

(2) unlawfully and maliciously wounding with intent to cause grievous bodily harm;

(3) unlawfully and maliciously causing grievous bodily harm with intent to resist or prevent the lawful apprehension or detainer of any person;

(4) unlawfully and maliciously wounding with intent to resist or prevent the lawful apprehension or detainer of any person.

As the wording is rather archaic, to assist your understanding, these options have been categorised further into 'ordinary' victims and 'police officer' victims. Bear in mind that this is not a legal definition and is an over-simplification because, for example, a police officer may be assaulted in the same way as any other member of the public, in which case the prosecution would need to prove that the accused intended grievous bodily harm. However, this summary provides an overview of the correct approach to take when analysing a defendant's liability under s 18.

The four varieties of a s 18 assault are:

'Ordinary' victim	
(1) AR - wound;	MR - intention to cause GBH
(2) AR - GBH;	MR - intention to cause GBH
'Police officer' victim	
(3) AR - wound;	MR - intention to resist/prevent arrest *and* intention/recklessness as to causing ABH
(4) AR - GBH;	MR - intention to resist/prevent arrest *and* intention/recklessness as to causing ABH

Having looked at the offences in summary, the detail of these assaults will now be analysed.

4.9.1 Actus reus

As mentioned above, there are two different ways of committing the actus reus of the offence, namely by wounding, or by causing grievous bodily harm to a person. The definitions of these terms are discussed above in the context of s 20 of the OAPA 1861. Indeed, the only difference between the actus reus of s 18 and s 20 assaults is the use of the word 'cause' rather than 'inflict'. Whether the defendant has 'caused' grievous bodily harm is purely a matter of causation and the normal rules will apply.

However, the question remains as to what the difference is between 'inflicting' grievous bodily harm for s 20 and 'causing' grievous bodily harm for s 18. Lord Steyn in *R v Burstow* [1997] 4 All ER 225 agreed that the word 'cause' is wider than the word 'inflict' and, later in his judgment, said: 'I am not saying that the words cause and inflict are exactly synonymous. They are not.' Unfortunately, he did not go on to explain what the difference was or give any examples, and indeed he also said '... in the context of the Act of 1861 there is no radical divergence between the meaning of the two words'.

We are at a loss to come up with an example that would be causing grievous bodily harm for s 18 but not inflicting it for s 20. Arguably, therefore, there is no longer any practical distinction between 'inflict' and 'cause' for the purposes of the actus reus of ss 20 and 18 of the OAPA 1861 and they can be treated as the same for both offences.

4.9.2 Mens rea

The mens rea of s 18 requires an intent either to cause grievous bodily harm; or to resist or prevent the lawful apprehension or detainer of any person. However, if the intention is to resist or prevent arrest, the prosecution must also prove that the defendant 'maliciously' (intentionally or recklessly) caused some bodily harm.

In most prosecutions for a s 18 assault, the defendant will be charged on the basis that they intended to cause grievous bodily harm. It is important to note that an intention to cause lesser harm or a wound will not suffice, and nor will recklessness.

Example

Valerie lunges at Samrita with a kitchen knife causing a deep cut to Samrita's face.

(1) Valerie admits that her aim or purpose was to scar Samrita permanently. She has the (direct) intent to cause grievous bodily harm and satisfies the mens rea for s 18.

(2) Valerie states that her aim was only to cut Samrita in a very minor way. Although she has an intention to wound, this is not sufficient for a s 18 assault. Furthermore, although she may be reckless as to causing grievous bodily harm in such circumstances, again, this would not satisfy the mens rea.

When deciding whether to charge a defendant with a s 18 offence, there are practical difficulties for the prosecution to overcome in establishing the mens rea as the threshold is so high. Evidence of clear planning, the use of a weapon, or repeated punching or stamping would all suggest an intention to cause grievous bodily harm, but each case will turn on its facts.

The alternative mens rea applies where the defendant intended to resist or prevent the lawful apprehension of any person. In simple terms, the accused intended to resist or prevent an arrest. However, this is only one of the requirements, and the other element needed to satisfy this mens rea is that the defendant intended or foresaw that some harm would be caused.

Example

PC Gore is called to attend a fight outside a public house. He tells Annie that she is under arrest for a public order offence. Annie's friend, Poppy, lashes out at PC Gore so that Annie can escape and causes a small cut to the officer's face. Poppy did not intend to cause grievous bodily harm but did foresee at least some harm as a possibility.

- *Actus reus: Poppy has the actus reus as she has wounded the officer by cutting his face. The cut resulted directly from Poppy's assault, and it is irrelevant that it is only 'small'.*
- *Mens rea: Poppy did not intend grievous bodily harm, but, as her intention was to help her friend to escape, the prosecution could prove an intention to prevent the lawful arrest of any person, in this case, Annie. Furthermore, Poppy was reckless as to causing at least some bodily harm as she admits foreseeing the possibility of some harm.*

To conclude, the only occasion when a defendant who is reckless as to causing at least some bodily harm or worse could be successfully prosecuted for a s 18 assault is where the prosecution can also prove the ulterior intent, namely an intention to resist or prevent the arrest of any person. However, this will be a rare occurrence in practice as the severity of the injury does not justify a charge of s 18 assault, and there are a number of other offences that a defendant could be charged with in such circumstances.

4.9.3 Summary

(a) Unlawfully wounding or causing grievous bodily harm with intent is a statutory offence under s 18 of the OAPA 1861.

(b) The only real difference to s 20 lies in the mens rea as both require a wound or grievous bodily harm for the actus reus.

(c) The mens rea is intention to cause grievous bodily harm unless the circumstances are such that the accused is resisting or preventing an arrest, where the defendant may intend or be reckless as to causing some bodily harm.

Set out below is an overview of wounding or causing grievous bodily harm with intent.

Figure 4.5 Wounding or causing grievous bodily harm with intent

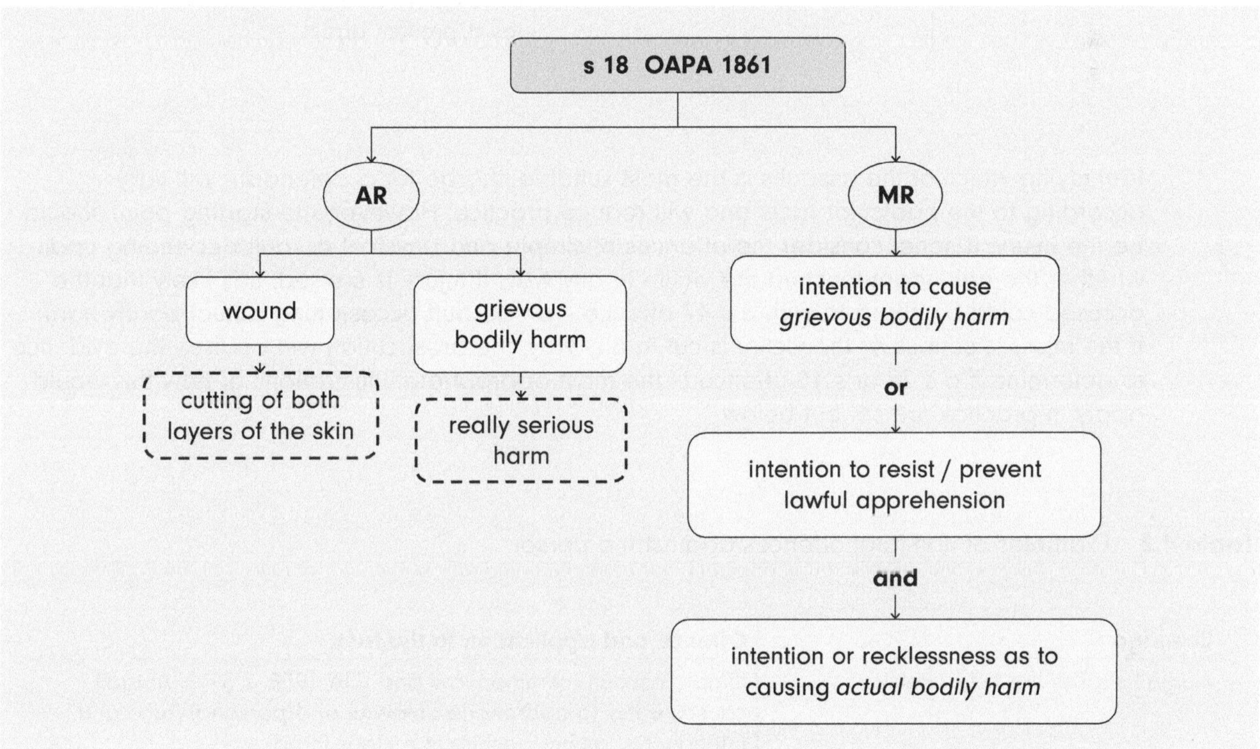

4.10 Overview of the assault offences

It is easy to confuse the different elements of the non-fatal offences, and so, to assist, the table below summarises the main requirements of each.

Table 4.1 Actus reus and mens rea of assaults

Offence	Actus reus	Mens rea
Simple assault - s 39 CJA 1998 and common law	Acts or words that cause the victim to apprehend immediate and unlawful personal force	Intention or recklessness as to causing the victim to apprehend immediate and unlawful personal force
Battery (physical assault) - s 39 CJA 1988 and common law	Infliction of unlawful personal force upon the victim	Intention or recklessness as to the infliction of unlawful personal force
s 47 OAPA 1861	Simple or physical assault causing actual bodily harm (which can include psychiatric harm)	Intention or recklessness as to the simple or physical assault (no need for the defendant to have intended or foreseen the actual bodily harm)
s 20 OAPA 1861	To wound or inflict grievous bodily harm (which can include really serious psychiatric harm)	'Maliciously' ie intention or recklessness as to actual bodily harm
s 18 OAPA 1861	Would or cause grievous bodily harm (as for s 20)	Intention to cause grievous bodily harm *Or* 'Maliciously' ie intention or recklessness as to actual bodily harm plus an intent to resist/prevent arrest

Identifying which of the assaults is the most suitable charge for a defendant will vary according to the particular facts and will require practice. However, the starting point should be the injury. If none, consider the offences of simple and physical assault depending upon whether the defendant touched the victim in any way. If injury is caused, it is likely that the accused could be charged with a s 47 offence - an assault occasioning actual bodily harm. If the injury is serious or the victim is cut in any way, the prosecution will analyse the evidence to determine if a s 20 or s 18 offence is the most appropriate. Illustrations of how this would apply in practice are set out below.

Table 4.2 Examples of non-fatal offences against the person

Scenario	Offence and application to the fact
Abigail shakes her fist at Betsy.	Simple assault (common law and CJA 1988, s 39) - Abigail causes Betsy to apprehend unlawful and personal force and intends this, as her gesture is a clear threat.
Candice slaps Debbie on the cheek during an argument.	Physical assault/battery (common law and CJA 1988, s 39) - Candice inflicts unlawful and personal force on Debbie and intends to do so as the slap is deliberate.
Errol hits Favour in the face causing him to suffer bruising to his jaw.	s 47 OAPA 1861 - Errol causes actual bodily harm and intends a battery as he hits Favour in the face.

Scenario	Offence and application to the fact
Gerry punches Howard once intending to hurt him but causes Howard to suffer from a severely fractured cheek bone.	s 20 OAPA 1861 - although Gerry inflicts grievous bodily harm, his intention is only to cause Howard to suffer some bodily harm, as evidence by the single punch.
Ivor stabs Jenny intending to really hurt her.	s 18 OAPA 1861 - Ivor wounds Jenny and does so intending grievous bodily harm.
In attempting to prevent his friend being arrested, Kamal pushes PC Lyle who falls onto the floor. Kamal is a careless as to whether he injures the officer but PC Lyle suffers a fractured skull.	s 18 OAPA 1861 - Kamal causes grievous bodily harm to PC Lyle and does so intending to prevent an arrest. He does not intend actual bodily harm, but may be reckless as to it.

4.11 Consent

Consent (or rather lack of it) can be a crucial element in the prosecution proving the offence. Usually, this issue will be raised by the defence, with the aim of persuading the court that the circumstances are such that the accused should not be found guilty of the assault for which they have been charged.

Because physical assault is defined as the intentional or reckless infliction of personal force, the courts would be overflowing if any time a person touched another, they were prosecuted. It is very difficult to get round a busy supermarket or travel on public transport without coming into contact with someone. Furthermore, normal social conduct involves touching, such as shaking hands or a kiss on the cheek as a sign of welcome. The law is not so foolish as to consider these criminal offences and implies consent in normal everyday situations.

However, a number of points remain for discussion including what amounts to a valid consent and whether consent should always absolve the defendant of criminal liability in all circumstances. These are controversial areas, giving rise to cases that have been widely reported in the media, such as when injuries are suffered during a football match or in the context of sexual activity.

4.11.1 What is a valid consent?

What if the victim is tricked into giving their consent, is very young, or suffers from some sort of mental disability? The law does not provide any detailed guidance on this issue, and deciding if a consent is valid will be a question of fact in each case. For example, if the case involves a child victim, their ability to consent will depend upon whether they have sufficient intelligence and understanding to do so.

Example

Sujata, who has severe learning difficulties, willingly allows her friend to practise his tattooing skills upon her arm. Because Sujata thinks that the ink will wash off, her consent is not valid.

The general position in criminal law had always been that the consent did not have to be fully informed to be valid. If the victim knew the identity of the assailant and the nature of the act they were agreeing to, that was sufficient. This led to controversial results. For example, in *R v Clarence* (1888) 22 QBD 23 the defendant had sexual intercourse with his wife knowing he was suffering from a sexually transmitted disease. His wife was unaware of this and was infected as a result. Clarence was charged under s 20 of the OAPA 1861, but the court held he had not assaulted his wife as she had consented. She knew the identity of the assailant (it was her husband) and the nature of the act (sexual intercourse), and this was so even though she would not have consented had she known of her husband's medical condition.

This approach was confirmed by the Court of Appeal in the case of *R v Richardson* [1999] Crim LR 62. The defendant was a registered dentist who was suspended from practice by the General Dental Council. While still suspended, she carried out dentistry on the victim who complained to the police. Richardson was charged with and convicted of assault occasioning actual bodily harm as the trial judge stated that the fraud about her professional status vitiated the apparent consent. However, the conviction was quashed on appeal as the court held the consent given was valid. The victim knew the nature of the act (dentistry) and the identity of the person (the defendant). The argument of the prosecution that the concept of the 'identity of the person' should be extended to cover their qualifications and attributes was rejected by the Court of Appeal.

The issue of what amounts to a valid consent was revisited in subsequent cases with differing results. The first was *R v Tabassum* [2000] Crim LR 686 where the defendant claimed that he was medically qualified and carrying out a study on breast cancer (neither of which were true). Three women allowed him to examine their breasts but complained that they would not have done so had they known the truth. The defendant was charged with indecent assault (an offence which has since been replaced by sexual assault under the Sexual Offences Act 2003).

If the law according to the *Richardson* case (see above) was applied, the women's consent would have been considered valid, and the defendant could not be convicted of indecent assault. This is because the victims were not deceived as to the nature of the act (a breast examination) or the identity of the person (the defendant), and a person's qualifications and attributes are not included within the concept of 'identity'. However, in *Tabassum*, the Court of Appeal stated that the victims must know the nature *and quality* of the act if their consent was to be valid. On this basis, the apparent consents were held to be invalid and the defendant was convicted of indecent assault. The victims thought they were consenting to an examination by a medically qualified person for medical purposes. They were not and thus did not know the 'quality' of the act.

4.11.2 Consent and sexual infection

The next case to come before the Court of Appeal was that of *R v Dica* [2004] 3 All ER 593. In this instance, the defendant infected his sexual partners with HIV. However, Judge LJ made it clear that, although the immediate case involved an HIV scenario, the issues raised and so the judgment given were not confined to that disease. The prosecution argued that the defendant had the relevant mens rea because he was reckless as to whether the victims might become infected - he foresaw a risk of causing some harm (knowing as he did that he was HIV positive). Furthermore, although both victims had been willing participants in the acts of intercourse, they would not have agreed had they known of the defendant's condition. Judge LJ ruled that the reasoning of the majority in *Clarence* had no continuing application. If the case was decided today, the conviction would be upheld as the defendant inflicted grievous bodily harm upon the victim (actus reus) and was reckless as to whether she might become infected (mens rea).

In summary, just because the victims consented to sexual intercourse with the defendant did not mean they had consented to any risk of infection from that sexual intercourse. The question of whether the victims consented was one of fact for the jury to decide.

In the later case of *R v Konzani* [2005] EWCA Crim 706, the issue of consent was again considered in the context of sexual infection. After the defendant had been informed that he was HIV positive, he had sexual relationships with three complainants. He did not inform them that he was HIV positive, and he repeatedly had unprotected sexual intercourse with them, knowing that by doing so he might pass on the infection. In consequence, all three complainants contracted the HIV virus. The defendant's case was that, by having consented to all the risks associated with sexual intercourse, the victims had consented to the risk of contracting HIV. The jury disagreed and convicted the defendant of a s 20 assault offence. Thereafter, the defendant's appeal against conviction was dismissed. A person's consent to the risks of contracting the HIV virus can only provide a defence to an assault charge if their consent is informed. In that regard, there was a critical distinction to be drawn between taking a risk of the various, potentially adverse and possibly problematic consequences of sexual intercourse, and giving an informed consent to the risk of infection with a fatal disease.

The decisions in *Dica* and *Konzani* confirm that *Clarence* is no longer good law, and valid consent is only given if both the identity of the defendant and the nature *and* quality of the act are known.

4.11.3 Consent as a defence to the common law assaults

It has long been recognised that consent can amount to a defence to simple or physical assault provided no harm was caused or intended. This is a common-sense approach in a modern society where people interact with each other on a frequent basis. Indeed, as discussed earlier, it would be nonsensical if every touch involved the criminal law. To cover the requirements of normal social conduct, it is the law that people impliedly consent to the inevitable physical contact that occurs as part of everyday life.

4.11.4 Consent as a defence to the statutory assaults

The general rule is that consent is not available to any assault where harm is intended or caused even if the consent is valid. In *Attorney-General's Reference (No 6 of 1980)* [1981] 2 All ER 1057, two youths decided to settle their differences by means of a fist fight. The outcome was that the victim sustained bruises to his face and a bleeding nose. The court held that his consent was no defence to a charge under s 47 of the OAPA 1861 as 'it is not in the public interest that people should try to cause, or should cause, each other actual bodily harm for no good reason' – Lord Lane CJ.

However, there are several exceptions to this general rule, and establishing the scope of these has been the subject of much judicial scrutiny. In *Attorney-General's Reference (No 6 of 1980)* (above), the court identified the following as examples of when consent would be a valid defence to an assault which caused harm:

(a) Surgical operations: otherwise operations and other essential medical examinations and procedures could not be carried out lawfully and doctors would be at constant risk of being prosecuted.

(b) Dangerous exhibitions (such as circus acts).

(c) Properly conducted sport, for example, boxing and rugby. In *R v Barnes* [2005] 1 WLR 910, the Court of Appeal looked carefully at this exception and endorsed a broad application of the defence of consent in cases involving sporting activities. In this case, the victim sustained a serious injury as a result of a tackle by the defendant in a football match. The judges stated that criminal conviction in the course of a sporting event was reserved for those situations where the conduct was sufficiently grave to be properly categorised as criminal, and this would depend on the circumstances. The fact that the play was within the rules and practice of the game and had not gone beyond it would be a firm indication that what had occurred was not criminal. However, in highly competitive sports, where conduct outside the rules could be expected to occur in the heat of the moment, such conduct still might not reach the threshold level required for it to be criminal. The Court of Appeal said that the level of criminality in such cases was to be assessed objectively (by the jury) and would be determined by the type of sport, the level at which it was played, the nature of the act, the degree of force used, the extent of the risk of injury and the state of mind of the defendant. On Barnes' appeal against conviction, it was held that the trial judge had inadequately summed up to the jury, as he had failed to explain to them that the fact that the tackle was a foul did not necessarily mean that the threshold of criminal conduct had been reached.

(d) The case of *R v Brown* [1994] 1 AC 212 also confirmed that consent can be a defence to other 'lawful activities' such as ritual circumcision, tattooing and ear-piercing, even though harm is caused.

Lord Lane CJ in *Attorney-General's Reference (No 6 of 1980)* based the exceptions on the grounds of their being in the public interest, or where there was 'good reason' for such harm being risked or caused. Deciding what harm individuals may consent to is a question of balance, and public policy is the determining issue, although some examples are easier to justify than others. With regard to tattoos and piercings, for example, they are not actually beneficial to society but, on the other hand, they are not harmful either. In any event, it would be difficult on a practical level to make such common body decorations illegal.

(e) A more controversial exception is that of 'rough and ill-disciplined behaviour', which is also known as 'horseplay'. In the case of *R v Jones* [1987] Crim LR 123, the Court of Appeal overturned the two defendants' convictions of inflicting grievous bodily harm on two school friends after they had thrown them into the air with the intention of catching them. Unfortunately, they had dropped the victims resulting in serious injury including a ruptured spleen. Evidence was produced that the boys had engaged in the activity before without injury and that it was taken by all as a joke with no intention to cause injury. The justification for this exception is that youngsters messing around is part of growing up, but attitudes change and in modern society such behaviour may now be regarded as bullying.

4.11.5 Developments in case law

Quite where to draw the line in determining criminal liability can be problematic, and, as a consequence of the emphasis on public interest, it has been ruled that sado-masochism and body modification are not exceptions.

R v Brown [1994]

The House of Lords considered the defence of consent in the highly publicised and controversial case of *R v Brown* [1994] 1 AC 212. The appellants belonged to a group of sado-masochistic homosexual men who, over a long period of time, willingly participated in the commission of acts of violence against each other, including genital torture, for the sexual pleasure which it engendered in the giving and receiving of pain. It was not disputed that the passive partner or victim in each case consented to the acts being committed and suffered no permanent injury. The appellants were charged with and convicted of offences under ss 47 and 20 of the OAPA 1861. They appealed to the House of Lords, arguing that the consent of the victims should amount to a defence to these offences, but the appeal was dismissed by a majority of three to two.

Lord Templeman (and the other Lordships giving the majority view) considered that homosexual sado-masochism was concerned with violence as well as sex, and as such fell within the OAPA 1861. Furthermore, they concluded that the activities were not in the public interest and could not, therefore, be a 'new' exception to the general rule that a victim cannot consent to the harm. Their Lordships were concerned, for example, about the risks of corrupting young men, of spreading disease, and of the level of pain inflicted getting out of control. As a result, Lord Templeman's view was that he could not see any 'good reason' to 'invent a defence of consent for sado-masochistic encounters which breed and glorify cruelty'. Even at the time, this was a controversial decision as many agreed with the views of Lord Mustill and Lord Slynn of Hadley, the judges in the minority in *Brown*, who argued that it was not for the court to decide to bring such consensual, private activities within the OAPA 1861.

The case was subsequently taken to the European Court of Human Rights by the appellants under the name of *Laskey v UK* (1996) 24 EHRR 39, on the basis that it breached Article 8 of the Convention – the right to respect for private life. The European Court of Human Rights held unanimously that it was not a breach of the Article as the interference of the State was necessary for the pursuance of a legitimate aim, namely, that of protection of health.

Development of the law of consent

In the case of *R v Wilson* [1996] 3 WLR 125, the Court of Appeal stated that the defence of consent was available to a man who branded his initials onto his wife's buttocks because the act was akin to tattooing. The judges held that it was not in the public interest to interfere with consensual activity between a husband and wife. Even at the time, this ruling was criticised.

Soon after, in *R v Emmett* [1999] All ER (D) 641, the Court of Appeal appeared to put the law back on track by ruling that consent would not act as a defence for a defendant charged with committing a s 47 offence against his female partner. The facts of the case involved sado-masochistic acts between two consenting heterosexual adults. The court held that the issue of consent was immaterial where there was a realistic risk of harm 'beyond a merely transient or trivial injury'. Also, following *Brown*, that the degree of harm made it appropriate for the criminal law to interfere, and so the defendant's appeal against conviction was dismissed.

This approach is apparent in the more recent case of *R v BM* [2018] EWCA Crim 560. The defendant, who was a tattooist and body piercer by trade, was charged with a s 18 offence after having (with the victim's consent) removed part of his ear, a nipple and split his tongue to resemble that of a lizard. The accused's argument that body modification should be a further exception failed, and it was ruled that a person could not consent to such serious, irreversible injuries. Furthermore, the judges rejected the defendant's argument that these procedures were analogous to piercings or tattoos, stating that they in fact constituted 'medical procedures performed for no medical reason and with none of the protections provided to patients by medical practitioners'.

In *R v Hobday* [2025] EWCA Crim 46, the Court of Appeal reconsidered the case of *Wilson* and strongly implied that it was decided on a flawed basis and that, with modern understandings of domestic abuse and coercive behaviour, the result would have been different today. In *Hobday*, a man and woman engaged in consensual sexual activity before the woman began carving the man's initials into her buttocks using a knife blade. She asked the man to help her finish off the letters, which he did. The man was subsequently convicted of a s 47 assault and appealed.

The Court of Appeal was obviously still bound by its own decision in *Wilson*; but it did state, firstly, that *Wilson* should now only be considered a case limited to its own specific facts, which is hard to justify as being in accordance with *Brown*. Secondly, that *Wilson* conflicted with *R v BM* over whether the law should be allowed to develop on a case-by-case basis. *BM* was to be preferred and so the categories of exceptions in *Brown* should stand and new categories should only be added by Parliament. Thirdly, that even if the court had been free to decide whether cutting a young person with an unsterile knife should be a lawful activity if she consented to it, they would decide that it should not be.

4.11.6 Overview of consent

In summary, the present position is:

(a) Consent must be valid and given by a fully informed and competent person. Consent is not valid if it is obtained by fraud as to the identity of the defendant or the nature and quality of the act.

(b) Consent is implied to simple and physical assault provided no harm is intended or caused.

(c) Consent is not a defence to an assault under ss 47, 20 or 18 of the OAPA 1861 unless the behaviour comes within one of the exceptions.

4.12 Summary

Identifying which of the assault offences apply to a given set of facts may be difficult and will require skills of analysis. Generally, you should begin by discussing the most serious offence the defendant could reasonably be liable for. With the assaults, this will usually be s 18 unless there is clearly only minor injury when you should consider s 47. Having done this, identify the actus reus of the offence and apply it to the facts. Sometimes the answer is clear cut, but often it is not and there will be areas that need further analysis; for example, does the injury amount to a wound or grievous bodily harm?

If the actus reus is present, identify the mens rea for the offence and apply it to the facts. Look for information in the evidence that will help determine whether the mens rea is satisfied. Next, consider whether any defences may be available to the defendant; if so, describe the elements of the defence and apply them to the facts.

In situations where you conclude that the actus reus or the mens rea for that particular assault is not present, you should explain why and move down the scale to the next offence. For example, from s 18 to s 20, or from s 47 to simple or physical assault and go through the same process again. Start high and work down as this is the approach the prosecution would take.

To assist you in practising these skills, you should attempt the activity below.

ACTIVITY

Consider the criminal liability of the defendants in the following cases for an offence of assault. You are not required to consider any possible defences.

(1) Humera strikes Ben with her fist, giving him a black eye. Chukwu, who is passing by, shouts at Humera to stop. Angry at his intervention, Humera turns around and slaps Chukwu in the face, causing him to suffer a cut to his lip.

COMMENT

Humera will be liable under s 47 of the OAPA 1861 for the black eye. She satisfies the actus reus as she applies unlawful force to Ben (she punches him) and causes actual bodily harm, as the injury sustained is more than 'transient or trifling' – *R v Miller* [1954]. Humera also has the mens rea for a physical assault (intention or recklessness as to the application of unlawful force) as punching Ben is an intentional act. She is not liable for a s 20 or s 18 offence, as these require an actus reus of a wound or grievous bodily harm, neither of which is present here.

When Humera gives Chukwu a cut lip, she could be liable under s 18 or s 20 of the OAPA 1861 because the injury satisfies the definition of a wound (a cutting of both layers of the skin – *Moriarty v Brookes* [1834]). Liability will hinge on Humera's mens rea. If she intended grievous bodily harm, she will be guilty under s 18; but this is unlikely as she only slapped Ben once and did not use a weapon. If she intended or foresaw some harm, Humera will be liable under s 20 and this seems more likely on the evidence. However, if the court is satisfied that she did not, Humera will be guilty only of an assault occasioning actual bodily harm under s 47.

(2) Gussy is walking along the road carrying a parcel. He is walking fast because he is in a hurry to get to the Post Office. Suddenly, he is accosted by Lyndon who grabs hold of his arm and asks him what he has got in the parcel. Gussy fears that he is about to be robbed and tries to escape. In the course of the struggle, Gussy breaks free, lashes out at Lyndon and knocks him to the ground. Lyndon hits his head on the pavement and fractures his skull. Unknown to Gussy, Lyndon is a plain clothes police officer.

COMMENT

(i) The actus reus of s 18 of the OAPA 1861 is satisfied as Gussy has clearly caused the fractured skull to Lyndon which would amount to grievous bodily harm. For the mens rea, he must have intended grievous bodily harm, which seems unlikely on the facts.

Alternatively, Gussy must intend to resist or prevent arrest and intend or be reckless as to the causing of some harm. Gussy would submit that his only intention was to escape, but he may have been reckless as to the causing of some harm (see below). However, he did not intend to resist arrest as Gussy was unaware he was being arrested. Lyndon was dressed in plain clothes and there is no indication that he identifies himself as a police officer.

(ii) The actus reus of s 20 of the OAPA 1861 is the same as for the more serious offence. For the mens rea, Gussy needs to have intended or been reckless as to the causing of some harm. This seems more likely as he 'lashes out' at the police officer and hits him hard enough to cause Lyndon to fall to the ground.

(iii) If Gussy did not foresee the risk of some harm, he would fulfil the actus reus and mens rea of a s 47 assault as he has intentionally assaulted Lyndon and caused actual bodily harm.

(3) Mateus owes his drug supplier a large sum of money. He goes to his father George's house to plead with him to lend him some cash so he can repay the dealer. An argument ensues in George's front garden. Mateus shakes his fist at George, calling him 'a tight-fisted old skinflint in need of a good hiding'. Terrified, George makes a dash for his front door but Mateus deliberately pushes him over onto the lawn. Fortunately, George is uninjured and Mateus walks away. George is upset that his son has attacked him and that he is a drug user and, as a result, he suffers mild clinical depression.

COMMENT

(i) Mateus has satisfied the actus reus of simple assault (common law/CJA 1988, s 39) as he caused George to apprehend the application of immediate personal force. His words and shaking his fist resulted in George being 'terrified'. As to the mens rea, Mateus seems to have intended to cause George to apprehend immediate unlawful physical force as he said that George was 'in need of a good hiding'. At the very least, he was reckless at to this. Mateus is guilty of simple assault.

(ii) Pushing George onto the lawn is an infliction of unlawful personal physical force and suffices for the actus reus of physical assault (common law/CJA 1988, s 39). There is no need for George to suffer any injury. Mateus 'deliberately' did this; thus, he had intention and he is guilty.

(iii) The actus reus of a s 47 assault requires a simple or physical assault - see above. Mild clinical depression may constitute the actual bodily harm element (*R v Ireland/Burstow* [1997]). In this instance, there is a causal link with the physical assault, because George suffered depression partly because his son attacked him. It only needs to be a cause, not the sole cause. As to the mens rea, Mateus must have the mens rea for simple or physical assault and he does (see above). There is strict liability in relation to the ABH element - *Savage and Parmenter* [1992]. Thus, Mateus is guilty.

5 Murder and the Partial Defences

LEARNING OUTCOMES

When you have completed this chapter, you should be able to:

- demonstrate how the current law of homicide is structured and understand the relationship between the different homicide offences;
- explain the definitions of murder and voluntary manslaughter and appreciate how the partial defences of diminished responsibility and loss of control may apply;
- discuss, in outline, the proposed changes to the current law of homicide.

5.1 Introduction

The unlawful killing of a person is generally regarded as one of the most heinous crimes it is possible to commit. As a consequence, there is extensive media coverage of such offences: for example, the mass murderers Dr Harold Shipman and Fred and Rose West, as well as the fatal stabbings of teenagers, and so-called 'mercy killings' where a person is killed by a relative to end their suffering.

5.2 Different types of homicide offences

Although there is currently no such offence in English law, the word 'homicide' is used as a generic term for unlawful killings. The term encompasses situations where the defendant is criminally liable for the death of the victim, and the most commonly reported such offences are murder and manslaughter. However, there are also different types of manslaughter, namely voluntary, unlawful act and gross negligence manslaughter, as well as corporate manslaughter. The other type of homicide covered in this textbook is the causing of death by dangerous or careless driving.

It is interesting to note that countries classify homicide offences in different ways. In England and Wales, the most serious offence is murder, followed by voluntary manslaughter, then unlawful act and gross negligence manslaughter. The Law Commission proposed that the current classification be changed (see the Law Commission Report No 304, referred to below), as a criticism of the current law is that the offence of murder covers such a wide range of behaviour. The mercy killer, motivated by a desire to help end the suffering of a much-loved relative, is treated in the same way as the terrorist who has caused indiscriminate multiple deaths – they are both convicted of the crime of murder and sentenced to life imprisonment. In contrast, in the United States of America the crime of murder is split into first and second degree murder, and in Denmark there are four different murder offences - 'general', child killings, mercy killings, and genocide. We will return to the proposals for reform of our law later in this chapter.

5.3 The actus reus of homicide

The common element in all homicide cases is that the accused has caused the death of a human being. The actus reus of murder or manslaughter cannot be established without this, and it will usually be very easy for the prosecution to prove - for example that the defendant shot or stabbed the victim to death. However, there are occasions where difficulties do arise in establishing this element.

5.3.1 The victim must be a human being

The defendant will only be guilty of murder or manslaughter if the victim is a human being, and (very occasionally) this aspect has been disputed, with one such scenario being in the context of an unborn child. The point for consideration here is when does a foetus become a human being so they are afforded the protection of the law of homicide.

It is not homicide to kill a child in the womb and abortion is not murder. There are, however, some statutory protections under s 58 of the Offences Against the Person Act 1861 and, where the child is capable of being born alive, the Infant Life (Preservation) Act 1929, but these are beyond the scope of this textbook. To be given the protection of the law of homicide, the child must be wholly expelled from the mother's body and be alive (*R v Poulton* (1832) 5 C & P 329), and have an existence independent of the mother. The courts have said this means the child should have independent circulation and have drawn breath after birth.

A high profile case in 2000 involved the decision by the courts on whether to allow the separation of conjoined twins that would result in the death of the weaker twin, Mary - *Re A (Children) (conjoined twins: surgical separation)* [2000] 2 WLR 480. One question for the court was whether the weaker twin was a human being. It had been argued that as Mary had an underdeveloped heart, lungs and brain, and depended on the stronger twin (Jodie) for survival, she was not a separate person and therefore it would not be murder if she was to be killed. This argument was unanimously rejected by the Court of Appeal. Brooke LJ stated:

> Here Mary has been born in the sense that she has an existence quite independent of her mother. The fact that Mary is dependent upon Jodie, or the fact that twins may be interdependent if they share heart and lungs, should not lead the law to fly in the face of the clinical judgment that each child is alive and that each child is separate both for the purposes of the civil law and the criminal law.

In very rare instances, the assault takes place whilst the unborn child is in the womb but the death occurs afterwards.

Example

Nazra is pregnant. Tuah knows this and, intending to kill the unborn child, she gives poison to Nazra. The child is born and dies two days later as a result of the poisoning. Tuah is liable for homicide of the baby because the child was born and had an existence independent of the mother. It does not matter that the injury occurred when the child was in the womb because it is the time of death that is the relevant consideration, not the time of the injury.

This was confirmed by the case of *Attorney-General's Reference (No 3 of 1994)* [1997] 3 All ER 936, where the defendant stabbed his girlfriend who was pregnant with their child. The stab wound penetrated the foetus, the baby was born prematurely as a result and died after 120 days. The House of Lords held that murder could not be committed where unlawful injury had been deliberately inflicted to a *mother* carrying a child where the child was subsequently born alive and then died as a result of the injuries inflicted while in the uterus. Their reasoning was that any mens rea the defendant had in relation to the mother could not be transferred to the unborn foetus. However, the House of Lords went on to conclude that in these circumstances the defendant could be liable for unlawful act manslaughter.

5.3.2 When does death occur?

The second point of general application to all homicide offences, having identified the victim as a human being, is the consideration of when the victim actually dies. This may sound an odd point, but there could be a difference of opinion particularly in light of medical advances. Does a person die when they stop breathing or are 'brain-dead'? What if they are being kept alive artificially on a life support machine? Is the victim dead only if the heart has stopped beating? Obviously, a person who is already dead cannot be killed.

In *R v Malcherek and Steel* [1981] 1 WLR 690, the defendant assaulted the victim, resulting in brain damage. The victim was put on a life support machine. Having concluded that she was brain dead, the doctors disconnected the machine and the victim was pronounced dead half an hour later. The defendant argued that it was the doctors, not he, who had caused the death by turning off the machine. Unsurprisingly, the argument was rejected by the Court of Appeal. The defendant's act was clearly an operating and substantial cause of death. During his judgment Lord Lane CJ stated the generally accepted legal definition of death as:

> ... the irreversible death of the brain stem, which controls the basic functions of the body such as breathing. When that occurs it is said that the body has died, even though by mechanical means the lungs are being caused to operate and some circulation of blood is taking place.

In conclusion, it is irrelevant that the task of switching off a victim's life support machine falls to the medical staff – the perpetrator of the injuries remains liable for the death.

5.3.3 Unlawful

Homicide requires that the death of the victim is unlawfully caused. Thus, if a police officer shoots a terrorist as they are about to detonate a bomb, this would be a lawful killing as it is justified to prevent a crime and defend others. As a consequence, there is no 'homicide' and the officer would not be guilty of a criminal offence.

5.3.4 Causation

The final element that is common to all offences of homicide is that the accused must cause the death of a human being. The usual rules of causation apply and these may be found in **Chapter 2**. This means that the prosecution must prove that the defendant was both the factual and legal cause of the victim's death. This is a question for the jury to determine.

5.4 Murder

Having considered the points relevant to all homicide offences, we can now turn to specific offences, starting with murder.

Murder is one of the most serious offences in the criminal justice system as it involves the deliberate taking of a human life. This is reflected in the mandatory life sentence imposed on anyone who is convicted. However, this does not mean that an individual will spend the rest of their life in prison (although the most dangerous offenders may receive a whole life sentence). The judge will decide the minimum term that a defendant must serve and thereafter, if deemed no longer a threat to society, they will be released. Once back in the community, they are subject to a life licence, which means they can be recalled to prison if they commit a further offence.

Whilst there are two statutes - the Homicide Act (HA) 1957 and the Coroners and Justice Act (CJA) 2009 - that deal with partial defences to murder, the offence itself is a common law offence. Coke's classic definition of murder is:

> The unlawful killing of a reasonable creature in being under the Queen's peace with malice aforethought.

5.4.1 Actus reus

Although the definition of murder refers to a 'reasonable creature in being', this is an outdated phrase and is rarely used. It is clear from the definition that the actus reus of the offence requires the defendant to cause the death of a human being as discussed above. The killing must take place under the Queen's (or King's) peace; thus, where a defendant kills an enemy combatant during times of war, they have a defence to a charge of murder.

5.4.2 Mens rea

The mens rea of the offence is 'malice aforethought' but this term is unhelpful and misleading. Even if a defendant kills with benevolent intentions to put a dying relative out of their misery (so-called 'mercy killings'), they will still be guilty of murder, as confirmed by the Court of Appeal in *R v Inglis* [2011] 1 WLR 1110. The term 'malice' is also confusing because, in the context of non-fatal offences against the person, 'malice' is defined as 'intentional or reckless' behaviour (see *R v Cunningham* [1957] 2 QB 396), whereas the mens rea for murder can only be established by an intention.

The mens rea for murder is more accurately defined in *R v Moloney* [1985] 1 AC 905 as either an intention to kill or an intention to cause grievous bodily harm. It is important to note that only such an intention is an adequate mens rea for murder; recklessness or any other type of mens rea will not suffice. It is an entirely subjective test, so the question is whether the individual defendant intended to kill or to cause grievous bodily harm.

There are two types of intention in the criminal law. Direct intention means that the defendant desired something to happen, or it was their aim, purpose or goal. In other words, the word 'intention' is given its ordinary meaning (*R v Moloney* [1985] 1 AC 905). Indirect or oblique intention occurs where the defendant's primary aim or desire was not the forbidden consequence but where they foresaw the consequence as virtually certain. Applying this to the case of murder, the jury *may* (but do not have to) find that the defendant intended the consequence of death or grievous bodily harm (*R v Woollin* [1999] 1 AC 82). This is a question for the jury to decide.

Examples

(1) Zoe and Yvonne are animal rights extremists, and Frank is the head scientist of a local laboratory that conducts experiments on animals. In order to disrupt the work of the laboratory, Zoe and Yvonne plant an incendiary device in Frank's house.

Zoe hates Frank as he sexually abused her as a child and wants him to burn to death. Yvonne wants Frank's house to burn down, hoping this will frighten Frank into abandoning animal testing. The incendiary device goes off, killing Frank and destroying his house.

Zoe intended to kill Frank as it was her direct intention that he would die; she desires that result. In contrast, Yvonne's direct intention is to cause criminal damage and prevent animal testing. However, if she foresaw Frank's death or serious injury as a virtually certain consequence of her actions, the jury may find that she intended it.

(2) Anton deliberately and intentionally breaks Sunita's arm. Due to a rare physiological disorder, Sunita dies. Anton would be liable for murder because an intention to cause grievous bodily harm is sufficient mens rea for the offence. Some academics have criticised this, arguing that the label of 'murderer' should be reserved only for those who intend to kill.

5.4.3 Summary of murder

(a) The actus reus of murder is the unlawful killing of a human being (not a foetus) under the Queen's (or King's) peace and this is common to all homicides.

(b) The mens rea for murder is the intention to kill or cause grievous (really serious) harm. It is an entirely subjective test – did this particular defendant have the relevant intention?

(c) Murder is a crime of specific intent so it cannot be committed recklessly.

(d) Either direct or indirect intent will satisfy the mens rea for murder.

Figure 5.1 Murder

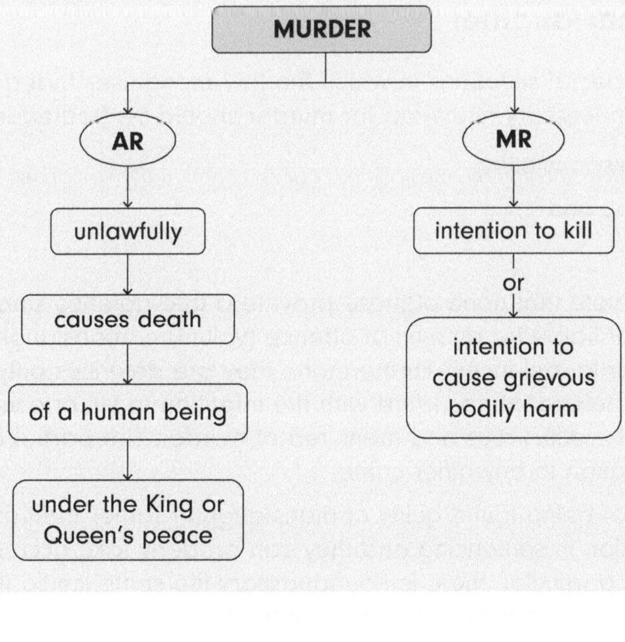

5.5 Manslaughter

Usually, if the actus reus and mens rea of murder are established, the defendant will be convicted and will receive a mandatory life sentence. Many consider this to be right, as taking another person's life can never be excused, and it is fair to say that in most homicides, the defendant deserves little or no sympathy. However, the reality is that there are degrees of culpability for this offence, and the law recognises that there are certain situations where someone who has killed should be treated differently and more favourably.

The case of *R v Ahluwalia* (1993) 96 Cr App R 133 illustrates this point. The defendant had been violently abused by her husband for over 10 years until she could take no more. One night, she poured petrol over her sleeping victim and then set fire to him. Her husband died from his burns. Most people would sympathise with Ahluwalia's predicament and even the fact that she killed her husband; after all, she was reacting to a violent bully. Arguably, she is not morally culpable at all, because she was provoked by the abuse she received over a period of time. However, although the law recognises a defence for those who are pushed to the edge so that they lose their self-control, the means adopted were extreme, particularly as Ahluwalia's husband was asleep at the time. This case illustrates the complexity of the issues that may arise. On the one hand, Ahluwalia has taken a life but, on the other, she herself is clearly a victim. This case was adopted by women's groups who were pressing for a change in the way the courts dealt with domestic violence cases, and her conviction for murder was subsequently reduced to manslaughter.

The case of *R v Martin (Anthony)* [2002] EWCA Crim 2245 is another example. Martin's home, known as Bleak House, had been plagued by burglars over the years. One night, he confronted a burglar in his house; then, as the burglar was fleeing his property, Martin shot him dead with a gun he used for shooting rabbits. Although there was much sympathy for Martin, he remains morally culpable. The fact that the victim was running away at the time of the shooting demonstrates that this is not a case of self-defence or prevention of crime.

Both these defendants were subsequently convicted of manslaughter, of which there are two different types - voluntary and involuntary manslaughter - and it is important to be able to distinguish them.

5.6 Voluntary manslaughter

There are three special situations in which the law recognises that a person who has killed another with the necessary mens rea for murder should be treated less harshly. These are:

(a) diminished responsibility;

(b) loss of control; and

(c) suicide pact.

It is important to note that none of these provide a true defence since, even if successful, the accused is still liable for a criminal offence (voluntary manslaughter). Hence, they are referred to as 'partial defences'. Furthermore, they are defences only to murder - they only apply where the defendant has killed with the intention to kill or cause grievous bodily harm and so satisfies the actus reus and mens rea of murder. The partial defences should not be considered in relation to any other crime.

The significance of being found guilty of manslaughter rather than murder is that the judge has discretion in sentencing and they can properly take account of all the relevant circumstances. In particular, there is no mandatory life sentence so that although life imprisonment may be appropriate, often a less severe penalty is imposed. This chapter concentrates on two of the partial defences, namely diminished responsibility and loss of control as the third, suicide pact (HA 1957, s 4), is very rarely raised as a defence and thus is not covered in this textbook.

To assist, the following flowchart illustrates whether the defendant has committed murder and the relationship between this offence and manslaughter.

Figure 5.2 Murder and voluntary manslaughter

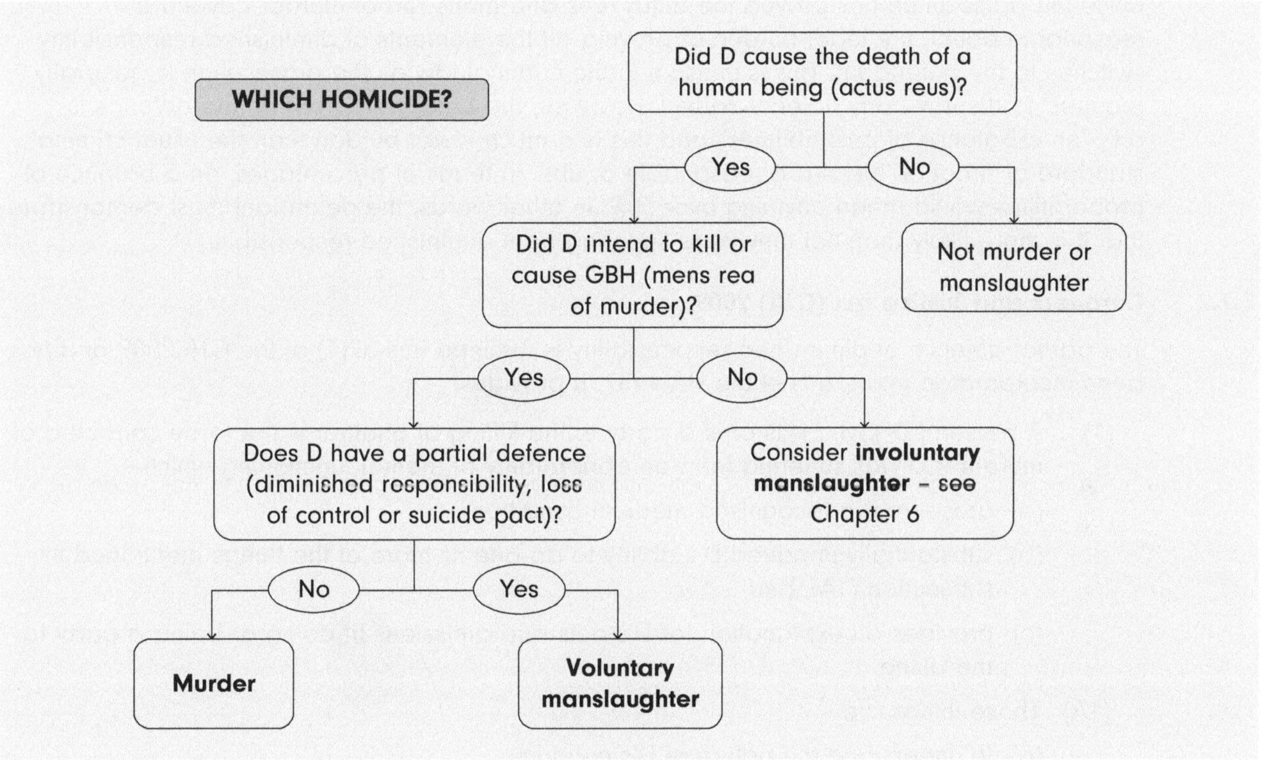

5.6.1 Background

Until October 2010, the partial defences of diminished responsibility and provocation were contained in ss 2 and 3 of the HA 1957. Over time, both defences were the subject of a large body of case law in which the courts concerned themselves with the exact meaning of these definitions. The defence of provocation proved particularly controversial, with different courts reaching different decisions in their efforts to interpret the intentions of Parliament. As a result, the Government asked the Law Commission to review this area of law.

In its report, 'Partial Defences to Murder' (Law Com No 290), the Law Commission recommended changing the definitions of the (then) existing partial defences of diminished responsibility and provocation, contained in ss 2 and 3 of the HA 1957 respectively. It later affirmed these recommendations in its report, 'Murder, Manslaughter and Infanticide' (Law Com No 304). In 2008 the Government responded by publishing its own Consultation Paper, 'Murder, manslaughter and infanticide: proposals for the reform of the law'. Whilst accepting some of the Law Commission's proposed changes, the Consultation Paper set out new proposals, notably to abolish the defence of provocation and replace it with a new defence labelled 'loss of control'.

Following a period of consultation, the Government incorporated proposed changes to the definitions of these partial defences in Part 2 of the Coroners and Justice Act 2009.

5.7 Diminished responsibility

The rationale for diminished responsibility is that, although the defendant has committed the actus reus of murder with the necessary mens rea, they were suffering from a recognised medical condition which, whilst it does not give them the legal defence of insanity, does provide them with a partial excuse for their actions.

5.7.1 Evidential issues

Once the prosecution has proved the actus reus and mens rea of murder beyond a reasonable doubt, the legal burden of proving all the elements of diminished responsibility switches to the defendant. This is unusual in the criminal law as the prosecution is generally required to disprove any defence raised. However, the burden of proof on the defence is only 'on a balance of probabilities', and this is a much lower burden than the usual criminal standard of proof of 'beyond a reasonable doubt'. In terms of percentages, on a balance of probabilities would mean anything over 50%; in other words, the defendant must demonstrate that it is more likely than not they were suffering from diminished responsibility.

5.7.2 Coroners and Justice Act (CJA) 2009

The partial defence of diminished responsibility is outlined in s 52(1) of the CJA 2009 and has been incorporated into s 2(1) of the HA 1957. It provides:

> (1) A person ('D') who kills or is a party to the killing of another is not to be convicted of murder if D was suffering from an abnormality of mental functioning which–
>
> (a) arose from a recognised medical condition,
>
> (b) substantially impaired D's ability to do one or more of the things mentioned in subsection (1A), and
>
> (c) provides an explanation for D's acts and omissions in doing or being a party to the killing.
>
> (1A) Those things are–
>
> (a) to understand the nature of D's conduct;
>
> (b) to form a rational judgment;
>
> (c) to exercise self-control.
>
> (1B) For the purposes of subsection (1)(c), an abnormality of mental functioning provides an explanation for D's conduct if it causes, or is a significant contributory factor in causing, D to carry out that conduct.

Thus, there are four elements to the defence that must be established for it to be pleaded successfully and these are:

(a) an abnormality of mental functioning; which

(b) arose from a recognised medical condition; and

(c) substantially impaired the defendant's ability to understand the nature of their conduct, and/or form a rational judgment, and/or exercise self-control; and

(d) provides an explanation for the defendant's acts and omissions in doing or being a party to the killing.

5.7.3 Abnormality of mental functioning

The first question for the jury to consider is whether the defendant was suffering from an abnormality of mental functioning when they killed their victim. There is no further definition in the Act as to what this actually means, although it tends to be interpreted widely, and it falls to the jury to decide having heard expert medical evidence.

The definition 'abnormality of mental functioning' replaces the old definition of 'abnormality of mind' contained in s 2 of the HA 1957 which, according to the Court of Appeal in *R v Byrne* [1960] 2 QB 396, meant a state of mind so different from ordinary human beings that the reasonable man would term it abnormal. The Government preferred the new definition as, unlike the phrase 'abnormality of mind', it is a term commonly used by medical experts who will testify in court on this issue. As Lord Bach said when introducing the second reading of the Bill in the House of Lords:

> The changes to the partial defence of diminished responsibility will ensure that this area of law is modernised and properly takes into account the needs and practices of medical experts. This is as it should be, given that it is the evidence of such experts which is crucial to determining whether any claim of diminished responsibility is properly made out.

5.7.4 Recognised medical condition

The second requirement for diminished responsibility is that the abnormality of mental functioning must arise from a 'recognised medical condition'. This phrase replaces the rather more convoluted wording under s 2 of the HA 1957, which stated that the abnormality of mind had to arise from 'a condition of arrested or retarded development of mind or any inherent causes or induced by disease or injury'. This complex wording caused some issues, particularly the phrase 'inherent causes' which was used in practice to include almost anything, including pre-menstrual tension and extreme stress.

During the Committee stage of Parliamentary debate, Maria Eagle (the Parliamentary Under-Secretary of State for Justice) said the Government envisaged that qualified medical experts giving evidence would refer to accepted classification systems encompassing recognised medical conditions (whether physical, psychiatric or psychological) such as the World Health Organization's international classification of diseases (ICD10). Furthermore, if a medical expert testified that, at the time of the killing, a defendant was suffering from a condition included in one of these lists, and this was accepted by the jury, the test will be met.

Ms Eagle also stated that conditions which are not included in such a list could still be deemed 'recognised medical conditions' for the purposes of the defence. She pointed out the need to cater for emerging conditions that had not yet been recognised and put on the classificatory lists. The defence could therefore call a recognised specialist to give evidence about such conditions, and it would then be for the jury to decide whether the partial defence requirement was met.

The Crown Prosecution Service confirmed this approach in its Legal Guidance on Homicide: Murder and Manslaughter:

> Examples of recognised medical conditions within these classificatory lists are schizophrenia, phobic anxiety disorders, bipolar affective disorder, depression and battered person syndrome.

Physical conditions, such as diabetes and epilepsy, are also included provided they impact on the defendant's mental state.

Example

Denise killed her friend. Her evidence is that she finds it almost impossible not to drink vodka every day, and once she has consumed the first drink, she cannot control her urge to drink more. If she does not drink vodka, she gets headaches, nausea, uncontrollable shaking and other symptoms.

Denise can plead diminished responsibility as a partial defence to her murder charge because she is suffering from a recognised medical condition according to the World Health Organization's international classification of diseases (ICD10), that of alcohol dependence syndrome. The relevant extract from ICD10 appears below.

> *V. Mental and behavioural disorders due to psychoactive substance use (F10-F19)*
>
> *2. Dependence syndrome*
>
> *A cluster of behavioural, cognitive, and physiological phenomena that develop after repeated substance use and that typically include a strong desire to take the drug, difficulties in controlling its use, persisting in its use despite harmful consequences, a higher priority given to drug use than to other activities and obligations, increased tolerance, and sometimes a physical withdrawal state.*
>
> *The dependence syndrome may be present for a specific psychoactive substance (for example tobacco, alcohol, or diazepam), for a class of substances (for example opioid drugs), or for a wider range of pharmacologically different psychoactive substances.*
>
> *Thus, it includes chronic alcoholism, dipsomania and drug addiction.*

Deciding whether an accused is suffering from an abnormality of mental functioning arising from a recognised medical condition may be challenging at times and even controversial. In the case of *R v Blackman* [2017] EWCA Crim 190, the defendant, then a member of the Royal Marines, shot and killed a badly wounded rebel while serving in Afghanistan. At his trial, Blackman was found guilty of murder as the evidence was that he acted calmly and deliberately. However, his original conviction for murder was overturned on appeal as a result of psychiatric evaluations that suggested the defendant was suffering from an adjustment disorder, compounded by the presence of several 'exceptional stressors'. As a consequence, Blackman was incapable of making rational judgements or exercising self-control, and a finding of manslaughter was substituted.

5.7.5 Diminished responsibility and intoxication

It is not unusual for offences to be committed while the defendant is under the influence of alcohol or drugs, and there have been several cases in which the judges have considered the relationship between intoxication and the partial defence of diminished responsibility. The issue becomes even more complex when a defendant relies on diminished responsibility due to alcohol dependence syndrome but was also drunk at the time of the offence. This question was considered by the House of Lords in *R v Dietschmann* [2003] 1 AC 1209. Although the case was decided according to the 'old' law under s 2 of the HA 1957, the decision was approved by the Law Commission in its report, 'Partial Defences to Murder' (Law Com No 290), and thus should be equally relevant to the 'new' definition of diminished responsibility.

In *Dietschmann*, the defendant began to drink heavily after the death of his aunt and was prescribed anti-depressants and sleeping tablets by his doctor. A few days later the defendant was drinking with friends and became involved in a fight with the victim, during which the victim was killed. The defendant was charged with murder and raised the defence of diminished responsibility. Evidence from two psychiatrists was adduced at trial – both agreed that at the time of the killing the defendant was suffering from an abnormality of mind. In summing up to the jury, the trial judge directed them that they could find the defence of diminished responsibility established only if they were satisfied that, if he had not been drinking, the defendant would have killed and would have been under diminished responsibility when he did so. The defendant was convicted of murder but appealed successfully.

The House of Lords said that s 2 of the HA 1957 did not require the abnormality of mind to be the sole cause of the defendant's acts; the question is whether the defendant was suffering an abnormality of mind at the time of the killing which substantially impaired their mental responsibility. If the jury considered that the impairment of responsibility may have been caused partly by drink and partly by an underlying abnormality, it was still open to them to uphold the defence of diminished responsibility provided they were satisfied that, despite the drink, the abnormality of mind substantially impaired their mental responsibility for the fatal act.

In *R v Wood* [2008] 2 Cr App R 507, the Court of Appeal followed *R v Dietschmann* and confirmed that the defence of diminished responsibility was not precluded by the mere fact that the defendant consumed alcohol voluntarily before committing the fatal act. In deciding whether the defendant's mental responsibility for the killing was substantially impaired as a result of his alcoholism, the jury should focus exclusively on the effect of the alcohol consumed as a direct result of the defendant's illness and ignore the effect of any alcohol consumed voluntarily - a somewhat difficult task.

In its report, the Law Commission confirmed that the law in connection with the impact of the voluntary consumption of alcohol on the availability of the defence is 'clear and satisfactory', and so these cases are equally valid to the current definition of diminished responsibility.

In *R v Dowds* [2012] EWCA Crim 281, the Court of Appeal considered whether voluntary acute intoxication which is uncomplicated by any alcoholism or dependence is capable, under s 2 of the HA 1957, of being relied upon to found diminished responsibility. The Court confirmed that such intoxication, whether from alcohol or other substance, cannot. There are public policy reasons at play here; an offender who voluntarily takes alcohol and drugs and then behaves in a way they would not have done when sober should not be excused from responsibility.

In summary:

(a) If the defendant commits murder while intoxicated but does not suffer from alcoholism or a dependency-related condition, they cannot rely on diminished responsibility.

(b) If the defendant suffers from a recognised medical condition such as schizophrenia and kills the victim when in a psychotic state which was triggered by their voluntary intoxication, they may successfully plead the partial defence of diminished responsibility. The law does not require the abnormality of mind to be the sole cause of the defendant's acts.

(c) If the defendant has alcohol dependence syndrome but is also intoxicated at the time of the murder, the jury must focus exclusively on the effect of the alcohol consumed as a result of their illness and disregard the effect of any alcohol consumed voluntarily.

5.7.6 Substantial impairment of D's ability

The next element of the defence is the 'substantial impairment' of the defendant's ability to do one or more of the things set out in s 2(1A) of the HA 1957. Whether there has been a 'substantial' impairment is a question of fact for the jury. The case of *R v Lloyd* [1967] 1 QB 175 (based on the 'old' law) found that for the impairment to be 'substantial', it must be 'more than trivial or minimal'.

In *R v Golds* [2016] UKSC 61, the Supreme Court reviewed the authorities from both England and Scotland on the meaning of this phrase and concluded that 'substantial' meant 'important or weighty'. This is not surprising when the context is borne in mind.; the partial defence only comes into play when the prosecution has proved that the defendant has committed murder. As such, the judges ruled that there must be a 'weighty' impairment of the defendant's abilities before this grave offence may be reduced to the lesser offence of manslaughter; a reason that is so minor it just passes the trivial will not be enough. Although ordinarily there would be no need to direct a jury on the meaning of 'substantial', they would be required to consider the question of degree when all the evidence has been heard.

Under the 'old' definition of diminished responsibility, there was a general requirement for a substantial impairment of the defendant's mental responsibility. However, under the amended s 2 the defendant's ability to do particular things must be substantially impaired, namely, to understand the nature of their conduct, and/or to form a rational judgment, and/or to exercise self-control. Set out below are illustrations of what incidents may satisfy s 2(1A) of the HA 1957.

Example

(1) Stefan enjoys playing violent computer games. He stabs Perry in the heart, believing that he will come back to life as the victims do when he replays his computer games.

In this example it appears that Stefan does not understand the nature of his conduct – s 2(1A)(a). He does not realise that stabbing someone in the heart has fatal consequences and that his 'real life' victim cannot be resuscitated.

(2) Stefan is obsessed with the belief that the security services want to question him on terrorist charges (which is totally untrue). He shoots the postman when he rings on the doorbell with a delivery, believing that the postman is an MI5 agent. Stefan appears to be suffering from some sort of neurosis which impairs his ability to form a rational judgment under s 2(1A)(b).

(3) Stefan hits his neighbour in the face with a hammer after his neighbour plays his music too loudly all evening despite Stefan's complaints. It may be that Stefan lacks the ability to exercise self-control under s 2(1A)(c).

5.7.7 The abnormality of mental functioning must provide an explanation for the killing

One major criticism the Law Commission identified under the old definition of diminished responsibility contained in s 2 of the HA 1957 was that there was no causal link required between the defendant's abnormality of mind and their act (or omission) in killing. As the Parliamentary Under-Secretary of State for Justice (Maria Eagle) stated during the Committee stage of Parliamentary debate:

> The Government agree with the Law Commission that it is necessary for there to be some causal connection between the abnormality of mental functioning and the killing in order for the partial defence to succeed. It is right for there to be some connection between the condition and the killing, otherwise the partial defence could succeed in cases when the defendant's mental condition made no difference to their behaviour, and they would have killed regardless of the medical condition. For that reason, subsection (1B) [of s 52 of the CJA 2009] provides that, for the partial defence to succeed, any such abnormality of mental functioning must have been at least a significant contributory factor in causing the defendant to do as he did. It need not have been the only cause, the main cause or the most important factor, but it must be more than merely trivial. The partial defence cannot succeed when the truth is that the recognised medical condition and the impairment were randomly present by coincidence and made absolutely no difference to the behaviour that ensued.

In other words, causation must be established. For the defence to succeed, the defendant must show that the homicide would not have occurred if the mental abnormality, which amounts to a recognised medical condition, had not been present. This is important because, otherwise, anyone who suffers from a psychiatric condition would automatically succeed in this defence even if the condition had no bearing whatsoever on their fatal act. Accordingly, if the accused suffers from a paranoid personality disorder but kills the victim in a fit of rage, unassociated with their personality disorder, they will not be able to rely on diminished responsibility as a defence, despite their abnormality of mental functioning arising from a recognised medical condition.

Determining this question will involve considering the extent to which the defendant is answerable for their behaviour in light of their state of mind and ability to control their physical actions. Realistically, the jury will not be able to answer these questions without medical evidence; for example, even the phrase 'abnormality of mental functioning' would be difficult for a lay person to interpret as it requires an understanding of the processes going through the defendant's mind – something that only an expert is likely to have.

Figure 5.3 Diminished responsibility

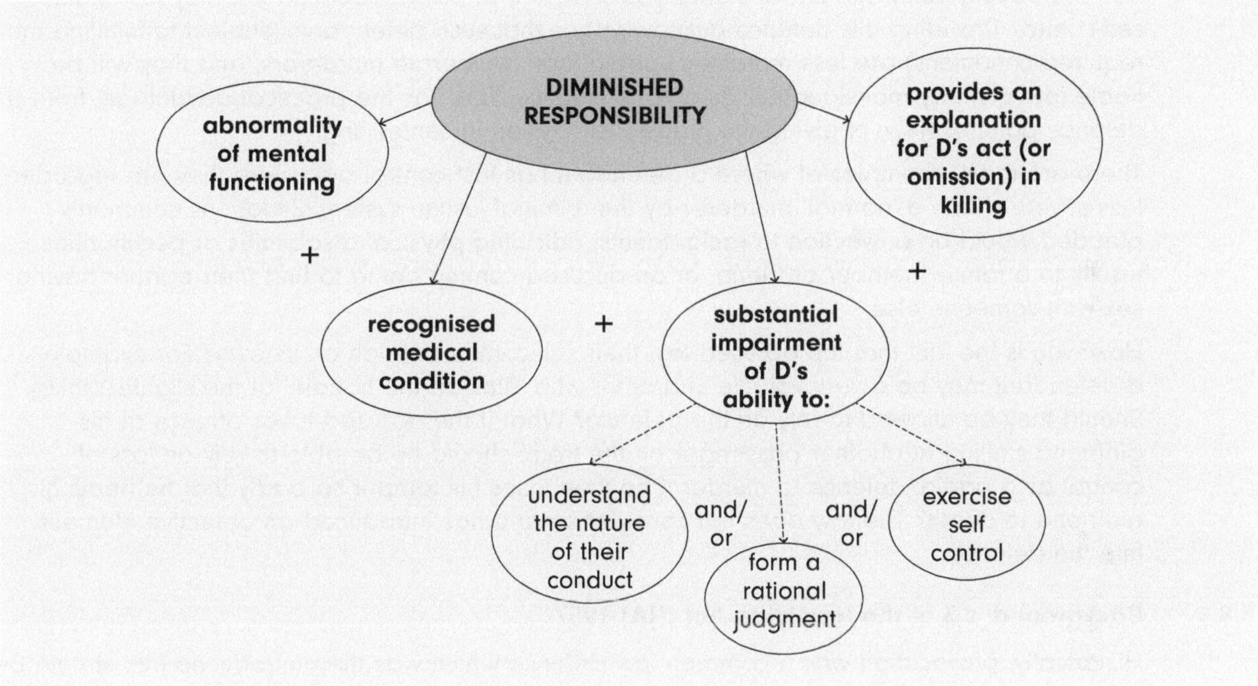

5.7.8 Diminished responsibility and legal insanity

Diminished responsibility is a partial defence to murder which, if successfully proved by the defendant on the balance of probabilities, reduces murder to voluntary manslaughter. It can only ever be pleaded as a defence to a murder charge, not to any other offence.

However, there is a different defence that a defendant may raise in relation to any crime with which they are charged, that of 'insanity'. This requires the defendant to prove, again on the balance of probabilities, that they were suffering from a 'disease of the mind' causing a 'defect in reason' so that either they did not know the 'nature and quality' of their act, or they did not know their act was legally and morally wrong. This defence arises from *M'Naghten's Case* (1843) [1843–60] All ER Rep 229.

The defence of insanity is rarely used and is only mentioned here so you are aware of its existence and the potential overlap with the defence of diminished responsibility. Unlike diminished responsibility, however, insanity is a complete defence, resulting in a special verdict of 'not guilty by reason of insanity'. A high-profile example of a defendant successfully pleading insanity as a defence to an attempted murder charge is Michael Abram, who attacked former Beatle member George Harrison in his own home in 1999. After Mr Abram successfully raised the defence, the judge ordered him to be held in a secure psychiatric hospital (from which he has now been released).

5.8 Loss of control

Loss of control is the second partial defence which, if successful, would reduce murder to voluntary manslaughter. Again, it does not come into play until the prosecution has proved that the defendant has killed with the intention to kill or cause grievous bodily harm, and so is liable for murder; thus, it should not be pleaded if the defendant is charged with an assault, for example. The rationale behind the defence is an acceptance by the law that everyone has a breaking point and circumstances may arise that push people so far, they lose their self-control. Providing this defence acknowledges that such defendants (subject to fulfilling the required conditions) are less morally culpable than deliberate murderers, and they will be liable for voluntary manslaughter as a consequence. This has the practical advantage, from a defence point of view, of giving the judge a discretion in sentencing.

There are many examples of where a defendant has lost control but where they are regarded less severely than a 'normal' murderer by the criminal justice system. Situations commonly pleaded would be a reaction to racial taunts, ridiculing physical disabilities or peculiarities, insults to a family member or friend, or an accused coming home to find their partner having sex with someone else.

However, is the fact that the accused lost their self-control enough on its own? For example, a defendant may be a very volatile character who 'flies off the handle' at the slightest thing. Should they be allowed to rely on the defence? What if the accused takes offence at his girlfriend smiling at another passenger on the train; should he be able to rely on loss of control as a partial defence to murder if he then loses his temper so badly that he beats his girlfriend to death? The law does not consider so and has introduced an objective element into the defence.

5.8.1 Background: s 3 of the Homicide Act (HA) 1957

Historically, provocation was a common law defence which was then introduced into statute by s 3 of the HA 1957. However, the definition of the defence proved controversial and was the subject of much case law. It consisted of two tests which the defendant had to overcome to be able to rely on it, namely:

(1) Was the defendant provoked by things said or done (or both) to suddenly and temporarily lose their self-control? (Subjective test)

(2) Would the provocation have made a reasonable person lose their self-control and do as the defendant did? (Objective test)

In its Consultation Paper, 'Murder, manslaughter and infanticide: proposals for the reform of the law', the Government argued that the defence of provocation was too generous in cases where a defendant killed in anger, and that the law relating to the objective test in particular was too complex and uncertain. There had been much debate and a whole line of case law on the issue of who, exactly, is the 'reasonable person' for the purposes of the objective test. For example, could any of the defendant's characteristics be taken into account?

It was generally agreed, following *DPP v Camplin* [1978] AC 705, that the reasonable person is the same sex and age as the defendant. However, the objective nature of the test was considerably compromised by the controversial case of *R v Smith (Morgan)* [1998] 4 All ER 387.

The majority decision of the House of Lords was that the jury could take into account any of the characteristics of the defendant it felt was just to do so when considering how the 'reasonable person' would have reacted. However, the position changed again with the decision of the Privy Council in *Attorney-General for Jersey v Holley* [2005] 2 AC 580. The majority view here was that the defendant's characteristics could only be taken into account when determining the gravity of the provocation towards the defendant. Having assessed how serious the provocation was, the defendant then had to be judged according to the standards of self-control to be expected of an ordinary person of the defendant's age and sex.

Because the definition under s 3 of the HA 1957 proved both complex to interpret and difficult for a jury to apply, the Government decided to abolish the defence of provocation and replace it with a new defence called 'Partial defence to murder: loss of control'. This defence is contained in ss 54 and 55 of the CJA 2009. Section 56 of the Act both abolishes the common law defence of provocation (by s 56(1)) and repeals s 3 of the HA 1957 (by s 56(2)(a)).

5.8.2 Definition of the partial defence of loss of control

The definition of loss of control is contained in s 54 of the CJA 2009 (extracts of which are set out below):

(1) Where a person ('D') kills or is a party to the killing of another ('V'), D is not to be convicted of murder if –

  (a) D's acts and omissions in doing or being a party to the killing resulted from D's loss of self-control,

  (b) the loss of self-control had a qualifying trigger, and

  (c) a person of D's sex and age, with a normal degree of tolerance and self-restraint and in the circumstances of D, might have reacted in the same or in a similar way to D.

(2) For the purposes of subsection (1)(a), it does not matter whether or not the loss of control was sudden.

(3) In subsection (1)(c) the reference to 'the circumstances of D' is a reference to all of D's circumstances other than those whose only relevance to D's conduct is that they bear on D's general capacity for tolerance or self-restraint.

In summary, the three elements of the defence that need to be established for it to be pleaded successfully are:

(a) the defendant must lose self-control;

(b) the loss of control must have a qualifying trigger; and

(c) a person of the defendant's sex and age, with a normal degree of tolerance and self-restraint and in the same circumstances, might have reacted in the same or similar way to the defendant.

Some 60% of those accused of murder rely upon the defence of loss of control, and, to succeed, all three requirements listed in s 54 of the CJA 2009 must be satisfied. Only then will their conviction for murder be reduced to manslaughter.

5.8.3 Evidential issues

There is one important difference between the two partial defences. Unlike diminished responsibility, the conventional burden of proof in criminal cases applies to loss of control. Section 54(5) places an evidential burden only on the defendant. The effect is that, provided the accused can produce some evidence that raises the defence, the burden will revert back to the prosecution to disprove loss of control beyond reasonable doubt. If the prosecution fails to do so, the jury must assume the defence is satisfied.

5.8.4 Defendant must lose control

When determining if the defendant has lost control, a number of issues arise and these are considered in turn.

First it must be established that the defendant lost self-control and this is a question of fact for the jury. Because the issue is subjectively assessed, they must be satisfied that this particular defendant lost self-control; it is not enough that the reasonable person would have done so but the accused actually did not.

Example

Felipe's wife, Moira, constantly criticises him both in public and at home. As soon as he steps through the front door, he faces a torrent of abuse. Moira has also thrown saucepans at him and scratched his car when she is angry. Felipe is an exceptionally calm individual but he decides that he can no longer tolerate her behaviour. However, he does not want to pay his wife a divorce settlement, so he decides that the next time she begins to insult him, he will kill her. Two days later, he strangles Moira to death.

Even though a reasonable person may well have 'cracked' under the continuous verbal onslaught, Felipe cannot rely upon the partial defence of loss of control. This is because Felipe, in fact, did not because he planned Moira's death.

Although the statute does not define the term loss of control, the courts have provided some assistance. In *R v Jewell* [2004] EWCA Crim 404, the accused shot and killed a work colleague. He alleged that the victim had intimidated and threatened him the previous evening and that he had armed himself for protection. He claimed that, when he saw the victim, he could not control himself. The Court of Appeal approved the meaning of loss of control as a loss of the ability to act 'in accordance with considered judgement, or a loss of normal powers of reasoning'. However, in this instance, the degree of planning was found to be such that the defendant was convicted of murder.

Example

Baxter is caught stealing a laptop computer by Gethan. Gethan calls Baxter 'a good for nothing thug' and says perhaps he should not be surprised as Baxter's family are all 'thieving bastards'. Baxter loses his temper and kills Gethan. Baxter may rely on the partial defence because he has lost his self-control, and the fact that Baxter induced Gethan's comments by stealing Gethan's laptop is irrelevant. However, to rely on the defence, Baxter must also satisfy the other elements too, and here there may not be a 'qualifying trigger' (see below).

5.8.4.1 No need to be sudden

Although the court must be satisfied that the defendant did indeed lose control, there is no requirement for the defendant to suddenly 'snap' so that they are acting, for example, in a fit of rage. This is because s 54(2) provides that the reaction need not be 'sudden'.

Returning to the case of *R v Ahluwahlia*, which was discussed earlier in this chapter, the defendant set fire to her husband and killed him while he slept. Initially, Ahluwalia was unsuccessful in her attempt to reduce her criminal liability to manslaughter. This was because, under the test that applied at the time, the loss of control had to be sudden. However, more understanding of how domestic violence victims react to their abusers led to a change in the law so that (now) the defendant need only prove that they actually did lose control at the time of the killing. The effect is that killings which occur in the domestic violence context, where the defendant's reaction builds up over a period of time, are not excluded. Nevertheless, in reality, the greater the level of deliberation, the less likely it is that the killing followed a true loss of self-control.

In summary, there may be a loss of control where the defendant 'snaps'; or their reaction is a response to a culmination of events, such as incidents of abuse, that occur over time.

5.8.4.2 Considered desire for revenge

Whilst the loss of self-control need not be sudden and without warning, it will not apply where the defendant acted in a considered desire for revenge (CJA 2009, s 54(4)). Although it may be difficult for the jury to distinguish between a planned attack and the reaction of a victim of abuse, this is a decision they must make. It is important that defendants who take deliberate steps to kill the victim should be distinguished from those who act on impulse or in fear or both.

As to what qualifies as a 'considered' desire for revenge, there is no guidance in the statute. However, during the consultation process, a number of concerns were expressed over so-called honour killings (in which the victim is killed because they are perceived to have brought dishonour on the family), and the need to prevent those charged with such from taking advantage of the defence. In its Impact Assessment Statement, the Government said: 'following consultation we are also amending the defence to ensure that it excludes killings carried out in a considered desire for revenge, which is likely to be relevant to "honour" killings.'

Other factors that may satisfy the test could include where the defendant arms themselves with a weapon, there is evidence of planning or there is a significant delay between the provoking words or conduct and the killing.

Examples

(1) Beryl has been subjected to physical abuse from her husband for some years. One day her husband threatens to slap her, and she loses her temper and kills him. Beryl has lost her self-control for the purposes of the defence in these circumstances. The fact that his final comment may not, on its own, be that serious does not matter – it can be 'the straw that breaks the camel's back'.

(2) As above, but Beryl leaves the house and goes to the park where she plans how she is going to kill him. She returns three hours later and carries out her plan. In this instance, the partial defence will almost certainly not apply. There is no evidence that Beryl lost her self-control at the time of the killing. The facts also suggest that she has had time to 'cool down' and has planned her attack; this points to revenge rather than to a loss of self-control.

(3) As in example 2 above, but when she returns her husband slaps her face, resulting in Beryl 'snapping' and stabbing her husband. Here, she may succeed. There is a significant difference from the previous example in that Beryl has lost her self-control at the time of killing due to a fresh action by her husband.

5.8.4.4 Multiple defendants

Finally, it is worth noting that, under s 54(8), just because one party to a killing successfully pleads the defence, this does not affect the criminal liability of any other party. Thus, if two defendants attack and kill the victim, one may still be liable for murder even if the other successfully pleads loss of control as a partial defence.

5.8.4.5 Summary of loss of control

When determining if there has been a genuine loss of control, the jury will need to consider all the facts. In particular, evidence of there being a delay does not automatically preclude a defendant from relying upon the partial defence of loss of control, but it may mean that the defence is less likely to succeed. Set out below is a summary of the law that applies to this aspect of loss of control.

Figure 5.4 Loss of control

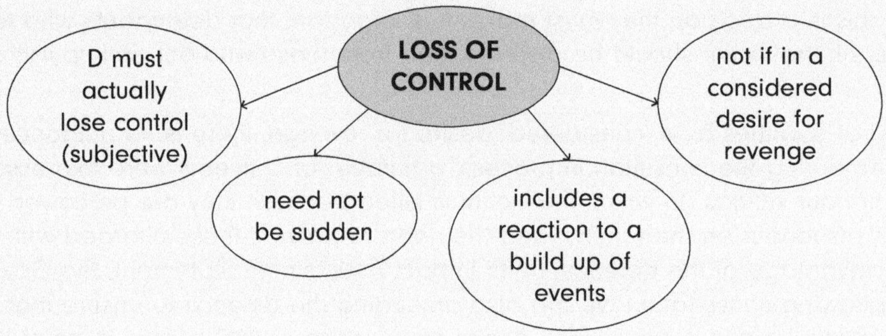

5.8.5 The 'qualifying trigger'

One of the criticisms of the 'old' defence of provocation is that it was a model based around anger. It acknowledged that, in certain circumstances, a defendant might get so angry they lost control and, as a result, killed someone. Both the Law Commission and the Government felt that a shift in emphasis was needed. As the Parliamentary Under-Secretary of State for Justice, Maria Eagle, stated during the Committee stage of Parliamentary debate:

> The Government are persuaded that in a small number of murder cases the existing partial defence of provocation is too generous to those who kill in anger and is poorly tailored to killings in response to fear.

She went on to point out that the partial defence of loss of self-control was intended to have a higher bar than the provocation defence, as there must now be a specified 'qualifying trigger', respectively known as the 'fear' and 'anger' triggers, which causes the loss of self-control. The loss of control must be the result of one of these or a combination of both. The Government's intention was to make the defence available in a smaller number of cases than the previous law. To achieve this, the statute provides:

> **55 Meaning of 'qualifying trigger'**
>
> (1) This section applies for the purposes of section 54.
>
> (2) A loss of self-control had a qualifying trigger if subsection (3), (4) or (5) applies.
>
> (3) This subsection applies if D's loss of self-control was attributable to D's fear of serious violence from V against D or another identified person.

(4) This subsection applies if D's loss of self-control was attributable to a thing or things done or said (or both) which –

(a) constituted circumstances of an extremely grave character, and
(b) caused D to have a justifiable sense of being seriously wronged.

(5) This subsection applies if D's loss of self-control was attributable to a combination of the matters mentioned in subsections (3) and (4).

It is important to note that, according to s 55(6)(a) and (b), the defendant's fear of serious violence must be disregarded, and their sense of being seriously wronged is not justifiable if they incited the thing said or done in order to provide an excuse to use violence in response. In such circumstances, the defendant cannot rely on the triggers and the partial defence will fail.

Example

Neil has had an argument with Pete. With the aim of starting a fight, Neil insults Pete and his family. Pete loses his temper and attacks Neil with a baseball bat. Neil reacts by stabbing Pete with a knife, killing him.

Neil is unlikely to be able to rely on the defence due to s 55(6)(a) as his fear of serious violence from Pete is disregarded to the extent that it was caused by a thing which Neil had done or said for the purpose of providing an excuse to use violence. In insulting Pete, Neil's intention was to start a fight, thus providing an excuse to use violence against Pete.

5.8.5.1 The fear trigger

The 'fear trigger' under s 55(3) will apply where the loss of control 'was attributable to the defendant's fear of serious violence from the victim against the defendant or another identified person'. The fear is subjectively assessed so that the jury must be satisfied that the defendant was genuinely afraid of such violence even if the fear is not reasonable; and the fear must be from the victim against the defendant or another identified person, rather than a more general fear.

Example

Jessie has been married to Pili for 3 years. During that time, he has subjected her to violence, especially when he has been drinking. One evening he returns from a night out, clearly drunk. Jessie picks up a kitchen knife and stabs Pili when he approaches her.

Provided Jessie has lost her self-control, she should be able to rely on the qualifying trigger under s 55(3) if she feared serious violence from Pili against her. The same would be true if she feared serious violence against someone else other than her personally, for example against their child. Unlike under s 55(4), there is no objective element to this subsection, so the question is not whether the jury would have been in fear of serious violence but whether Jessie herself was in fear of such violence from Pili at the time of the killing.

5.8.5.2 The anger trigger

The anger trigger under s 55(4) applies where the defendant's loss of control was attributable to things said and/or done that amounted to circumstances of an extremely grave character and caused the defendant to have a justifiable sense of having been seriously wronged. No definitions are included in the Act. However, in its Consultation Paper, 'Murder, Manslaughter and Infanticide' (Law Com No 304), the Law Commission gave a parent coming home to find their child being raped as an example of when s 55(4) might apply.

Whether the defendant's sense of being seriously wronged is justifiable is an objective question to be determined initially by the judge, who must decide whether a properly directed jury could reasonably conclude that it was. Only then should the judge leave the question as one of fact to be decided by the jury. Effectively, the judge is acting as a filter here.

Example

Deepak finds out that his sister, Amina, has a boyfriend. She has kept this a secret as she is aware that her family will be extremely angry. In a fit of rage, Deepak kills Amina because of her relationship as he believes it will bring shame to his family.

Deepak may personally feel that his sister's relationship brings dishonour to the family, thus constituting circumstances of an extremely grave character and causing him to have a justifiable sense of being seriously wronged. However, he would not be able to rely on s 55(4) as a qualifying trigger because of the objective elements within the Act. In particular, whether or not the circumstances are of an 'extremely grave character' is to be decided by the jury, and it is highly doubtful they would consider that Amina's relationship meets this requirement. Furthermore, the sense of being 'seriously wronged' must be 'justifiable', and a jury is unlikely to share Deepak's belief in this regard. Thus, Deepak would be guilty of murder.

5.8.5.3 Sexual infidelity

Historically and statistically, the partial defence of loss of control (or its equivalent) was used by defendants who reacted violently to their partner's adultery. To combat this, the statute deliberately excludes such an excuse, providing that the fact that a thing done or said constituted sexual infidelity is to be disregarded (s 55(6)(c)). This subsection caused a great deal of debate in its passage through Parliament. The Government stated that the 'words and conduct' partial defence would apply only in circumstances of an extremely grave nature, so eliminating its possible application to routine relationship and domestic conflicts. This would be reinforced by the explicit statement in s 55(6) that sexual infidelity on its own could not constitute grounds for the defendant to have a justifiable sense of being seriously wronged to an extent that would warrant reducing murder to manslaughter.

Example

Dewi returns home to find his partner, Steve, having sex with another man. He loses his temper and attacks Steve ferociously, killing him instantly. Dewi has clearly lost his self-control under s 55(4). However, sexual infidelity on its own is to be disregarded as a qualifying trigger under s 55(6) and, thus, he is liable for the offence of murder.

However, although understandable, such a rigid approach is perhaps not realistic. Difficulties arise where, for example, the victim taunts the defendant with their infidelity amongst a torrent of other abusive comments. Should one be ignored and others taken account of?

In *R v Clinton, Parker and Evans* [2012] EWCA 2, the Court of Appeal was asked to determine whether sexual infidelity is entirely excluded from consideration in a case involving other potential qualifying triggers. The court ruled that where sexual infidelity is the only 'provocation', such evidence must be excluded. However, to avoid potential injustice, the judges also confirmed that sexual infidelity is 'not subject to a blanket exclusion' and that where it 'forms an essential part of the context', it may be considered.

The effect of this decision is that where the sexual infidelity is part of the background or context to other possible triggers, then evidence relating to it may be relevant when assessing that other potential qualifying trigger.

Example

Gawain and his wife, Jody, have been married for eight years and have three young children. However, Jody wishes to separate and has contacted a lawyer about divorce proceedings. Gawain is devastated about the break-up of his marriage and tries to dissuade her. The two begin to argue and Jody taunts Gawain about a range of matters including her repeated sexual infidelity, his visits to suicide websites (specifically that he did not have the courage to kill himself), and also her lack of care for their children. Gawain suddenly flips, beating Jody to death.

Jody's sexual infidelity may be considered as part of the background, but it cannot be the qualifying trigger on its own. In Gawain's case there are other factors, namely the taunts about his suicidal thoughts and his wife's attitude to the children, that can (in the context of the sexual infidelity) count as a potential trigger. Combined together, the things said and done were such as to constitute circumstances of an extremely grave character, which caused Gawain to have a justifiable sense of being seriously wronged. The effect is that Gawain's conviction for murder may be reduced to voluntary manslaughter.

The fact that sexual infidelity cannot be relied upon on its own as a qualifying trigger, but can be taken into account as one of a number of factors, is generally regarded as a sensible compromise reflecting the complexities of relationships and the fact that murders are often committed when passions are roused, which may be for several reasons.

In summary:

(a) Sexual infidelity cannot be relied upon on its own as a qualifying trigger, but its existence does not prevent reliance on the defence where there are other qualifying triggers.

(b) Where other factors suggest a qualifying trigger, sexual infidelity may be also taken into account in assessing whether things done or said amounted to circumstances of an extremely grave character and gave the defendant a justifiable sense of being seriously wronged.

Note that sexual infidelity may be taken into account in the third component of the defence in examining whether a person of the defendant's sex and age, with a normal degree of tolerance and self-restraint and in the circumstances of the defendant, might have reacted in the same or in a similar way.

5.8.5.4 Overview of the qualifying triggers

Figure 5.5 Qualifying triggers for loss of control

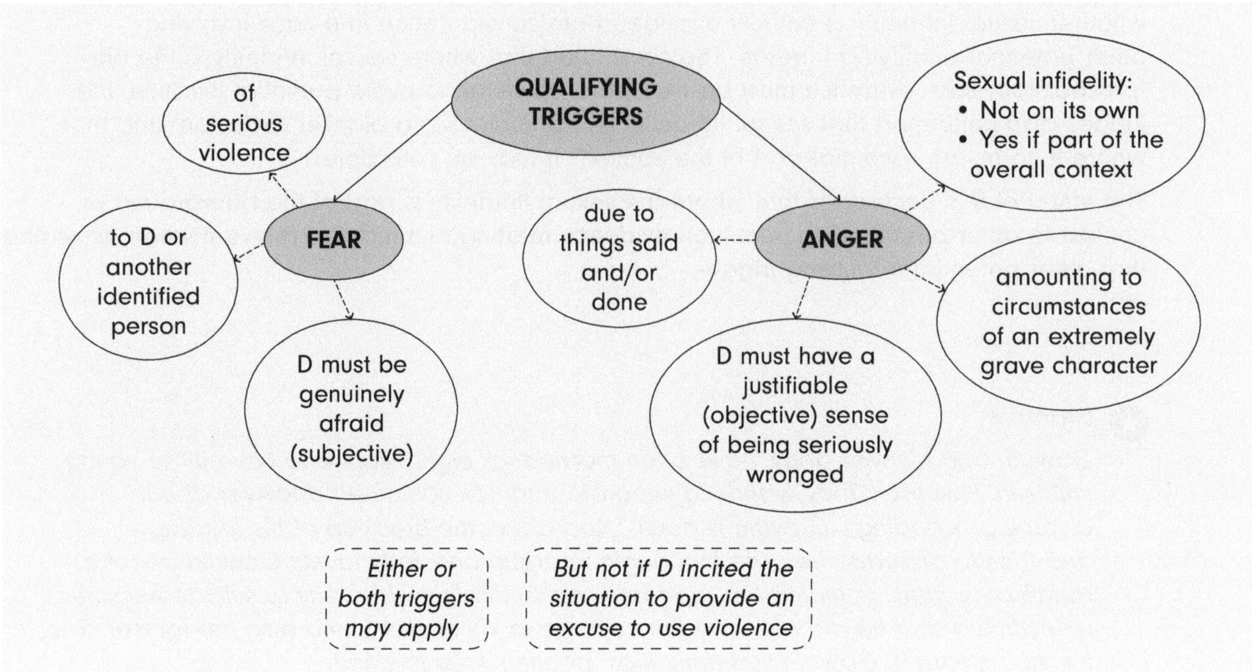

5.8.6 Similar reaction of a person of the defendant's sex and age

Loss of control is subject to a third requirement, which is primarily objective in content. The reason is that, to maintain the rule of law and a peaceful society, there are standards of behaviour that must be adhered to whenever possible. The partial defences provide a compassionate outcome to those who are unable to meet this standard in specific circumstances, but it does not mean the killing is acceptable.

The third element of the defence is set out in s 54(1)(c):

> A person of D's sex and age, with a normal degree of tolerance and self-restraint, and in the circumstances of D, might have reacted in the same or in a similar way to D.

The 'circumstances of D' are defined in s 54(3) as:

> all of D's circumstances other than those whose only relevance to D's conduct is that they bear on D's general capacity for tolerance or self-restraint.

In making this assessment, the 'normal' person will have the same history and characteristics as the defendant in so far as they are relevant to the qualifying triggers that prompted the loss of self-control. However, if the defendant is particularly aggressive or short tempered, they will not be able to rely upon these characteristics as an excuse for the killing.

This part of the defence adopts the approach of the majority decision of the Privy Council in *Attorney-General for Jersey v Holley* [2005] (discussed above), and was designed to replace the old 'objective' test of provocation under s 3 of the HA 1957. The aim was to overcome concerns that the objective test in provocation had become too subjective, particularly as there were conflicting cases and confusion over who, exactly, was the 'reasonable person'. The provision is interesting in itself since, as loss of control can only ever be a partial defence to murder, the law is accepting that a person with a 'normal' degree of self-restraint might intentionally kill another in some circumstances. In doing so, the statute aims to put 'clear water' between the two partial defences of loss of control and diminished responsibility.

The Act includes age and sex as general characteristics to be taken into account, although the relevance of both has been questioned. The Government, by including the defendant's sex as a factor in this test, seems to imply that people of different sexes may have different levels of self-control in some situations, although no examples are given as to when this may apply. It has been argued that the defendant's sex may be most relevant when considering the fear of serious violence trigger, as set out in s 55(3) of the CJA 2009. This is presumably on the basis that females are generally less physically powerful than men or that they react differently to threats of serious violence, and thus have a lower capacity for self-restraint when faced with such threats.

With regard to the second characteristic, age has long been a factor in determining this aspect of the partial defence. When considering reform of the law, both the Law Commission and the Government agreed that age has an influence on the amount of self-control to be expected of a person. A child generally has a lower capacity to control themselves and their emotions than an adult, and so the defendant should be judged according to the level of tolerance and self-restraint to be expected of a 'normal' person of their age. To judge a child defendant against the level of self-control expected of an adult would not be fair. There are some who argue that age is not really the issue - maturity is. However, age is an objective, if somewhat crude, way of measuring this.

Set out below are three examples of how this element of the offence would apply in practice.

Examples

(a) Jay, who is 19 years of age, is waiting for a train with his girlfriend, Amy. As they enter the train, Tobias, who is boarding at the same time, smiles at Amy. Jay is convinced that Tobias is flirting with Amy despite his protestations to the contrary. Jay becomes more and more agitated and then loses his control completely, stabbing Tobias to death with a flick knife.

In this scenario, a 19-year-old male with a normal degree of tolerance and self-restraint would not have stabbed Tobias to death just because he smiled politely at the defendant's girlfriend, so the partial defence would fail.

(b) Ariana is a 14-year-old girl who has been sexually abused by Richard for over two years. One day, after she has been drinking heavily, Richard sexually assaults Ariana and then laughs at her distress. Ariana hits Richard with a vase and kills him.

Ariana must satisfy the jury that a 14-year-old girl with a normal degree of tolerance and self-restraint might have killed her abuser when taunted in this way. Her voluntary intoxication will not be taken into account and she will be assessed as if she were sober. Even so, the defence is likely to succeed.

(c) Nyofi is 25 years of age and recently entered into a civil partnership with her girlfriend, Marnie. However, Marnie has just announced that she is leaving Nyofi and taking their five-year-old daughter, Jemma, with her. The two argue and Marnie screams at Nyofi that she is sick of her partner's 'disapproving African family' and that she does not want to be in a lesbian relationship any longer. Nyofi is devastated as she has cut all ties with her family to be with Marnie. As Marnie

is leaving the house, she yells: 'Lesbians are all bitchy and African ones are the worst – I need to get Jemma out of this toxic atmosphere.' Nyofi grabs a kitchen knife and fatally stabs Marnie.

Nyofi would have to establish that a 25-year-old female with a normal degree of tolerance might have reacted by stabbing her partner to death, when taunted about being a lesbian and her African heritage and confronted with the loss of her daughter. Because Nyofi is being taunted about her sexual orientation and racial origin, the normal person will have the same sexual orientation and racial origin. It is likely that Nyofi could rely successfully upon the partial defence of loss of control to reduce her criminal liability to manslaughter.

Set out below is a summary flowchart of similar reaction.

Figure 5.6 Similar reaction for loss of control

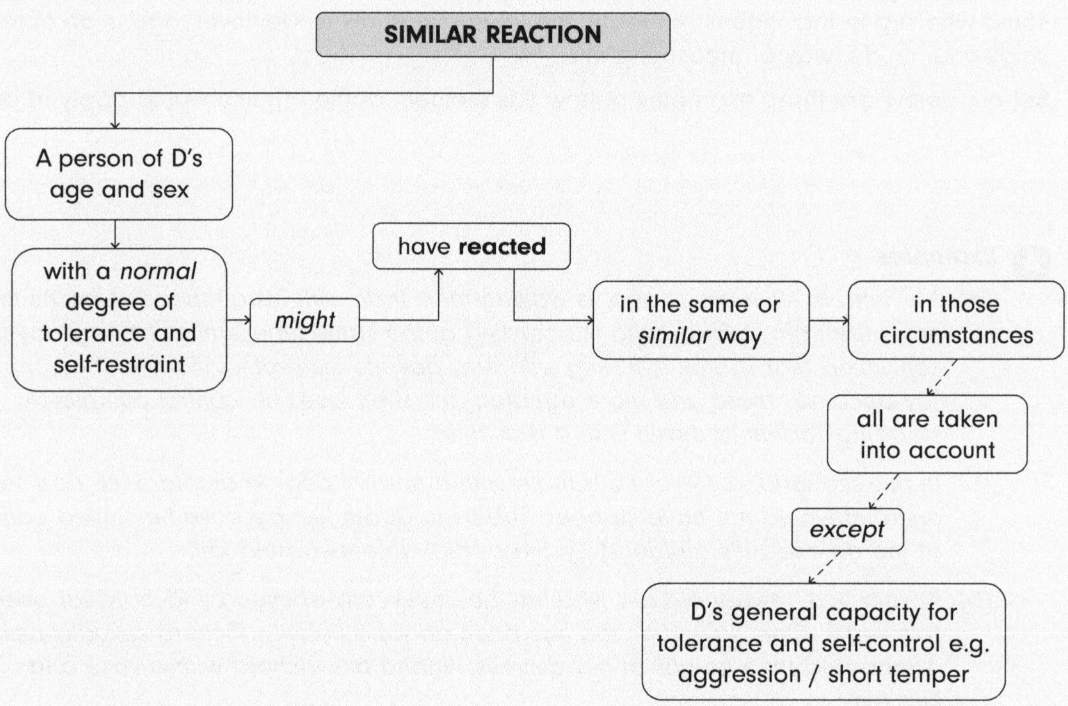

5.8.7 'Sufficient evidence'

Unlike the 'old' defence of provocation under s 3 of the HA 1957, there is now a 'filter' on whether the issue is to be brought before the jury. In the past, if the defendant raised any evidence of provocation, the judge had no discretion. In *R v Doughty* (1986) 83 Cr App R 319, the defendant appealed against his murder conviction when the trial judge refused to allow the defence of provocation to be left to the jury. The defendant had claimed that the persistent crying of his baby caused him to lose his temper and to kill the child. The Court of Appeal held that, since there was evidence of a causal link between the crying of the baby and the defendant's response, it was wrong for the trial judge to withhold the matter of provocation from the jury.

Now, under s 54(6) of the CJA 2009, the defence of loss of control can only be presented to the jury if there is sufficient evidence that 'in the opinion of the trial judge, a jury, properly directed, could reasonably conclude that the defence might apply'.

How this works in practice is that, at the conclusion of the evidence, the trial judge will consider whether enough evidence has been raised in respect of all the components of the defence. If any one element is missing, that is the end of the matter and the partial defence will not apply. The jury will have no involvement at this stage. In *R v Jewell* (see earlier in this chapter), when giving evidence, the defendant recited as if from legal textbooks: 'I did it because I lost control. I could not control my actions.' The Court of Appeal judges confirmed that a mere assertion by the defendant that he had lost control was not on its own sufficient evidence upon which a jury could reasonably conclude that the defence might apply.

Other examples of circumstances where the judge could intervene to remove the partial defence entirely from consideration by the jury include deaths in response to a baby's persistent crying or a threat to prevent the defendant seeing his children unless he agreed to the victim's divorce settlement terms. However, these would rarely arise in practice.

5.9 Summary

To conclude:

(a) Murder is a common law offence committed when the defendant unlawfully causes the death of the victim with an intention to kill or cause grievous bodily harm.

(b) The actus reus and mens rea for murder and voluntary manslaughter are the same.

(c) In certain situations, the law accepts that the accused's culpability for murder should be reduced. The defendant remains liable for causing the death, but their behaviour is excused in some way. These are referred to as the partial defences. If the defendant succeeds in establishing all the elements required for one of the partial defences, their conviction for murder will be reduced to manslaughter.

(d) For the partial defence of diminished responsibility, the defendant must suffer an abnormality of mental functioning; arising from a recognised medical condition; which substantially impairs their ability to understand the nature of their conduct, form a rational judgment or exercise self-control; and explains the defendant's acts or omissions in doing the killing.

(e) For the partial defence of loss of control, the defendant must actually lose control; this must be attributable to a qualifying trigger so that the defendant feared serious violence from the victim against either the defendant or another identified person; and/or something was said or done that constituted circumstances of an extremely grave character and caused the defendant to have a justifiable sense of being seriously wronged. Sexual infidelity cannot be relied upon on its own as a qualifying trigger, but it can be taken into account as one of a number of factors. Thus, its mere presence does not prevent reliance on the defence where other qualifying triggers exist. Finally, it must be shown that a person of the defendant's sex and age with a normal degree of tolerance and self-restraint might have reacted in the same or a similar way in the circumstances.

Having completed our study of murder and voluntary manslaughter, test your understanding using the activity below.

ACTIVITY

(1) Barney is an alcoholic and has a paranoid personality disorder. He is staying at his friend, Tamara's house. He drinks a great many whiskies and decides to start a fire in the living room as he believes that Tamara is haunting him. The fire spreads rapidly and Tamara is burnt to death. Is Barney guilty of either murder or voluntary manslaughter in respect of Tamara's death?

COMMENT

Barney commits the actus reus of murder as he unlawfully caused Tamara's death. However, he may lack the necessary mens rea for this offence because there is no evidence to suggest that he wanted to kill or cause serious bodily harm, although he does believe that Tamara is 'haunting' him. The prosecution may submit that Barney indirectly intended Tamara's death as he set fire to the living room of her house, and this will be satisfied if they can prove that Barney appreciated that death or serious harm was virtually certain to result from his actions.

If Barney does satisfy the mens rea, he could try to prove diminished responsibility based on an abnormality of mental functioning caused by a recognised medical condition (his paranoid personality disorder and alcohol dependence syndrome). The jury would then decide whether Barney's ability to understand the nature of his conduct, and/or to form a rational judgment, and/or to exercise self-control, was substantially impaired by the abnormality of mental functioning. In determining this, they would have to ignore the effects of any voluntarily consumed alcohol and focus only on his personality disorder and the effect of the alcohol consumed as a direct result of his alcoholism.

(2) Eithne is 35 years of age. She has been married to Aaron for 10 years and they have a six-year-old daughter, Iona. Eithne is significantly overweight and was bullied at school because of this. Furthermore, during the marriage, Aaron has punched and kicked Eithne on a frequent basis, and constantly taunted her about her weight. In each of the scenarios below, consider whether Eithne lost control when she carried out the fatal act.

(a) One evening, Aaron returns from work in a foul mood. He starts shouting at Eithne, calling her an 'ugly fat bitch' before grabbing her hair and slapping her face. This is usually the prelude to a violent assault. Eithne is chopping vegetables when Aaron enters the kitchen and uses the knife to stab him to death.

(b) As for scenario (a) above, except that Eithne does not respond immediately. Aaron continues with the violence, punching his wife in the face and then repeatedly kicking her as she cowers on the floor. When he leaves the kitchen, Eithne hides in the under-stairs cupboard and waits until Aaron falls asleep in front of the television, which he does two hours later. When she emerges, Eithne sees him lying there and, unable to take any more, she grabs a kitchen knife and stabs Aaron to death.

(c) One morning during breakfast, Aaron looks at Eithne and says contemptuously: 'You really could make a bit of effort – you look a right state!' Eithne storms out of the kitchen and grabs Aaron's golf club, which is in a bag in the hallway. She runs towards him and smashes Aaron repeatedly over the head with the club, killing him.

(d) As for scenario (c) above, but instead of reacting immediately, Eithne walks out of the house to go to work. During the day, she plans how she is going to kill Aaron. That evening, she goes into the garage and finds a hammer and then, while he is playing computer games, she hits Aaron repeatedly over the head, killing him.

COMMENT

(a) Here, there is a clear loss of control - Eithne 'snaps' and reacts instantly to Aaron's assault.

(b) In this example, there is not (on the face of it) a lack of control because Eithne did not react spontaneously to the assault but, instead, waited for a couple of hours until Aaron was asleep. However, her action was a response to an accumulation of years of provocation, something that has been described as 'a snapping in slow motion, the final surrender of frayed elastic' - a quote from the book 'Eve was Framed: Women and British Justice' by Helena Kennedy. It is now established that certain defendants, such as those who have been the victim of domestic violence, may lose control in a manner that is not obviously so.

(c) Here, the evidence is clear that Eithne lost her temper when she killed her husband, satisfying the test for loss of control. The fact that the final comment on its own may not be the most offensive does not matter as it can be the so-called 'straw that breaks the camel's back'.

(d) On this evidence, the jury would not find a loss of control at the time of the fatal act. Not only has Eithne had time to 'cool down' but she planned the attack and carried it out deliberately.

(3) When Shania returns home one day, she is shocked to find her husband, Charlie, pushing and slapping her 86-year-old mother, who suffers from dementia. In a rage, Shania throws a heavy plant pot at Charlie. He is killed by the blow. In her police interview, Shania admits that she wanted to hurt Charlie badly. Is Shania guilty of either murder or voluntary manslaughter?

COMMENT

The actus reus of murder is complete as Charlie is dead, as is the mens rea because, although Shania did not want to kill Charlie, she intended to cause him really serious bodily harm. Shania will be guilty of murder unless she can rely on a partial defence to reduce this offence to voluntary manslaughter. Shania would have to provide sufficient evidence to raise the defence as an issue. The trial judge must be satisfied that a jury, properly directed, could reasonably conclude that the defence might apply. If so, the issue goes before the jury and the Crown must disprove it beyond reasonable doubt.

It appears that Shania's act in throwing the heavy vase at Charlie resulted from a loss of self-control as she is 'in a rage'. Did this have a qualifying trigger? Possibly yes, as under s 55(4) of the CJA 2009 there appear to be circumstances of an extremely grave character which cause her to have a justifiable sense of being seriously wronged. If so, the question is then whether a woman of the same age as Shania, with a normal degree of tolerance and self-restraint and in her circumstances, might have reacted in the same or a similar way. A jury may find that such a person might have reacted by throwing a vase at a man who was abusing her elderly and vulnerable mother. Thus, Shania may be guilty of voluntary manslaughter due to the partial defence of loss of control, instead of murder.

6 Involuntary Manslaughter

LEARNING OUTCOMES

When you have completed this chapter, you should be able to:

- understand the elements of unlawful act manslaughter and gross negligence manslaughter;
- explain the driving offences that apply when a death occurs;
- appreciate how involuntary manslaughter and the driving offences are applied in practice.

6.1 Introduction

This chapter deals with situations where a defendant kills a victim but does so without intending either death or grievous bodily harm. Thus, although they have committed the actus reus of murder, they have not satisfied the mens rea. The accused may only have intended minor harm or indeed no harm at all, but despite this and perhaps due to pure misfortune, they cause the victim's death.

6.2 Murder, voluntary and involuntary manslaughter

For all homicides, the defendant must unlawfully cause the death of a human being. However, as discussed in the previous chapter, a murder conviction is reduced to voluntary manslaughter if the defendant has the benefit of an excuse in the form of a partial defence, such as diminished responsibility or loss of control. Involuntary manslaughter is distinguished by the mens rea, as there is no requirement to prove that the defendant intended to kill or cause grievous bodily harm.

The flowchart below summarises the three types of homicide.

Figure 6.1 Types of homicide

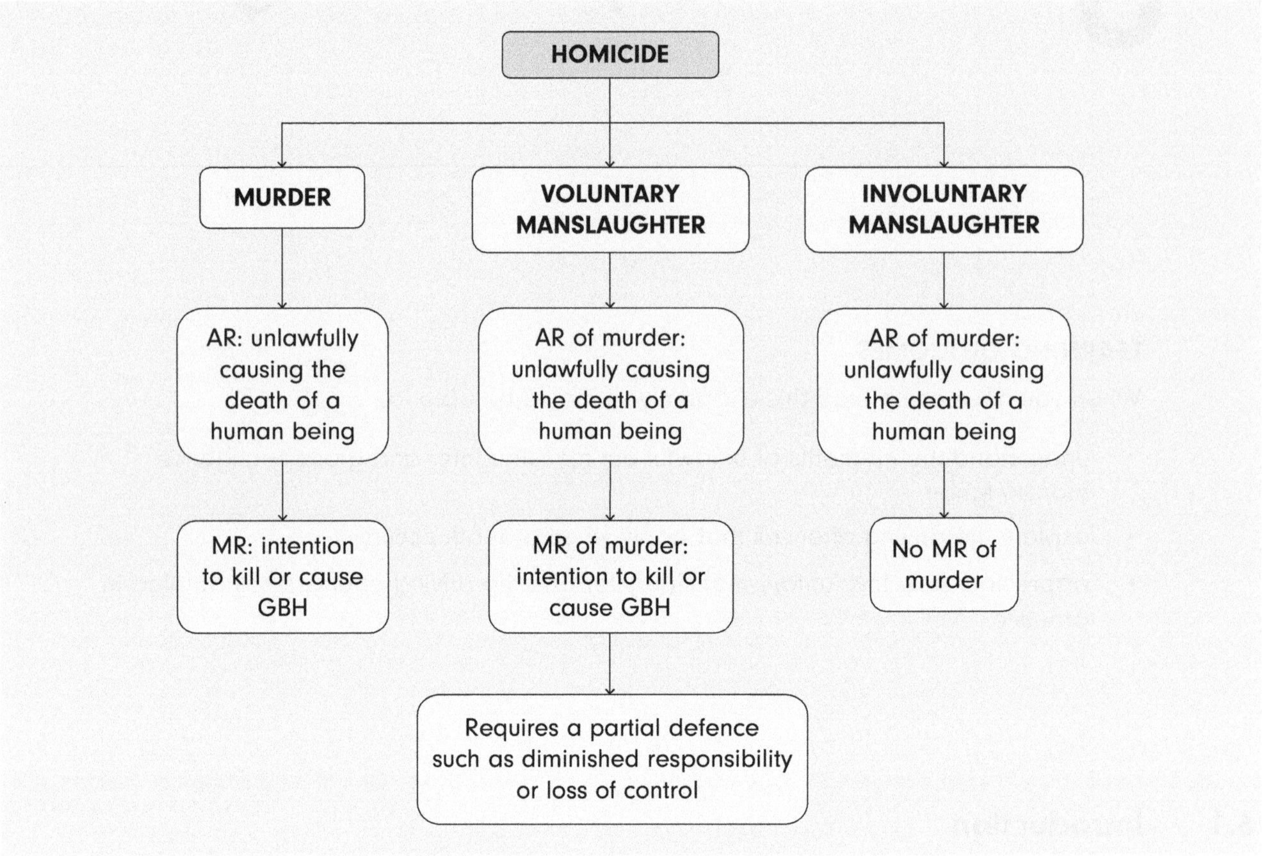

6.3 Unlawful act manslaughter

Unlawful act manslaughter is also referred to as unlawful and dangerous act manslaughter – a title that includes many of the elements required to establish the offence. There is also an alternate description of the offence as constructive manslaughter because liability for the death is 'constructed' from the fact that the defendant has committed a lesser crime. However, it is important to remember that these are just different names for the same offence.

For unlawful act manslaughter the defendant must:

(a) do an unlawful act;

(b) that is dangerous; and

(c) which causes the victim's death.

The first two elements will be considered below; whilst the third is purely the issue of causation that was covered earlier in this textbook. If the defendant did not cause the death, in the legal sense, they are not liable for murder or manslaughter, although they may be liable for another criminal offence, for example an assault.

6.3.1 The unlawful act

The first element the prosecution must prove is that the defendant has committed an unlawful act, namely a crime with a mens rea of intention or recklessness. Crimes of negligence, such as careless driving, will not suffice for unlawful act manslaughter. Note that, when dealing with a case where the unlawful act is an assault, there is no need to worry about which type – the prosecution will choose the easiest level of assault to prove and this will usually be a physical assault.

Example

Solly is angry at his teenage son for staying out late. They begin arguing and Solly pushes Benjy in the chest, causing him to fall backwards and strike his head on the concrete floor. Benjy dies as a result of a bleed to the brain.

The unlawful act here is physical assault (the application of unlawful personal force). As this is an offence that may be committed either intentionally or recklessly, it counts as an unlawful act for the purposes of involuntary manslaughter.

Although the unlawful act is often an assault, any offence requiring proof of intention or recklessness will do. In the case of *DPP v Newbury and Jones* [1977] AC 500, the defendants pushed a paving stone over a bridge into the path of a train. It smashed through a window of the train, killing the guard. The defendants were convicted of manslaughter, presumably on the basis of their criminal damage, and appealed. The Court of Appeal confirmed that the issue was whether there was an unlawful act; thus, the defendant need not intend or foresee the risk of harming anyone. As a consequence, the unlawful act could be criminal damage, burglary or theft, for example.

Example

Dawood breaks into his neighbour's property in the middle of the night. The house is owned by Harold, a frail 85-year-old man with chronic asthma. Harold hears a noise and comes out of his bedroom where he is confronted by Dawood. Harold is terrified and suffers a severe asthma attack from which he dies. The unlawful act here is the burglary and, as it causes Harold's death, Dawood is likely to be convicted of unlawful act manslaughter.

The defendant must have committed a positive act for this element of the offence to be established, so it follows that a failure to act cannot give rise to a charge of unlawful act manslaughter. In the case of *R v Lowe* [1973] QB 702, the defendant was convicted of unlawful act manslaughter of a child based on the evidence that the defendant had neglected the child causing death. However, the Court of Appeal quashed the conviction as no unlawful *act* had been committed.

The only requirement is that the unlawful act is a criminal offence in law and there will be the (rare) occasions where this element is not satisfied. In *R v Lamb* [1967] 2 QB 981, the defendant and the victim were fooling about with a revolver. As a practical joke, and unaware the bullets rotated in the chamber, the defendant pointed the gun at his friend. He pulled the trigger and shot the victim dead. Lamb was found not guilty of manslaughter on appeal because there was no unlawful act of assault. The reason was that by simply pulling the trigger of a revolver, the defendant did not commit an unlawful act as he believed they were just playing a game, and this in itself was not a criminal offence.

6.3.2 Dangerous act

In addition to being unlawful, the act must also be dangerous. In the case of *R v Ball* [1989] Crim LR 730, the defendant loaded a shotgun with two cartridges taken from his pocket which contained both live and blank cartridges. He fired the gun at his neighbour, without checking the cartridge, and killed him. The defendant claimed that he only intended to frighten the victim as he thought he was firing a blank cartridge. However, he was found guilty of unlawful act manslaughter on the basis of simple assault.

The question of whether the unlawful act was dangerous falls to the jury to decide, but what would they need to know to determine this? This question has been answered by case law as set out below.

6.3.2.1 Test for dangerousness

The test for dangerousness is entirely objective. In *R v Church* [1966] 1 QB 59, the Court of Appeal held that the unlawful act must be one which 'all sober and reasonable people would inevitably recognise must subject the other person to, at least the risk of some harm ... albeit not serious harm'. Whether this particular defendant did or did not is irrelevant. In simple terms, the act must be dangerous from the point of view of the (ordinary) reasonable person, and this is decided by the jury based upon the evidence put before them. Furthermore, the risk of harm must be to a person and not to property.

6.3.2.2 Knowledge required

In determining whether the reasonable person would have recognised a risk of some harm, they are deemed to have the knowledge the defendant had, or should have had, at the time of the offence.

In *R v Dawson* (1985) 81 Cr App R 150, three defendants attempted to rob a petrol station wearing masks and armed with a pickaxe handle and replica guns. The petrol attendant was aged 60 and suffered from heart disease. After the defendants fled, he suffered a heart attack and died. On appeal, the defendants' conviction for manslaughter was quashed because, although the jury were aware of the attendant's heart condition, a sober and reasonable person who was present at the scene of the robbery would not have been.

Whether an act is categorised as objectively dangerous will depend upon the particular facts, and the knowledge held by the reasonable person may be apparent in advance or gleaned during the crime. In *R v Bristow* [2013] EWCA Crim 1540, the defendants carried out a burglary at a vehicle repair business that was situated in a remote rural location. As they were driving their van away from the scene, they ran over and killed the victim. Significantly, access to the premises was by a single lane track, and as a consequence the unlawful act of burglary was held to be objectively dangerous. This was because a reasonable and sober person would recognise that if anyone tried to intervene, there would be a risk of harm to them. Also important was the finding that the act did not become dangerous simply at the point the burglars were disturbed, but from the very outset of the burglary.

In conclusion, 'dangerous' may summarised as follows:

(a) 'Dangerous' means the act carries the risk of some harm to some person, but not necessarily serious harm.

(b) The defendant need not foresee the precise form or sort of harm that ensues.

(c) The test is objective, namely, whether all sober and reasonable people would think the act was dangerous; not whether the defendant themselves did.

(d) The reasonable person is deemed to have the knowledge that the defendant had, or should have had, at the time of the offence, had they been present at the scene of the crime and watched the whole act being performed.

6.3.3 Causes death

The final element of the actus reus of unlawful act manslaughter is that the unlawful act causes the victim's death. The usual rules of causation apply so it must be proved that the defendant was both the factual and legal cause of the victim's death. These principles are analysed in detail in **Chapter 2**. If the prosecution is unable to do so, the accused will not be liable for either murder or manslaughter, although they may be guilty of another criminal offence, for example an assault. This requirement has caused some difficulties in the drugs offences, where the defendant supplies the victim with illegal drugs from which they die. If the victim freely and voluntarily injects themselves, the chain of causation will be broken and the defendant will not be guilty of unlawful act manslaughter.

6.3.4 Mens rea

The mens rea of this type of manslaughter will change depending upon the circumstances, as it will be linked to the unlawful act. Although it will usually be the mens rea of an assault, it need not be.

Example

Hughie has become aware that his neighbour, Keni, is a convicted paedophile. When Keni goes on holiday, Hughie decides to set fire to Keni's empty house to drive him out of the area. Unfortunately, and unknown to Hughie, Keni has returned home early and he dies in the fire.

Although Hughie thought the house was empty, he remains criminally responsible for Keni's death. The unlawful act for manslaughter is arson. Arson is objectively dangerous as all sober and reasonable people would regard it as such, particularly when it relates to a domestic property. The unlawful act caused Keni's death.

There is no single definition of mens rea for unlawful act manslaughter - it simply needs to match the unlawful act. Thus, Hughie must have the mens rea for arson, which he does as he intentionally sets fire to the property. In legal terms he has the direct intent to destroy the house that belongs to another (Keni).

6.3.5 Summary of unlawful act manslaughter

Having studied the components required for unlawful act manslaughter, it is apparent why it is so named. **Figure 6.2** summarises the main issues that arise when analysing whether the defendant is guilty of this offence.

Figure 6.2 Unlawful act manslaughter

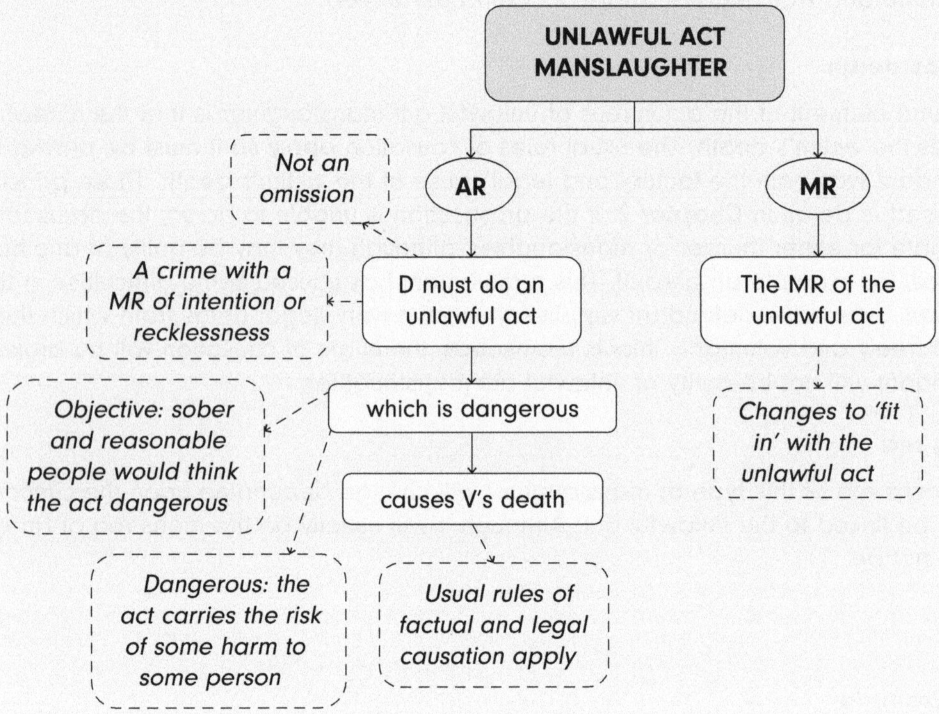

6.4 Gross negligence manslaughter

A person can be charged with murder or unlawful act manslaughter only in circumstances where they had a criminal state of mind: intention to cause death or grievous bodily harm is needed for murder; and at least recklessness is needed for unlawful act manslaughter. Furthermore, an act is required for this type of manslaughter – an omission to act will not suffice. These requirements can cause difficulties in holding someone responsible for causing the death of an individual in certain situations.

Example

Scenario 1

Dr Ho is on duty at the local hospital. She is suffering from a hangover and lack of sleep after an all-night party. She administers a fatal dose of morphine to a seriously ill patient who dies two hours later as a result of the overdose. Dr Ho claims she misread the instructions as to the correct dosage to be administered. She is devastated by the patient's death.

Scenario 2

Dr Walters is also on duty at the local hospital. He is a junior doctor who has been working without sleep for the last 36 hours. He fails to arrange for X-rays to be taken of a newly admitted patient who is complaining of severe pains and breathing difficulties. The patient dies of blood poisoning caused by a perforated ulcer. An X-ray would have identified the problem and immediate treatment could have saved the patient's life. Dr Walters says that he was so tired he did not think to obtain X-rays and there was no one he could call on for help.

COMMENT

In both situations, it can be said that the doctor has caused the patient's death. Dr Ho has caused death by the positive act of administering the fatal dose of morphine, and Dr Walters has caused death by his failure to give prompt treatment to the patient in a situation where he was under a duty to act.

However, in neither case could it be argued that the doctor intended to kill or to cause grievous bodily harm to their patient, and therefore a charge of murder would fail due to lack of mens rea.

It would also be impossible to convict either doctor of unlawful act manslaughter because neither of them has committed a criminally unlawful act. Dr Ho was acting with the consent of the patient in administering the dose of morphine (and therefore cannot be said to have committed an assault); Dr Walters has failed to act and a positive act, rather than an omission, is required for this type of manslaughter. Although they have both behaved negligently as they have fallen below the standard of the competent doctor, there is no general criminal liability for negligence.

However, there is an offence which 'mops up' defendants who would not usually expect to be caught by the criminal justice system, including professionals doing their job such as medical practitioners. In the above scenarios, both doctors could be prosecuted for manslaughter by gross negligence.

To convict a defendant of this offence, the court must be satisfied that:

(a) the defendant owed the victim a duty of care;

(b) the defendant breached that duty;

(c) the breach caused the death of the victim; and

(d) the defendant's conduct was grossly negligent.

This definition looks very similar to the civil wrong of tort, but there is a key difference – the breach must be gross.

6.4.1 Duty of care

That a duty of care is owed by the defendant to the victim is a prerequisite of this offence. In most cases, determining whether there is a duty to act is quite straightforward; for example, it is well established that a duty of care exists between, for example, a parent and child; employers and employees; and drivers and other road users. In these circumstances, the judge will direct the jury that a duty of care does exist.

However, new situations may arise requiring a consideration of both law and fact. In *R v Willoughby* [2004] EWCA Crim 3365, the Court of Appeal stated that whether a duty of care exists is usually a matter for the jury once the judge has decided that there is evidence capable of establishing a duty.

Example

Olivia supplied her friend, Lydia, with heroin. Lydia overdosed but, instead of seeking medical assistance, Olivia just kept her under observation overnight as she was afraid of getting into trouble. Lydia died. As this situation was not covered by the established duties, the court was required to determine the issue. After some consideration, Olivia was held to owe a duty of care on the basis that she had created or contributed to a state of affairs that was life-threatening and ought to have taken reasonable steps to save Lydia's life.

6.4.2 Breach of duty

The prosecution must also prove that the defendant breached their duty of care towards the victim, whether by a positive act, an omission, or negligent behaviour. In the case of *R v Khan* [1998] Crim LR 830, the Court of Appeal confirmed that the general principles with regard to duties to act apply to cases of manslaughter by gross negligence. Thus, a person could be liable for this offence for failing to act but only where there was a duty to do so.

This principle was applied in the case of *R v Evans* [2009] 1 WLR 1999, in which the defendant supplied heroin to the victim, her half-sister. Unfortunately, the victim overdosed. The defendant realised this, as it was a condition with which she was familiar, but despite her knowledge she chose not to seek medical assistance and the victim died. The Court of Appeal upheld the defendant's conviction for gross negligence manslaughter on the basis of her omission to act.

Whether an individual may be successfully prosecuted for gross negligence manslaughter due to their failure to act is considered below.

Examples

(1) Gwenda leaves her 18-month-old son, Hayden, unattended in the bath for 30 minutes while she talks with a friend on the telephone. Hayden drowns.

(2) Hassan is an electrician who fails to notice that he has wrongly connected a central heating programmer when the householder, Kavita, complains that she is suffering electric shocks from the radiators. Kavita is killed by electrocution when she touches the radiator in the bathroom after stepping out of the bath.

(3) Bharti is a junior surgeon who fails to notice that a piece of gauze has not been removed from the patient's stomach before the end of an operation. The patient later develops complications as a result of the gauze being left in place and dies.

In these scenarios, all three people could face liability for manslaughter by gross negligence as they have failed to act when there was a duty on them to do so.

Gwenda has a duty of care towards Hayden since she has a special relationship with him as his mother. Hassan had a contractual duty towards Kavita (his customer) to carry out his investigation with reasonable skill and care, and he has breached this duty by failing to identify his mistake. Bharti had a duty of care towards her patient, not least under her contract of employment.

(4) Padraig sees a child struggling in a pool. The child is clearly in distress but Padraig, who has never seen the child before, does nothing to help the child who drowns.

Padraig would not be liable for manslaughter by gross negligence as he is not under a duty to act to help the child.

The ordinary principles of negligence will apply to ascertain whether a breach has occurred. A defendant will breach their duty of care to the victim where their conduct falls below that expected of a reasonable person. There is no need to establish that the defendant was aware their conduct may fall below this standard - just that it did. Furthermore, where the defendant has special knowledge or expertise, such as a doctor, they will be expected to meet the standard of care expected of a reasonable person with that knowledge or expertise.

6.4.3 Causes death

It must be shown that the defendant's breach of duty caused the death of the victim, and the usual rules of causation will apply here. These are set out in detail in **Chapter 2**. In practice, this aspect will not usually cause any significant difficulties to the jury. Indeed, it is the final part of the test that makes the difference between a negligent act and a criminal one.

6.4.4 Gross negligence

The breach of duty must be grossly negligent. This means that the conduct of the defendant must be sufficiently bad as to justify the law imposing a criminal penalty and not just one under the civil law.

The issue of when a person could be prosecuted, other than for murder or unlawful act manslaughter, for causing the death of a person has been the subject of much consideration by the courts over the last 100 years. In 1925, the Court of Appeal, in *R v Bateman* (1925) 19 Cr App R 8, concluded that a defendant could be criminally liable for causing death if they had been grossly negligent. In this case, a patient died following negligent medical treatment and the doctor was charged with causing the death. In the Court of Appeal, Lord Hewart CJ said that:

> In order to establish criminal liability the facts must be such that, in the opinion of the jury, the negligence of the accused went beyond a mere matter of compensation between subjects and showed such disregard for the life and safety of others as to amount to a crime against the state and conduct deserving punishment.

The approach taken in *Bateman* was approved by the House of Lords in *Andrews v DPP* [1937] AC 576. This case involved a death caused by dangerous driving, and in the House of Lords, Lord Atkin said that:

> Simple lack of care such as will constitute civil liability is not enough. For the purposes of the criminal law there are degrees of negligence: and a very high degree of negligence is required to be proved before the felony is established.

A number of years passed before the principle was considered again in detail.

The leading case on gross negligence manslaughter is *R v Adomako* [1995] 1 AC 171 and set out below are the facts and extracts from the judgment.

Facts

The defendant, an anaesthetist, was acting as such during an eye operation which involved paralysing the patient, when a tube became disconnected from a ventilator. The patient suffered a cardiac arrest and subsequently died. The defendant was convicted of the manslaughter of the patient by breach of duty.

Extracts from the judgment of Lord Mackay of Clashfern

In my opinion the law as stated in these two authorities [*R v Bateman and Andrews v DPP*] is satisfactory as providing a proper basis for describing the crime of involuntary

> manslaughter. Since the decision in *Andrews* was a decision of your Lordships' House, it remains the most authoritative statement of the present law which I have been able to find ... On this basis in my opinion the ordinary principles of the law of negligence apply to ascertain whether or not the defendant has been in breach of a duty of care towards the victim who has died. If such breach of duty is established the next question is whether that breach of duty caused the death of the victim. If so, the jury must go on to consider whether that breach of duty should be characterised as gross negligence and therefore as a crime. This will depend on the seriousness of the breach of duty committed by the defendant in all the circumstances in which the defendant was placed when it occurred. The jury will have to consider whether the extent to which the defendant's conduct departed from the proper standard of care incumbent upon him, involving as it must have done a risk of death to the patient, was such that it should be judged criminal.
>
> It is true that to a certain extent this involves an element of circularity, but in this branch of the law I do not believe that is fatal to its being correct as a test of how far conduct must depart from accepted standards to be characterised as criminal. This is necessarily a question of degree and an attempt to specify that degree more closely is I think likely to achieve only a spurious precision. The essence of the matter which is supremely a jury question is whether having regard to the risk of death involved, the conduct of the defendant was so bad in all the circumstances as to amount in their judgment to a criminal act or omission.

In the later case of *R v Sellu* [2016] EWCA Crim 1716, the Court of Appeal provided further guidance by confirming that the test for gross negligence manslaughter is whether an individual's conduct was 'truly exceptionally bad and was such a departure from [the standard of a reasonably competent doctor] that it consequently amounted to being criminal'. This demonstrates the high bar that the prosecution must reach to succeed in a conviction for gross negligence manslaughter.

The Court of Appeal's judgment in the case of *Adomako* clarified that one aspect in deciding whether the defendant's conduct was so bad as to be worthy of criminal sanction is the risk of death involved.

In *R v Singh* [1999] Crim LR 582, the trial judge directed the jury that, in order to establish a charge of manslaughter by gross negligence, 'the circumstances must be such that a reasonably prudent person would have foreseen a serious and obvious risk not merely of injury or even of serious injury but of death'. This statement was not criticised on the defendant's appeal against conviction by the Court of Appeal. In *R v Rose* [2018] QB 328, the Court of Appeal allowed the appeal of an optometrist against her conviction for the manslaughter of a 7-year-old boy who died because of the defendant's failure to properly examine the back of his eyes when conducting an eye examination. The judges confirmed that 'in assessing reasonable foreseeability of serious and obvious risk of death in cases of gross negligence manslaughter, it is not appropriate to take into account what the defendant would have known but for his or her breach of duty'.

Examples

A risk of death was found in the case of a defendant who smuggled illegal immigrants into the country in the back of his lorry. He sealed the air vent to reduce the chance of discovery and the immigrants died of suffocation.

In contrast, the test was not satisfied where a doctor failed to attend a 12-year-old boy who subsequently died from a very rare disease. The mere possibility that an assessment may reveal something life-threatening is not the same as an obvious risk of death.

6.4.5 Assessing liability for manslaughter by gross negligence

To convict, a jury must conclude that the defendant fell so far below the standards of the reasonable person in that situation that they can be labelled grossly negligent and deserving of criminal punishment. Furthermore, the case of *Adomako* makes it clear that the defendant is punished for gross negligence, and it need not be proved they had any 'criminal' state of mind such as intention or recklessness. The decision is also of importance as it confirms that liability for a charge of homicide can be incurred through the defendant's omission to act if there is a duty to act, as well as through positive steps taken by the defendant.

Having analysed the requirements for gross negligence manslaughter, the examples that follow demonstrate how the law is applied in practice.

Examples

Returning to the two scenarios considered earlier in this chapter in relation to Dr Ho and Dr Walters, it is clear that they owe a duty of care to their patients. It is equally apparent that both doctors in the scenarios breached that duty and in doing so caused the deaths of their patients. There was a risk of death from their conduct, and therefore the factor that will determine whether or not they are convicted of manslaughter by gross negligence is the final issue, namely, whether the jury consider that the breach of duty amounts to gross negligence. Is the doctor's conduct so bad in all the circumstances that it amounts to a criminal act or omission? Jurors may have differing views on this question, particularly in the case of Dr Walters, and this is one of the main criticisms of the test for manslaughter by gross negligence.

6.4.6 Summary of gross negligence manslaughter

This homicide offence can be established if all the elements in **Figure 6.3** are present.

Figure 6.3 Gross negligence manslaughter

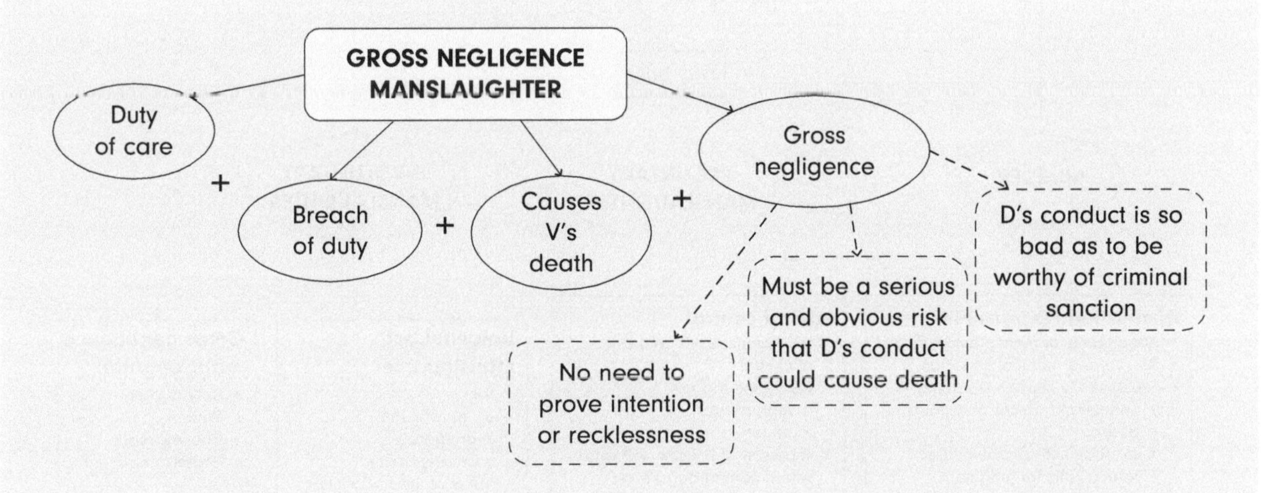

To establish gross negligence manslaughter, the prosecution must prove:

(a) A duty of care was owed by the defendant to the victim; in most instances, there will be a clear and established duty of care.

(b) The duty was breached; this will be determined based upon the particular facts of the case. Liability may be incurred through the defendant's omission to act (if they have a duty to do so) as well as by a positive act.

(c) There was a risk that the defendant's conduct could cause death.

(d) The breach of duty did cause the victim's death and the usual rules of factual and legal causation apply here.

(e) The defendant fell so far below the standards of the reasonable person that they can be labelled grossly negligent and deserving of criminal punishment. It is clear that ordinary negligence will not suffice: just because a victim's family might be able to sue for compensation for a victim's death in the civil courts, it does not automatically follow that criminal charges could be brought. Furthermore, there is no need for the prosecution to establish intention or recklessness - the defendant is punished for their negligence.

6.5 Summary of homicide

Having considered the involuntary manslaughters of unlawful act and gross negligence manslaughter, these have now been added to the flowchart (below) to provide a complete picture of homicide.

Figure 6.4 Summary of homicide

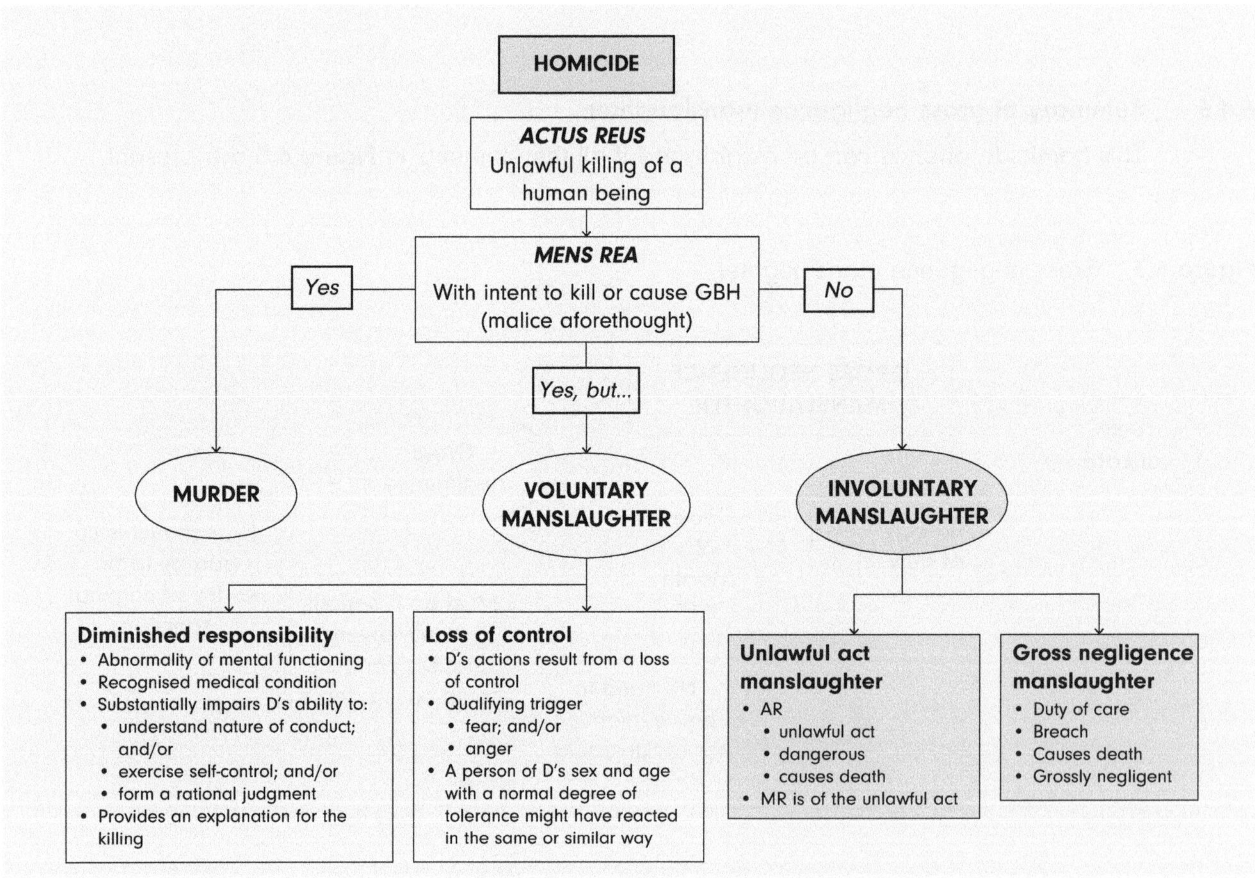

6.6 Driving offences

There are two other homicide offences covered in this chapter, namely, causing death by dangerous driving and causing death by careless driving.

6.6.1 Causing death by dangerous driving

Earlier in this textbook, we studied the offence of dangerous driving. However, if someone is killed by such driving, the accused will face a more serious charge, that of causing death by dangerous driving. The definition of the offence is found in s 1 of the Road Traffic Act 1988:

> A person who causes the death of another person by driving a mechanically propelled vehicle dangerously on a road or other public place is guilty of an offence.

The prosecution will require proof of the dangerous driving and must also establish causation – that the death was caused as a result of the dangerous driving. Examples could include a defendant who races through a red light at 80 mph, knocking down and killing a pedestrian who is crossing the road; or one who, knowing their brakes are faulty, drives at speed into an oncoming vehicle, unable to stop, and kills the other driver.

6.6.2 Comparing gross negligence manslaughter and s 1 of the Road Traffic Act 1988

Causing death by dangerous driving cannot lead to a charge of unlawful act manslaughter because there is no criminally unlawful act. The unlawful act must be a crime requiring proof of intention or recklessness on the part of the defendant, and the offence of dangerous driving does not require proof of such mens rea as it is a crime of negligence. However, there is clearly some overlap between these offences. Indeed, the prosecution may have a choice as to which to charge as both require evidence that the defendant has been grossly negligent and that they have fallen far below the standards expected of them. Nevertheless, there are also some differences.

(a) Obviously, an offence under s 1 of the Road Traffic Act 1988 can be committed only if the defendant was driving a mechanically propelled vehicle at the time, whereas the offence of manslaughter by gross negligence has a much wider application.

(b) Rightly or wrongly, an offence under s 1 of the Road Traffic Act 1988 is often regarded as less serious than a charge of gross negligence manslaughter. This is reflected in the sentencing options available: the maximum sentence following a conviction under s 1 is 14 years' imprisonment, whereas a conviction for gross negligence manslaughter can lead to a sentence of life imprisonment.

(c) There are differences in the matters to be proved against the defendant. On a s 1 offence, there is no need to establish a risk of death as there is under the *Adomako* test for manslaughter by gross negligence. Because s 2A(3) of the Road Traffic Act 1988 defines 'dangerous' in terms of danger of injury or serious damage to property, there is no requirement for the reasonable person to fear that someone might be killed (or even seriously injured) by the defendant's actions before the driving can be said to be dangerous. In this respect, therefore, it may be easier to secure a conviction under s 1 than in respect of a charge of manslaughter by gross negligence.

6.6.3 Causing death by careless or inconsiderate driving

Previously, if a driver caused the death of a victim by driving carelessly, as opposed to dangerously, the only conviction that driver would face would be one of careless driving. This sometimes led to press reports where the family of the victim were, understandably, outraged by the 'leniency' of the sentence imposed on such a driver.

These criticisms of the law led the Government to introduce the offence of causing death by careless, or inconsiderate, driving, under s 20 of the Road Safety Act 2006. This introduced a new s 2B into the Road Traffic Act 1988, which states:

> A person who causes the death of another person by driving a mechanically propelled vehicle on a road or other public place without due care and attention, or without reasonable consideration for other persons using the road or place, is guilty of an offence.

This is an either-way offence which carries a maximum term of imprisonment of five years. The driver must have caused the death of a person by driving carelessly.

Example

Precious drives along a motorway late one dark and foggy night, at 90 miles an hour, accompanied by her 2-year-old son, Jonathan. She runs into the back of a lorry, which is being driven slowly in the fast lane by River. He had forgotten to turn into the slow lane after overtaking another lorry a few moments earlier. Jonathan is killed in the crash.

Precious' driving would almost certainly be regarded as falling far below the standards of a competent and careful driver and the danger would surely have been obvious to a competent driver (Road Traffic Act 1988, s 2). Thus, Precious must be guilty of dangerous driving. As to whether this was a substantial cause of Jonathan's death, she is unlikely to succeed in arguing that the accident would still have occurred and Jonathan would still have died, even if she had been driving competently. Accordingly, she is guilty of causing death by dangerous driving under s 1 of the Road Traffic Act 1988, and also death by careless driving under s 2B of that Act.

River's driving is unlikely to be far enough below the standard of the competent driver to be dangerous, so he will not be guilty of causing death by dangerous driving. However, it is possible that River has committed careless driving by going slowly in the fast lane, as arguably this falls below the standard expected of a competent and careful driver. Provided this is held to be a cause of Jonathan's death, River will be liable for causing death by careless driving.

6.7 Proposals for reform

On 29 November 2006, the Law Commission published Report No 304 entitled 'Murder, Manslaughter and Infanticide', which suggested reforming the whole area of homicide law and recommended that there should be a new Homicide Act for England and Wales. Proposals included a three-tier structure of homicide offences, the most serious being 'first degree murder', which would deal with situations where the defendant intentionally killed or intended to cause serious injury while being aware of a serious risk of causing death. There would then be a 'middle' offence of 'second degree murder', which would cover:

(a) killings where the defendant intended to cause serious injury;

(b) killings where the defendant intended to cause injury, or the risk or fear of injury, while being aware their conduct had a serious risk of causing death; and

(c) killings where the defendant successfully pleaded provocation (loss of control), diminished responsibility or suicide pact.

Next would be a third offence of manslaughter, which would broadly cover the existing offences of unlawful act and gross negligence manslaughter, with some changes.

The Law Commission also proposed that the Government should undertake a public consultation on whether the law should recognise a separate offence or partial defence of 'mercy killing'. The outcome was that the Government adopted the new definitions of the partial defences of diminished responsibility and loss of control (see **Chapter 5**) but rejected the remainder of the Law Commission's recommendations.

6.8 Summary

The homicide offences are among the most serious crimes a defendant can commit. Accordingly, a good understanding of the details of these offences, and how they relate to each other, is essential for any criminal lawyer.

(a) To be liable for murder, the accused must cause the death of the victim with the intention to kill or cause grievous bodily harm.

(b) If the prosecution cannot establish the mens rea for murder, the defendant may be liable for involuntary manslaughter. There are two types, namely, unlawful act manslaughter and gross negligence manslaughter. However, there are some key differences and these are summaried in **Table 6.1**.

Table 6.1 Comparison of unlawful act and gross negligence manslaughter

Similarities	Differences
In both gross negligence and unlawful act manslaughter: • D unlawfully causes the death of V • D does not intend to kill V or to cause serious bodily harm	Unlawful act manslaughter: • only applies where D has a criminal state of mind (intention or recklessness) • cannot be committed negligently • requires an act Gross negligence manslaughter: • only requires negligence • may be committed by an act or by omission

Having completed your study of involuntary manslaughter, test your understanding by completing the activity below.

ACTIVITY

Caspian and Lola are standing beside a waterfall at a well-known beauty spot. Lola wants a selfie for her Instagram account and asks Caspian to photograph her with her phone. Lola keeps posing and, eventually, Caspian begins to lose patience. He lunges at Lola, intending to frighten her into believing that he is about to push her over, but, unfortunately, Lola steps back in response, trips on a tree root and falls over the ledge dying instantly. Analyse Caspian's liability for murder and involuntary manslaughter.

COMMENT

Caspian is not guilty of murder as he does not have the requisite mens rea of an intention to kill Lola or cause her grievous bodily harm, as he only intended to frighten her. If Caspian is charged with unlawful act manslaughter, the prosecution must prove an unlawful act. Caspian does not have the mens rea for an assault under either s 18 of the OAPA 1861 (intention to cause grievous bodily harm) or s 20 (intention or recklessness as to causing some harm). However, all that is required is for the prosecution to establish any unlawful act even if this does not seem to match the seriousness of the event. Caspian caused Lola to apprehend the application of unlawful force and did so intentionally, as his stated aim was to frighten her. Thus, he satisfies both the actus reus and the mens rea of the offence of simple assault.

The unlawful act must be objectively dangerous. Given that Lola was standing at the edge of a waterfall, Caspian's act would be regarded by all sober and reasonable people as carrying the risk of some harm to some person, in this case Lola. The unlawful and dangerous act caused Lola's death as she fell over the ledge and died from her injuries.

In this instance, Caspian would be criminally liable for unlawful act manslaughter.

7 Corporate Liability for Manslaughter

LEARNING OUTCOMES

When you have completed this chapter, you should be able to:

- appreciate the historical background to the Corporate Manslaughter and Corporate Homicide Act 2007, and its practical and economic context;
- demonstrate a sound knowledge and understanding of the key concepts relating to corporate manslaughter;
- recognise a company defendant's potential criminal liability for corporate liability and the liability of an individual within that company for a homicide offence.

7.1 Introduction

Thus far we have considered the liability of individuals for criminal offences, but each year there are significant numbers of employee fatalities which occur in the workplace. Establishing liability for these deaths is complex as, whilst the person who directly causes the death of the victim is clearly at fault, there may be underlying organisational reasons that contribute. Indeed, poor decisions by companies, or carelessness in ensuring adequate safety systems, can result in deaths or huge losses to the victims who suffer as a consequence.

This issue came to the public's notice primarily due to the failure to convict companies following major disasters, such as the sinking of the *Herald of Free Enterprise* ferry in 1987. In this case 193 passengers and crew were drowned when a cross-Channel ferry capsized in Zeebrugge harbour. In the subsequent investigation, it became apparent that the ferry had sailed with the bow door open. Furthermore, the ferry company had not installed any warning devices on the bridge of the vessel which would have informed the captain of this and had operated inadequate safety systems. Despite this, the prosecution of the owners of the ferry failed on charges of manslaughter by gross negligence. In the Ladbroke Grove train crash in 1999, 31 people died when two trains collided after the driver failed to stop at a red light. The causes were identified as insufficient driver training, a lack of automatic protection systems and a partially obscured railway signal that was a known risk. Despite the multiple deaths, the only charge that was successfully pursued was under the health and safety at work laws.

These cases highlighted that the criminal law had developed in such a way as to make convicting organisations of corporate manslaughter under the common law notoriously difficult.

7.2 Problems with corporate liability for crime

Under the law in England and Wales, a company is treated as a separate person from those who run it and so, because a company has its own legal identity, it can be prosecuted for committing crimes.

The company is generally owned by shareholders who act as financial backers because they buy shares in it. The company is, however, usually run by a group of senior executives known as directors who manage the organisation. They take the business decisions and make up a Board of Directors, with a Managing Director who is responsible for the day-to-day operation of the company. Public companies must have a Company Secretary who is responsible for the administrative side. They are usually a director and will often be a professional person such as a solicitor or an accountant. Different rules apply to private companies and, often, the directors and shareholders are the same people. In larger companies, whilst the directors may own shares, there will be many other shareholders too.

As a company is a separate legal entity, it has been acknowledged for many years that a company can be convicted of a crime. Indeed, the commencement of the prosecution of the ferry company (above) shows an acceptance that the company could, legally, be criminally liable on a manslaughter charge in addition to, or instead of, the individual employees with immediate responsibility for the vessel.

However, although the Court of Criminal Appeal confirmed, in the case of *R v ICR Haulage Ltd* [1944] KB 551, that a company could incur criminal liability, two limitations to the concept of corporate criminal liability were highlighted.

(a) Many offences, by their very nature, cannot be committed by a company. These include assault, burglary and rape, as such crimes need a physical act by the defendant and are therefore clearly inappropriate charges to bring against a company.

(b) A company cannot be convicted of any offence where the only sentence that can be imposed is 'physical', such as a term of imprisonment.

The other major stumbling block to securing a conviction against a company is the difficulty of proving that the company had the mens rea required for the crime. A company may be a separate legal entity, but it has no body or mind in the way that a human being does. How can a company as a separate legal entity be said to have intended something to happen (or indeed be described as reckless)?

To overcome this hurdle, in cases such as *Tesco Supermarket Ltd v Nattrass* [1972] AC 153, the courts developed a particular approach. The idea appeared simple: if the prosecution could prove that senior executives of the company (the 'directing mind and will of the company') had the necessary mens rea required for an offence, the company itself, as a separate legal entity, could be prosecuted and convicted of the crime. This became known as 'the identification principle'. Unfortunately, prosecutors found it difficult to determine who was the 'directing mind' of the company and whether they had the necessary mens rea.

In larger companies, issues arose as case law held that at least one senior executive, for example a director, effectively had to know everything that was going on that was relevant to the crime before the company could be said to be criminally liable. This meant that if a number of senior executives knew pieces of information but no one individual knew 'the full story', the identification principle would fail, and the company could not be convicted.

Problems with the identification principle led to the failure of the prosecution of P&O European Ferries (Dover) Ltd for manslaughter following the Zeebrugge disaster. This case and public demands for criminal prosecutions following several major train disasters, such as at Southall, Hatfield and Ladbroke Grove, eventually led to an announcement by the Government that it would urgently review the law relating to corporate liability for killing. Although senior executives could be individually prosecuted, it was felt that holding a company liable for corporate manslaughter would be more effective. In small companies, the imposition of a substantial fine could force them to cease trading. In larger companies, such a prosecution would ensure that senior management were more vigilant both in order to avoid incurring liability themselves and because of pressure for increased safety from shareholders, anxious not to lose their stake in the company or their dividends following a hefty fine and attendant adverse publicity.

The outcome of that review was the offence of corporate manslaughter, which does not rely on the identification principle for a successful conviction.

7.3 The Corporate Manslaughter and Corporate Homicide Act 2007

When the Government introduced the Corporate Manslaughter and Corporate Homicide Bill to Parliament, Justice Minister, Maria Eagle, stated:

> The Corporate Manslaughter Act is a ground-breaking piece of legislation. This is about ensuring justice for victims of corporate failures. For too long it has been virtually impossible to prosecute large companies for management failures leading to deaths.
>
> Today's Act changes this, for the first time, companies and organisations can be found guilty of corporate manslaughter on the basis of gross corporate failures in health and safety. The Corporate Manslaughter and Corporate Homicide Act will make it easier to prosecute companies who fail to protect people.
>
> We are sending out a very powerful deterrent message to those organisations which do not take their health and safety responsibilities seriously.

The main provisions of the Corporate Manslaughter and Corporate Homicide Act (CMCHA) 2007 are covered in this chapter. However, it should also be borne in mind that, unfortunately, accidents do happen and the company involved may not necessarily be at fault.

Example

The Concrete Manufacturing Company is involved in the construction industry and has 100 employees and several directors. There are various health and safety policies filed at the company's head office. Last year, there was a 'near miss' with a conveyor machine, and an employee narrowly avoided serious injury. Today, a new employee has been killed in an accident involving the same machine.

When determining corporate liability, establishing exactly how and why the employee died is crucial, but the focus should be on the role of the company itself in the incident. For example:

- *Were there any special precautions necessary for operating this machine safely and were these in place at the relevant time? Had the new employee been given the appropriate training for using this machine?*
- *Did the company have the necessary health and safety policies in place and were these actually put into operation? Were the employees aware of their responsibilities under these policies?*
- *Was anyone, for example one of the directors, responsible for health and safety issues; and did they monitor the operation of the policies 'on the ground' including reporting back to the Board of Directors?*

- *Was there an investigation following the 'near miss' with the same machine in the previous year and, if so, what lessons were learned from the findings?*

If the answer to some, or all, of these questions was 'No', the conclusion may be that the company's approach to safety was flawed and it should be responsible, in criminal law, for the death of the employee.

We shall now move on to analyse how the Act operates in practice, beginning with an overview of its key features.

7.4 The corporate manslaughter offence

The offence of corporate manslaughter (or 'corporate homicide' as it is called in Scotland) is set out in s 1 of the CMCHA 2007, and the penalty is an unlimited fine. This offence differs from the old law because it does not rely on the successful prosecution of an individual for manslaughter before a case against the company can succeed. Instead, the prosecution will focus on the collective conduct of the company's senior management, and it is the organisation itself that will be charged.

The main provisions of s 1 of the CMCHA 2007 are set out below:

1 The offence

(1) An organisation to which this section applies is guilty of an offence if the way in which its activities are managed or organised–

(a) causes a person's death; and

(b) amounts to a gross breach of a relevant duty of care owed by the organisation to the deceased.

(2) The organisations to which this section applies are–

(a) a corporation;

(b) a department or other body listed in Schedule 1;

(c) a police force;

(d) a partnership, or a trade union or employers' association, that is an employer.

(3) An organisation is guilty of an offence under this section only if the way in which its activities are managed or organised by its senior management is a substantial element in the breach referred to in subsection (1).

(4) For the purposes of this Act–

(a) 'relevant duty of care' has the meaning given by section 2, read with sections 3 to 7

(b) a breach of a duty of care by an organisation is a 'gross' breach if the conduct alleged to amount to a breach of that duty falls far below what can reasonably be expected of the organisation in the circumstances;

(c) 'senior management', in relation to an organisation, means the persons who play significant roles in–

(i) the making of decisions about how the whole or a substantial part of its activities are to be managed or organised, or

(ii) the actual managing or organising of the whole or a substantial part of those activities.

In summary, to establish the offence of corporate manslaughter, the prosecution must prove that:

(a) the defendant is a relevant 'organisation';

(b) the organisation owes a relevant duty of care to the deceased;

(c) the organisation breaches that duty;

(d) the breach causes death;

(e) the breach is a gross breach; and

(f) a substantial element of the breach is in the way the activities were managed or organised by senior management.

An important point to notice is that liability depends on how the organisation's activities have been managed or organised, so the test of breach is not linked to a particular rank of senior executive but requires the court to consider how an activity has been managed by the organisation overall. However, under s 1(3) there cannot be a conviction unless a substantial element of the breach of duty rests with the way in which senior management dealt with activities. This requirement will be studied in more detail later in the chapter.

The breach must have caused death, and the normal principles of causation will apply.

A final general point to note is how many different types of organisations are covered by the Act. It is not just companies in the United Kingdom that can be guilty of corporate manslaughter but, as is apparent from s 1(2), it also includes police forces, trade unions, employers' associations, and partnerships such as law firms. Importantly, as mentioned above, Crown immunity has been removed and certain government departments are identified as owing the same duties of care as corporations. These include the Home Office, the Department for Transport, and the Department for Defence (amongst others). However, some of the functions of these government departments are specifically excluded from the Act, for example, any strategic decision on the allocation of public resources or the formulation of public policy, such as a decision by a hospital on how to prioritise its resources. The same is also true of certain operational and military activities, including those dealing with terrorism, civil unrest or serious disorder. The rationale for this is that these are public and government functions, the management of which involves wider questions of public policy and which are already subject to other forms of accountability.

The different elements of the offence will now be considered in more detail.

7.4.1 The 'relevant duty of care'

Section 1(1) of the CMCHA 2007 refers to a breach of a 'relevant duty of care owed by the organisation to the deceased'. The term 'duty of care' is similar to that of gross negligence manslaughter, which is covered earlier in this textbook, whilst s 2 provides more guidance on the phrase in this context.

Section 2 states that a 'relevant duty of care' in relation to an organisation means a duty owed under the law of negligence:

(a) to its employees or to other persons working for the organisation or performing services for it;

(b) as occupier of premises;

(c) in connection with the supply by the organisation of goods or services (whether for consideration or not), the carrying on of any construction or maintenance operations, or of any other activity on a commercial basis, or the use or keeping of any plant, vehicle or other thing; and

(d) a duty owed to a person who is someone for whose safety the organisation is responsible.

The 2007 Act does not create new duties - they are already owed in the civil law of negligence and the corporate manslaughter offence is based on these. A duty of care exists, for example: in respect of the systems of work and equipment used by employees; in respect of the condition of worksites and other premises occupied by an organisation; and in relation to products or services supplied to customers.

What is also apparent, from the statute itself, is that the question of whether an organisation owes a duty of care to an individual is a question of law, to be decided by the judge and not by the jury.

7.4.2 A 'gross breach'

Central to the offence is that the organisation must have committed a 'gross breach' of the duty of care that it owed to the deceased. Under s 1(4), a breach of duty will be 'gross' if the conduct falls far below what can reasonably be expected of the organisation in the circumstances. To assist the jury in deciding this, s 8 sets out a number of factors to be taken into account.

The jury *must* consider whether the organisation failed to comply with any health and safety legislation that relates to the alleged breach; and, if so, how serious that failure was and how much of a risk of death it posed. The jury *may* also consider:

(a) the extent to which the evidence shows that there were attitudes, policies, systems or accepted practices within the organisation that were likely to have encouraged any such failure, or to have produced tolerance of it. An example of this might be where a company does not enforce its policy of its employees wearing high-visibility jackets.

(b) any health and safety guidance that relates to the alleged breach. This means any code, guidance, manual or similar publication that is concerned with health and safety matters and is made or issued (under a statutory provision or otherwise) by an authority responsible for the enforcement of any health and safety legislation.

Furthermore, the jury may have regard to any other matters they consider relevant. Having considered these factors, the court will decide whether the breach of duty is 'gross'.

What is interesting is that these sections dealing with a 'gross breach' incorporate the concept of 'corporate culture' into the legislation. It represents a move away from just considering documented policies and so on, to include what is actually happening 'on the ground'. Expert evidence is likely to be called upon to help the jury when considering how s 8 applies in any particular case.

7.4.3 Management failure by 'senior management'

Although corporate liability no longer depends on proving the liability of any one individual 'controlling mind', the CMCHA 2007 does state that an organisation is guilty of the offence only if the way in which its activities are managed or organised by its senior management is a substantial element in the gross breach of duty (see s 1(3)).

7.4.3.1 Who are 'senior management'?

Who would count as a senior manager is an issue that causes difficulties for the court. Under s 1(4)(c), 'senior management' is defined to include people who play significant roles in the making of decisions about how the whole or a substantial part of an organisation's activities are to be managed or organised; and the actual managing or organising of these activities.

This definition is intended to cover two strands of management responsibility – those of the decision-making process and the actual 'hands-on' management. The aim is for the management conduct to be considered collectively as well as individually, so that the failures of different managers can be aggregated together. A practical example will assist.

Examples

Set out below are a number of personnel, all of whom have some level of responsibility; but are they a 'senior manager' under the statutory definition in s 1(4)(c)?

(1) A director of X Co, a small family-run business.

(2) A director of Waitway (a large supermarket chain).

(3) A non-executive director of Waitway (someone who is a director with voting rights but has no management role in the company).

(4) A partner in a very large international law firm.

All these individuals play a role in the making of decisions about how the organisation is managed or organised even if they are one of many, and, in the case of the non-executive director, they are not involved in any actual 'hands-on' management. Perhaps the only potential issue for those who are directors or partners of very large organisations is whether their role could be described as 'significant'.

(5) The chief buyer for Waitway's clothing range.

(6) The manager of a local Waitway store.

(7) The manager of the bakery section of a local Waitway store.

(8) The manager of one of four restaurants in London, owned by Z partnership.

(9) A county sales manager for AB Sales Co. The company has a county sales manager for each county in England and Wales, responsible for eight sales representatives each. The county sales managers each report to either the Northern or Southern sales manager, who in turn report to the sales director.

All the people in Examples (5) to (9) are playing significant roles in actually managing or organising (and quite probably, making decisions about) a part of an organisation. The issue is whether it is a 'substantial part' of the organisation. The answer is likely to be 'No' in relation to the manager of the bakery section of a local Waitway store (Example (7)); and 'Yes' for the manager of one of four restaurants in London (Example (8)). However, with regard to the others, more information is required about the organisation they work for and how it is structured and run.

Organisations cannot avoid liability for the corporate manslaughter offence by delegating responsibility for health and safety to people who could not come within the definition of 'senior management'. Guidance on the offence from the website of the Ministry of Justice (www.justice.gov.uk) makes this clear:

> Failures by senior managers to manage health and safety adequately, including through inappropriate delegation of health and safety matters, will leave organisations vulnerable to corporate manslaughter/homicide charges.

7.4.3.2 What is management failure?

Imagine that a train driver went through a red light and caused a fatal accident: who is to blame for that accident? Very often, human error (in this case, on the part of the train driver) is the most immediate cause of such an incident. However, the CMCHA 2007 aims to look beyond human error by workers in the 'front line' and to ask whether the organisation itself was at fault, in the way that it was organised and managed so as to control and minimise risks. Management failure involves failing to put proper health and safety systems in place, or failing to monitor and enforce those systems effectively. For example, if the train driver (mentioned above) had not been trained in accordance with industry standards, that would be a clear management failure.

The Health and Safety Executive publication, *Reducing Error and Influencing Behaviour*, makes the same point:

> It is estimated that up to 80% of accidents may be attributed, at least in part, to the actions or omissions of people ... Many accidents are blamed on the actions or omissions of an individual who was directly involved in operational or maintenance work. This typical but short-sighted response ignores the fundamental failures which led to the accident. These are usually rooted deeper in the organisation's design, management and decision-making functions ... The immediate cause [of accidents, ill health and incidents] may be a human or technical failure, but they usually arise from organisational failings which are the responsibility of management.

Common failures of management include poor training of frontline employees, procedures not followed properly by employees, and poor management at an operational level of the business.

7.4.4 Health and safety legislation

The CMCHA 2007 refers to health and safety legislation specifically. For example, s 8 (see above) provides that when a jury is deciding if there has been a gross breach of the duty of care, they must consider whether the evidence shows that the organisation failed to comply with any health and safety legislation that relates to the alleged breach. The jury may also have regard to any health and safety guidance that may apply. Clearly, the health and safety legislation will play a vital role in corporate manslaughter cases, and many commentators have pointed out that if an organisation is complying with the Health and Safety at Work, etc Act 1974, it should be safe from a successful prosecution under the 2007 Act too. It is therefore obviously important to be aware of the main provisions of the 1974 Act.

- Section 2(1) requires an employer 'to ensure, so far as is reasonably practicable, the health, safety and welfare at work of all his employees'.
- Section 3 provides that employers and the self-employed should conduct their undertakings in such a way as to ensure that those who are not in their employment should not be exposed to risks to their health and safety.
- Regulation 3 of the Management of Health and Safety at Work Regulations 1999 (SI 1999/3242) requires employers to make 'suitable and sufficient assessment' of risks.

Although these requirements had existed for over 30 years, the CMCHA 2007 provides a good reason for organisations to check how they are managing risk. Failure to carry out adequate risk assessments, in particular, is likely to be a key factor used to justify prosecutions for corporate manslaughter.

7.4.5 The penalties for corporate manslaughter

At the beginning of this chapter, the inability to imprison a company or other organisation was discussed as one of the problems with corporate liability for homicide. How, then, can a company be punished effectively?

Example

BP Global is a huge company employing over 67,600 people in nearly 62 countries, with total assets in 2022 of over $288 billion. If such a company were to commit corporate manslaughter, a financial penalty is the obvious one to be imposed. However, it would have to be an extremely substantial fine if it were to have any significant impact on a large multi-national company like BP.

BP has previously faced very considerable financial penalties following the Deepwater Horizon disaster in April 2010 when an explosion on one of its rigs in the Gulf of Mexico killed 11 crew men and caused the largest oil spill ever in US waters. Recent figures suggest that BP has set aside a total sum of $56.4 billion to settle all Deepwater Horizon claims.

The maximum penalty for a conviction under the CMCHA 2007 is an unlimited fine. Under the most recent sentencing guidelines for corporate manslaughter, the seriousness of the offence is measured by considering the harm and culpability involved. The court assesses factors that affect the seriousness within this context by asking questions such as how foreseeable was serious injury, how far short of the appropriate standard did the offender fall, how common is this kind of breach in the organisation, and was there more than one death or a high risk of further deaths. The court then has to consider what type of organisation is the defendant. There are four categories ranging from micro organisations with a turnover of up to £2 million, to large organisations with a turnover of more than £50 million. The fines vary to reflect these differences – a minimum of £180,000 for a micro organisation up to a maximum of £20 million for a large one.

The court must then check whether the proposed fine based on turnover is proportionate to the overall means of the defendant. The fine imposed should meet the objectives of punishment, the reduction of offending through deterrents and removal of gain being derived from the commission of the offence. It must be sufficiently substantial to have a real economic impact that will bring home to management and shareholders the need to achieve a safe environment for workers and members of the public affected by their activities.

In finalising the sentence, the court should have regard to the following:

(a) The profitability of an organisation will be a relevant factor. If an organisation has a small profit margin relative to its turnover, downward adjustment may be needed; if the opposite applies, an upward adjustment is appropriate.

(b) Any quantifiable economic benefit derived from the offence, including through avoided costs or operating savings, should normally be added to the fine.

(c) Whether the fine will put the offender out of business will be relevant; however, in some cases this may be an acceptable consequence.

In addition to any financial penalty, there are two other key sentencing options available to the court on conviction:

(a) Under s 9, the organisation can be ordered to remedy the breach of duty. This might involve the organisation having to review its policies, procedures and so on, as well as taking steps to remove the danger that caused the death. Failure to comply with any such order will itself be a criminal offence punishable by a fine (s 9(5)).

(b) Under s 10, the court will also have the power to 'name and shame' by making a publicity order. Potentially, this goes far beyond any 'ordinary' press report of the criminal proceedings, as it has to be publicised by the organisation itself, giving details of the offence, the conviction, the fine, and any remedial order made. Any failure to comply will be a criminal offence punishable by a fine (s 10(4)). Combined with the disruptive nature of any investigation for corporate manslaughter, a publicity order may have the most significant effect on guilty companies due to the resulting public stigma and adverse consequences for future business, including on the organisation's reputation and shares. The Sentencing Council has recommended that ordinarily a publicity order should be imposed on every offender convicted of corporate manslaughter.

7.4.6 Prosecutions under the CMCHA 2007

Before instituting proceedings for corporate manslaughter against an organisation, the consent of the Director of Public Prosecution is required (s 17). Investigations will be carried out jointly by the police and the Health and Safety Executive. Typical ways in which an investigation may arise are if the police are called to the scene of a death and instigate a prosecution; if the papers are referred to the police after an 'unlawful killing' verdict at a coroner's inquest; or as a referral following an investigation by another regulatory authority, such as the Civil Aviation Authority following an aeroplane crash.

It is open to the prosecuting authorities to prosecute for both corporate manslaughter under the 2007 Act and existing health and safety offences - and they will usually choose to do so. Having said this, the number of prosecutions was always expected to be small as the guidance on the offence from the website of the Ministry of Justice made clear:

> The Government expects that cases of corporate manslaughter following a death at work will be rare as the new offence is intended to cover only the worst instances of failure across an organisation to manage health and safety properly.

Similarly, Justice Minister Maria Eagle MP, speaking at a Corporate Manslaughter Conference in October 2007, said:

> This law will ensure that there is proper accountability when very serious management failings lead to people being killed. This is not about over-regulation. Businesses should see this as an opportunity to make sure they have proper arrangements in place for managing health and safety.

For most organisations, a health and safety prosecution is more likely than one for corporate manslaughter, but one of the aims of the CMCHA 2007 is to provide an extra incentive for organisations to treat health and safety as a high priority.

The first conviction under the CMCHA 2007 came in February 2011. Cotswold Geotechnical Holdings Ltd was convicted under the new law for the death of one of its employees, a junior geotechnical engineer, who died when the sides of an excavation pit collapsed on him. The original list of charges also included a charge for breach of health and safety legislation against the company. The company was a 'one-man band' with an annual turnover of £154,000. Although the fine of £385,000 was payable by 10 instalments, this did not prevent the company from going into liquidation. This result was described by the Court of Appeal, when it dismissed the appeal against sentence, as 'unfortunate but unavoidable'.

In another example, Baldwins Crane Hire Ltd was convicted of corporate manslaughter and health and safety offences in December 2015, following the death of an employee in 2011 whilst driving one of the company's cranes. The crane crashed after failing to negotiate a steep bend. The crash was found to have been caused by serious problems with the braking system of the crane which had not been properly maintained, and the company was fined £700,000 together with costs.

There have been several further prosecutions since this date but primarily of small companies. However, this may be because health and safety statistics suggest this is where most fatalities occur; indeed, according to the European Commission, small and medium sized companies account for 90% of work-related deaths. The tragedy at Grenfell Tower, in which 72 people died in a fire at a tower block, is likely to be the real test of the Act. In July 2017, the police stated that there were 'reasonable grounds' to suspect Kensington and Chelsea Council and the Chelsea Tenant Management Organisation of corporate manslaughter. However, as at that date, the criminal investigation had seized 31 million documents and identified 336 companies and organisations linked to the construction, refurbishment and management of the tower – figures which will certainly have increased since then. There is no doubt that proving criminal responsibility in such a complex case will be a challenge for the prosecuting authorities.

7.5 The liability of individuals

In addition to the liability of the company or organisation collectively for a death, individuals such as directors, partners or other senior managers may also be liable.

Example

The following case was reported on the Health and Safety Executive's website.

Arnold, aged 27, and several others had been employed by Lee Harper (managing director of Harper Building Contractors Ltd) to remove and replace the roof of a warehouse in Salford. No safe system of work had been prepared before the work began and no safety precautions were in place at the time of the incident. Arnold had never worked on a roof before.

While working on the roof, Arnold stepped backwards onto a fragile roof light on an adjoining warehouse, which gave way. He fell approximately 6.75m, landing on the ground floor directly below and died as a result of his injuries.

The court was told that Lee should have ensured that people could not stand directly on top of the fragile roof light and also installed safety netting underneath the roof of the warehouse to catch anyone who fell. Alternatively, individual workers could have been issued with safety harnesses to break their fall. Lastly, Lee should have ensured that the roof work was properly supervised and provided Arnold – who had never worked on a roof before – with suitable training and instruction. In court, Lee accepted that he had not given any thought to health and safety measures.

In this scenario, the company itself could be convicted of corporate manslaughter and of health and safety offences. However, the director involved could also incur personal criminal liability for the death, and the most appropriate offence for which Lee Harper would be liable is gross negligence manslaughter. He clearly owed his employee a duty of care, and it seems from the facts that he breached that duty in a grossly negligent way and caused death (R v Adomako).

It is well established that an individual can be personally liable for gross negligence manslaughter as a result of a work-related death. It is also true that failure to comply with the health and safety legislation, referred to above, may result in a criminal prosecution of both the organisation itself and individual directors, officers and managers. Under s 37 of the Health and Safety at Work etc Act 1974, where an offence under Part 1 of that Act (including for example under ss 1 or 2) has been committed by a body corporate, a director, manager or similar officer will also be guilty of that offence if it has been committed with their consent or connivance or was attributable to their neglect. What is more, the introduction of the Health and Safety (Offences) Act 2008 means that serious breaches of health and safety rules, which were previously punishable with fines, can attract a custodial sentence of up to two years.

One final possible penalty to consider is disqualification of a director. Obviously, this is not a basis of criminal liability as such, but it is an alternative sanction, the threat of which any director is going to take very seriously indeed. Section 2 of the Company Directors Disqualification Act 1986 gives the court the power to make a disqualification order in relation to a person who has been convicted of an indictable offence in connection with the way a company is managed. The offences under the Health and Safety at Work, etc Act 1974 mentioned previously, and gross negligence manslaughter, are indictable offences, so disqualification may be used as a legal sanction against those directors who have played a part in the commission of such offences.

7.6 Summary

(a) The Corporate Manslaughter and Corporate Homicide Act 2007 was a decade in the making and has a lot to live up to. Its effectiveness, both as a deterrent and as a means of convicting and punishing organisations that are responsible for deaths, is still questioned. However, the Act is a significant piece of legislation in this area of the law.

(b) In addition to establishing corporate manslaughter against the company or organisation, prosecutions may be brought under the health and safety legislation; and individuals such as company directors or senior managers may be criminally liable for the offence of gross negligence manslaughter.

The issue of determining corporate manslaughter remains a complex one, and the scenario below highlights how the law applies in a practical context. Completing the activity should assist your understanding in this regard.

ACTIVITY

The Small Business and Home Workers Association ('the Association') is a fictional unincorporated association that provides advice and support to its clients, which comprise small businesses. The Association has a Chief Executive and 10 Regional Directors who make up the Board of Management. Each Regional Director is responsible for clients who carry on business in their region, with England and Wales being divided into 10 such geographical regions. Each Regional Director then works with a team of four deputy directors, who, in turn, oversee the employees.

The work involves a lot of travelling, and, from time to time, it is necessary for staff to be seconded at short notice to a different region. In order to minimise transport costs, and because of recent road traffic accidents involving employees, the Association's policy is to encourage employees to use public transport wherever possible. Further to the above, a recent policy statement appeared on the Association's Intranet:

'Colleagues,

Due to the increased focus from the Police on road traffic accidents caused by business drivers, we have reviewed and revised the Association's Driving on Business Protocol. Although the majority of travel is still to be undertaken by public transport, if you do have to use your own car, you need to be aware of the revised Protocol. In particular, you should never drive when tired, or under the influence of alcohol or prescribed medication.'

Late one Monday afternoon, the Regional Director for the North-West Region, Callum, e-mails all of the other Regional Directors to say that he is exceptionally short of staff and has a number of important client visits scheduled for the following day that must be covered. Callum asks each of his colleagues to lend him one of their staff.

The Regional Director for the South-West Region, Leona, asks Kevin, one of her deputies, to suggest a member of his team to go to Lancashire. Kevin orders Harry to drive overnight to Preston (a journey of 280 miles), in order to be ready to start work at 8.30am on Tuesday. Harry is unhappy with this instruction, as he has been on call over the weekend and had worked the previous night helping a local farmer deal with the impact of recent flooding on their farm. On his journey north, Harry falls asleep at the wheel, the car goes off the road, rolls down an embankment and Harry is killed.

(1) Should the Association be charged with corporate manslaughter?

(2) Further or in the alternative, could Leona or Kevin be personally liable for gross negligence manslaughter?

COMMENT

Liability of the Association for corporate manslaughter

- The defendant is a relevant 'organisation' under s 1(2)(d), namely 'a partnership, or a trade union or employers' association, that is an employer'.
- The organisation must owe a relevant duty of care to the deceased; and here, Harry is an employee.
- The Association breaches their duty due to the deputy director's insistence on Harry making the journey at that time.
- The breach must cause death. Harry falls asleep at the wheel, crashes the car and dies. However, it is possible that the Regional and deputy directors' involvement was a more than negligible cause of his death, and the consequence of their employee falling asleep at the wheel was reasonably foreseeable. (See the general principles on causation.)
- The issue is whether the breach is a gross breach. To decide this, the jury would have to consider the factors set out in s 8 (see above). The e-mail suggests that the Association is complying with its health and safety obligations by having an appropriate policy which it reviews regularly, communicates to its employees, and makes available on its Intranet. However, any investigation would also want to know whether the organisation monitored how its policy was actually working in practice. Furthermore, the Association may try to argue that the accident was caused solely by the employee, for example, by Harry's failure to take a break when tired.
- The prosecution must also prove that a substantial element of the breach is in the way the activities were managed or organised by senior management. The definition of

'senior management' is contained within s 1(4)(c) and it seems very likely that the Chief Executive and the Regional Directors will be covered by this. Arguably it may well also include the deputy directors, as they could all be said to 'play significant roles' in the managing of a 'substantial part' of the organisation. However, it is improbable that any of the other personnel mentioned would count as 'senior management'.

- If convicted of corporate manslaughter, the Assocation is liable to an unlimited fine. The court can also impose a remedial order and/or a publicity order.

Liability of Kevin and Leona for gross negligence manslaughter

When dealing with individual liability, according to *R v Adomako*, the prosecution must prove that the Regional and deputy directors:

(a) owed a duty of care; and

(b) breached that duty in a grossly negligent way; and

(c) caused death.

The issues of duty of care and causation have been mentioned above. The question for the jury is whether the Regional and deputy directors breached the duty in such a grossly negligent way as to justify a criminal conviction for gross negligence manslaughter. This may be difficult to prove.

8 Sexual Offences

LEARNING OUTCOMES

When you have completed this chapter, you should be able to:

- understand the legal elements of selected statutory sexual offences under the Sexual Offences Act 2003;
- appreciate the social and practical context of these offences.

8.1 Introduction

The law relating to sexual offences is one of the most sensitive areas of criminal law, heavily influenced by social and moral issues and beset by practical, evidential difficulties.

This area of the law has long been controversial, with accusations that it has been ineffectual in delivering justice to victims. 'Archaic, incoherent and discriminatory' and failing 'to reflect changes in society and social attitudes' – this is how the Government described the law on sexual offences as it existed in 2002. At that time, there had been no significant legislative change in the law on sexual offences since the Sexual Offences Act 1956, and many offences were unaltered since Victorian times. Prompted by this fact, and also by the passing of the Human Rights Act 1998, the Government published a White Paper, 'Protecting the Public' (Cm 5668), based on the recommendations of earlier Home Office reviews, including 'Setting the Boundaries: Reforming the Law on Sex Offences' (2000). As a result, the Sexual Offences Act (SOA) 2003 was given Royal Assent on 20 November 2003 and, for the most part, came into force on 1 May 2004.

Despite this law reform and efforts to increase the conviction rate, there are still significant concerns about the high number of sexual offences being committed, the low reporting rates and the rate of conviction for such offences. In the year ending September 2022, 70,633 rapes were recorded by the police – a figure that has increased significantly in recent times – but of these only 2,616 were charged, with even fewer being convicted. The situation is complicated by differing views on who the law should punish, and what activities should be prosecuted as sexual offences and why? Are there certain members of our society who need extra protection from the law? If so, how should this be balanced with fairness towards potential defendants?

Putting this into context, if a man threatens a woman with violence to have sex with him, this would certainly be regarded as a sexual offence; but what if two 14-year-olds kiss each other behind the bike sheds at school? Or an 18-year-old man has sex with a girl aged 13, who looks much older than her age, at her suggestion? Two of these scenarios involve young but apparently willing victims and all would, under the current law, be categorised as sexual offences. This may be considered somewhat harsh if there is little difference in age between the 'victim' and the perpetrator.

8.2 Sexual Offences Act 2003

The SOA 2003 resulted in widespread reforms to sexual offences. It amended the definitions of some existing offences such as rape but also created many new crimes, not all of which are covered here. Indeed, this chapter will concentrate on the offences of rape (SOA 2003, s 1), assault by penetration (SOA 2003, s 2), sexual assault (SOA 2003, s 3) and offences where children are victims (SOA 2003, ss 5 to 7, 9 and 13).

8.3 Rape

The law on rape has been subject to significant changes over the years. One of the most notable was the House of Lords decision in *R v R* [1991] 4 All ER 481, which overturned the matrimonial exception to rape. This removed an outdated rule that said, in effect, that on marriage a woman was consenting to sexual intercourse with her husband whenever he wanted it. Thereafter, s 142 of the Criminal Justice and Public Order Act 1994 amended the offence of rape so that potential victims included men as well as women. Finally, the offence was further amended by s 1 of the SOA 2003 which defines rape as follows:

> **1 Rape**
>
> (1) A person (A) commits an offence if–
>
> (a) he intentionally penetrates the vagina, anus or mouth of another person (B) with his penis,
>
> (b) B does not consent to the penetration, and
>
> (c) A does not reasonably believe that B consents.
>
> (2) Whether a belief is reasonable is to be determined having regard to all the circumstances, including any steps A has taken to ascertain whether B consents.
>
> (3) Sections 75 and 76 apply to an offence under this section.
>
> (4) A person guilty of an offence under this section is liable, on indictment, to imprisonment for life.

Having set out the statutory definition, we shall now move on to analyse each element of the offence in detail.

8.3.1 Actus reus of rape

The actus reus of rape is:

(a) the penile penetration by the defendant of the vagina, anus or mouth of another person;

(b) who at the time does not consent to the penetration.

Note that this is an extension of the previous law which was limited to penetration of the vagina or anus. The inclusion of penetration of the mouth of the complainant also means that non-consensual oral sex is capable of amounting to rape, whereas previously it would have been charged as a less serious offence.

The definition refers to 'a person' as the defendant. However, the requirement for the penetration to be with the defendant's penis means the defendant must be male; a woman cannot therefore commit the offence of rape. However, she could be an accomplice to a rape committed by a male defendant if, for example, she suggested the rape or gave physical assistance to the male defendant by restraining the victim (see **Chapter 15** for issues of accomplice liability). In this context it is important to note that s 79(3) of the SOA 2003 states that 'references to a part of the body include references to a part surgically constructed (in particular through gender reassignment surgery)', which makes it clear that the law covers transgender persons.

Any degree of penetration will satisfy the actus reus of rape. Furthermore, penetration is a continuing act (s 79(2)) and withdrawal of consent by the victim during penetration suffices to commit the actus reus. This was also the position under the old law, as evidenced by *R v Kaitamaki* [1985] AC 147. It would not, however, be rape if the defendant withdrew as soon as the complainant changed their mind.

Penetration alone, of course, is not sufficient to establish the actus reus of rape. There must also be a lack of consent on the part of the victim.

8.3.1.1 Consent

Consent is defined by s 74: a person consents if they agree by choice, and have the freedom and capacity to make that choice. This is a wide definition, but it does appear that the victim must know what they are consenting to.

One particular issue that has arisen and caused debate is that of consent when the complainant is intoxicated. In *R v Dougal* (24 November 2005), Swansea Crown Court, the prosecution decided not to proceed with the case due to the lack of proof that the alleged victim had not consented because she was very intoxicated at the time and had little recollection of events. This left open the possibility that the complainant had given consent, albeit a drunken consent. However, some commentators have argued that the jury should have been left to consider whether, given the complainant's level of intoxication, she was actually capable of consenting at all.

The issue was considered again by the Court of Appeal in the case of *R v Bree* [2007] 2 All ER 676. In his judgment, Sir Igor Judge P made the following comments:

> In cases which are said to arise after voluntary consumption of alcohol the question is not whether the alcohol made either or both less inhibited than they would have been if sober, nor whether either or both might afterwards have regretted what happened, and indeed wished that it had not. If the complainant consents, her consent cannot be revoked. Moreover it is not a question whether either or both may have had very poor recollection of precisely what had happened. ... In our judgment, the proper construction of s 74 of the 2003 Act, as applied to the problem now under discussion, leads to clear conclusions. If, through drink (or any other reason) the complainant has temporarily lost her capacity to choose whether to have intercourse on the relevant occasion, she is not consenting, and subject to questions about the defendant's state of mind, if intercourse takes place, this would be rape. However, where the complainant has voluntarily consumed even substantial quantities of alcohol, but nevertheless remains capable of choosing whether or not to have intercourse, and in drink agrees to do so, this would not be rape.

And, importantly, the judge added:

> We should perhaps underline that, as a matter of practical reality, capacity to consent may evaporate well before a complainant becomes unconscious.

The common perception of rape is that it includes a degree of physical force. However, from the definition of consent in s 74, it is clear that the victim may not be consenting to the penetration even though no violence or force is used or threatened by the defendant. In the example below, a number of scenarios are considered where the existence of consent may be questioned.

Examples

(1) A man uses physical force to make a woman have sex with him.

(2) A man holds a knife to the victim's throat and says that unless the victim has anal sex with him, he will 'cut him up'. The victim agrees.

In each of these examples, the victim has not consented as they were effectively forced to have sex against their will.

(3) Florin says to Yasmin, who has always previously refused to have sex with him, that if she will have sex with him now, he will marry her. Yasmin agrees. Florin never intended to marry Yasmin. Although Florin has acted dishonourably, Yasmin did give her consent in this situation.

(4) Malcolm employs Chelsey. He goes into Chelsey's office after normal working hours and says that unless she agrees to have sex with him, he will dismiss her. Chelsey agrees. What if Malcolm was aware that Chelsey was a lone parent with four children and the job was her only source of income?

Traditionally, the courts have distinguished between actual consent, on the one hand, and mere submission, on the other. In R v Kirk*, unreported, 4 March 2008, CA, the complainant was a young girl who had been sexually abused by the defendant (and others). When homeless, hungry and, in the words of the trial judge, 'desperate', she had sex with the defendant in return for some money for food. The defendant was convicted of rape on the basis that the complainant had submitted rather than consented. This case may be relevant here, particularly if Malcolm knew of Chelsey's financial vulnerability.*

(5) As above, but Malcolm says he will ensure that Chelsey gets the promotion she has applied for if she has sex with him. This scenario is the most likely to result in differing views, with attitudes being influenced by greater awareness of the complexities of consent and how power and status is used to obtain sex, and various campaigns, for example, on social media.

(6) Eric, a police officer, threatens to report Sally, a 16-year-old girl, for a criminal offence unless she has sex with him. Sally does so. Although Sally acquiesces, she does not give true consent as she only agrees due to Eric's abuse of power.

To assist the prosecution, the SOA 2003 establishes various presumptions about consent under ss 75–76 and these are considered later.

8.3.2 Mens rea of rape

Establishing non-consensual penetration of the complainant by the defendant proves he committed the actus reus of rape. However, in order to be guilty of rape, it must also be proved that the defendant had the requisite mens rea. There are two mens rea requirements in the definition of rape in s 1 of the SOA 2003: one positive element and one negative.

First, the defendant must intentionally penetrate the victim. This means he must do so deliberately, and this aspect of the mens rea should be reasonably easy to prove in the majority of cases. Secondly, the negative mens rea requirement is that there must be an absence of reasonable belief in consent. This is therefore an objective test. Under s 1(2), whether a belief in consent is reasonable is determined with regard to all the circumstances, including any steps the defendant took to ascertain whether the complainant consented.

It is apparent that the issue of consent features twice in the offence of rape:

(a) as an element of the actus reus - there must be a lack of consent on the part of the complainant; and

(b) as an element of the mens rea - whether the defendant reasonably believed the complainant was consenting.

These are two separate issues and both need to be considered by the jury before a conviction for rape can be returned.

As mentioned earlier, ss 75–76 of the SOA 2003 establish various presumptions about lack of consent (actus reus) and lack of a reasonable belief in consent (mens rea). These will be considered in detail later in the chapter.

8.4 Assault by penetration

The next offence created by the SOA 2003 is assault by penetration, which is defined in s 2 of the SOA 2003. Note that although the statute refers to the defendant as 'he', both men and women can commit these crimes.

> **2 Assault by penetration**
>
> (1) A person (A) commits an offence if—
>
> (a) he intentionally penetrates the vagina or anus of another person (B) with a part of his body or anything else,
>
> (b) the penetration is sexual,
>
> (c) B does not consent to the penetration, and
>
> (d) A does not reasonably believe that B consents.

The actus reus elements are the penetration by the defendant of the vagina or anus of another person (B) with a part of the defendant's body or anything else; the penetration must be sexual; and B does not consent to the penetration. The mens rea elements are an intentional (deliberate) penetration of B's vagina or anus by the defendant; and a lack of reasonable belief by the defendant that B consents.

Until the SOA 2003, assault by penetration was not a separate offence. Under the old law if, for example, the defendant penetrated the victim's vagina or anus with their tongue, finger or an implement such as a bottle, this would have been charged as a lesser offence of indecent assault, carrying a maximum of 10 years' imprisonment. The creation of this new offence ensures that a defendant can be sentenced to up to life imprisonment for such conduct - the same as rape.

Note that in theory the definition of this offence is wide enough (penetration ... by a part of the defendant's body or anything else) to include penile penetration, but the assumption is that the latter will usually be charged as rape. As in rape, there needs to be a lack of consent on the part of the complainant (actus reus) and a lack of reasonable belief in consent on the part of the defendant (mens rea).

8.5 Sexual assault

Another new offence created by the SOA 2003 is that of sexual assault under s 3, which carries a maximum sentence of 10 years' imprisonment. This is a less serious offence, the essence of which is the intentional sexual touching of one person by another.

The definition of the offence is that a person (A) commits the offence of sexual assault if:

(a) he intentionally touches another person (B);

(b) the touching is sexual;

(c) B does not consent to the touching; and

(d) A does not reasonably believe that B consents.

'Touching' includes penetration and also touching with any part of the body or anything else and through anything, including clothing.

8.5.1 Sexual

'Sexual' is defined in s 78. Any penetration, touching or any other activity is sexual if a reasonable person would consider that:

(a) whatever the circumstances or any person's purpose in relation to it, it is because of its nature sexual (clearly sexual);

(b) because of its nature it may be sexual and because of its circumstance or the purpose of any person in relation to it (or both) it is sexual. This covers the situations where a scenario may or may not be sexual depending on the circumstances and/or the purpose of the defendant. For example, touching a woman's breasts could be sexual, but such a scenario would require full consideration of the circumstances and the defendant's motive or purpose.

It seems clear that the test is an objective one - would a reasonable person regard the conduct as 'sexual'? If the conduct is ambiguous, then the jury can consider the circumstances and purpose of the defendant in deciding whether the conduct is sexual (s 78(b)); but if the conduct is clearly 'non-sexual', it cannot be classed as sexual, irrespective of the defendant's motive.

Examples

(1) A stranger squeezes a man's penis on a crowded train; and a man smacks the bottom of a 20-year-old. In both these circumstances, the touching would be clearly sexual regardless of the circumstances or the defendant's purpose.

(2) A doctor carries out a medical examination of a woman's breasts to check for signs of cancer; this would not be sexual.

(3) A man pretends to be a doctor so he can examine a woman's breasts. In this instance, the man's purpose would make the act sexual in nature.

(4) A man kisses a woman. Whether this is sexual depends upon the circumstances and the defendant's purpose: was it, for example, a kiss on the lips or the cheek? Was the kiss just a greeting between friends?

*(5) A woman takes off a child's shoe. There are some scenarios that are incapable of being construed as sexual, and no sexual assault is committed regardless of the circumstances. Removing a shoe is not sexual even if the woman has a 'foot fetish'. This was certainly the position under the old law (*R v George *[1956] Crim LR 52).*

In the case of *R v H* [2005] EWCA Crim 732, the question of what constituted a sexual touching was considered specifically. The victim had been approached by a man who asked her: 'Do you fancy a shag'. The victim walked away but was subsequently approached by the same man who asked if she was shy. The man then tried to pull the victim towards him by grabbing at a pocket that was located at the side seam of the victim's trousers. The Court of Appeal held that the touching of an individual's clothing was sufficient to amount to 'touching' under s 3. The Court also confirmed that, where it was not clear whether touching was by its nature 'sexual', it was appropriate to ask the jury to consider two questions:

(a) Would the jury, as reasonable people, consider that the touching *could* be sexual?

(b) Whether the jury, as reasonable people and in all the circumstances of the case, would consider that the purpose of the touching had *in fact* been sexual?

The affirmative answer to both questions would lead to a finding that the touching was sexual. In this judgment, the Court of Appeal followed the approach taken in cases pre-dating the SOA 2003.

8.6 Presumptions as to consent

In all the offences outlined above, a lack of consent on the part of the victim is central to establishing the actus reus of the offence. The definition of consent is contained under s 74 above; but in addition, ss 75–76 of the SOA 2003 establish certain presumptions relating to consent. These presumptions exist to help the prosecution show lack of consent (actus reus) and lack of belief in consent (mens rea).

8.6.1 Section 76

Section 76(2) sets out two circumstances in which an irrebuttable presumption arises. This means that lack of consent and lack of belief in consent are conclusively established. The circumstances are that:

(a) the defendant intentionally deceived the complainant as to the nature or purpose of the relevant act;

(b) the defendant intentionally induced the complainant to consent to the relevant act by impersonating a person known personally to the complainant.

The Court of Appeal considered what it means to deceive a complainant 'as to the nature or purpose of the relevant act' in the case of *R v Jheeta (Harvinder Singh)* [2007] EWCA Crim 1699. The defendant deceived the complainant into believing that she would be fined by the police if she did not have sexual intercourse with him. The Court of Appeal interpreted s 76(2)(a) narrowly and held that, although there had been deceptions involved, the complainant had not actually been deceived as to the nature or purpose of the relevant act, namely, the sexual intercourse. Therefore, the conclusive presumption in s 76(2)(a) did not apply. However, this does not mean the defendant cannot be found guilty; indeed, in this case, he was convicted on the basis that the complainant had not consented, applying s 74 generally, and so the defendant had the necessary mens rea for rape.

A very similar approach was taken by the Divisional Court in *Assange v Swedish Prosecution Authority* [2011] EWHC 2849 (Admin). The case concerned the application by Sweden for the extradition of Julian Assange (the founder of WikiLeaks) to Sweden to face certain charges of sexual assault and rape. The court had to consider whether the alleged offences in Sweden would also be offences in this country under the SOA 2003. Here the complainant stated that she had only agreed to sexual intercourse if the defendant wore a condom, and the defendant had failed to do so. The court held that the presumption under s 76 was not triggered because there was no deception as to the nature and purpose of the act. The court did, however, observe that the prosecution could still succeed on the complainant's lack of consent under s 74, because she had not consented to unprotected sex.

By contrast, in *R v Devonald* [2008] EWCA Crim 527, the Court of Appeal held that the jury was entitled to find that the defendant had deceived the complainant as to the 'purpose' (if not the 'nature') of the act. The defendant wanted to take revenge on the complainant for jilting his daughter. He posed over the Internet as a woman - 'Cassey' - and persuaded the complainant to masturbate on a webcam for the sexual gratification of 'Cassey'. His purpose was to embarrass and expose the complainant. He was charged with causing a person to engage in sexual activity without consent under s 4 of the SOA 2003 (which is not an offence covered in this textbook). Here, the Court of Appeal took a broader approach to the scope of s 76(2)(a), deciding that the fundamental purpose of the act was for the sexual gratification of 'Cassey', rather than for whoever might happen to watch the webcam. The complainant had been deceived as to this purpose.

8.6.2 Section 75

Section 75 sets out six circumstances in which a rebuttable presumption arises. Under s 75(1), if the prosecution proves that:

(a) the defendant did the relevant act (for example, the penetration or sexual touching);

(b) any of the six specified circumstances existed; and

(c) the defendant knew the circumstance existed,

then it is presumed that the complainant did not consent and that the defendant did not have a reasonable belief in consent. The defendant can rebut this presumption by producing evidence to the contrary. Given that many such incidents occur in private without any witnesses, the practical effect is that the defendant will almost certainly have to go into the witness box to give evidence, thus exposing themselves to being cross-examined about their account. However, if the defendant successfully produces such evidence, the prosecution must then prove the issues of lack of consent (actus reus) and lack of reasonable belief in consent (mens rea) beyond reasonable doubt in the usual way.

Under s 75(2), the six specified circumstances are that:

(a) any person was, at the time of the relevant act or immediately before it began, using violence against the complainant or causing the complainant to fear that immediate violence would be used against them;

(b) any person was, at the time of the relevant act or immediately before it began, causing the complainant to fear that violence was being used, or that immediate violence would be used, against another person;

(c) the complainant was, and the defendant was not, unlawfully detained at the time of the relevant act;

(d) the complainant was asleep or otherwise unconscious at the time of the relevant act;

(e) because of the complainant's physical disability, the complainant would not have been able at the time of the relevant act to communicate to the defendant whether the complainant consented;

(f) any person had administered to or caused to be taken by the complainant, without the complainant's consent, a substance which, having regard to when it was administered or taken, was capable of causing or enabling the complainant to be stupefied or overpowered at the time of the relevant act.

The application of these presumptions is analysed next.

Example

The following defendants have been charged with various offences under the SOA 2003. All the cases turn on the issue of whether the complainant consented, and/or the defendant had a reasonable belief in consent.

(1) *Kiyansh is charged with rape. The complainant alleges that the penetration was non-consensual. Although she did not struggle, she says the defendant (Kiyansh) threatened to cut her throat immediately before he had sex with her.*

Under s 75(1) and (2)(a) of the SOA 2003, there is a presumption that the complainant did not consent, and that Kiyansh did not reasonably believe she consented, if Kiyansh caused his victim to fear that immediate violence would be used against her. If the prosecution's version of events is accepted, this presumption would apply as Kiyansh effectively forced her to submit by threatening to cut her throat immediately before he engaged in intercourse.

However, the presumption is rebuttable. Kiyansh would need to produce evidence to raise an issue as to whether he reasonably believed the complainant was consenting. If such evidence was available, the prosecution would then need to establish both a lack of consent and a lack of reasonable belief in consent beyond reasonable doubt.

(2) *Finley is charged with sexual assault. The complainant alleges that Finley put on a wig and deliberately set out to pretend to be her boyfriend, and so induced her to engage in sexual activities with him.*

Finlay's case falls under s 76 of the SOA 2003. If Finlay intentionally induced his victim to consent to sexual activities by impersonating her boyfriend ('a person known personally to the complainant': SOA 2003, s 76(2)(b)) then there is a conclusive presumption that the complainant did not consent to the act and that Finlay did not believe she consented. If the prosecution's evidence is accepted, there is nothing Finlay can do to rebut the s 76 presumption.

(3) *Tanisha is charged with assault by penetration. The complainant alleges that she was intoxicated at the time of the act because of a drug that Tanisha had provided for her.*

Tanisha's situation is similar to that of Kiyansh. If Tanisha did supply the complainant with drugs that caused her to be intoxicated, this gives rise to circumstances under s 75(2)(f) of the SOA 2003 which, in turn, leads to a presumption that the complainant did not consent and that Tanisha did not have a reasonable belief in her consent. Whether the presumption applies will depend on whether Tanisha administered or caused her victim to take the drug without her consent. If she did, the prosecution must also establish that the drug was one that was capable of causing the complainant to be stupefied or overpowered at the time of the assault. The presumption is rebuttable by evidence, but further information would be required.

8.7 Children as victims

Sections 5–7 of the SOA 2003 replicate the offences under ss 1–3 where the victim is a child under 13. The only difference is that under ss 5–7 neither the consent of the victim nor the defendant's belief in consent is a relevant issue. They simply do not feature as elements of the offence.

Also, there is strict liability as to the age of the child. If, for example, a defendant has sexual intercourse with a girl the day before her 13th birthday, he is guilty of rape under s 5. The fact that the girl may have consented to, or indeed instigated, the intercourse is not relevant. Furthermore, the fact that the defendant reasonably believed she consented, or believed (reasonably or otherwise) that the girl was over 13 years of age, is also irrelevant.

8.8 Sexual offences against children

Section 9 of the SOA 2003 creates an offence of intentionally sexually touching a child.

Under s 9(1), a person aged 18 or over (A) commits an offence if:

(a) he intentionally touches another person (B);

(b) the touching is sexual; and either

(c) B is under 16 and A does not reasonably believe that B is 16 or over; or

(d) B is under 13.

If the victim is aged 13 to 15, therefore, the defendant will have a defence if they reasonably believed the victim was 16 or over, but no such defence is available if the victim is under 13. In these cases, the issue of the age of the victim is one of strict liability.

Section 9(2) provides that the offence is indictable only, and the maximum penalty is 14 years' imprisonment if a person commits an offence under s 9 by touching which involves penetration of B's anus or vagina with a part of A's body or anything else; penetration of B's mouth with A's penis; penetration of A's anus or vagina with a part of B's body; or penetration of A's mouth with B's penis. Otherwise (that is if the touching does not fall within the penetration scenarios above), the offence is either-way, but again, following a Crown Court trial, would attract a maximum of 14 years' imprisonment.

The offence under s 9 can be committed only by a defendant who is aged 18 or over. However, there is a corresponding provision under s 13 of the SOA 2003 for those defendants who are under 18. Under s 13, the maximum penalty is five years' imprisonment.

It is apparent that there is a significant degree of overlap between some of the offences outlined above. What is also interesting is that, whilst the sexual offences against children were clearly aimed at protecting young people from exploitative sexual activity with adults, the effect of ss 5–7 and s 13 is actually to make any consensual sexual touching between two adolescents potentially a criminal offence. Much is left to the discretion of the prosecuting authorities, following guidelines intended to ensure that inappropriate or unnecessary prosecutions are not pursued in such cases.

8.9 Summary of the sexual offences

This chapter has considered some of the most important offences under the SOA 2003, and a summary of the main points may assist you at this stage. However, this is just a reminder of the key areas and is not a substitute for knowing and understanding all the detail discussed above. Set out below is an overview of ss 1–3 of the SOA 2003 and the statutory presumptions.

Figure 8.1 Sexual offences

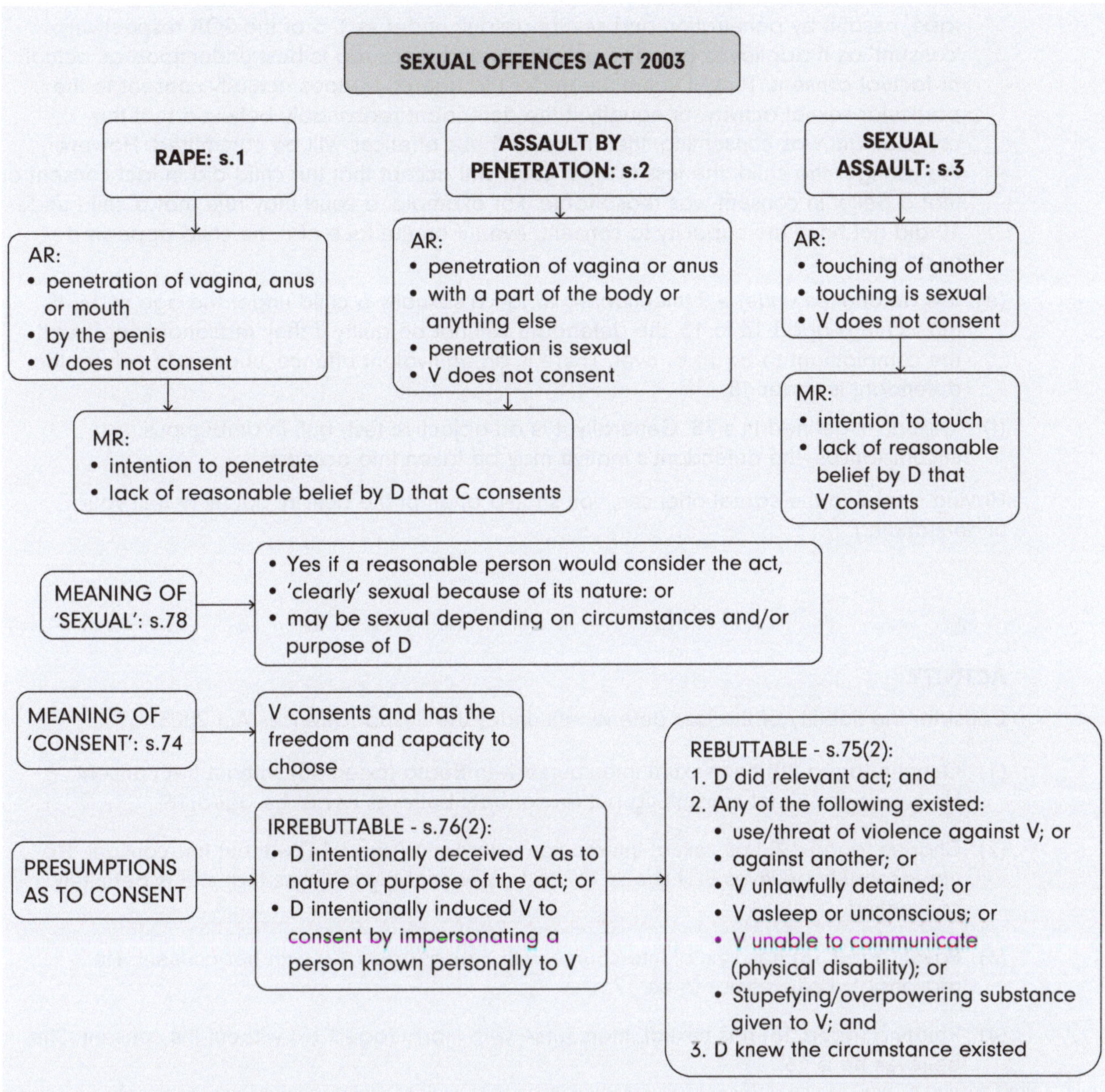

To conclude:

(a) The offences of rape (s 1), assault by penetration (s 2) and sexual assault (s 3) all revolve around a lack of consent from the complainant (actus reus) and a lack of a reasonable belief in consent from the defendant (mens rea).

(b) These elements are presumed to exist if any of the presumptions set out in s 75 or s 76 apply. The two presumptions in s 76 are irrebuttable; whereas the presumptions set out in s 75 can be rebutted if the defendant succeeds in producing evidence to the contrary.

(c) 'Consent' is defined in s 74: 'a person consents if he or she agrees by choice and has the freedom and capacity to make that choice'.

(d) Sections 5, 6 and 7 establish equivalent offences to ss 1–3, but where the complainant is under 13 years old. For these offences, consent is irrelevant and there is also strict liability in relation to the victim's age.

Note that the term 'age of consent', which you may have come across, is not helpful here as it is only relevant to the range of child sex offences from s 5 to s 7, s 9 and s 13. For rape, assault by penetration and sexual assault under ss 1–3 of the SOA respectively, 'consent' as it applies to both the actus reus and mens rea is best understood as actual or factual consent. Thus, if someone under the age of 16 does actually consent to the particular sexual activity, or equally if the defendant reasonably believed that the complainant was consenting, then none of these offences will be committed. However, the younger the child, the less likely a court will accept that the child did in fact consent or that a belief in consent was reasonable. For example, a court may rule that a child under 10 did not have the capacity to consent, even if on the face of it the child appeared to do so.

(e) It is an offence under s 9 intentionally to touch sexually a child under the age of 16. If the victim is aged 13 to 15, the defendant will not be guilty if they reasonably believed the complainant to be 16 or over. There is an equivalent offence, under s 13, where the defendant is under 18.

(f) 'Sexual' is defined in s 78. Generally it is an objective test, but, in ambiguous circumstances, the defendant's motive may be taken into account.

Having analysed the sexual offences, you should attempt the activity below to test your understanding.

ACTIVITY

Consider the liability of the four defendants under the Sexual Offences Act 2003:

(1) Quentin (aged 20) has sexual intercourse with Beata (aged 15) without her consent. He knows she is not consenting but reasonably believes her to be aged 16.

(2) Charles (aged 19) has sexual intercourse with Aoife (aged 14) without her consent. He unreasonably believes that she is 16; and unreasonably believes that she is definitely consenting.

(3) Pavel (aged 16) has sexual intercourse with Freda (aged 12) with her consent. He reasonably believes her to be 17.

(4) Rhianna (aged 18) has sexual intercourse with Harry (aged 15) without his consent. She believes he is 16.

COMMENT

(1) Quentin will be guilty of offences under s 1 (rape), s 2 (assault by penetration) and s 3 (sexual touching), as Beata does not consent to the sexual intercourse (actus reus) and he knows this (mens rea). He will not be guilty of a s 9 offence (sexual activity with a child), as he reasonably believes her to be aged 16.

(2) Charles will be guilty of rape, assault by penetration and sexual touching under ss 1–3. Aoife does not consent (actus reus), and although he believes that she is consenting to sex, this belief is unreasonable so the mens rea is complete. He is also guilty of sexual activity with a child (s 9), as although Charles believes Aoife to be 16, this belief is also unreasonable.

(3) As Freda is under 13, Pavel will be guilty of offences under s 5 (rape of a child under 13), s 6 (assault by penetration of a child under 13) and s 7 (sexual touching of a child under 13). Her consent is irrelevant for the purposes of these offences, as is Pavel's (reasonable) belief that she is older than 16.

Pavel will also be guilty of an offence under s 13 (child sex offences committed by children or young persons). Again, his reasonable belief that Freda is 17 is irrelevant, as she is under 13. Pavel is guilty under s 13, rather than s 9, because he is under 18 so his sentence will be lower - a maximum of five years' imprisonment instead of 14 years.

Freda does not commit any offence, as she is the 'victim' and thus cannot be a secondary party to the offences committed against her by Pavel - see *R v Tyrrell* [1894] 1 QB 710.

(4) Rhianna will not be guilty of rape (s 1) as she is not male. She is not guilty of assault by penetration (s 2) as she has not 'penetrated' Harry. She will be guilty of sexual touching (s 3) unless she reasonably believed that Harry consented to sex. She will be guilty under s 9 (sexual activity with a child) unless she reasonably believed Harry to be aged 16 or over.

9 Theft and Robbery

LEARNING OUTCOMES

When you have completed this chapter, you should be able to:

- demonstrate a sound knowledge and understanding of the key concepts relating to theft and robbery, having regard to statutory provisions and case law;
- appreciate how these offences are applied in practice.

9.1 Introduction

There are a number of property offences, many of which are set out in the Theft Act 1968. This chapter considers two such crimes, beginning with theft, before moving on to its aggravated form - robbery.

9.2 Theft

Theft, or larceny as it was originally known, is historically a very important crime and remains so today, as it is probably the most commonly committed property offence. Theft covers a wide range of criminal activity from simple shoplifting to sophisticated conduct, such as the taking of thousands of pounds of stock as a result of organised theft from a factory. It is important to understand from the outset that theft can encompass a wide variety of types of behaviour - it is not just restricted to the 'obvious' situations.

9.2.1 Definition

Theft is defined in s 1(1) of the Theft Act 1968 (TA 1968), and many of its concepts have an impact on other property offences.

The offence of theft can also involve consideration of various aspects of civil law. For example, theft usually involves taking something from someone, such as the pickpocket snatching a mobile phone from a pocket, or the art thief removing a valuable oil painting. In these situations, there is no disputing the fact that the 'thief' does not own the goods. However, questions of who owns the property and when ownership passed to another can be critical. This means that, sometimes, the civil law must be considered in order to explain the criminal law.

Section 1(1) of the TA 1968 provides:

> A person is guilty of theft if he dishonestly appropriates property belonging to another with the intention of permanently depriving the other of it; and 'theft' and 'steal' shall be construed accordingly.

Theft is an 'either way' offence and carries a maximum penalty of seven years' imprisonment. As ever, when studying a criminal offence, the actus reus and mens rea must be identified first, before the detail of those elements is analysed. For this offence, the actus reus is the appropriation of property belonging to another, whilst the mens rea is dishonesty coupled with an intention to permanently deprive.

When considering liability for theft it is important to ensure that all five elements are present at the same time. If one (or more) is missing, the offence is not committed, however much one may feel that the defendant should be liable. For example, a person who assumes ownership of a piece of their neighbour's garden is not guilty of theft because land is generally not within the definition of property under s 4 of the TA 1968 (see below). As soon as all five elements are present at the same time, the offence is complete.

Sections 2 to 6 of the TA 1968 give guidance on the interpretation of each element of theft, but some of these statutory provisions have been supplemented by a considerable amount of case law and, initially, these concepts can be quite difficult to grasp. It is important to remember that each of the elements forms part of the jigsaw that makes up the crime of theft, and often it is only when all five have been studied that the offence becomes clear.

9.2.2 Actus reus

This section begins by analysing the actus reus of theft, looking at each of the three requirements in turn.

9.2.2.1 Appropriation

The physical act required by a defendant in order to establish the actus reus of the offence is that of 'appropriation' and this is usually very easy to establish. It is therefore particularly important to remember that appropriation is just one of the five elements needed to secure a conviction for theft.

The dictionary definition of 'appropriate' is 'to make to be the private property of anyone: to take to oneself as one's own: to filch'. However, the legal meaning is much wider than this. Appropriation is defined in s 3(1), which provides:

> Any assumption by a person of the rights of an owner amounts to an appropriation, and this includes, where he has come by the property (innocently or not) without stealing it, any later assumption of a right to it by keeping or dealing with it as owner.

An appropriation under the TA 1968 therefore is any assumption of the rights of an owner.

Example

Hafsa owns a book. What rights does Hafsa have over that book which may be 'assumed' by a potential thief? In other words, what does being the owner of the book allow Hafsa to do to it or with it?

The potential list is very long. It would include the right to read the book, sell it, have possession of it, lend it to someone, exchange it for something else, or even destroy it. Thus, if someone came and took possession of Hafsa's book, they would have appropriated it. Similarly, they would appropriate the book if they made out that they were the owner of her property and offered to sell it to someone else, or if they chose to keep it for themselves. It is Hafsa's right, as the owner, to do these things. If someone else exercises those powers, they have assumed her rights as the owner.

Consent of the owner

In some cases of theft, the defendant has appropriated property with the consent of the owner (often obtained by fraud). The House of Lords, in four notable cases, ruled on how this impacts on the offence, and what is meant by an assumption of the rights of an owner (and therefore the meaning of appropriation). The first two, *R v Morris* [1984] AC 320 and *Lawrence v Metropolitan Police Commissioner* [1972] AC 626, unfortunately conflicted.

In *R v Morris*, the defendant, who was in a supermarket shopping, switched the price labels on two pieces of meat. This meant he would have paid £2.73 for a piece of meat originally priced at £6.91. The House of Lords had to decide whether the act of switching the price labels amounted to an appropriation of the meat. Their Lordships decided that it did, as it was the owner's right (in this case the supermarket) to decide at what price to sell the goods. The judges decided that an appropriation was:

(a) an act which adversely interferes with or usurps 'any right of an owner'. It is an act which is unauthorised;

(b) an assumption of any *one* right of an owner. In other words, to appropriate, the defendant had to usurp only one of the many rights of an owner, not all of them.

In *Lawrence v MPC*, a foreign student, who did not speak English very well, took a taxi ride, the correct fare for which should have been in the region of 50p. The student offered a £1 note. When the taxi driver (the defendant) intimated that this was not sufficient, the student offered his wallet, whereupon the defendant took a further £6. He was charged with theft of the £6. The House of Lords confirmed that the defendant's act did amount to an appropriation. Section 3(1) of the TA 1968 did not contain the words 'without the consent of the owner', and it therefore followed that it was irrelevant if the owner consented to the taking of the money.

Uncertainty arose as these two judgments are inconsistent. In *Morris*, the House of Lords stated that an appropriation had to be an 'unauthorised act', thus something to which the owner had not consented. However, in *Lawrence*, the same court said that the issue of whether or not the owner had consented was irrelevant. The conflict between *Morris* and *Lawrence* was finally resolved in a subsequent House of Lords case.

In *DPP v Gomez* [1993] AC 442, the defendant was the assistant manager in a shop. A customer asked to be supplied with goods for which he would pay with two cheques. Both the customer and the defendant knew the cheques were stolen and therefore worthless. The defendant asked the shop manager to authorise the transaction without telling him that the cheques were of no value. The manager did so, and the goods were handed over. The defendant was charged with and convicted of theft at his trial. He appealed and the matter ultimately went to the House of Lords.

The question the court was asked to consider was:

> When theft is alleged and that which is alleged to be stolen passes to the defendant with the consent of the owner, but that has been obtained by a false representation, has (a) an appropriation within the meaning of s 1(1) of the Theft Act 1968 taken place, or, (b) must such a passing of property necessarily involve an element of adverse interference with or usurpation of some right of the owner?

The House of Lords answered 'Yes' to question (a) and 'No' to question (b).

Their Lordships agreed with the decision in *Morris* that the accused only had to assume one of the rights of an owner for an appropriation. Lord Keith gave the leading judgment for the majority. He stated:

> While it is correct to say that appropriation for purposes of section 3(1) includes [an act of adverse interference with the rights of the owner], it does not necessarily follow that no other act can amount to an appropriation and in particular that no act expressly or impliedly authorised by the owner can in any circumstances do so. Indeed, *Reg v Lawrence* [1972] AC 626 is a clear decision to the contrary since it laid down unequivocally that an act may be an appropriation notwithstanding that it is done with the consent of the owner.

Lord Keith went on to conclude:

> In my opinion it serves no useful purpose at the present time to seek to construe the relevant provisions of the Theft Act by reference to the report which preceded it, namely the Eighth Report of the Criminal Law Revision Committee on Theft and Related Offences (1966) (Cmnd 2977) [which clearly intended 'appropriation' to be interpreted as 'without the consent of the owner']. The decision in *Lawrence* was a clear decision of this House upon the construction of the word 'appropriate' in section 1(1) of the Act, which had stood for 12 years when doubt was thrown upon it by *obiter dicta* in *Morris*. *Lawrence* must be regarded as authoritative and correct, and there is no question of it now being right to depart from it.

The majority of the House of Lords in *Gomez* therefore confirmed that an appropriation occurred even though the property passed with the consent or authorisation of the owner.

The decision in *Gomez* has a considerable practical effect, as virtually anything a person does to property that is not theirs is an appropriation (although it does not follow that it is theft, as the other four elements of the offence must also be present).

Example

Blessing is going around a supermarket doing her shopping. She picks up a pint of milk, a bar of chocolate and a loaf of bread that she wants to buy, and puts them into her supermarket trolley. On her way out, she sees a shop assistant stacking the shelves with some tins of beans.

Blessing's acts and those of the shop assistant are acts of appropriation. By picking up the goods, both assume some of the rights of an owner, as they have control over them. The fact that the supermarket positively wants Blessing to put the goods in her trolley is irrelevant; likewise, the fact that it is the shop assistant's job to fill the shelves. R v Gomez *confirms that the consent of the owner (or lack of it) is irrelevant in deciding whether an appropriation has taken place.*

There has been much debate over the case of *Gomez*. For example, Professor JC Smith, in his commentary on the case in the Criminal Law Review ([1993] Crim LR 306), made the following points:

> *The ratio decidendi.* The certified question was limited to the case where the consent of the owner has been obtained by a false representation and the House might have confined its decision to that point. It did not. The fact that, in the instant case, consent

was obtained by a false representation is nowhere treated as material. Cases where the defendant makes no representation, like the taker of goods in a supermarket, are regarded as the same in principle as the deception cases. The decision is that the consent of the owner to the act done, or the fact that he authorised that act, is irrelevant.

... *The effect on the law of theft*. The full effect on the law of theft can be appreciated only when account is taken of the approval given to the ruling in *Morris* that the assumption of any of the rights of an owner amounts to an appropriation; and that it may amount to theft even though *that* act will not deprive the owner permanently, or at all, of his property; it is sufficient that the defendant has a present intention to deprive by some future act. Merely switching the labels in a supermarket, dishonestly intending to buy the article for the lower price, amounts to the complete offence of theft, even though the enterprise is immediately interrupted or abandoned. We now have to couple this extraordinary ruling with the proposition that consent and authority are irrelevant and we reach this conclusion:

Anyone doing anything whatever to property belonging to another, with or without the authority or consent of the owner, appropriates it: and, if he does so dishonestly and with intent, by that act or any subsequent act, permanently to deprive, he commits theft.

Of course the object of the Theft Act was to get away from the troublesome concepts of taking and carrying away but this reduces the actus reus of theft almost to vanishing point. Acts which common sense would regard as attempts or merely preparatory acts are the full offence of theft.

Appropriation and gifts

Despite the comment and criticism, in 2000, the judges went even further on the meaning of appropriation.

In *R v Hinks* [2000] 3 WLR 1590 the House of Lords was asked to consider whether the receipt of a gift could be held to be an appropriation. In this case, the defendant befriended a man (X) who was described as being of limited intelligence. Over a period of some months, X drew £60,000 from his savings account and these sums were then deposited in the defendant's account. Hinks was convicted of theft and appealed.

When the case came before the House of Lords, the certified question was: 'Whether the acquisition of an indefeasible title to property is capable of amounting to an appropriation of property belonging to another for the purposes of section 1(1) of the Theft Act 1968.' The judges clarified that this meant the question was whether a person can 'appropriate' property belonging to another where the other person makes them an indefeasible gift of property, retaining no proprietary interest or any right to resume or recover any proprietary interest in the property.

In Hinks' previous appeal hearing, the Court of Appeal (Rose LJ) had said that: 'Belief or lack of belief that the owner consented to the appropriation is relevant to dishonesty.' It was not relevant to 'appropriation' since a defendant could appropriate something even if they had the consent of the owner.

The legal basis of the defendant's appeal to the House of Lords was that the conviction of a donee for receiving a perfectly valid gift was a departure from the current law – backed up by Professor Sir John Smith's academic arguments. However, the decision in *Gomez* destroyed the appellant's argument as it treated 'appropriation' as a neutral word meaning 'any assumption by a person of the rights of an owner', so an indefeasible gift of property can amount to an appropriation. Thus, the conviction of Hinks and the Court of Appeal decision were not departures from the existing law.

In the House of Lords, the defendant's conviction was upheld. Lord Steyn rejected the defendant's suggested revision of the definition of 'appropriation', arguing that if the law was restated by adopting a narrower definition, the outcome was likely to place beyond the reach of the criminal law dishonest persons who should be found guilty of theft. The suggested revision would unwarrantably restrict the scope of the law of theft and complicate the fair and effective prosecution of theft. The judge was satisfied that the decisions in *Lawrence* and *Gomez* can be applied by judges and juries in a way that does not result in injustice. Furthermore, the mental requirements of theft (particularly the element of dishonesty) are an adequate protection against injustice.

Regarding the appellant's suggestion that the criminal and civil laws conflicted in this area, Lord Steyn said:

(a) yes, there was conflict;

(b) it was wrong to assume the criminal law was wrong rather than the civil law;

(c) the conflict did not justify a departure from *Lawrence* and *Gomez*; and

(d) the conflict was good because it meant there was no need to explain difficult civil law concepts of ownership to juries.

In conclusion, the House of Lords held that there can still be an appropriation, even when there was a valid gift of property to the defendant according to civil law (for example, when it was not obtained by fraud, duress or undue influence). In legal terms, the acquisition of an indefeasible title to property is capable of amounting to an appropriation.

The decision has attracted criticism because, if a person is gifted property, under civil law it is theirs. Logically, they cannot be said to be assuming the right of an owner – they are the owner!

Limitations on appropriation

The combined effect of *Gomez* and *Hinks* makes it difficult to imagine any situation where a person will not be appropriating property if they deal with it in any way. How the individual came to deal with that property, for example with or without the consent of the owner, is immaterial to the issue of appropriation (although it could be very relevant to issues relating to other elements of the offence such as dishonesty). However, some limit on the extent of appropriation was introduced by the Court of Appeal in *R v Briggs* [2004] 1 Cr App R 34. In this case, the defendant's aunt and uncle (Mr and Mrs Reid) were selling their home and buying another closer to the defendant (Briggs). A firm of licensed conveyancers was dealing with the transaction. Briggs sent the conveyancers a letter of authority signed by the Reids telling the conveyancers to send the sum of £49,950 to solicitors acting for the vendors of the Reids' new house. This was done and title in the new house was vested in Briggs and her father.

Briggs was charged with theft of the Reids' account as Mr and Mrs Reid argued that their consent to the transaction had been induced by fraud. This was because they thought the money would be used to ensure that title (ownership) in the new house would be transferred to them. Briggs appealed against her conviction and that appeal was upheld by the Court of Appeal. The judges stated that the word 'appropriation' connoted a physical act on the part of the defendant rather than a more remote action that had triggered the payment in question. The fact that Briggs had caused her relatives to perform an act in relation to their bank account that would have been an appropriation if she had performed it herself did not render her dishonest and deceptive conduct an appropriation. Although she could now possibly be charged with an offence under the Fraud Act 2006 (see below), the Court held that there was no theft.

Note that if the facts had been slightly different so that Ms Briggs had direct control over her relatives' bank account and had authorised the payment to be made, then a clear act of appropriation could have been established (via the innocent agency of a bank employee) and she would have been guilty of theft of a thing in action by assuming a right of an owner over the credit balance in their bank account.

Later assumptions of the rights of an owner

Usually the appropriation (and other elements of theft) can be established at the time the defendant first 'deals' with an item of someone else's property, but what if all the elements of theft cannot be made out at that initial stage? Can there be a subsequent appropriation of property once the defendant is in possession of the property? Within the definition of appropriation, under the second half of s 3(1), is the phrase '... and this includes, where he has come by the property (innocently or not) without stealing it, any later assumption of a right to it by keeping or dealing with it as owner'. This allows a defendant who comes into possession of property legitimately but later does something which assumes the rights of an owner to be liable for theft. Although not a common occurrence, examples of where this would apply are set out below.

Examples

(a) Himesh is given some beer to deliver to a local business. When he arrives, Himesh realises that he has been given too much and decides to drink the excess.

(b) Betsy borrows a book from her college library in February. In April, she decides to keep it permanently.

(c) Gareth accidentally picks up his friend's watch. When he discovers his mistake, instead of returning it, Gareth decides to sell the watch using an online market site.

Drinking the excess beer, keeping the library book and selling the watch would all be appropriations. In each case, the defendant came by the item innocently but later assumed the rights of an owner in some way. If the other elements of theft are also present at that later stage, the offence of theft is established.

Multiple appropriations

It is apparent how easy it is to appropriate property, but can the defendant continue to do so indefinitely so as to establish multiple charges of theft, in other words, can property be stolen more than once? The answer is no – once the defendant has stolen the property, thus appropriated it with full mens rea, a later assumption of rights by them will not amount to another theft of the property.

This can be established, first, by considering the latter part of s 3(1), which deals with an assumption of a right when the defendant has come by the property 'without stealing it' and says that such can be an appropriation. This implies that if a defendant had come by the item originally by stealing it, later assumptions of the rights of an owner would not be an appropriation.

The point was confirmed in *R v Atakpu* [1994] QB 69. In this case the defendants were arrested at Dover, driving cars which had been hired abroad by using false documents. The prosecution alleged that the defendants intended to disguise the identity of the cars and sell them in England. The defendants were convicted of conspiracy (an agreement) to steal. On appeal, the Court of Appeal held that all the elements of theft had been made out when the cars were hired. Any later dealing with the cars could not found a charge of theft or of conspiracy to steal because there could be no appropriation. The defendants had already stolen the cars when they hired them, and any later assumption of rights (such as changing the number plate, re-spraying the car, driving it and selling it) could not be an appropriation for theft. Their convictions were consequently quashed.

In *Atakpu*, the prosecution submitted that the initial appropriation was a continuing one, and if this argument had succeeded, the charges would stand. The Court of Appeal accepted that there could be situations where the appropriation was continuing, and here the jury would have to apply its common sense as to when the appropriation ended. In reality, thefts are invariably 'instantaneous' so that all elements of the definition are established instantly, but if there is any doubt, the jury must decide as a question of fact whether the appropriation was continuous so the defendant was still engaged 'on the job'.

Example

Joy picks up a necklace in a jewellers' shop. Her intention is to take it without paying for it. All elements of theft seem to be established when she picks the necklace up. What happens if Billy walks into the shop and helps Joy by restraining the shopkeeper while Joy makes her escape. Is Billy an accomplice to the theft, or is the theft already complete by then so that he cannot be charged? It will be a question of fact for the jury to decide as to when the appropriation is complete, although it seems likely that it was here.

This point can be important in determining issues of accomplice liability and for charges of burglary (see later in this textbook).

The innocent purchaser for value

The last issue to be considered on appropriation returns to those people who acquire property without stealing it but later, with the mens rea of theft, assume rights of an owner. Usually such defendants are guilty of theft because of the provisions of s 3(1). However, there is an exception to this general rule. Section 3(2) of the TA 1968 makes it clear that a person is not liable for theft if, when they acquired the goods, two major conditions apply:

(a) The transfer was 'for value', so payment must have been made. This need not necessarily be money, for example the person could have exchanged other goods for the property.

(b) The purchaser has acted 'in good faith' so they had no doubts or concerns about the transaction and its legality, and believed that the seller was acting entirely properly. Thus, if a person bought the item for a price which they knew was considerably less than its true value, in circumstances that raised doubts in their mind, it is certainly arguable they were not acting in 'good faith' when they bought it.

Example

Scenario 1

Ursula buys an antique vase from Tahir. She pays £1,000 for it and at no time does she suspect anything untoward is going on. She subsequently discovers that Tahir had stolen the vase from Vera. This means that the vase still belongs, in law, to Vera. If Ursula keeps the vase, she will be able to rely on s 3(2) to protect her from liability for theft as she acted in 'all innocence' at the time of the purchase and therefore in good faith. She also paid £1,000 for the vase and so gave value.

Note that if Ursula then sold the vase to someone else, she could be liable for fraud by false representation - an offence under the Fraud Act 2006 - by implying that she was the owner. However, she commits no offence of theft either by keeping or selling the vase as she falls within the s 3(2) exception.

Scenario 2

Tahir gives the vase to Ursula who subsequently discovered it belonged to Vera. In this instance, Ursula would not be able to rely on s 3(2) of the TA 1968 because she would not be a 'purchaser' as she received the vase as a gift. She therefore has appropriated the vase under the second part of s 3(1), as she came by it innocently but later assumed the rights of an owner by keeping it, in the sense that she continued to exercise those rights. However, remember that this would be theft only if the other four elements of the offence were also present.

9.2.2.2 Property

The second part of the actus reus of theft is that there must be an appropriation of 'property', and this is defined in s 4(1) of the 1968 Act:

> 'Property' includes money and all other property, real or personal, including things in action and other intangible property.

There are some qualifications to the basic definition in subsections (2), (3) and (4) and these will be studied later. Most of the items listed in s 4(1) are self-explanatory but others require further consideration.

(a) *Money*. Money simply means any currency (British or foreign), so the normal notes and coins that are used every day.

(b) *Real property*. Real property means land and things attached or fixed to it. For home owners, 'real property' would therefore include the plot of land, the house and, if present, a garage. However, it is important to note that the circumstances in which land can be stolen are actually very limited due to the provisions of s 4(2) of the TA 1968 (see below).

(c) *Personal property*. This means any tangible object that is not real property and would include, for example, cars, books, televisions, furniture, mobile phones, jewellery, clothes, and even prohibited drugs unlawfully in the complainant's possession (*R v Smith, Plummer and Haines* [2011] EWCA Crim 66). This list is virtually endless.

(d) *Things in action*. 'Things in action' (which is sometimes referred to as 'chose' in action) is a more difficult concept to grasp. It comprises property which cannot be touched or felt but is something that can be enforced by a legal action.

Example

Jacinta writes a book and, thus, has copyright in it. Eli writes his own book and copies Jacinta's wording before claiming it as his own. In these circumstances, Jacinta can sue Eli for infringing her copyright; it is therefore a thing in action for the purposes of the TA 1968.

By contrast, if Eli steals an actual copy of Jacinta's book, the book is personal property (see (c) above).

The most common example of a thing in action for the purposes of theft is a bank or building society account. When a person opens an account, they deposit money into it. What they have is a thing in action - the credit balance in the account, in other words, a right to sue the bank for that money. Similarly, an overdraft is a thing in action. If the bank has given a person an overdraft facility of £500, that is their property as they have a contractual right to enforce it. The bank is contractually obliged to give them that £500 or honour payments up to that amount.

In *Chan Man-sin v R* [1988] 1 All ER 1, the defendant was a company accountant who forged company cheques. These were used to take money out of the company's accounts and the monies were then paid into other accounts controlled by the defendant. He was convicted of theft but argued that he had not appropriated property. The Privy Council disagreed. It found that the bank owed a debt to the company (the credit balance of the company's account) and this was a thing in action. If the account balance was reduced, the company had the right to sue the bank to recover its losses. The defendant had therefore appropriated by dealing with the company's account. By drawing, presenting and negotiating cheques, he had assumed the rights of an owner (appropriation). The account (the credit balance and any agreed overdraft facility) was a thing in action and so amounted to property. All other elements of theft were also established and so the defendant was guilty.

The two main things in action to be aware of, therefore, are:

(a) the credit balance of another's account;

(b) another person's overdraft facility.

Interestingly, a person does not commit theft from a bank if they overdraw on their own account without authority. In *R v Navvabi* [1986] 3 All ER 102, the defendant knew his bank account was overdrawn but continued to use his bank card to support cheques. He was charged with theft from the bank. It was held that the defendant was not guilty as he had dealt only with his own account, so he had not assumed the rights of an owner over someone else's thing in action.

As is usual in cases of offences against property, it is important to remember that a defendant cannot 'get away with' fraudulent use of their own account. *Navvabi* suggests that although not guilty of theft, there are offences under the Fraud Act 2006 which could be charged (see **Chapter 10**), and the bank could, of course, take civil proceedings to recover outstanding monies.

(e) *Other intangible property.* This phrase in the 1968 Act covers intangible property which is not, technically, a thing in action. An example is a patent or an application for a patent for a new drug or vaccine. This is because s 30 of the Patents Act 1977 states that they are not things in action but personal property. As a patent cannot be touched, it is clearly 'other intangible property'.

Land

Despite the definition of property in s 4(1) of the TA 1968 including a reference to 'real property', there are in fact only very limited circumstances in which land can be stolen.

Under s 4(2):

> A person cannot steal land, or things forming part of land and severed from it by him or by his directions, except in the following cases, that is to say—
>
> (a) when he is a trustee or personal representative, or is authorised by power of attorney, or as liquidator of a company, or otherwise, to sell or dispose of land belonging to another, and he appropriates the land or anything forming part of it by dealing with it in breach of the confidence reposed in him; or
>
> (b) when he is not in possession of the land and appropriates anything forming part of the land by severing it or causing it to be severed, or after it has been severed; or
>
> (c) when, being in possession of the land under a tenancy, he appropriates the whole or part of any fixture or structure let to be used with the land.

The effect of s 4(2) is that land cannot generally be stolen except in the specific circumstances set out in the rest of that section.

Under s 4(2)(a), a relevant situation would include where a person owns the land on trust for someone else. A common example would be where one joint owner of property forges the other owner's signature in order to sell the land they owned jointly. Another would be the executor of an estate, where the person who had died had left their house to a named beneficiary. The executor holds the land on trust until such time as it is formally transferred to the beneficiary. If they transferred the property into their own name by forging documentation, they could be liable for theft of the land.

Example

Florence dies, leaving her house, Bramble Cottage, to her granddaughter, Emma, who is aged 12. In her will, she appoints her nephew, Ray, as executor to hold the property on trust for Emma until she reaches 18 years of age. Ray forges a signature on the documentation and transfers the cottage into his own name. Ray may be liable for theft of the land.

Next, s 4(2)(b) provides an exception which applies to someone who is not in possession of the land; hence, this would not cover the owner or a tenant. This provision relates to the appropriation of anything forming part of the land by severing it or causing it to be severed, or after it has been severed. Thus, if a person went onto another's land and cut down a tree, this would be an exception to the usual rule that land cannot be stolen.

Example

Jade is annoyed that her neighbour is refusing to cut down a bush that overhangs her garden. She leans over the fence and chops down the bush. Jade may be guilty of theft as she has severed the bush from her neighbour's land.

Later that same day, Jade is walking through her local allotments when she sees a pile of vegetables that one of the gardeners has just dug up. She picks up several carrots and walks away. As Jade is not in possession of the allotment, she has committed theft because the carrots have been severed from the land.

Finally, s 4(2)(c) covers tenants who take something fixed to the land which they are not supposed to take.

Example

Gethan rents a house in the country. When he leaves the property, he takes the shelving from the kitchen (a fixture) and the greenhouse from the garden (a structure). Subject to the prosecution establishing the other four elements of the offence, Gethan is guilty of theft of these items.

Wild plants and flowers

The TA 1968 provides specifically the circumstances in which wild plants, mushrooms, flowers, fruit or foliage from a plant are deemed to be property and therefore capable of being stolen. Under s 4(3):

> A person who picks mushrooms growing wild on any land, or who picks flowers, fruit or foliage from a plant growing wild on any land, does not (although not in possession of the land) steal what he picks, unless he does it for reward or for sale or other commercial purpose.
>
> For purposes of this subsection 'mushroom' includes any fungus, and 'plant' includes any shrub or tree.

Set out below are some examples to illustrate when the thing appropriated amounts to property capable of being stolen under s 4(3):

Examples

(1) *Marina goes for a walk in the countryside and picks some buttercups and daisies growing on the side of the road.*

There is no property here. Marina has picked flowers that are growing wild, and s 4(3) specifically states that wild flowers are not capable of being stolen.

(2) *Whilst on her walk, Marina looks over a hedge and sees a large field full of tulips. She goes into the field and picks an armful before taking them home.*

There probably is property here that is capable of being stolen. As the tulips are in a field, they are highly likely to be growing commercially and are therefore not 'wild'.

(3) *Marina is aware of a farmer's field that has a large variety of wild mushrooms growing in it. She knows the local vegetarian restaurant specialises in mushroom dishes and therefore picks all the mushrooms she can find, intending to sell them to the restaurant.*

There is property here capable of being stolen. Although wild mushrooms are normally excluded, when Marina picks them, she does so for 'reward ... sale ... or other commercial purpose'.

Wild creatures

Section 4(4) of the TA 1968 covers situations when wild creatures may be stolen, as set out below:

> (4) Wild creatures, tamed or untamed, shall be regarded as property; but a person cannot steal a wild creature not tamed nor ordinarily kept in captivity, or the carcase of any such creature, unless either it has been reduced into possession by or on behalf of another person and possession of it has not since been lost or abandoned, or another person is in course of reducing it into possession.

It is apparent from the statutory provision that, although wild creatures are generally excluded as property, there are some exceptions.

Examples

(1) Hans breaks into the local zoo and takes a penguin. The penguin does amount to property as it is a wild creature, and s 4(4) states that wild creatures shall be regarded as property and can be stolen when they are ordinarily kept in captivity.

(2) Hans goes onto Lord Bridgerley's estate at night and poaches three salmon from the river that runs through it. The salmon cannot be stolen contrary to s 1 as they are neither tamed nor ordinarily kept in captivity.

(3) Lord Bridgerley is shooting grouse on his estate. When a grouse is shot and falls to the ground, Hans, who has been hiding in the bushes, takes it before Lord Bridgerley can get to it. The grouse is property for the purposes of the TA 1968. Although normally Hans would not be able to steal it (because it is a wild creature not tamed nor kept in captivity), he falls within the exception stated in s 4(4) as Lord Bridgerley is in the course of reducing the grouse into possession – he merely has to go and pick it up.

What else cannot be stolen?

The definition of property in s 4(1) is very wide, but case law provides two examples of what cannot be stolen.

In *Oxford v Moss* [1979] Crim LR 119, the defendant went into an office and read the examination paper that he was due to sit in the next few days. He then replaced it in the filing cabinet where he had found it. This was not theft of the actual paper because he had no intention permanently to deprive the university of that piece of paper (see below). The court held that the only thing he could have 'taken' therefore was the information on the paper, namely, the examination questions. However, the court held that this confidential information was not property within the meaning of the TA 1968.

In *Low v Blease* [1975] Crim LR 513, the court confirmed that electricity could not be stolen as it was not property. Although there is a separate offence under s 13 of the TA 1968 to deal with unlawful extraction of electricity, it is not theft contrary to s 1(1) of the 1968 Act.

9.2.2.3 Belonging to another

The final part of the actus reus of theft is that the property appropriated must 'belong to another'. Obviously property belongs to its legal owner, but under s 5(1) of the TA 1968, the definition is wider than this and property can actually belong to several different people.

Section 5(1) of the TA 1968 states:

> Property shall be regarded as belonging to any person having possession or control of it, or having in it any proprietary right or interest (not being an equitable interest arising only from an agreement to transfer or grant an interest).

There are many examples of where a thief may take property from someone other than a sole owner, and set out below are illustrations of this point.

Examples

(1) Cheung lends his mobile phone to his friend, Liu. Liu hands it to his partner, Xi, so he can use the navigation app to check their route. Joel grabs the phone from Xi and runs off. Joel has taken the property from Cheung (the owner) but also from Liu, as he has possession of the phone at the time of the theft, and Xi, who has control of it.

(2) Anwar and Kay hold property on trust for the benefit of Clare and Balbinder. As a consequence, the property belongs to four people – Anwar and Kay are the legal owners; and Clare and Balbinder are the beneficial or equitable owners. Thus, if a defendant takes the trust property, they have stolen it from all four people.

Establishing whether property belongs to another is usually straightforward. However, it is always important, when considering whether the property belongs to another, to remember the extended definition and that it potentially includes people other than the actual legal owner.

Companies

In this context, it is relevant to emphasise the position of a company. Legally, a company is a separate legal entity which means the company can sue and be sued in its own right. Therefore, if one of the company directors takes some of the company assets, they have stolen property 'belonging to another' (the company). This is so even if the people who took the property are the sole shareholders in the company and therefore own it completely. Because the company is a separate legal entity, the property belongs to it and therefore falls within s 5(1).

Theft of own property

It is also possible for a legal owner to be guilty of stealing property, perhaps from another legal owner, or from someone else who has an interest in the property or possession or control of it. This may seem illogical as, if property belongs to the defendant, how can they be said to have appropriated property belonging to another? It is important, however, to bear in mind the extended definition of this term under s 5(1).

Example

(1) Dorothy owns a book which she lends to Arthur for one week in return for £1. However, after two days she takes her book back. She remains the owner of the book at all times, but by the terms of the loan she has parted with possession and control of the book to Arthur. By taking the book back early, she has appropriated property 'belonging to another'. Section 5(1) clearly states that property belongs to someone in possession or control of it. The actus reus of theft is present.

(2) *Barbara and Owen own a horse jointly. Barbara forges Owen's signature on a sale agreement transferring ownership of the horse to her. Although Barbara is the joint owner of the horse, Owen (as a co-owner) has a 'proprietary right or interest' in the animal, so the horse belongs to him for the purposes of the TA 1968.*

The concept of someone being able to steal their own property has been accepted by the courts in a number of decisions. For example, in *R v Turner (No 2)* [1971] 2 All ER 441, T took his car to B's garage for repairs. B did the work and T then removed his car from the garage without paying for the repairs. T argued that he could not be guilty as he had appropriated his own property and so the actus reus of theft was not satisfied. Despite this, T was convicted. On appeal, the Court of Appeal in *Turner (No 2)* held that the garage had a 'lien' over the car. Basically, this means it is lawful for the garage to retain possession of the car until T has paid his bill. As a consequence, B lawfully had possession or control of the car and hence the property did belong to another under s 5(1). T was therefore guilty of theft by dishonestly removing it, and the fact that T owned the car did not prevent him from being liable.

The principle that a legal owner can be guilty of stealing their own property (because it also belongs to another) is clearly of particular importance when dealing with jointly owned property, for example, partnership property. In addition, it is relevant when dealing with theft by trustees, as although they are the legal owners of trust property, that property also belongs to the beneficiaries who have an equitable interest in it.

Timing of 'belonging to another'

When considering the offence of theft, it is important to remember that the property must belong to another *at the time* of the dishonest appropriation, as all five elements of the offence must be established simultaneously. The fact that the property belonged to another one minute before the dishonest appropriation does not give rise to liability. If ownership, possession and control of the property had already passed to the defendant at the time of their dishonest appropriation, they are not guilty of theft.

This is particularly problematic with items such as food (because obviously it disappears into the defendant's stomach) and petrol, which mixes with the petrol inside the vehicle's tank. This issue may arise in a scenario where the defendant eats a meal and then decides not to pay for it. As they only form the mens rea of theft after the meal, do they dishonestly appropriate property belonging to another?

To answer the question and understand the criminal law position, we must turn to the civil law for assistance. Under the law of contract, property (or ownership in the property) passes when the parties intend it to. The effect is that property in petrol passes at the moment a person starts to fill their tank; and with the meal, at the moment they begin to eat it. This is because, at that point, the petrol and the food are irretrievably mixed with the petrol in the tank and the contents of the stomach respectively, and it is not possible to retrieve them in the exact same condition. A person is still contractually obliged to pay and can be sued for the debt, but that is a question of civil law not criminal law.

This issue was considered in the case of *Edwards v Ddin* [1976] 1 WLR 942. The defendant entered a garage and filled up his car with petrol, intending to pay for it. However, he then realised that he did not have the money to pay for it and drove off. The Divisional Court held that the defendant had not appropriated property belonging to another. It concluded that at the time the defendant was dishonest, when he decided not to pay, the property had already passed to him. As a result, the actus reus element of belonging to another did not co-exist with the mens rea elements of theft and so the defendant was not guilty of theft.

Example

Errol drives into a petrol station to fill up his car. Because he is short of money, Errol has already decided before he enters the garage that he is not going to pay; thus, he is dishonest. As soon as he starts to dispense the petrol, Errol is guilty of theft. This is because when he appropriates the petrol (by assuming the rights of the owner), at this moment, the petrol still belongs to the garage and so combines with his mens rea to make him guilty of the offence.

It is apparent from the case of *Edwards v Ddin* and the illustration above that the crucial question is when does the defendant form their dishonest intent? There are clearly practical difficulties in establishing this, and so, as a fall-back provision, the offence of making off without payment (TA 1978, s 3) was introduced, which is considered later in this textbook.

Similar problems to those identified above can arise with money (cash). As far as civil law is concerned, ownership of cash transfers when it is handed over. If the prosecution can prove that a defendant was dishonest all along, there is no difficulty in establishing the coincidence of the actus reus and mens rea of theft, but what if this is not possible?

Example

A group of people wish to attend an important rugby match. Luke agrees to organise the trip and collect money from Xavier, Yvette and Zara in order to buy the tickets and hire a car. When he collected the money, Luke fully intended to use it as he should. However, he changes his mind and absconds with it. Has Luke appropriated property belonging to another?

The first important point to note is that when Luke received the money, he was going to use it for the intended purposes. At that stage, therefore, although he committed the actus reus of theft (he appropriated property belonging to another), he lacked the mens rea element of dishonesty.

It is only once Luke has received the money that he decides to abscond with it. Under civil law, at the time of his dishonesty, ownership of the money has passed to him and he also has possession and control of it. Luke still owes Xavier, Yvette and Zara the equivalent sum they paid him, but that is a matter of civil law. Luke is in breach of contract by not providing the tickets and car, and therefore the three victims can sue for the return of their money. But how are the prosecution to prove that he dishonestly appropriated property belonging to another in order to establish a criminal charge of theft?

A potential solution to this problem is to use s 5(3) of the TA 1968 which is discussed in the next section.

Obligation to deal with property in a particular way

Section 5(3) of the TA 1968 states:

> Where a person receives property from or on account of another, and is under an obligation to the other to retain and deal with that property or its proceeds in a particular way, the property or proceeds shall be regarded (as against him) as belonging to the other.

This was introduced to cover a situation where the owner (A) parts with their property to B on the understanding that B must deal with that property in a particular way. If s 5(3) applies then, contrary to the normal rule that ownership of cash passes when it is handed over, ownership of the property will remain with the person who hands it over, thus making it possible to establish a coincidence of all five elements of theft.

In order for s 5(3) to apply, the accused must be under a legal obligation, not just a moral one. If the accused is under no such legal obligation and they can lawfully do what they like with the property, it does not belong to another and therefore cannot be stolen. For example, in *DPP v Huskinson* [1988] Crim LR 620, the defendant had applied for and received Housing Benefit. He received £479 but paid only £200 to his landlord even though his rent arrears amounted to more than £800. He spent the rest of the money on himself. He was charged with theft, but the Divisional Court held he was not guilty. Huskinson had ownership, possession and control of the money and therefore the only way the money could belong to another was if s 5(3) of the TA 1968 applied. The court held that it did not as there was no legal obligation to deal with the money in a particular way because there was nothing in the Social Security regulations to say that he must spend the Housing Benefit money on rent.

The case of *R v Hall* [1973] 1 QB 126 provides further insight into when such an obligation arises. In this case, the defendant was in business as a travel agent. He received money from various clients to pay for flights and paid the money into his general business account. However, the flights were not booked and no money was refunded. The Court of Appeal decided that he had not committed theft. Although the defendant was under a contractual duty to buy his clients their tickets in due course, he was not required to use the money they specifically had given him, or its proceeds, for that purpose. He was therefore not under an obligation to deal with the property or its proceeds in a particular way and s 5(3) did not apply.

By way of contrast, Lord Edmund-Davies quoted an example given in the Eighth Report of the Criminal Law Revision Committee where the Committee felt that s 5(3) would apply. The example given was that of a treasurer of a holiday fund who misapplies the fund or its proceeds. There appears to have been an obligation to keep the money or its proceeds in a separate fund. Because the Act refers to 'or its proceeds', the exact same notes and coins that had been given need not be kept separate as long as the understanding was that an equivalent sum would be. The legal obligation is to use that fund for the particular purpose.

Indeed, in *R v Wain* [1995] 2 Cr App R 660, the Court of Appeal upheld the conviction of the defendant who had misappropriated money which he had raised for charity and collected in a special bank account. He then transferred it into his own account. He handed a cheque over to the charity drawn on his account, but the cheque was not met as there were insufficient funds in the account. He was charged with theft of the money raised for charity – £2,833.25. The Court held that the defendant was clearly under an obligation to retain, if not the actual notes and coins, at least their proceeds, namely the money credited to the account he had opened. The money remained the proceeds of the notes and coins collected even after the transfer into his own account, and therefore belonged to the charity by virtue of s 5(3).

Returning to the example considered above:

Example

Continuing the previous example, you will recall that Luke collected money from Xavier, Yvette and Zara in order to buy tickets and to hire a car. When he did so, Luke fully intended to use the money as he should; however, he then changes his mind and absconds with it.

Whether s 5(3) of the TA 1968 applies to Luke will depend on what the agreement between the parties was. If it was understood by all concerned that Luke would keep the money given to him, or its equivalent, separate from his own and use it for the purpose of buying the tickets and the hiring of the car, then s 5(3) would apply. However, if it was understood that the only obligation on Luke was for him ultimately to provide the tickets and car, but there was no understanding that he should deal with the 'money or its proceeds' in that particular way, s 5(3) would not apply. In this instance, Xavier, Yvette and Zara would merely have a civil claim against Luke for the return of the money owed.

It is clear that a difficult distinction must be made, as a question of fact and civil law, between:

(a) the case where the defendant's obligation to the victim is to use the property or proceeds in a particular way; and

(b) the case where the defendant has a mere contractual obligation to the victim, not relating to the specific property or proceeds.

In (a) the property still belongs to the victim and so (if all other elements are established) the defendant can be guilty of theft. In (b) the property belongs to the defendant alone and so they cannot be guilty of theft, unless of course the prosecution can prove that they had already formed a dishonest intent at the time the money was handed over.

The important point here is that s 5(3) provides a way round problems concerning whether cash belongs to another where there is no evidence that the defendant was dishonest throughout.

Abandoned property

The final point on this element of the actus reus relates to abandoned property. If property has been abandoned, it does not belong to anyone; consequently, it does not 'belong to another' and cannot be stolen. Whether the property is abandoned depends on the intention of the owner when they disposed of it. If they intended to relinquish their interest in the property entirely without giving any interest to another, they have abandoned it. This will obviously depend on the facts in every case. However, it is important to distinguish abandoned property from that which the owner has merely lost.

Example

If Uzair loses his wallet, searches for it but then gives up the search, the wallet is not abandoned. It is still Uzair's property as he has not relinquished his interest in it. He would still like the wallet back – he has just given up hope of finding it. If anyone else finds the wallet, they will be appropriating property belonging to another.

On the other hand, if Uzair has bought a new wallet and throws his old one into a hedge, it is likely that the old wallet has been abandoned, and anyone who subsequently appropriated it would not be guilty of theft as the property does not belong to another – it is 'ownerless' or abandoned.

In *Williams v Phillips* (1957) 41 Cr App R 5, the Divisional Court was required to consider whether rubbish left outside a house for a local authority to collect could be regarded as abandoned property. The court held that, where it was left outside for a specific purpose, here for the local authority to collect, it remained property belonging to the householder. Moreover, once the rubbish was placed into a local authority waste vehicle, it then became the property of the local authority.

This question was revisited in *R (Ricketts) v Basildon Magistrates' Court* [2011] 1 Cr App R 15. The claimant was caught on CCTV, in the early hours of the morning, taking clothing that had been left outside two charity shops. It was held that the property either still belonged to the unknown donors of the clothing, or, alternatively, it would be inferred that in one of the cases the charity shop had taken possession of the clothing when it had been placed in its bin outside the shop. Importantly, in both of the above cases, the Divisional Court agreed that the property had not been abandoned.

9.2.2.4 Overview of actus reus

Before moving on to consider the mens rea elements of theft, the following flowchart summarises the issues that may arise in relation to the actus reus.

Figure 9.1 Actus reus of theft

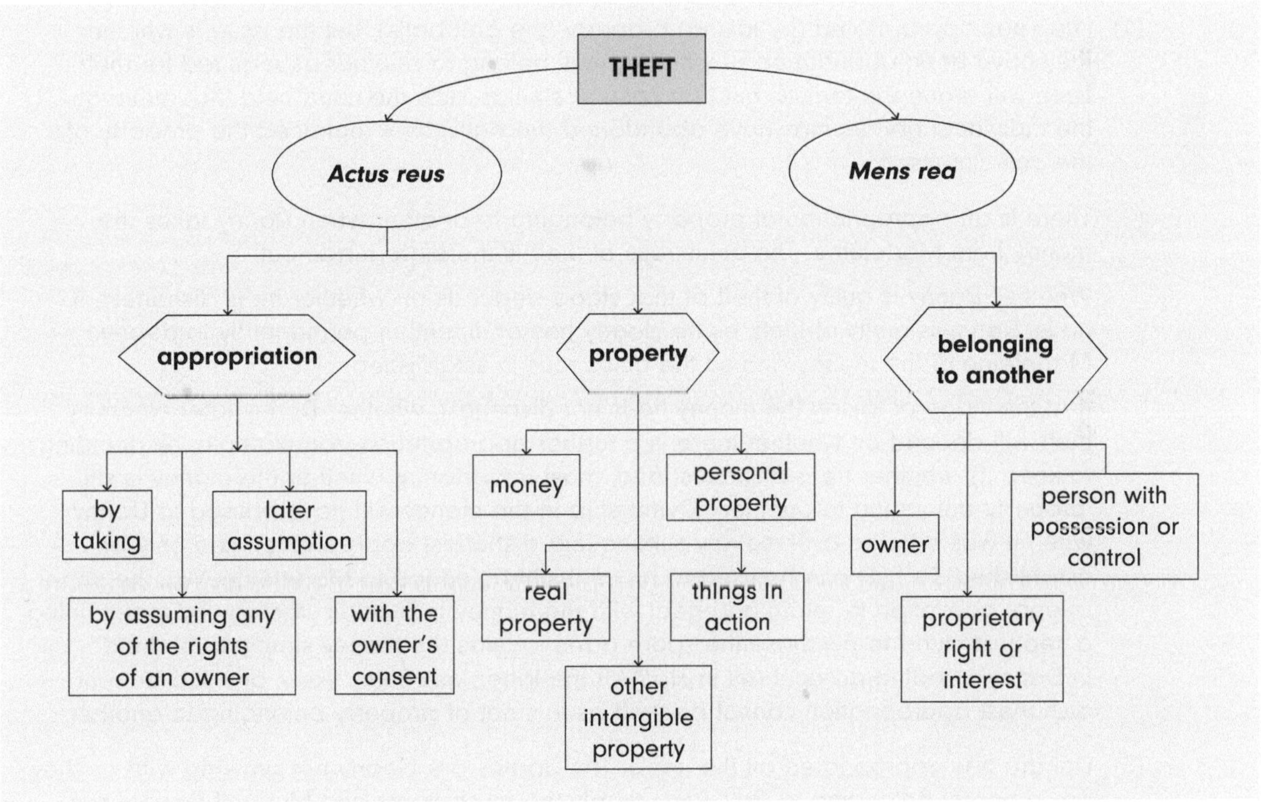

Now apply your knowledge of the actus reus elements in the following activity.

ACTIVITY

Has there been an appropriation of property belonging to another in the following circumstances?

(1) Leon goes to a local golf club at night with sub-aqua diving equipment and retrieves a large number of golf balls from the bottom of a lake on the course, which he sells online. The balls have been left in the lake after being mis-hit by golfers.

(2) Danny, a mechanic, agrees to carry out repairs to Madeleine's car. The agreement requires Madeleine to pay £100 to Danny in advance, to enable Danny to buy the necessary spare parts. Shortly after Madeleine has paid this sum, Danny goes out of business and is unable to perform the contract or to return Madeleine's money to her.

(3) Deirdre has a fruit and vegetable stall in a London street market. She picks the apples from trees in Guy's orchard and the mushrooms from a wood on land also owned by Guy. In addition, she sells bluebells picked from the wood and has uprooted some of the bluebell plants to put in her own garden.

COMMENT

(1) Leon has appropriated (by taking) property (the golf balls), but the issue is whether they have been abandoned or whether they belong to another as required for theft. Leon will argue the former, but in a case of similar facts the court held that although the individual golfers may have abandoned the balls, they remained the property of the golf club itself.

(2) There is an appropriation of property belonging to another when Danny takes the money from Madeleine. The actus reus of theft is therefore made out.

Whether Danny is guilty of theft at that stage depends on whether he is dishonest. If he is, Danny is guilty of theft, as he clearly has an intention permanently to deprive Madeleine of the money and so the actus reus is established.

If at the stage of taking the money he is not dishonest, whether Danny later commits theft will depend on whether there is a further appropriation (for example, by deciding to keep it), whether he is dishonest and, most importantly, whether the money is still 'property belonging to another'. Ownership in the money will have passed to Danny when it was handed over, so any subsequent dishonest appropriation can only be established if s 5(3) can be used to prove it still belonged to Madeleine. Was he under a legal obligation to retain and deal with the money in a particular way by maintaining a separate fund to purchase the spare parts, or was the money simply to be held in Danny's trading account (as in *Hall*)? If the latter, as seems likely, any subsequent dishonest appropriation cannot be theft as it is not of property belonging to another.

(3) Deirdre has appropriated all the items. The apples are clearly not growing wild as they are property belonging to Guy. Presumably the mushrooms and bluebell flowers are wild, and so s 4(3) gives immunity from the crime of theft in respect of these. However, the immunity is lost if the picking (as here) is done for commercial gain. As for the bluebell plants she uprooted, this is not done for commercial gain, but because it is more than mere 'picking', as she has taken the whole plant, s 4(3) will not assist her.

Having finished our consideration of the actus reus of theft, we shall move on to analyse the mens rea.

9.2.3 Mens rea

It is clear that, after *Gomez* and *Hinks*, it is usually very easy for people to commit the actus reus of theft. However, it is important to remember that, in order to secure a conviction for this offence, there are also mens rea elements to be established, namely, dishonesty and an intention permanently to deprive.

9.2.3.1 Dishonesty

In many cases of theft, whether someone is dishonest is the key issue in determining their guilt. Although the TA 1968 provides no working definition of this term, it does give a partial definition of three circumstances that will *not* amount to dishonesty and one circumstance that *may* still be regarded as dishonest.

Dishonesty under statute

Section 2(1) lists the three situations which, if applicable, mean that the defendant is not dishonest, and these should always be considered first. If any of the provisions are relevant, that section will apply.

Section 2(1) of the Theft Act 1968 provides:

> (1) A person's appropriation of property belonging to another is not to be regarded as dishonest–
>
> (a) if he appropriates the property in the belief that he has in law the right to deprive the other of it, on behalf of himself or of a third person; or
>
> (b) if he appropriates the property in the belief that he would have the other's consent if the other knew of the appropriation and the circumstances of it; or
>
> (c) (except where the property came to him as trustee or personal representative) if he appropriates the property in the belief that the person to whom the property belongs cannot be discovered by taking reasonable steps.

In each case the test is purely subjective, so the issue is whether the individual defendant believed that one of the situations outlined in the subsection existed, whether it was a reasonable belief or not. It does not matter whether *in fact* the particular circumstance existed, as dishonesty is a mens rea concept.

Dealing first with s 2(1)(a), where the defendant relies on a right in law, an example would be where the defendant thought the property the victim had was theirs and, furthermore, that they had the legal right to take it back.

> ***Example***
>
> *Musa has lent £20 to Taiwo. Taiwo has not repaid Musa despite frequent requests for him to do so. Musa therefore takes £20 from Taiwo's wallet without his knowledge. In this instance, Musa may argue that he does have the right in law to deprive Taiwo of the £20 because it was a debt owed to him.*

It is because of this subsection that people who appropriate property which belongs to themselves (see *R v Turner (No 2)* discussed when studying the element of belonging to another above) are often not liable for theft. Even if the property does belong to another under s 5(1) of the TA 1968, the owner usually believes that they have the right in law to take it back, meaning they are not dishonest. Note that if the defendant knew they did not have a legal right but thought they had a moral entitlement to take the property back, that would not suffice for s 2(1)(a).

Next, under s 2(1)(b), the defendant is not dishonest if they believed the owner would have consented had they known of the circumstances.

Example

Suki has a ticket to a music concert but cannot attend. Dana has lost her ticket, and because Suki is a friend, she decides to take Suki's ticket from the kitchen table where it has been left. Dana may argue that she was not dishonest because she honestly believed that Suki would have consented to the taking of the ticket if she had known of the circumstances.

The circumstances are important. The court is far more likely to hold that the accused was dishonest if the ticket was sold and the proceeds retained, rather than being taken knowing that, otherwise, the ticket would be wasted. It is also important to be aware that the defendant must believe the other *would* have consented. An argument by the defendant that they believed the other ought to have consented, or possibly/probably would have consented, is not enough.

The third situation in which the defendant may rely on their honest belief is where the owner cannot be discovered by taking reasonable steps – s 2(1)(c).

Example

Ari finds a watch in the street. He looks around and cannot see anyone the watch could possibly belong to. There is nothing on it, such as an inscription, to indicate to whom the watch belongs, and so Ari decides to keep it. If he honestly believed that the owner could not be found by taking reasonable steps and the jury accepts this, Ari will not be dishonest.

Again, it is important to remember that the issue is not whether the owner could have been traced, for example, by contacting the police. This is a mens rea issue, and so the question is whether this particular defendant honestly believed that the owner could not be traced. As with s 2(1)(a) and (b), there is no need for the belief to be reasonable.

In s 2(1)(c) scenarios, however, if the defendant subsequently realises the owner can be found (perhaps, for example, because the loss is publicised in the local paper), they could now be guilty of theft. This is because they appropriate the property by keeping it (see s 3(1) of the TA 1968 above), it belongs to another, they intend permanently to deprive (see below) and they can no longer argue s 2(1)(c) so they are probably dishonest.

Lastly, in relation to s 2(1)(c), note that the provisions do not apply when the property came to the accused as a trustee or personal representative. Therefore, for example, if the defendant was a trustee who was unable to trace a beneficiary, they would not be able to claim they were not dishonest under s 2(1)(c) if they kept the property for their own personal use.

Section 2(1) only covers these three very specific situations where there will be a lack of dishonesty. The only other statutory provision relevant to the issue of dishonesty can be found in s 2(2) of the TA 1968. This provides that:

(2) A person's appropriation of property belonging to another may be dishonest notwithstanding that he is willing to pay for the property.

It is apparent from this section that willingness to pay is not necessarily an answer to an allegation of dishonesty. Section 2(2) is not stating that the person is dishonest despite a willingness to pay; it is saying that a willingness to pay is not an automatic defence to a charge of theft – it will be a question of fact for the jury to decide. The application of this subsection can produce different outcomes depending on the evidence.

Examples

(1) *Lucy is at work on a hot sunny day and is very thirsty. She notices that someone has left a carton of orange juice on the table. Lucy takes the orange juice and drinks it, leaving one pound in its place to pay for it. Lucy may be able to argue a lack of dishonesty under s 2(1)(b) as outlined above. Furthermore, Lucy's willingness to pay may be a factor in helping the jury conclude that she was not dishonest.*

(2) *Petra owns a valuable vase valued at £15,000. Hannah wants to buy it, but Petra refuses to sell it. Knowing Petra's views, Hannah takes the vase, leaving £15,000 in payment. Hannah argues a lack of dishonesty due to her willingness to pay, but on these facts, it is unlikely that she will escape liability. Having been directed by the judge that a willingness to pay is not automatic proof of lack of dishonesty, the jury may well conclude that she was dishonest because of the value of the vase and her knowledge that Petra did not want to sell.*

In the vast majority of cases, the issue of dishonesty will be clear but, if not, it is apparent that the assistance provided by the provisions of the TA 1968 is limited. This will rarely cause difficulties in practice, as having heard the evidence in the case, the jury will apply their common sense and experience to the question of whether the defendant was dishonest. However, on those rare occasions where the jury does need further assistance, there is other guidance available.

Dishonesty under case law

There are some situations where dishonesty is less than clear, and where the magistrates or the jury may have differing views on whether the defendant is dishonest. For example, the defendant who takes a pen from the stationery cupboard at work to use at home, or who receives a small overpayment in change at their local supermarket and keeps it.

In each of these situations, if the defendant argues they were not dishonest, the first place to start would be s 2(1) of the TA 1968. However, if that does not assist, the jury can be referred to a test known as the '*Ivey* test' to help them to resolve the issue.

Previously, the test for dishonesty had, since 1982, been the *Ghosh* test, as set out by the Court of Appeal in *R v Ghosh* [1982] QB 1053. However, there were concerns about this approach as a consequence of which the Supreme Court felt the need, some 35 years later in 2017, to replace it and suggest it had been the wrong test all along. Set out below is an extract from Lord Lane's judgment in *Ghosh*.

> This brings us to the heart of the problem. Is 'dishonestly' in section 1 of the Theft Act 1968 intended to characterise a course of conduct? Or is it intended to describe a state of mind? If the former, then we can well understand that it could be established independently of the knowledge or belief of the accused. But if, as we think, it is the latter, then the knowledge and belief of the accused are at the root of the problem.
>
> Take for example a man who comes from a country where public transport is free. On his first day here, he travels on a bus. He gets off without paying. He never had any intention of paying. His mind is clearly honest; but his conduct, judged objectively by what he has done, is dishonest. It seems to us that in using the word 'dishonestly' in the Theft Act 1968, Parliament cannot have intended to catch dishonest conduct in that sense, that is to say conduct to which no moral obloquy could possibly attach. This is sufficiently established by the partial definition in section 2 of the Theft Act itself. All the matters covered by section 2(1) relate to the belief of the accused. Section 2(2) relates to his willingness to pay. A man's belief and his willingness to pay are things which can only be established subjectively. It is difficult to see how a partially subjective definition can be made to work in harness with the test which in all other respects is wholly objective.
>
> If we are right that dishonesty is something in the mind of the accused (what Professor Glanville Williams calls 'a special mental state'), then if the mind of the accused is honest, it cannot be deemed dishonest merely because members of the jury would have regarded it as dishonest to embark on that course of conduct. So we would reject the simple uncomplicated approach that the test is purely objective, however attractive from the practical point of view that solution may be.
>
> There remains the objection that to adopt a subjective test is to abandon all standards but that of the accused himself, and to bring about a state of affairs in which 'Robin Hood would be no robber': *Reg v Greenstein* [1975] 1 WLR 1353. This objection misunderstands the nature of the subjective test. It is no defence for a man to say 'I knew that what I was doing is generally regarded as dishonest; but I do not regard it as dishonest myself. Therefore I am not guilty.' What he is however entitled to say is 'I did not know that anybody would regard what I was doing as dishonest.' He may not be believed; just as he may not be believed if he sets up 'a claim of right' under section 2(1) of the Theft Act 1968 ... But if he is believed, or raises a real doubt about the matter, the jury cannot be sure that he was dishonest.

Having considered what dishonesty involved, the judges set out the *Ghosh* test which was then used for many years to determine this aspect of mens rea. The test required the jury to ask themselves two questions:

(a) Was what the defendant did dishonest according to the standards of reasonable and honest people?

(b) If so, did the defendant realise that reasonable and honest people would regard what they did as dishonest?

Only if the answer to both questions is 'Yes' could the jury find the defendant to have been dishonest.

The *Ghosh* test had its critics over the years and the issue was considered by the Law Commission on more than one occasion. Many commentators felt that there should be more guidance on the meaning of dishonesty and that different juries might apply the test in different ways.

In 2017, the Supreme Court intervened and, interestingly, the Court did so in a civil, not criminal, case. In *Ivey v Genting Casinos* [2017] 3 WLR 1212, the claimant, a professional gambler, sued the defendant casino which had failed to pay him a sum in excess of £9 million which he had won over two days playing a card game called Punto Banco. The casino refused to pay on the basis that he had cheated - and cheating was a breach of the casino rules. The trial judge, Court of Appeal and finally the Supreme Court all found in favour of the defendant. There was no requirement for the Court to establish that he had been dishonest, but the Supreme Court took the opportunity to review the criminal test for dishonesty as laid down in *Ghosh*. It decided that the criminal test for dishonesty should be the same as the civil test - basically the first limb of *Ghosh* but not the second. The test is set out in para 74 of the judgment of Lord Hughes - with whom all the other judges agreed:

> When dishonesty is in question, the fact-finding tribunal must first ascertain (subjectively) the actual state of mind of the individual's knowledge or belief as to the facts. The reasonableness or otherwise of his belief is a matter of evidence (often in practice determinative) going to whether he held the belief, but it is not an additional requirement that his belief must be reasonable: the question is whether it is genuinely held. When once his actual state of mind as to knowledge or belief as to facts is established, the question whether his conduct was honest or dishonest is to be determined by the fact-finder by applying the (objective) standards of ordinary decent people. There is no requirement that the defendant must appreciate that what he has done is, by those standards, dishonest.

The effect was that the Supreme Court in *Ivey* removed the second limb of *Ghosh* and the defendant is now judged on the basis of their actual knowledge or belief as to the facts.

Set out below are various scenarios, together with a consideration of whether the accused is likely to be found guilty under the *Ivey* test.

Table 9.1 Examples of dishonesty

Scenario	Dishonest under *Ivey*?
Alicia takes £10 from the till at the shop where she works to buy cigarettes.	Alicia's actions are clearly dishonest by the standards of ordinary, decent people.
Alicia takes £10 from the till because she has forgotten her bus fare. She leaves a note for her boss explaining the situation and that she will repay the money the next day.	This example is less clear. Factors such as whether Alicia actually intends to repay the money as soon as she can, whether she knows if borrowing from the till is allowed under any circumstances and her relationship with her boss would all be relevant to her (subjective) view of the facts. Having determined this, the question is whether Alicia was (objectively) dishonest, and this will depend upon the jury's assessment of the situation.
Alicia takes £10 from the till because she has forgotten her bus fare. She is aware from company policy that it is forbidden to take money from the till under any circumstances.	In this scenario, Alicia is aware of the company policy forbidding the taking of money, so she is likely to be found dishonest.
Alicia takes £10 from the till because her bus is not running due to poor weather. Her route home, had she walked, would have been through a crime-ridden area late at night. She is aware from company policy that it is forbidden to take money under the till under any circumstances, but she repays the £10 the next day.	The outcome of this scenario would depend upon the weight the court gives to Alicia's particular circumstances given that she knows of the company policy forbidding the taking of money from the till.

Overview of dishonesty

Dishonesty and the *Ivey* test are vital concepts because they can be applied to all crimes that have a mens rea of dishonesty. These include not only theft, but also other offences against property such as fraud and making off without payment, burglary and robbery (see later in the textbook).

To conclude, when deciding if the accused is dishonest, the court should first determine if the dishonesty is clear, for example, a shoplifting scenario. If so, that is the end of the matter and the defendant will be guilty of theft. If not, the court will refer to the partial definitions contained in s 2 of the TA 1968 for guidance; only if these do not assist should the jury or magistrates turn to the common law test from the *Ivey* case.

The flowchart set out below will assist your understanding of dishonesty.

Figure 9.2 Examples of dishonesty

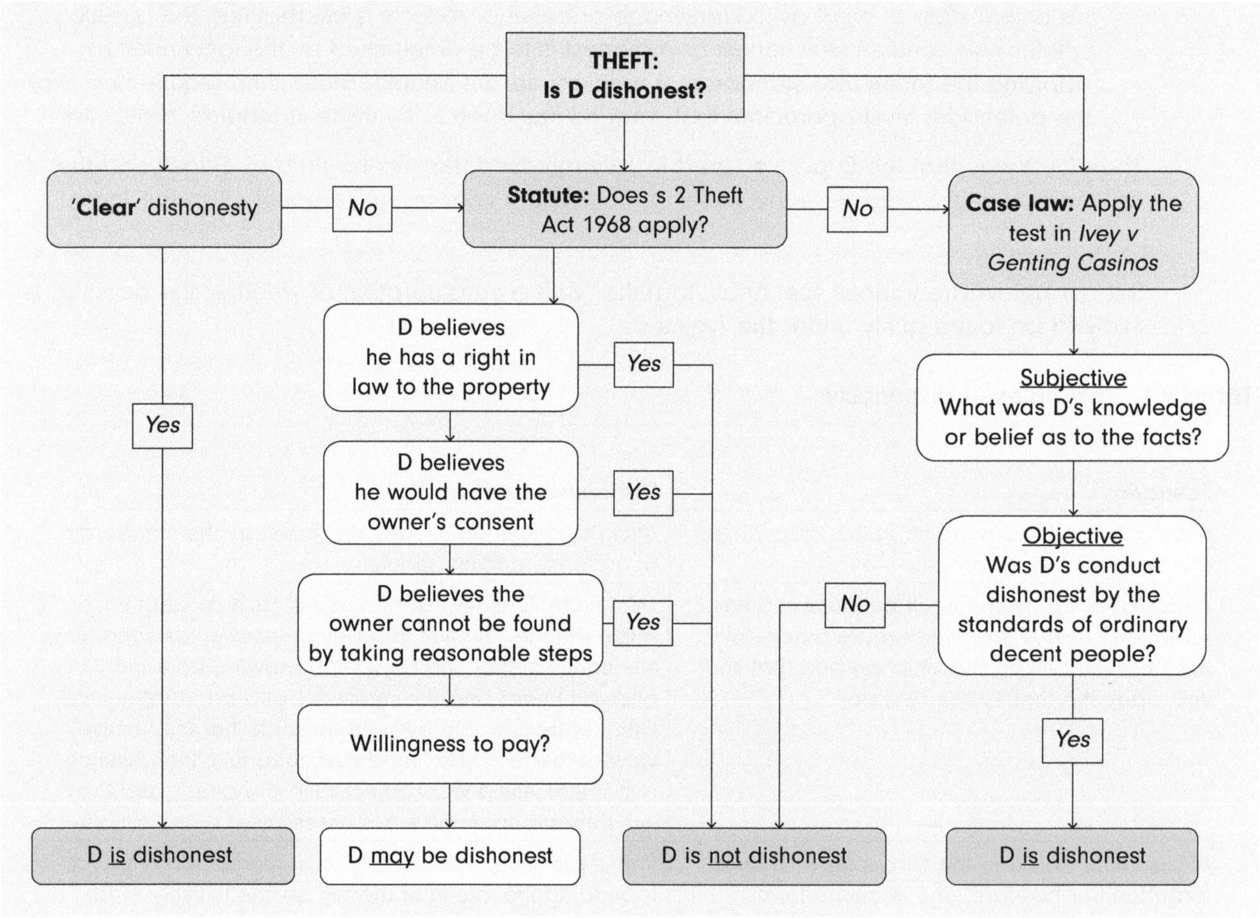

We will complete our consideration of dishonesty issues with an activity.

ACTIVITY

Has the defendant dishonestly appropriated property belonging to another in the following circumstances?

(1) Richard, while walking to work, takes a newspaper from his newsagent's display counter without paying. He leaves a note saying what he has done, giving his name and address, and asking the newsagent to add the cost to his next bill.

(2) Philip owes his ex-wife, Iona, maintenance arrears amounting to £500. While Iona is picking up their children from Philip's home where they have been spending the weekend, she removes an antique carriage clock belonging to Philip, which she knows is worth almost £500. When questioned later by the police, Iona admits taking the clock and says: 'It's no more than he owes me'.

(3) Donna, a shopper in a supermarket, removes a tin of baked beans from the shelf and places it in her jacket pocket. She then leaves the shop without paying for the beans.

COMMENT

(1) It is unlikely that Richard has acted dishonestly. Section 2(2) provides that a defendant may be dishonest, notwithstanding his willingness to pay. However, Richard may well honestly have believed that the owner would consent to his actions, and so would not be dishonest – s 2(1)(b). Even if this is not the case, applying the test in *Ivey*, it is possible that a jury would decide that reasonable and honest people would not regard Richard's actions as dishonest.

(2) If prosecuted, Iona may claim that she has not acted dishonestly and will rely on s 2(1)(a) – she believed that she had a legal right to take the clock to satisfy the maintenance arrears owing to her. The only question for the jury is whether Iona genuinely believed she had that right. If she did, she is not dishonest and is innocent of theft. The jury are not determining whether her belief would have been held by a reasonable person. However, if Iona thought she only had a moral claim, she would not be able to rely on s 2(1)(a), so the jury would apply the *Ivey* test to her situation.

(3) Clearly, if Donna put the beans in her pocket intending never to pay for them, then she has acted dishonestly. On the other hand, if she had placed the beans in her pocket absent-mindedly, she is not dishonest. This is a question of fact for the jury. This is not a case where it would be either appropriate or necessary for the judge to give the jury a direction in the *Ivey* form.

9.2.3.2 Intention permanently to deprive

The final element the prosecution must prove is that the accused intended to permanently deprive the other of the property that they have appropriated. In most cases a jury will not need any guidance on the phrase 'intention of permanently depriving' used in s 1(1) of the TA 1968, and the words will just be given their ordinary meaning.

Examples

(1) Sunil takes Ashley's sandwich when he is not looking and eats it.

(2) As (1) above, but Ashley notices what Sunil has done and retrieves his sandwich before Sunil eats it.

(3) Miho wants to mow her lawn but her lawnmower is broken. She goes next door and borrows Hugh's without telling him. She returns it after she has finished.

There is clearly an intention to permanently deprive in Example (1); on the other hand, in Example (3), there is no such intention as Miho always intended to return the lawnmower after she had used it. This illustrates that, generally speaking, a person is not liable for theft if they intend only to borrow something (subject to s 6(1) of the TA 1968: see below). There is also an intention permanently to deprive in Example (2). The fact that Ashley retrieves his sandwich before it is consumed is irrelevant. The intention permanently to deprive is part of the mens rea, not the actus reus of the offence, and so whether someone was in fact permanently deprived of their property is immaterial. Sunil clearly intended permanently to deprive Ashley of his sandwich when he appropriated it, and this is sufficient.

Although usually a straightforward matter, this element of the mens rea can sometimes cause difficulties. Before analysing the statutory provision relating to intention permanently to deprive under s 6 of the TA 1968, there are two general points to note.

(1) It is possible to intend permanently to deprive someone who has only a limited interest in the property.

Example

Pierre lends Salome his laptop for one week. Pierre is still the owner of the laptop, but Salome has possession and control of it. If Jo takes the laptop from Salome, intending to return it to Pierre after the week is over, she intended permanently to deprive Salome of her interest if she was aware that Salome had the use of the laptop only for a week.

(2) It is necessary to check whether the defendant intended permanently to deprive the owner of the specific thing that they have appropriated.

Example

Anya is thirsty and takes Cliff's can of lemonade, intending to replace it later with another one. Here, Anya has an intention permanently to deprive as she always intended to deprive Cliff of the specific can of lemonade that she took, and this is sufficient. The fact that Anya intended to replace it is only relevant to the question of whether she is dishonest.

A common error is made in this respect when dealing with the scenario of people 'borrowing' money intending to replace it. The case of *R v Velumyl* [1989] Crim LR 299 confirmed that if a person takes money from someone (in this case an employer) intending to repay it, there is an intention permanently to deprive. This is because the defendant always intended to deprive the owner of the particular notes and coins that they took. Again, the fact that they intended to pay the owner back an equivalent sum is relevant only to the question of dishonesty.

Treating the property as one's own

One area that poses a potential difficulty for jurors is where the defendant argues a lack of intent permanently to deprive because they intended to return the property in due course. Generally, an intention to borrow property does not suffice to establish a charge of theft.

Example

Padma takes Alison's debit card and returns it but only after she has bought herself a dress. Padma has no defence to the actus reus elements of theft as she has clearly appropriated property belonging to another by taking Alison's debit card. On the facts, she seems also to be dishonest, but Padma will argue that she had no intention permanently to deprive Alison of the property as her intention was always to return the card, once she had used it.

It is possible that, left to apply the ordinary meaning to the words 'intention of permanently depriving', a jury might acquit a defendant of theft in these circumstances as this element of mens rea appears to be lacking. However, the prosecution may be able to secure such a conviction by using the provisions of s 6(1) of the TA 1968 which states:

> A person appropriating property belonging to another without meaning the other permanently to lose the thing itself is nevertheless to be regarded as having the intention of permanently depriving the other of it if his intention is to treat the thing as his own to dispose of regardless of the other's rights; and a borrowing or lending of it may amount to so treating it if, but only if, the borrowing or lending is for a period and in circumstances making it equivalent to an outright taking or disposal.

Despite the wording of the statute (treating the property as his own to dispose of regardless of the other's rights), the defendant does not actually need to dispose of the property to satisfy the test, and the definition is perhaps best understood by removing the reference to this phrase. Indeed, a defendant who intends to return the property to its owner, but only after it has been used, will have an intention to permanently deprive on this basis.

Another example of the type of case s 6(1) was aimed at, according to the courts, is where a defendant takes items and then offers them back to the owner for the owner to buy (see *R v Raphael* [2008] EWCA Crim 1014).

Example

Jon secretly takes Gurpreet's valuable watch, intending to offer it back to Gurpreet for £200. If Jon intends to return the watch to Gurpreet only if Gurpreet pays the £200, then he would fall within s 6(1) and have the necessary intention permanently to deprive.

Section 6 has also been used to destroy some inventive defences. In *R v Marshall* [1998] 2 Cr App R 282, the defendant was charged with theft after implementing a scheme which involved acquiring used but unexpired tickets from passengers on London Underground. The defendant then sold the tickets on. He claimed that he had no intention permanently to deprive the Underground of the tickets as they would in due course be returned via the second wave of passengers! The Court of Appeal upheld his conviction, holding that by acquiring and reselling the tickets, the defendant had intended to treat them as his own to dispose of regardless of the rights of the Underground company. The Court said that their decision reflected the dictionary definition of 'dispose' which is to get rid of, sell and so on.

Similarly, in *Chan Man-sin v R* [1988] 1 All ER 1, where the defendant forged company cheques, one of his submissions was that he lacked an intention permanently to deprive the company of the balance of its account. He argued that he believed (correctly) the bank would have to reimburse the company. This submission was rejected by use of s 6(1) - he had, by writing out the cheques, treated the company's property as his own to dispose of regardless of the company's rights.

Borrowing equivalent to outright taking

Although simple borrowing does not make someone a thief, there are occasions where the borrowing has a greater effect, and this is dealt with in s 6(1).

Example

Julia's friend, Oscar, has a ticket for a balloon ride. He leaves the ticket lying around, and Julia takes it intending to return it at the end of the day. Understandably irate, Oscar complains to the police who charge Julia with theft. Her defence is that she had no intention of permanently depriving Oscar of the ticket as her plan was to return it after the balloon ride - she only borrowed it.

This is unlikely to succeed as s 6(1) can be used to argue that the borrowing was for a period (until after the ride) and in circumstances (only to be returned once it had been 'used up'), making it equivalent to an outright taking. In other words, the circumstances of the borrowing were such that Julia might as well have intended to take the ticket and never return it.

However, s 6 does not apply to all 'borrowing' cases. A borrowing which is not equivalent to an outright taking cannot be theft, whatever economic losses flow to the victim.

In *R v Lloyd* [1985] QB 829, the defendant was a projectionist in a cinema. He removed films to make 'pirate' copies and then returned the films to the cinema within a few hours. The Court of Appeal held that 'a mere borrowing is never enough to constitute the necessary guilty mind unless the intention is to return the "thing" in such a changed state that it can be truly said that all its goodness and virtue has gone.' In this case, the Court ruled that there was still a practical value to the films as they could continue to be projected to paying audiences. Consequently, the borrowing was not equivalent to an outright taking or disposal under s 6(1).

Parting with property under a condition as to its return

An intention permanently to deprive also arises under s 6(2) of the TA 1968 which states:

> Without prejudice to the generality of [s 6(1)] above, where a person, having possession or control (lawfully or not) of property belonging to another, parts with the property under a condition as to its return which he may not be able to perform, this (if done for purposes of his own and without the other's authority) amounts to treating the property as his own to dispose of regardless of the other's rights.

The clearest example of where this section applies is pawning.

> **Example**
>
> *Yamato takes Ira's ring and pawns it, intending to redeem it in due course. Under s 6(2), this would amount to an intention permanently to deprive because Yamato has parted with the property (the ring) under a condition as to its return (paying the money owed) which he may not be able to perform. It is irrelevant whether Yamato believes the chances of paying back the money due and getting the ring back are very good or unlikely.*

Overview of intention to permanently deprive

The important points are as follows:

(a) Usually the words 'intention of permanently depriving' will be given their ordinary meaning and s 6 should be referred to in exceptional cases only.

(b) In those cases where the jury need further guidance or assistance, s 6 can be used to establish an intention permanently to deprive:

  (i) If the defendant's intention was to treat the item as if it was their own, s 6(1) should enable the prosecution to establish the relevant mens rea.

  (ii) Similarly, in a case where the defendant is arguing that they simply 'borrowed' the property, s 6(1) can assist if the borrowing equates to an outright taking. If, however, there is still value attached to the property when it is to be returned, the provision may not assist.

  (iii) If the defendant parts with the property under a condition as to its return that they may not be able to perform, s 6(2) may be relied upon to establish the required intention to permanently deprive.

The situations which may prove problematic are summarised in the flowchart below.

Figure 9.3 Intention permanently to deprive

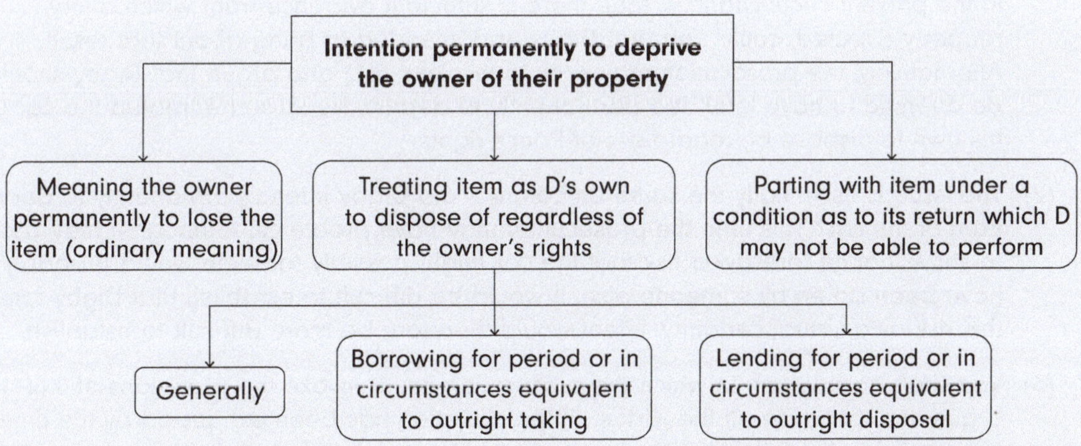

Finally, to check your understanding of this element of theft, you should complete the following activity.

ACTIVITY

Does each defendant have the intention of permanently depriving the owners of their property in the following situations?

(1) Digby breaks into and drives away a car belonging to Pam. He spends the day in the car and then leaves it parked on an area of waste ground, where the car is soon vandalised and stripped down by others.

(2) Would your answer in question (1) differ if Digby, instead of abandoning the car on waste ground, had left the car unlocked outside Pam's house with the keys in the ignition, from where it was subsequently stolen by someone else?

(3) Vanisha works as a personal assistant for Kehinde, a well-known socialite. One day, while her employer is out, an invitation to attend a garden party is delivered to Kehinde's house. Vanisha keeps the invitation, attends the garden party herself and later returns the invitation to Kehinde through the post, to convey the impression that it had merely arrived late.

(4) Aqib, a milkman employed by Unifence Ltd, takes a £10 note from the money he has collected from his customers and uses it to place a bet on a horse race. The bet is successful and Aqib uses £10 from his winnings to replace what he had taken.

(5) Peter hires a car in London from Squertz Ltd for use on a three-week touring holiday of Devon with his wife, Della. Two days before the expiry of the hire period they have a violent argument, which culminates in Della taking the car keys and driving back to London alone, where she returns the car to Squertz Ltd. Peter is left to make his own way home by train.

COMMENT

(1) As Digby abandoned the car, the question for the jury to decide is whether he intended to deprive Pam of the car permanently. If it can be proved that he knew it was virtually certain that Pam would lose the property permanently, which is likely in the present circumstances, then there is sufficient evidence from which a jury, properly directed, could find that Digby had intended to bring about that result. Alternatively, the prosecution may seek to invoke s 6(1) and argue that Digby should be deemed to have intended permanently to deprive because he treated the car as his own to dispose of, regardless of Pam's rights.

(2) The issue is essentially the same as before – did Digby intend permanently to deprive Pam of the car? This time the prosecution may have problems. Although it may be able to show that he foresaw a risk that the car might possibly (or even would probably) have been stolen by someone else, it would be difficult to establish that Digby foresaw this risk as a virtual certainty. Intent would therefore be more difficult to establish.

(3) Vanisha's case is one in which the prosecution could invoke the provisions of s 6(1) and argue that, because all the 'virtue' in the invitation has been exhausted by the time it is returned to Kehinde, Vanisha can properly be convicted of theft. The only possible argument for the defence is that, unlike (say) a railway ticket which confers a legally enforceable right, this social invitation has no legally recognisable 'virtue'.

(4) Although Aqib had intended throughout to replace the money, he clearly intended to deprive his employers permanently of the specific £10 note which he had taken. He therefore does have an intention permanently to deprive the employers of that property. Whether he is guilty of theft will depend upon whether his conduct is held to have been dishonest, in accordance with the test in *Ivey*.

(5) Della has not committed theft of the car from Squertz Ltd because it is clear from her conduct that she had no intention of depriving the company permanently of the vehicle.

Has she stolen the car from her husband, Peter? He did not own the car but merely had possession of it under the hire contract. However, this is sufficient to render Della's act an appropriation of property 'belonging to' another. Furthermore, she intended to deprive Peter permanently of the whole of his short-term interest. The key issue here will be whether she was dishonest.

9.2.4 Summary of theft

Set out below is a flowchart which provides you with an overview of the offence of theft.

Figure 9.4 Overview of theft

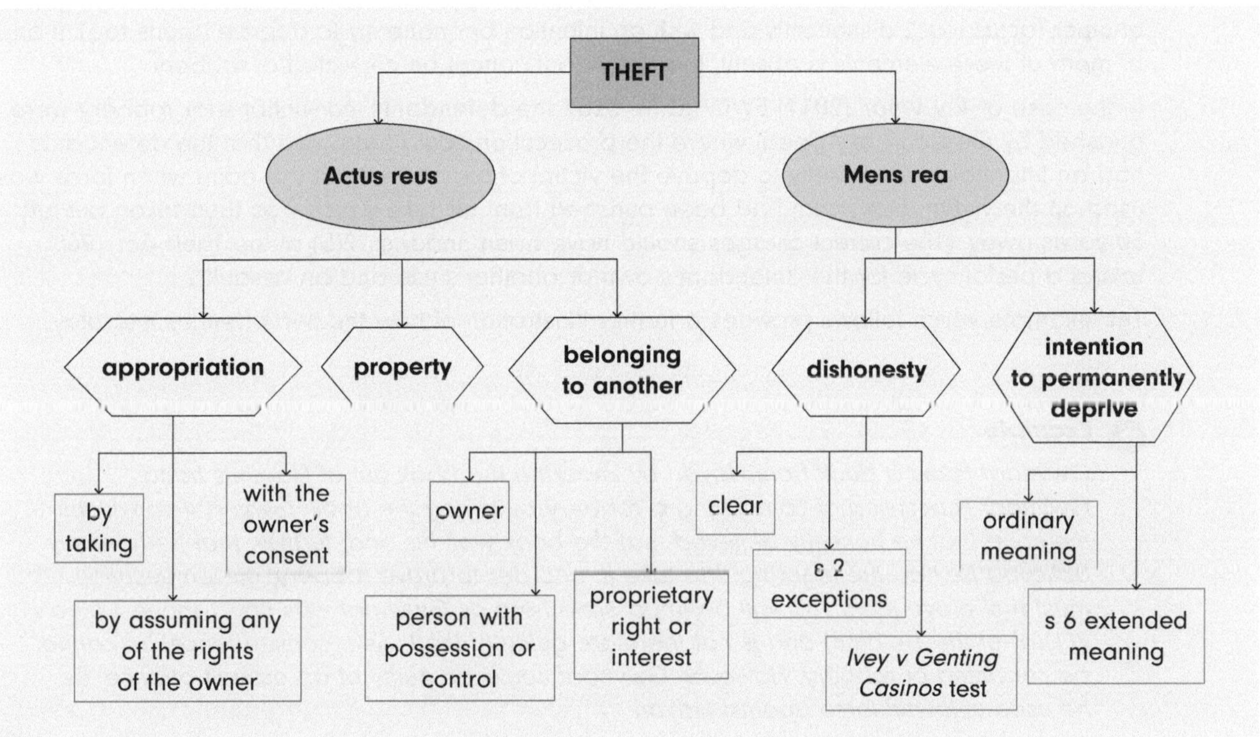

9.3 Robbery

Robbery is a far more serious charge than that of theft. Theft is an either-way offence and carries a maximum sentence of seven years' imprisonment where the matter is dealt with by the Crown Court. Robbery, however, is an indictable only offence with a maximum sentence of life imprisonment (under s 8(2) of the TA 1968).

Robbery covers a wide range of criminality from an armed gang of robbers who actually use their weapons during the commission of the offence, to a teenager threatening a classmate to make them hand over their mobile phone. The offence of robbery is contained in s 8 of the TA 1968 which provides:

> (1) A person is guilty of robbery if he steals, and immediately before or at the time of doing so, and in order to do so, he uses force on any person or puts or seeks to put any person in fear of being then and there subjected to force.

There are four key components which the prosecution must prove for robbery:

(a) that the defendant committed an offence of theft;

(b) they either used or threatened force on any person; and

(c) did so immediately before or at the time of the theft;

(d) in order to steal.

Each of these elements will be examined in turn.

9.3.1 Requirement for a theft

It is vital to appreciate as a starting point that one of the key elements of the offence of robbery is the requirement to establish that a theft has occurred: without this, there cannot be a charge of robbery. It is, therefore, important to check that all five elements of theft considered earlier in this chapter are present: specifically, there must be an appropriation of property belonging to another (actus reus), dishonestly and with an intention permanently to deprive (mens rea). If one or more of these elements is absent, the defendant cannot be convicted of robbery.

In the case of *R v Vinall* [2011] EWCA Crim 6252 the defendants' convictions for robbery were quashed by the Court of Appeal where the prosecution could not prove that the defendants had an intention permanently to deprive the victim of his property at the point when force was used on the victim. The victim had been punched from his bike which was then taken but left 50 yards away. (The correct charges should have been under s 12(5) of the Theft Act 1968 – taking a pedal cycle for the defendant's own or another's use and an assault.)

The example which follows provides a further illustration of how the two offences interplay.

Example

Gwyndaf takes a book from Haydn by knocking the book out of Haydn's hand. Gwyndaf is accused of committing a robbery by taking the book. Gwyndaf convinces the court that he honestly believed that the book was his and, further, that he honestly believed he had the legal right to take it. In order to prove robbery, the prosecution must first prove theft. This will be impossible here as Gwyndaf was not dishonest (see s 2(1)(a) of the TA 1968) and is not therefore guilty of theft. As a consequence, he cannot be convicted of robbery. However, Gwyndaf could be guilty of an assault offence, as he used unlawful force against Haydn.

Although the elements of theft are essential ingredients to robbery, proving these alone is not sufficient to substantiate a charge for this offence. Force (actual or threatened) is the additional requirement which converts a simple theft into a charge of robbery.

9.3.2 The meaning of 'force'

The meaning of the word 'force' was considered in *R v Dawson* (1976) 64 Cr App R 170. In this case the two defendants jostled the victim, making it difficult for him to keep his balance, and at the same time another man took the victim's wallet. The defendants appealed against their conviction for robbery on the basis that the jostling could not, in law, amount to the use of 'force'. The Court of Appeal disagreed and upheld the convictions for robbery. In so doing, the Court stated that 'force' is a word in ordinary use and one which is understood by jurors. It confirmed that it was a matter for the jury in each case to determine whether force had been used (or threatened).

At the trial of the defendants in *Dawson*, the judge had directed the jury that the force used must be 'substantial' to justify a conviction for robbery. The Court of Appeal declined to pass judgment on whether it was correct to put this adjective in front of the word 'force', stating only that it was a matter for the jury. However, in the case of *Dawson,* one of the defendants was found guilty of robbery when the victim's bag was grabbed. This would suggest that the amount of force used does not need to be significant.

In *Dawson*, the force used was applied directly to the victim's body (the jostling); but what if the force is directed against the victim's property instead? Will this still be sufficient for a charge of robbery instead of theft? This question was answered in the affirmative by the Court of Appeal in *R v Clouden* [1987] Crim LR 56. In this case the defendant approached the victim from behind and wrenched her basket out of her hands. The judges confirmed that whether the defendant used force on any person in order to steal is an issue that should be left to the jury, but there was no distinction between applying force to the person or their property.

It is apparent that only a minor degree of force may be enough, although this will ultimately be a question of fact for a jury to decide. However, where only slight touching is used, say, for example, where a pickpocket takes items from a victim's jacket pocket, then this will not be sufficient to justify a conviction for robbery and a charge of theft would be more appropriate. Thus, in *P v DPP* [2013] 1 Cr App R 7, a defendant who snatched a cigarette from the victim, without making any contact with the victim, was held only to be guilty of theft and not robbery.

9.3.3 Against whom must force be used or threatened?

Usually, the threat or use of force will be against the person to whom the property belongs, but it need not be so and may be against 'any person' according to s 8.

Example

Ryan sees that Jennifer is wearing a large diamond ring and decides to steal it from her.

(1) He grabs Jennifer and refuses to let her go until she gives him the ring.

(2) He waves a knife at Jennifer and says he will cut her unless she gives him the ring.

(3) He tells Jennifer that he will cut her child's throat unless she hands over the ring.

(4) He ties up Jennifer's friend and refuses to release her until Jennifer hands over the ring.

Because it does not matter that the force used or threatened is against someone other than the owner of the property, in each of the above scenarios Ryan would fulfil the force element of robbery. However, in cases where force is threatened rather than actually used, the intended victim of the force must be aware of the threat. In scenario (3) above, provided the child is present, the charge of robbery will be made out.

In summary:

(a) whether the defendant has used or threatened the victim is ultimately a question of fact for the jury;

(b) the force need not be substantial;

(c) it does not matter against whom the force is used or threatened; and

(d) the force can be directed against property.

9.3.4 When must the force be used or threatened?

The use or threat of force must be broadly simultaneous with the theft in order to establish robbery as it must be 'immediately before or at the time' of the theft (TA 1968, s 8(1)). It is therefore essential to check that the force or threat does not occur a long time before the theft. It is also necessary to determine when the theft is complete, as any force used or threatened after the theft will not give rise to a charge of robbery (although the defendant could be charged with theft and assault).

Example

Zoe is at a nightclub and has a fight with Gina who has been flirting with Zoe's boyfriend. During the fight, Zoe notices that Gina has dropped her mobile phone onto the floor and so, after the fight has ended, she picks up the phone and keeps it. Zoe is not guilty of robbery as the theft takes place after the use of force.

In *R v Hale* (1978) 68 Cr App R 415, the Court of Appeal held that the issue to be determined was whether the appropriation was still continuing at the time the force was used. If so, the force had been used at the time of the theft and the defendant could be guilty of robbery. In *Hale*, the defendant stole various items from the victim's home and then, on the way out, threatened her young son if she rang the police within five minutes of his leaving. Eveleigh LJ clarified that the question of whether the appropriation was continuing was to be determined by the jury, and in this case the defendant was found guilty of robbery.

9.3.5 Reason for the force

The definition in s 8(1) makes it clear that the threat or use of force must be made in order to steal. Although this will usually be easy to establish, occasionally, the requirement may not be satisfied.

Example

Vincent hits Raymond because he does not like the look of him. Having knocked him unconscious, he spots Raymond's phone, which has fallen to the floor and decides to take it. He picks up the phone and walks away with it.

Vincent is not guilty of robbery as, although he used force against Raymond immediately before he stole the phone, he did not do so in order to steal. He hit Raymond because he did not like the look of him and the decision to take the phone was taken after using violence.

Vincent would be guilty of theft and an assault offence under either s 18 or s 20 of the OAPA 1861, as he appears to have caused grievous bodily harm to Raymond and presumably has the relevant mens rea at least for s 20.

9.3.6 The mens rea of robbery

Because theft is a requirement of robbery, the defendant must be proven to have had the mens rea of theft - to be dishonest and to intend permanently to deprive the owner of the property. If either of these elements are missing, the charge of theft will fail; and without a theft, there cannot be a conviction for robbery.

However, there are additional elements of mens rea that need to be established for this offence. Applying the normal rules of mens rea as far as assault offences are concerned, presumably, to be convicted of robbery, the defendant must at least be reckless as to the use or threat of force. Whether an intention to use force or to put someone in fear of being then and there subjected to force is required appears undecided, but Professor JC Smith, in his book *The Law of Theft*, suggests that recklessness will suffice and that an intention on the part of the defendant to use or threaten force need not be established. This would equate with the usual mens rea requirements of a simple or physical assault.

9.3.7 Summary of robbery

It is apparent that the crime of robbery may be approached in a less traditional way than for most offences. Instead of working through the actus reus and then the mens rea, it may be preferable to discuss the elements of theft first and then focus on the three issues relating to the use or threat of force. The flowchart (below) gives a complete picture of what the prosecution needs to prove to convict a defendant of robbery. This is because robbery is effectively an aggravated theft.

Figure 9.5 Theft and robbery

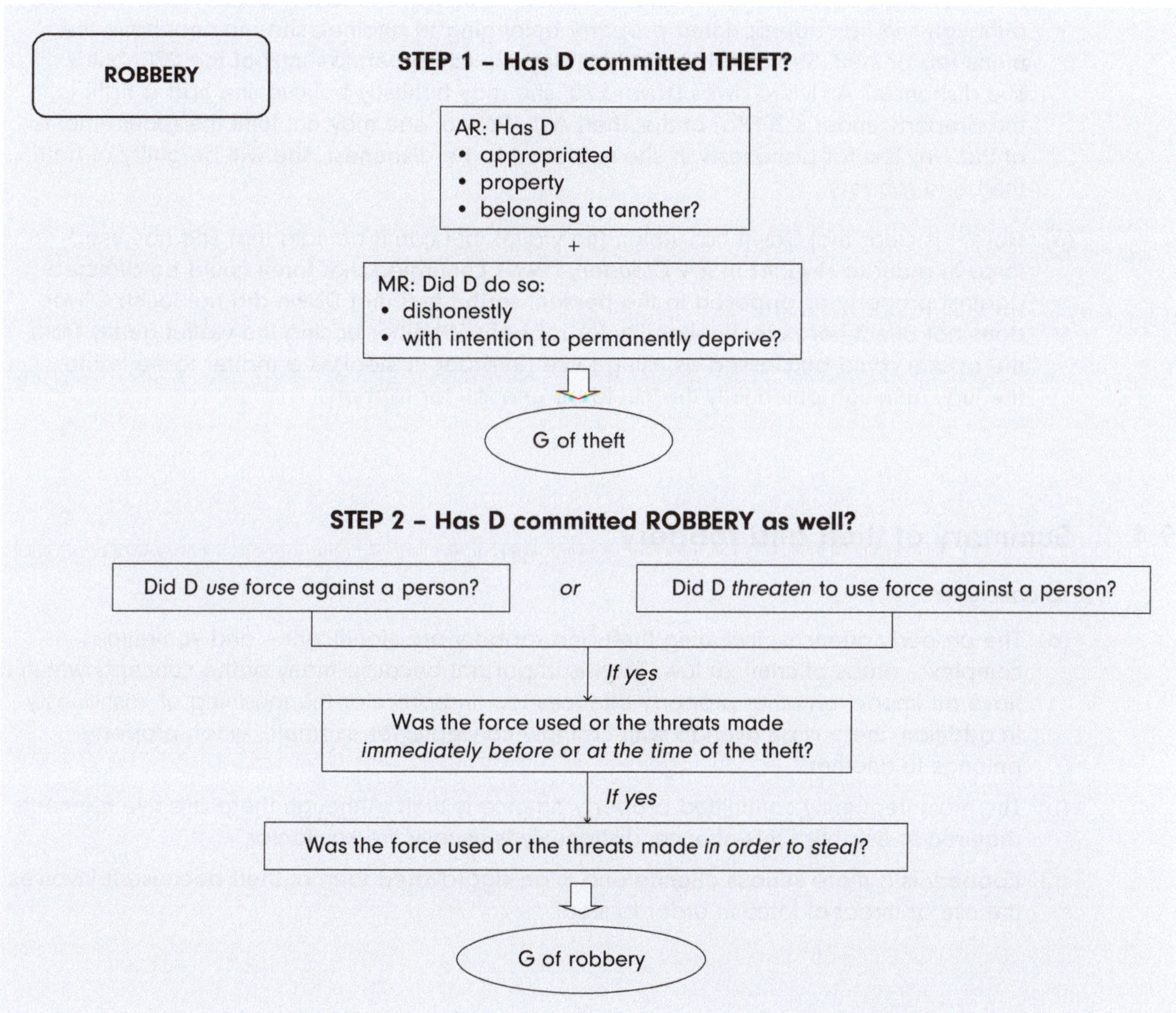

ACTIVITY

Consider the situations below and decide whether Dawn could be guilty of robbery in each case. Give reasons for your answers.

(1) Dawn accidentally bumps into Penny while out shopping, causing Penny to drop her handbag. Dawn notices that Penny's purse has fallen out of the bag, so she takes it without Penny noticing.

(2) Ichiro owes Dawn £20. Dawn sees Ichiro in the street and threatens to punch him if he does not give her the money. Ichiro hands over a £20 note.

(3) Dawn sees Oliver's wallet sticking out of his back pocket. She gently eases it out of his pocket and walks off, without Oliver noticing.

COMMENT

(1) As Dawn has accidentally bumped into Penny and only then takes the purse, this will not be robbery because, although Dawn did use force, it was not 'in order to' steal. The incident will be charged as theft instead.

(2) In this case Dawn has put Ichiro in fear of being there and then subjected to force (the threat that she will punch him) and has done so in order to take the £20 note. However, although she has appropriated property belonging to another, she may not have the mens rea of theft. She clearly intends to deprive Ichiro permanently of the £20, but is she dishonest? As Ichiro owes Dawn £20, she may honestly believe she had a right to the property under s 2(1)(a) of the Theft Act 1968, or she may not fulfil the requirements of the *Ivey* test for dishonesty. If she is proved to be dishonest, she will be guilty of both theft and robbery.

(3) Here it is clear that Dawn has stolen the wallet, but can it be said that she has used force in order to steal it? In *R v Clouden*, it was confirmed that force could be directed against property as opposed to the person, so the fact that Dawn did not touch Oliver does not affect her potential liability for robbery. Whether easing the wallet gently from the pocket could be classed as using force (in order to steal) is a matter to be left to the jury, although potentially this could be enough for robbery.

9.4 Summary of theft and robbery

To conclude:

(a) The property offences, including theft and robbery are significant – and sometimes complex – areas of criminal law. Theft is important because many of the concepts within it have an impact on other property offences too, in particular the meaning of 'dishonesty'. In addition, there is an overlap with civil law concepts, for example, when property belongs to another.

(b) The most frequently committed property offence is theft. Although there are five elements required to establish this offence, dishonesty is usually the key factor.

(c) Robbery is a more serious offence and is an aggravated form of theft because it involves the use or threat of force in order to steal.

10 Fraud and Making Off Without Payment

LEARNING OUTCOMES

When you have completed this chapter, you should be able to:

- define the offence of fraud and understand the three ways in which fraud may be committed;
- identify the elements required for the offence of making off without payment and appreciate how it complements the other property offences.

10.1 Introduction

In this chapter, you will be introduced to the law relating to fraud as contained in the Fraud Act (FA) 2006. Fraud may be committed in three different ways, namely, fraud by false representation, fraud by failing to disclose information and fraud by abuse of trust, and these will be analysed in turn.

Thereafter, the offence of making off without payment, under s 3 of the Theft Act 1978, will be discussed. This offence was introduced to plug a potential gap in the law that allowed some defendants to escape liability in situations where they ran off without paying for a taxi-ride or for a meal in a restaurant.

The offences of theft (which was covered previously), fraud and making off without payment often overlap so that a defendant may face more than one charge on the same evidence. Throughout this chapter, you will be examining statutory provisions and the relevant case law to build up an understanding of when, and how, the different offences may apply and their relationship to each other.

10.2 Offences under the Fraud Act 2006

Fraud is the most commonly experienced offence according to the National Crime Agency, and victims of fraud range from individuals to businesses to the public sector. The availability of technology means that it has become a global phenomenon, and a recent report estimated the annual cost to the UK economy as £190 billion. However, until the 2006 Act, there was no general offence of fraud, and the prosecution was forced to rely upon the old deception offences which, although heavily used, had become increasingly inadequate.

The FA 2006 is a piece of legislation designed to implement recommendations made by the Law Commission (Law Com No 276) to overhaul the law in relation to those situations where the defendant deceives someone. It was introduced to replace the multiple deception offences that applied previously, as these were regarded as too complex and outdated. The offence has been widely drafted to ensure that a broad range of behaviour is caught within its provisions, with the aim of ensuring that the law can keep pace with developing technology and the increasingly inventive ways in which criminals are committing fraud.

10.3 The offence of fraud

The 2006 Act creates a general offence of fraud which can be committed in three different ways. Section 1 of the Act provides for the offence of fraud, but does not define it, and s 1(2) sets out the methods by which fraud may be committed:

(a) by making a false representation (s 2);

(b) by failing to disclose information (s 3); and

(c) by abuse of position (s 4).

Sections 2, 3 and 4 contain further information on specifically how the offence of fraud may be satisfied. A common theme is that there is no requirement for the prosecution to prove the defendant actually obtained anything (such as goods or services) by their actions, just that they intended to do so. As with theft, dishonesty is a key element of the mens rea.

The offence is classified as an either-way offence (s 1(3)). If convicted in the Crown Court, the maximum sentence is a term of imprisonment of 10 years and an unlimited fine.

10.4 Fraud by false representation

The most common offence is that of fraud by making a false representation. This is dealt with in detail in s 2 of the Act, which provides that:

> (1) A person is in breach of this section (and so guilty of an offence under section 1) if he—
>
> (a) dishonestly makes a false representation, and
>
> (b) intends, by making the representation—
>
> (i) to make a gain for himself or another, or
>
> (ii) to cause loss to another or to expose another to a risk of loss.

Section 2(1) raises several issues to consider. The actus reus consists of making a representation (conduct), and that representation must be false (circumstance). All other aspects of the offence relate to mens rea, so the defendant must:

(a) be dishonest; and

(b) intend, by making the representation, to make a gain for themselves or another, or to cause loss to another or to expose another to a risk of loss.

There is also a third element of mens rea relating to the falsity of the representation, and this is discussed in the next paragraph. In the meantime, set out below is a flowchart which summaries the actus reus and mens rea of the s 2 offence.

Figure 10.1 False representation

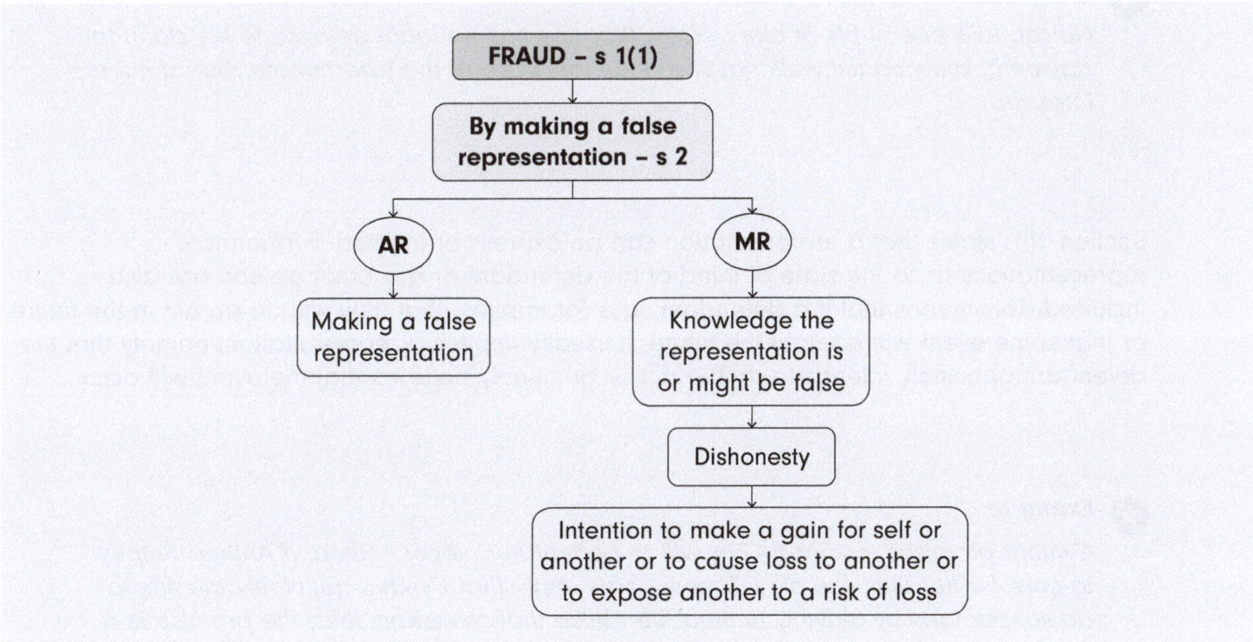

Central to the commission of the offence is the requirement that a false representation should be made, but what is meant by a 'representation' and when is such a representation false?

10.4.1 False representations

The term 'false representation' conjures up thoughts of a person being misled by something said to them that is untrue; for example, a burglar tricks their way into a home by pretending to be an employee from a gas company or a police officer. However, it also includes situations where nothing is said but the individual's behaviour creates a false impression, such as using a stolen credit card to pay for goods in a shop.

Section 2(2) of the Act states that a representation is false if:

(a) it is untrue or misleading, and

(b) the person making it knows that it is, or might be, untrue or misleading.

The definition includes elements of both the actus reus and the mens rea. First, any representation made must actually *be* false or misleading; and secondly, the defendant must have some awareness of this.

10.4.1.1 What is a representation?

Further guidance is provided in the Act as to what constitutes a representation. Under s 2(3), a representation means any representation as to fact or law, including a representation as to the state of mind of: (a) the person making the representation, or (b) any other person. In reality, most representations will be representations as to fact, but there may, on occasion, be a false representation as to the law.

Example

Nelson tells one of his debtors, Holly, that she has no legal defence to his claim for payment, knowing full well that she does, because of the extortionate rate of interest imposed.

Section 2(4) states that a representation can be express or implied. Furthermore, representations as to the state of mind of the defendant or any other person are also included. This means that if a defendant says (or implies) that they will do an act in the future, or that some event will occur in the future, it usually implies a representation, namely that the defendant genuinely intends to do the act or genuinely believes that the event will occur.

Example

Cynthia promises to change her will to benefit her niece, Anthea, if Anthea helps to care for her until she dies. These words imply that Cynthia genuinely intends to do so, perhaps by leaving Anthea the house that she owns; thus, the promise is a representation.

Even if a defendant states something as being merely their opinion, they impliedly represent that it is their genuine opinion.

Clearly, the most typical representation would be when a person says something that is untrue, so tells a lie, but the definition is wider than this. The Explanatory Notes to the Bill (Note 14) confirm that the representation can 'be stated in words or communicated by conduct. There is no limitation on the way in which the words must be expressed. So they could be written or spoken or posted on a website.' It is apparent from this Note that a representation which is in words may be expressed in a variety of ways, whether it be verbally, by email, in a text message, in a letter or even on an internet site.

The meaning of representation under the FA 2006 is summarised in the table below.

s 2(3)	**s 2(4)**	**Explanatory Notes to the Bill**
A representation may relate to: • a fact; • the law; or • the state of mind of the person making the representation and any other person.	A representation may be: • express; or • implied.	A representation may be: • in words; or • communicated by conduct. There is no limitation on how this is expressed, which may be: • in writing; • spoken; or • posted on a website.

The examples below illustrate how the law applies in practice.

Examples

(1) Jordan applies for a mortgage and declares he has a salary of £45,000.

(2) Hamish e-mails Euan, telling him his mother has died.

Scenarios 1 and 2 are representations, as they clearly fall within the provisions of the Explanatory Note referred to above.

(3) Cameron sends a text message to Len, telling him he owns a Scottish castle.

As a representation includes items posted on a website, it covers text messages too, as in this instance.

(4) Elisha uses a credit card to pay for her shopping.

(5) Gill orders food at a restaurant.

These scenarios involve representations made by the conduct of the defendant. Elisha is making a representation that she has authority to use the credit card by offering it as payment; similarly, Gill is making a representation that she is a legitimate customer willing to pay for the food by her conduct in ordering it.

10.4.1.2 When is a representation false?

Whether the defendant has made a false representation is a question of fact to be determined by the jury. However, it would usually involve a victim being deceived or misled by something said to or written about them.

Example

Marlon has befriended Hannah, a vulnerable young woman, over the internet. He tells her that he owes £5,000 and will be violently assaulted if he does not pay the money immediately. Marlon has made up the story to elicit money from Hannah. This is an express false representation by words.

However, the actus reus will not be established if a defendant says something that they believe to be false but is in fact true.

Example

Rodney sells Zeenat a watch, telling her it is made of '9 carat gold' but believing that it consists of a non-precious metal. When Zeenat has the watch valued a few days later, it transpires that the watch is, in fact, gold. There is no false representation and, thus, no s 2 offence. (However, Rodney could be guilty of an attempted offence, impossibility being no defence to an attempt charge - see later in this textbook.)

On occasion, a question will arise as to whether a representation by conduct is false, and this issue was considered in the authority discussed below. Although the case was generated by the previous law relating to deception offences, the principles established seem to fit squarely within the remit of the current offence. Note that any judgments which discuss deception would, under the new law, refer to false representations instead.

In *DPP v Ray* [1974] AC 370, the defendant and four friends went to a Chinese restaurant, intending to have a meal there and pay for it. After eating the main course, they decided not to pay but remained at the table until the waiter left the room and then they ran from the restaurant. The House of Lords held (Lord Reid and Lord Hodson dissenting) that the transaction had to be regarded as a whole. Further, that the defendant's conduct was a continuing representation of their present intention to pay and their change of mind produced a deception, the effect of which was that they were treated as an honest customer whose conduct did not call for precautions. Accordingly, the defendant had been rightly convicted.

Under the current law, the conduct of the defendant, from when he first entered the restaurant to just before he ran out without paying, impliedly represented that he had the means and intention of paying. That representation by his conduct became false when the defendant decided not to pay.

What if a defendant ate the meal, and *then* realised they did not have the means to pay? This situation is different as the defendant makes no conscious decision not to pay and only dashes out of the restaurant once they realise they have no money. It is difficult to argue that there is a real false representation with mens rea at the point when the truth dawns on the defendant. Indeed, it could be argued that their (true) representation as to payment ceases at that point and a fresh representation that they are *not* going to pay (also true) begins!

Note that the defendant would not be guilty of theft of the food under s 1 of the Theft Act 1968 on these facts (see *Edwards v Ddin* [1976] 1 WLR 942 discussed in **Chapter 9**), but they could, however, be guilty of making off without payment, under s 3 of the Theft Act 1978 covered later in this chapter.

With regard to representations made by the use of credit cards as payment, the Explanatory Notes (Note 15) specifically refer to this as an example of a representation. Again, this mirrors the case law under the old legislation. In *R v Lambie* [1981] 2 All ER 776, the defendant exceeded the limit on her credit card but continued to use it. The House of Lords held that she had falsely represented that she had authority to use the card by continuing to do so in these circumstances.

The next three cases provide interesting but clear examples of false representations. In *Idrees v DPP* [2011] EWHC 624 (Admin), the defendant had failed his driving theory test on 15 occasions. He then got another, unknown person to impersonate him to sit the test. Here, the false representation was made by the defendant when he booked the test online. In *R v Nizzar* (unreported, July 2012), the defendant worked on the till in a shop and informed a woman who had a £1 million winning lottery ticket that her ticket had not won anything. Finally, in *R v O'Leary* [2013] EWCA Crim 1371, the defendant visited the homes of two elderly victims who suffered from dementia, claiming that he had done roofing repair work to their properties and demanding payment for this. In fact, he had not done any such work.

Although juries should be capable of knowing if a representation is 'untrue', the absence of a definition of the word 'misleading' in s 2(2)(a) can cause difficulties. Indeed, in his article, 'The Fraud Act 2006 – Criminalising Lying?' [2007] Crim LR 193, David Ormerod criticised the lack of full definitions within the Act, and it has been left to the courts to decide what is meant by these words. To assist, the Home Office issued some guidance, suggesting that 'misleading' means 'less than wholly true and capable of an interpretation to the detriment of the victim' and provided the following scenario to illustrate what is meant by this phrase.

> **Example**
>
> *Dennis drafts an email with the heading 'Sponsored Swim to Support Cancer Research' and sends it to family, friends and neighbours. Dennis carries out the swim but only donates five per cent of the sponsorship money collected, keeping the rest for himself. Although Dennis has completed the swim and donated some money to the relevant charity, it is likely a jury would find his email to be misleading.*

Nevertheless, Ormerod remains concerned that this interpretation opens up an extremely wide scope of liability. He argues that it could criminalise street traders' repartee, so the only defence for a street trader who sells a jacket 'just like Beckham wears' may be lack of dishonesty. However, the passage of time may have provided some reassurance as prosecutors have adopted a sensible approach to charging this offence.

10.4.1.3 Effect of a representation

For the offence of fraud under s 2 of the FA 2006, the prosecution need only establish that a false representation was made; there is no need to prove that anyone was actually deceived. As a consequence, it is possible to commit the offence by making a false representation to a machine. Section 2(5) states that:

> a representation may be regarded as made if it (or anything implying it) is submitted in any form to any system or device designed to receive, convey or respond to communications (with or without human intervention).

> **Example**
>
> *Claire does her shopping at her local supermarket before using one of the self-service checkouts at the store. She scans her items through the checkout then swipes her mother's debit card into the machine to pay. Claire does not have her mother's permission to use the card. Claire has made a false representation by her conduct. She has implied by her use of the card that she has authority to do so, and she knows this is untrue. It does not matter that Claire has made the false representation to a machine rather than to a person.*

The statute is drafted so that the representation need only be 'submitted' and not necessarily communicated. The reason was to ensure that the FA 2006 remains relevant in a modern society, enabling its use in convicting those engaged in fraudulent conduct in the context of ever-changing technology. The practical effect is that:

(a) A representation by email is made as soon as it is sent, whether the intended victim reads the contents or even receives it at all.

(b) Withdrawing money from a cash point machine is covered by the Act and the representation is made when the PIN (personal identification number) is keyed into the machine.

(c) Entering stolen bank details onto an internet site to purchase items is a representation.

10.4.2 Mens rea

For the mens rea elements of the offence, it must be established that the defendant:

(a) is dishonest; and

(b) intends, by making the representation, to make a gain for themselves or another, or to cause loss to another or to expose another to a risk of loss; and

(c) knows the representation is untrue or misleading, or knows that it might be so.

Knowing that the representation is untrue or misleading is self-explanatory and has been discussed previously. However, in situations where the prosecution cannot prove certain knowledge on the part of the defendant, it will have to establish that the defendant knew the representation *might* be untrue or misleading. There is no guidance in the Explanatory Notes to the Fraud Bill (now the Act) to assist in determining how to deal with this aspect, but, following the approach to the deception offences, this element of the mens rea is akin to recklessness and is met by knowledge of falsity or a perception by the defendant that the representation might be false.

10.4.2.1 Dishonesty

The next mens rea requirement is dishonesty. There is no definition of dishonesty in the Act but, in most cases, the court will need no assistance in determining this aspect - it will simply be left to its common-sense when considering the evidence that has been heard. However, if further guidance is required, the Explanatory Notes (Note 10) indicate that the common law test (now the *Ivey* test) that was considered in the context of the offence of theft will apply. The court will take into account the question established under that test, namely whether a defendant's behaviour would be regarded as dishonest by the ordinary standards of reasonable and honest people.

10.4.2.2 Intention to gain or cause a loss

Finally, the defendant must dishonestly make the false representation with the intention, by making the representation, of making a gain for themselves or another, or of causing loss to another or exposing another to a risk of loss. A careful reading of this statutory requirement makes it apparent that it is 'by' making the false representation that the defendant must intend to make the gain or cause the loss. Thus, there must be an intended causal link; the defendant must intend the gain or loss to be as a result of the false representation.

This mens rea requirement is common to several offences created by the FA 2006 and is dealt with in detail in s 5 which states:

> (2) 'Gain' and 'loss'—
>
> (a) extend only to gain or loss in money or other property;
>
> (b) include any such gain or loss whether temporary or permanent;
>
> and 'property' means any property whether real or personal (including things in action and other intangible property).
>
> (3) 'Gain' includes a gain by keeping what one has, as well as a gain by getting what one does not have.
>
> (4) 'Loss' includes a loss by not getting what one might get, as well as a loss by parting with what one has.

The issues raised by s 5 are considered in the following examples.

Examples

Benedict and Laura are brother and sister. In each case Benedict has deliberately made a false representation to Laura and is dishonest.

(1) Benedict tells Laura he is dying, and his last wish is to see his favourite group in concert. The concert is a sell-out, but Laura has a ticket. Benedict has a view to gain by getting what he does not have - the ticket - and also intends to cause loss to Laura by making her part with what she has.

(2) Benedict sends a text to Laura, asking if he can borrow her car for an hour to visit his employer. He has a view to gain the car (and again an intent to cause loss to Laura). The fact that the gain and loss would only be temporary is immaterial (s 5(2)(b)).

(3) Benedict writes a note to Laura, apologising that he has lost the book she lent him last week. He has a view to gain by keeping what he has (the book) and an intent to cause loss by Laura not getting what she might get (the return of the book).

(4) Benedict telephones Laura and tells her that he is homeless. He asks if he can borrow £100. Benedict has a view to gain and an intent to cause loss as the intent can relate to money as well as to property.

(5) Benedict tells Laura that he is the sole beneficiary under their uncle's will and that he alone inherited their uncle's farm. Here, he has a view to gain real property (the farm) and an intent to cause loss to Laura, by Laura not getting what she might get (a share of the inheritance).

Note that in all these examples there is both a view to gain and an intent to cause loss. Only one or the other is required, although frequently (as here) it will be easy to establish both.

Let us conclude our consideration of the offence created by s 2 by looking at when the offence is committed.

10.4.3 When is the offence committed?

It is important to appreciate that the offence occurs as soon as the false representation is made - there is no need for any consequence to follow from the representation. The Explanatory Notes (Note 13) make it clear that it is immaterial whether anyone is in fact misled, and this is apparent from a further consideration of s 2(1) set out above. There is no reference in the provision to anyone *being* misled, simply a reference to the defendant dishonestly making a false representation with the *intention* of making a gain or causing loss. The offence should therefore be reasonably easy to prove, and the need to charge a defendant with attempting to commit an offence under s 2 should be rare. The full offence is complete as soon as the false representation is made provided the defendant has the requisite mens rea.

10.5 Fraud by failing to disclose information

Moving on to the next offence, under s 1 of the FA 2006, a person is guilty of fraud under s 3 if they:

(a) dishonestly fail to disclose to another person information which they are under a legal duty to disclose, and

(b) intend, by failing to disclose the information, to make a gain for themselves or another, or to cause loss to another or to expose another to a risk of loss.

As with s 2 (and indeed s 4) of the FA 2006, this offence is entirely offender focused as it is committed as soon as the accused does the act, and it is irrelevant whether anyone is actually deceived or any property lost or gained. In common with other crimes, the actus reus and mens rea elements must be proved by the prosecution and these are outlined in the flowchart below.

Figure 10.2 Failing to disclose information

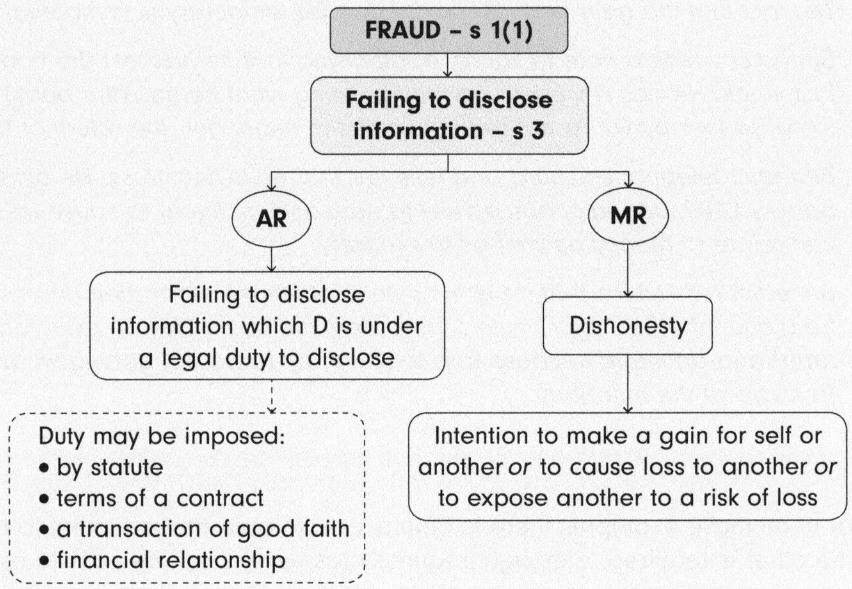

10.5.1 Actus reus

Not all information must be disclosed, and it only becomes a criminal offence if the defendant fails to do so when under a legal duty.

The FA 2006 does not define a 'legal duty', but the Explanatory Notes state that it includes 'duties under oral contracts as well as written contracts'. Examples where there is a legal duty to disclose would include those derived from statute (such as the provisions governing company prospectuses or the requirement to notify a change in circumstances in relation to a welfare benefits claim); the fact that the transaction is one of utmost good faith, for example, contracts of insurance; the express or implied terms of the contract; the custom of a particular trade or market; and the existence of a fiduciary relationship between the parties (such as agent and principal).

A failure to disclose such information may arise in a variety of situations.

Example

(1) Bradley applies for travel insurance to cover his trip to Australia to see his family but fails to disclose that he has previously been treated for a heart condition. Three days after arriving in Australia he suffers a heart attack. The contract of insurance is a transaction of good faith, so Bradley was under a legal duty to disclose his previous medical condition.

(2) Ravinder applies for a post as a social worker at a local authority. An express requirement of the position is that the successful applicant is a person of good character. Ravinder sends off her CV and is delighted to be awarded the job. Unfortunately, she was disciplined for cheating in her first year at university, and, here, a legal duty to disclose arises due to the express term of the employment contract.

The legal duty to disclose information applies not only if the defendant's failure to disclose the relevant facts gives the victim a cause of action for damages, but also if the law gives the victim a right to set aside any change in their legal position to which they may consent as a result of the non-disclosure.

Example

Petros often travels abroad due to his employment and so he decides to appoint his brother, Mehmet, as a trustee of his young son. However, Mehmet fails to tell Petros that he has recently been made bankrupt. Mehmet is being placed in a fiduciary position with Petros, and as a consequence he is under a duty to disclose material information. His failure to do so means that Petros can rescind or cancel their contract and reclaim any monies transferred under it. Furthermore, if Mehmet has invested the trust fund unwisely, Petros may also have a claim for damages for the monies which he has lost.

10.5.2 Mens rea

The mens rea required for an offence of fraud by failing to disclose information under s 3 is dishonesty and an intention to make a gain for themselves or another, or to cause loss to another, or to expose another to risk of loss. These mirror two of the mens rea elements of the s 2 offence of making a false representation, which have already been discussed in this chapter.

10.6 Fraud by abuse of position

There is a further means of committing fraud, and this covers those defendants who are in some form of privileged position in relation to the victim. The offence is complete once the defendant carries out the act that is the abuse of their power; and it is irrelevant whether they succeed and whether any loss or gain is actually made.

Section 4 of the FA 2006 provides that a person is in breach of this section if they:

(a) occupy a position in which they are expected to safeguard, or not to act against, the financial interests of another person;

(b) dishonestly abuse that position; and

(c) intend, by means of the abuse of that position, to make a gain for themselves or another, or to cause loss to another or to expose another to a risk of loss.

This offence of fraud is summarised below.

Figure 10.3 Abuse of position

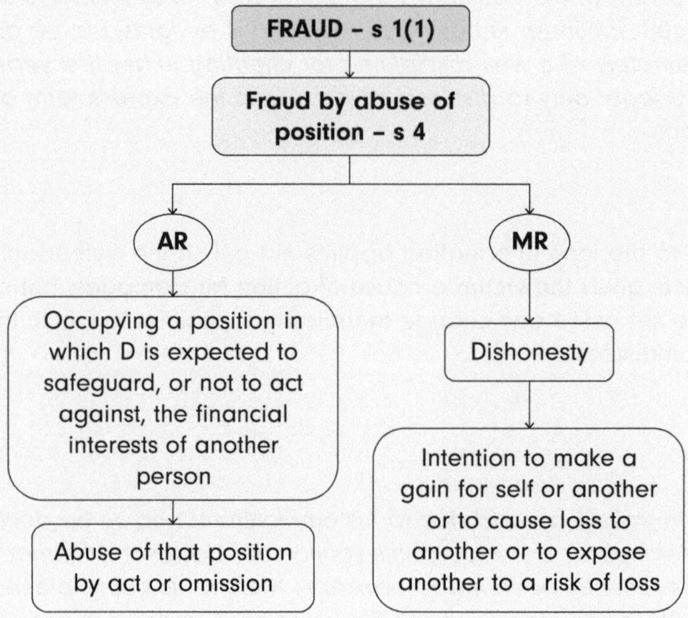

10.6.1 Actus reus

The actus reus of fraud by abuse of position comprises two elements, the first of which relates to the position held by the defendant, whilst the second concerns their behaviour.

Fraud under s 4 requires the existence of a position of financial trust between the defendant and the victim. This is further defined as one in which the defendant is expected to safeguard or not to act against the financial interests of another person. The FA 2006 does not define the word 'position', but suggested examples are between a trustee and beneficiary; a director and the company; a professional person and their client; an agent and their principal; an employee and employer. A position of financial trust may also arise in other circumstances, such as within a family or in the context of voluntary work. In all these examples, the victim has voluntarily placed the defendant in a privileged position with respect to their financial interests, so that the defendant is able to act in relation to those interests without reference to the victim.

Example

An employee of a software company who can access their employer's databases to clone software products occupies such a position, as they could use their access to sell products to a rival business.

The offence is interpreted widely and may be committed in a number of ways, not just where the defendant owes a specific fiduciary duty to the victim. This is demonstrated by the case of *R v Valujevs* [2014] EWCA Crim 2888 where unlicensed gang-masters abused their position by exploiting migrant workers, making unlawful deductions from their wages and charging excessive rent payments. They were found to occupy a position that was capable of being one in which they were expected to safeguard the financial interests of another.

Many people are in positions of trust, but to be liable for fraud, the defendant must go on to abuse their position. Thus, the employee of the software company referred to in the example above must actually clone the software products with the intention of selling them on.

The abuse can be committed either by a positive act or by an omission. In *R v Rouse* [2014] EWCA Crim 1128, the defendant was found guilty of fraud under s 4. He was the deputy manager of a care home with access to residents' bank and credit cards, and account details. As such, he was in a position in which he was expected to safeguard, or not to act against, the financial interests of the residents. However, the defendant abused that position by using the cards to withdraw money from a cash machine which he then spent on himself and to pay his personal bills.

Professionals such as lawyers and accountants clearly occupy positions in which they are expected to safeguard, or not to act against, the financial interests of another person – their clients. The criminal law will intervene when an abuse takes place and, in such instances, more than one offence may be committed.

10.6.2 Mens rea

The mens rea required for an offence of fraud by abuse of position under s 4 is dishonesty and an intention to make a gain for themselves or another, or to cause loss to another, or to expose another to risk of loss. These mirror two of the mens rea elements of the s 2 offence of making a false representation, which have already been discussed earlier in this chapter.

10.7 Overlap between the fraud offences

It is not unusual for a defendant to be criminally liable for different offences under the FA 2006, particularly as ss 2 to 4 describe three ways in which the offence of fraud may be satisfied.

Examples

(1) *Lee is an estate agent who has been instructed by Devon to sell her property. Lee undervalues the property and does not market it effectively so that his brother may purchase it at the lower price. Lee is guilty of an offence under s 3 as he fails to disclose to the seller, Devon, that a close relative is the prospective purchaser. This is material information that he is under a legal duty to disclose. Furthermore, Lee is in a fiduciary position with the seller of the property (Devon) in which he is expected to safeguard or not to act against the client. This would require him to market the property and to obtain the best price for it. Because he intends to make a gain for another (his brother) and a corresponding loss to Devon, provided the court is satisfied as to his dishonesty, Lee will also be guilty of an offence of fraud by abuse of position under s 4 of the FA 2006.*

(2) *Carys is a care worker who runs her own business. She is instructed by Grace, a very elderly and infirm woman, to carry out caring duties for Grace and to help her with chores around her house. Grace believes Carys to be an honest worker. However, when Grace's daughter looks into the arrangement, it becomes apparent that Grace has been charged a grossly excessive sum for what Carys has done. Carys is liable under s 2 as there was an implied representation that the price would be fair and reasonable due to the relationship of trust between Carys and Grace. However, Carys may also be guilty under s 4 due to her commission of a fraud by abuse of position of trust.*

10.8 Summary of fraud

To conclude, here is an overview of the offence of fraud:

(a) The FA 2006 creates a general offence of fraud under s 1, but it may be committed in three different ways: s 2 provides for fraud by false representation, s 3 by failing to disclose information, and s 4 by abuse of a position of trust.

(b) All three types of fraud share the same mens rea, although s 2 also has an additional requirement.

(c) Dishonesty is a key element; if the defendant is not clearly dishonest, the *Ivey* test will apply.

(d) The defendant must intend, by making the representation, to make a gain for themselves or another, or to cause loss to another or to expose another to a risk of loss. 'Gain' and 'loss' are defined under s 5 of the FA 2006.

(e) To be criminally liable for s 2 fraud, the defendant must make a false representation, knowing it to be untrue or misleading or that it might be.

(f) In order to be guilty of fraud by failing to disclose information under s 3, there must be a legal duty to disclose the information.

(g) To be guilty of fraud by abuse of position of financial trust under s 4, there must be a position of financial trust, which is abused. Such a position is one in which the defendant is expected to safeguard or not to act against the financial interests of another person.

10.9 Offence of making off without payment

The offence under s 3 of the Theft Act (TA) 1978 was introduced to fill a perceived hole in the legislation. Making off without payment was created to deal with the situation where the defendant has committed the actus reus of theft or fraud but only later forms the appropriate mens rea. An example is where a defendant eats a meal at a restaurant, fully intending to pay for it, but subsequently decides to leave without paying.

In this scenario, the defendant cannot be guilty of theft, as the actus reus and mens rea do not coincide in time (see *Edwards v Ddin*). Although they may be guilty of an offence under s 2 of the FA 2006, this would not apply if, for example, no false representation is made – the defendant may have intended to pay for the meal and then just run off at its end. In this situation, the prosecution may turn to s 3 of the TA 1978. Indeed, the offence of making off without payment is of considerable practical importance as it can be charged in circumstances where securing a conviction for theft or fraud might be difficult.

The offence is to be found in s 3(1) of the TA 1978 which is set out below:

> (1) Subject to subsection (3) below, a person who, knowing that payment on the spot for any goods supplied or services done is required or expected from him, dishonestly makes off without having paid as required or expected and with intent avoid payment of the amount due shall be guilty of an offence.

It is an either-way offence and has a maximum sentence of two years' imprisonment. The actus reus requires that:

(a) goods must be supplied or a service done;

(b) the defendant must make off from the spot where payment is required. Note that s 3(2) of the TA 1978 defines 'payment on the spot' as including payment at the time of collecting goods on which work has been done or in respect of which service has been provided;

(c) without paying as required or expected.

To satisfy the mens rea, the prosecution must prove three elements, namely, dishonesty; knowledge that payment on the spot was required or expected; and an intent to avoid payment.

10.9.1 Actus reus

For this offence to apply, the defendant must have had goods supplied to them, for example by the victim giving the items or allowing the defendant to take them; or had a service done, such as their car being repaired or shelves fitted in their house. The main restriction on this part of the actus reus is provided by s 3(3) of the TA 1978, which states:

> Subsection (1) above shall not apply where the supply of the goods or the doing of the service is contrary to law, or where the service done is such that payment is not legally enforceable.

This would apply to illegal and immoral services.

Example

Ben visits Hazel, who is a prostitute, and negotiates to have sex with her. Sexual intercourse takes place and Ben runs off without paying. Ben cannot be liable under s 3(1) of the TA 1978 - making off without payment - as a prostitute cannot legally enforce the contract. Thus, s 3(3) applies and no service has been done for the purposes of the offence. There is therefore no actus reus.

However, if Ben never had any intention of paying Hazel, then he could be guilty of fraud by false representation under s 2 of the FA 2006 - see above.

The second part of the actus reus is the requirement for the defendant to 'make off'. This term conjures up ideas of someone running away or dashing out of a shop or restaurant without paying. Such a situation would certainly be included, but the phrase also includes a person who left very casually or as a result of a deception, for example, telling a waiter that they had already paid the manager when they had not.

To be criminally liable, the defendant must make off from the spot where payment is required, but this is subject to interpretation. In certain situations, this may be clear, for example, if a defendant drives off the garage forecourt without paying for the petrol they put in their car. However, it is submitted that a person does not make off from a large department store until they leave the store, even though they may have left the actual department where the goods are sold. Therefore, if the defendant is found trying to escape through a window in the toilets of a restaurant without paying, this is likely to be an attempt (see later in the textbook), not the full offence.

Finally, the defendant must make off without payment as required or as expected. One issue that arose in case law concerned the situation where the accused 'pays' by a worthless cheque because, for example, it is stolen. As payment by a cheque with no value means the victim remains unpaid, it is not payment as 'required or expected', and it is submitted that the defendant would be liable. However, given the exponential increase in online payments, this scenario will rarely occur in the modern world.

10.9.2 Mens rea

As with many of the property offences, the prosecution must establish that the accused was dishonest: if the jury require guidance on this issue, the *Ivey* test will apply. In addition, it must be proved that the accused knew that payment on the spot was required or expected of them. This will normally be obvious; for example, if the defendant had just eaten a meal in a restaurant or had goods delivered, they know they must pay for them. However, there may be occasions where a defendant might argue that they did not know payment on the spot was required or expected of them, perhaps because they believed somebody else had already paid or was going to pay, or they were buying the goods or service on credit.

Another situation where this could apply is where the defendant has (possibly by a false representation) obtained the agreement of the 'victim' that payment can be made in the future. In *R v Vincent (Christopher James)* [2001] Crim LR 488, the defendant left a hotel without paying his bill. His defence was that he had arranged with the manager of the hotel to pay when he could, and thus payment was not expected on the spot when he left. The Court of Appeal agreed that this would amount to a defence to s 3, and the fact that the agreement was or may have been obtained dishonestly did not change that fact.

The main reason for the decision seems to be a desire to keep the offence a simple one and prevent complex investigations into the surrounding circumstances of any 'agreement'. However, such a defendant may now be liable for fraud by false representation under s 2 of the Fraud Act 2006 in this situation.

What if someone leaves, intending to return later and pay? Does the prosecution need to establish an intent to avoid paying permanently? The House of Lords considered this issue in the case of *R v Allen* [1985] AC 1029. The defendant had stayed at a hotel and incurred a bill of £1,286.94. He left the hotel without paying, but subsequently explained that he was in financial difficulties and said that he genuinely hoped to be able to pay the bill. Nevertheless, he was arrested and charged with making off without payment, contrary to s 3 of the TA 1978. His argument was that he had acted honestly and had genuinely expected to pay the bill from the proceeds of business ventures. The judges decided that the only correct way to construe s 3 was that the intention had to be to avoid payment permanently. Therefore, someone who makes off intending to return at a future date and pay cannot be liable for this offence.

10.9.3 Summary of making off without payment

Theft and fraud are two of the most common offences committed on a daily basis and, in most instances, will be more than sufficient to ensure the deserving defendant is found guilty. However, on rare occasions, they will fall short, perhaps because there is no clear evidence of dishonesty at the appropriate time or that the representation is false. To overcome this, theft and fraud are complemented by the offence of making off without payment (s 3 of the TA 1978), and prosecutors in practice may charge this offence as it is simpler to prove.

To test your understanding of this offence, you should attempt the activity below.

ACTIVITY

Joseph decides to purchase a computer. He is aware there are special offers on computers at the electrical store, and he decides to look at reviews on the Internet to select the best one. He goes to an Internet café which charges in arrears based on the time spent online. Joseph spends 20 minutes researching online but gets frustrated as the computer screen keeps freezing. He storms out of the café without paying.

Is Joseph liable for an offence under s 3 of the Theft Act 1978?

COMMENT

Actus reus: A service has clearly been provided (the access to the Internet), and payment on the spot is expected as this is usual commercial practice in such situations. Joseph has 'made off' as he 'storms out' of the café; thus, he has gone beyond the point at which payment is expected. The facts state that he has done so without paying 'as required or expected'.

Mens rea: Joseph appears to know that payment on the spot was required, and the facts suggest that he intended to make permanent default, as there is no suggestion he intends to return to the cafe. His liability seems to rest on whether or not he is dishonest, and the *Ivey* test should be applied to this situation. As the computer screen kept freezing, Joseph may (subjectively) believe that his conduct was honest in the circumstances. But would his conduct be regarded as dishonest by the standards of ordinary, decent people (an objective test)? It is more likely that an honest person would not storm off without paying anything; they would simply complain and possibly seek a reduction.

11 Burglary and Aggravated Burglary

LEARNING OUTCOMES

When you have completed this chapter, you should be able to:

- understand how burglary and aggravated burglary contain elements of offences against property and offences against the person;
- interpret complex sections of statute to identify correctly the actus reus and mens rea elements of burglary and aggravated burglary;
- analyse how these offences are applied in practice.

11.1 Introduction

This chapter covers burglary and aggravated burglary. Analysing these crimes will involve some careful statutory interpretation, as the definition of burglary is more complex and wide-ranging than the traditional view of it as an offence of breaking into property in order to steal. Indeed, although burglary usually involves entering premises as a trespasser with an intention to steal and/or actually stealing property, it can be committed in a number of different ways under s 9(1)(a) and s 9(1)(b) of the Theft Act (TA) 1968. Furthermore, because it combines elements of both offences against property and against the person, an analysis of burglary requires crimes such as causing grievous bodily harm to be discussed.

11.2 Burglary

Burglary and the more serious related offence of aggravated burglary are regularly reported in the press and frequently make headline news, especially when a victim is badly hurt or a large sum of money is stolen. It is an either-way offence – on conviction in the Crown Court, the maximum term of imprisonment is 10 years for burglary of commercial premises and 14 years for burglary of domestic premises. The higher sentence for burglary of a dwelling recognises that being a victim of a dwelling burglary can be a frightening and upsetting experience and reflects public concern about this common offence.

The common perception of burglary is that it is connected in some way to stealing property belonging to someone else. It must, however, involve more than theft, otherwise why have an offence of theft under s 1 of the TA 1968 and a separate offence of burglary under s 9 of the same Act? The critical additional element that sets the offences apart is that burglary must occur within a property belonging to someone other than the defendant. However, the legal definition of burglary is more wide-ranging.

Under s 9 of the TA 1968:

> (1) A person is guilty of burglary if–
>
> (a) he enters any building or part of a building as a trespasser and with intent to commit any such offence as is mentioned in subsection (2) below; or
>
> (b) having entered any building or part of a building as a trespasser he steals or attempts to steal anything in the building or that part of it or inflicts or attempts to inflict on any person therein any grievous bodily harm.
>
> (2) The offences referred to in subsection (1)(a) above are offences of stealing anything in the building or part of a building in question, of inflicting on any person therein any grievous bodily harm therein, and of doing unlawful damage to the building or anything therein.

Because of the distinct requirements of s 9(1)(a) and s 9(1)(b), effectively, there are two types of burglary, although they do have similarities. Both require the defendant to:

(a) enter;

(b) a building (or part of a building);

(c) as a trespasser; and

(d) know or be reckless that they are a trespasser.

However, there are also key differences. Section 9(1)(a) focuses on the thoughts that are going through the defendant's mind when doing so, and for this reason it may be referred to as 'burglary with intent'. In contrast, criminal liability in s 9(1)(b) rests upon the defendant's actions once inside the property, and so it can be referred to simply as 'burglary'. Furthermore, there is no consistency as to which offences the defendant must intend or actually carry out.

(a) Under s 9(1)(a), the defendant must *intend* theft, infliction of grievous bodily harm or criminal damage.

(b) Under s 9(1)(b), the defendant must *commit* or *attempt* theft or grievous bodily harm.

11.2.1 Actus reus

Common to the actus reus of both s 9(1)(a) and s 9(1)(b) burglary offences are the requirements that the defendant must enter a building or part of a building as a trespasser. The meaning of these terms will be considered in more detail below.

11.2.1.1 'Entry'

Although 'entry' is a word in everyday use, there have been a number of cases where the courts have considered its meaning in the legal context. Usually it is clear that the defendant entered the property, for example, if they walked into a stranger's house or broke into a school premises at night. However, on occasion, this is not so.

In the rather bizarre case of *R v Collins* [1973] 1 QB 100, the defendant climbed up a ladder to the window of the victim, who was asleep in her bedroom, after having removed all his clothes except for his socks (which he kept on believing this would enable him to escape more quickly!). The victim awoke and, adding to the already unusual circumstances of the case, invited Collins in, assuming that he was her boyfriend. Sexual intercourse then took place. Afterwards, however, she became suspicious, switched on the light, and saw that it was not her boyfriend but the defendant.

At the time of the incident, burglary could be committed by entry as a trespasser with intent to rape. One of the crucial questions for the jury in deciding guilt was where Collins was at the time he was invited in. If he was outside the building kneeling on the window sill, he was innocent of burglary: however, if he had entered the building with any part of his anatomy before being invited in, he was guilty. The case went to the Court of Appeal which held that the defendant should not be convicted unless the jury were satisfied that Collins had made an 'effective and substantial entry' into the bedroom when the complainant caused him to believe that she was consenting to his entry.

Although this authority provides some assistance, the issue of what is meant by 'entry' for the purpose of burglary has been debated by the courts on subsequent occasions, and some of those decisions will now be discussed.

In *R v Brown* [1985] Crim LR 212, the defendant leant in through a shop window for the purpose of stealing items from within the shop. He was convicted of burglary but argued on appeal to the Court of Appeal that he was not guilty as his whole body had not entered the building, the lower half having stayed outside the shop. The judges rejected his argument and upheld his conviction. The Court confirmed that there must be an 'effective' entry for the purpose of burglary, but whether there had been such an entry was a question of fact for the jury.

In the later case of *R v Ryan* [1996] Crim LR 320, the defendant was convicted of burglary after being discovered by an elderly householder, firmly stuck with his head and arm inside a window. He was convicted of burglary but appealed, arguing that he had not effectively entered the property as he was incapable of stealing anything. The Court of Appeal upheld his conviction, finding that entry of some part of the defendant's body into the premises could amount to an effective entry, and it was irrelevant they were not yet in a position to commit a crime. The Court did not say that entry of any part of the defendant's body into the premises would always amount to an entry: it simply confirmed that it could do so.

Following these decisions, it would appear that jurors can conclude that the entry of part of the defendant's body is sufficient to prove they have entered the building, and it is no defence that the defendant cannot at that point commit a crime such as theft or the infliction of grievous bodily harm.

What if a defendant uses an innocent party to enter the building for them, for example, by using a young child to climb through a window and open the door so the defendant can gain access? There is no authority on this point, but the defendant could be said to have entered when the child goes in. The question will be decided by a determination by the jury of whether the defendant has made an entry: the fact that no part of the defendant's body has entered the building may deter them from finding that they have entered, but, in this type of case, is the child not akin to an instrument inserted into the property to facilitate entry?

In order to answer this question, it is necessary to know whether a defendant is deemed to have entered a property if they insert an instrument into a building either to gain entry or to commit a criminal offence, for example, by inserting a hook or magnet on a stick through the letterbox to steal something from the property. The appeal courts have not considered this point, but under the old law (prior to the introduction of the TA 1968), the insertion of an instrument into a building was an entry by the defendant if it was used to commit an offence (such as theft), as in such a case the instrument would be regarded as an extension of the defendant's body. However, it was not an entry if the instrument was used simply to enable the defendant to get into the property, for example, to force open a door or window. Professor Griew, in his work *The Theft Acts 1968 and 1978*, suggests that this would still be the case if the matter fell to be decided by the courts under s 9 of the TA 1968.

The issues relating to entry as a trespasser are summarised in the example below:

Example

Has Majid entered a building in these circumstances?

He climbs through the open window of his neighbour's property.	Yes
He breaks down the door of an office building and goes inside.	Yes
He puts his arm through an open window to take the owner's purse which is lying nearby.	Yes: as entry need only be 'effective' – *R v Brown* [1985]. Majid does not need to enter the building entirely.
He smashes a window and tries to get into the house through the hole, but he gets stuck. Majid is discovered by the owner bending over, so that his feet and legs are outside the building and his upper body and head are inside the building.	Yes: it is irrelevant that Majid was incapable of committing a crime – *R v Ryan* [1996].
He inserts a wire hanger through a letter box and hooks the keys that are hanging near the door.	Maybe: if an instrument is used to commit an offence, such as the theft of keys, it may be treated as an extension of Majid's body.
He pushes his fingertips through the door of a house, which is slightly ajar.	No: if only Majid's fingertips are inserted, the entry is not 'effective'.
He uses a crowbar to force open the window of an office building.	No: as the instrument (the crowbar) is only being used to effect entry by forcing the window.

It is apparent that there are occasions where the entry is clear, and this will apply in the majority of instances. However, there are circumstances in which the law remains unclear, and the lack of recent case law on how an instrument should be treated in the context of burglary is just one example.

11.2.1.2 Building

Entry into a building or part of a building is required for the offence of burglary. Case law suggests that a building must have some degree of permanence about it: a house, factory, shop or garden shed, for instance, would be covered. As far as such properties are concerned, they fall within the definition of a building whether or not someone is actually living in the house, or occupying the factory premises.

Further assistance can be found in s 9(4) of the TA 1968 which makes it clear that the term includes inhabited vehicles and vessels, whether or not the inhabitant is there at the time of the burglary. A houseboat, for example, would qualify as it is inhabited: someone lives on that houseboat, and therefore it counts as a 'building' even if no one was actually there at the time of the burglary. Whether a camper van falls within the definition of property depends on whether the van is inhabited: it will count as a building if it is a permanent home to someone; or if someone is using it as a holiday home at the time of the burglary.

Example

Josie breaks the lock of a camper van which is parked near her home. She enters the van and steals a laptop. Whether she is guilty of burglary or just theft will depend upon the particular facts of the case. If Josie enters a camper van (or a caravan) parked on the victim's drive at home in November, it will not fall within the definition of a building if the van is occupied for only two weeks in August. If, however, Josie entered it within that two-week period in August, for example when the victim had parked the van on a camping site for a holiday, it would count as a building as it is then an inhabited vehicle.

The law which applies to buildings for burglary is summarised below.

Figure 11.1 Definition of a building for burglary

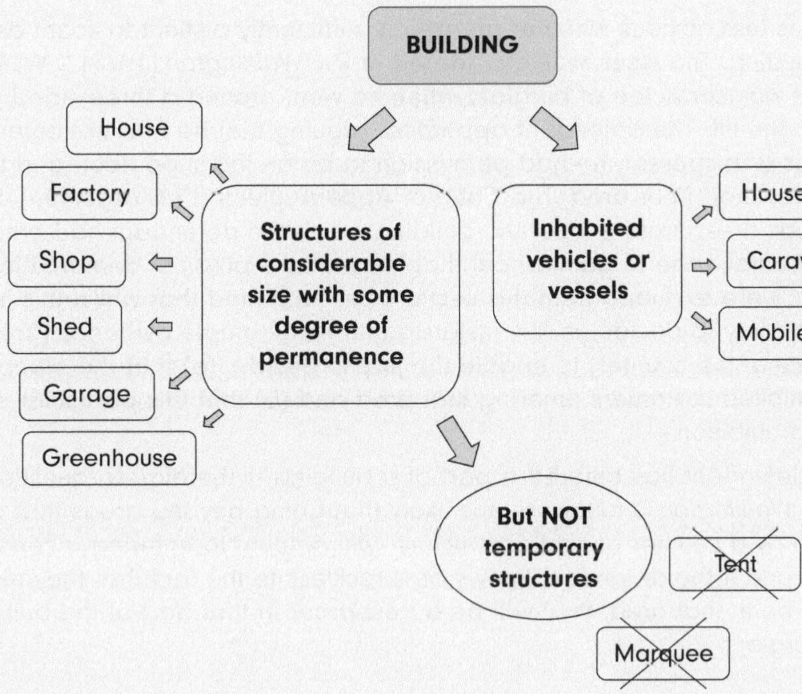

'Part of a building'

The definition under s 9(1) confirms that the initial elements needed to establish an offence of burglary (entry to a building as a trespasser) can be committed either by entry into a building or into part of a building. In situations where the defendant has no right at all to be in the building that they have entered, there is usually no difficulty in establishing the elements of s 9(1)(a) and/or s 9(1)(b) burglary. However, problems may arise where the prosecution has to prove that the defendant entered part of a building as a trespasser, and this would include a defendant who enters a building lawfully but who moves to another part where they do not have the authority to go.

Examples

(1) Mario is lawfully in Flat A as a guest and goes through an open door into Flat B: the door to Flat B has been left open accidentally by the occupier.

(2) Alessia is wandering round Arcos Stores as she wants to buy a new jumper for work. She sees a jumper that she likes inside a stockroom and goes inside despite the door being labelled: Staff Only.

Mario and Alessia were initially invited into the building; thus, they are not trespassers on entry, but do they become trespassers subsequently? To establish that the defendant is a trespasser, it is necessary to show they entered a separate part of the building without permission. It is generally accepted that moving to a different apartment or to a separate room of a building without permission would count. Hence, both Mario and Alessia would satisfy the requirement of entering a part of the building.

Sometimes, it is less obvious whether an area is sufficiently distinct to count as a separate part of the building. This issue was considered in *R v Walkington* [1979] 1 WLR 1169 in which the defendant was convicted of burglary when he went around a three-sided counter in a shop to get to the till. The defendant appealed, arguing that he had not entered 'a part' of the building as a trespasser: he had permission to be on the shop floor, and the till area was part of that shop floor area. The Court of Appeal rejected his argument, holding that the till area was a separate part of the building which the defendant had entered as a trespasser. Geoffrey-Lane LJ pointed out that there was a physical demarcation suggesting that the public were excluded from this section. He confirmed that whilst this issue was a question for the jury to decide, in this instance there was ample evidence (presumably due to the presence of the counter) to enable the jury to decide '(a) that the management had impliedly prohibited customers entering that area and (b) that this particular defendant knew of that prohibition'.

Whether the defendant has entered a part of a building is therefore a question of fact for the jury. If *Walkington* is followed, it is likely that going beyond areas that are roped off, or marked by a counter or similar structure, will amount to entering a separate part of a building; and if the defendant knows or is reckless to the fact that they may not have permission to be in that area, they will be a trespasser in that part of the building for the purpose of burglary.

11.2.1.3 Trespasser in fact

It is an essential element of both the actus reus and the mens rea of burglary that the defendant should enter as a trespasser. If this is not established, there can never be a conviction for burglary, no matter what the defendant does once they are inside the property and whatever they intend to do on entering the property.

As far as the criminal offence of burglary is concerned, trespass requires proof that the defendant entered without consent or permission and that they knew or were reckless as to this. The state of mind of the defendant on entry will be discussed later in this chapter. Although, establishing that the defendant is a trespasser will usually be straightforward, it is not always so.

Examples

(1) *Sinead breaks a window to gain access to a house when the owners are out.*

She is a trespasser as she is clearly entering the property without the consent of the owner. It is this type of situation that is most frequently associated with burglary.

(2) *Martin has been banned from entering the local store but goes in wearing a face mask to buy alcohol.*

He is a trespasser as he has no express permission to enter, and any implied permission to enter the store to browse the goods has been revoked.

There is no direct authority under the TA 1968 on whether fraudulently obtained permission to enter premises is sufficient to establish trespass for the purpose of a charge of burglary. However, under the old law (prior to the TA 1968), the courts held that permission to enter obtained by fraud was not a true permission (*R v Boyle* [1954] 2 QB 292). Professor JC Smith, in his book *The Law of Theft* (8th edn, p 194), says that 'it seems to be entirely clear that where the defendant gains entry by deception he enters as a trespasser'.

Examples

(1) *Jackie has been served with a court order banning her from her former husband's home, but she persuades a neighbour to let her in with a spare key, telling the neighbour that she has forgotten her own key.*

Jackie is a trespasser as she has been banned from entering the house and only obtained access by lying. Furthermore, the neighbour would not have allowed Jackie in had she been aware of the court injunction.

(2) *Nick falsely tells Ida, an elderly lady, that he is a police officer, and Ida lets him into her home.*

As with the previous scenario, Nick has obtained permission to enter through fraud, and therefore he is a trespasser because he has no true permission to enter. Ida only allowed Nick in because of her belief that he was a police officer.

What if a person is asked to leave a property? In this instance, they have an implied right to leave by the most direct route.

Example

Chiara has been invited to her friend's house for a coffee. When they have an argument, Chiara is told to leave immediately but, on the way out, she decides to go upstairs to use the toilet. Because she has exceeded the implied licence, Chiara is a trespasser when she goes to a separate part of the house.

In the case of *R v Jones and Smith* [1976] 1 WLR 672, the Court of Appeal considered a different scenario. It was accepted that the defendant (Smith) clearly had permission to enter his father's house. However, the question for the judges was whether he could be a trespasser given that, when Smith entered, he did so intending to steal - presumably not something that was within his father's contemplation when he gave his consent. If Smith was not a trespasser, he could not be guilty of burglary; therefore, the issue was an important one. The Court of Appeal concluded that a defendant could be a trespasser where they had permission to enter for lawful purposes but instead entered for an unlawful purpose, and they knew or were reckless that they were exceeding the terms of the permission given.

The case of *R v Jones and Smith* is authority for the fact that entering a building with the intention of doing something contrary to a general permission to enter can amount to trespass. The implications of this case are considered in the examples below.

Examples

(1) *Jamil has general permission to go to his father's house and has his own key. One night, he goes to the house planning to watch a football match on his father's TV. His father would be in agreement with this. However, once Jamil is inside the house, he spots a £20 note on the table and decides to steal it.*

Jamil is not a trespasser as, at the time of entering his father's home, he had no intention of exceeding the terms of his father's consent to enter. The fact that he decided to steal the £20 once he was inside could render Jamil liable for theft, but he cannot be guilty of burglary as he did not enter as a trespasser. Forming the intention to do something contrary to the terms of the consent given after entering the property is too late; in order for the principle in R v Jones and Smith *to apply, the defendant must at the time of entry intend to exceed the terms of the consent given, or at least be reckless as to whether those terms will be exceeded.*

(2) *Chloe goes to the local department store, planning to steal some perfume. The doorman at the store holds the shop door open for her and invites her in. Although shops do, of course, give a general permission to customers to enter their premises, that authority is given on the understanding that customers will browse around and, it is hoped, buy their products: not on the basis that customers will steal their goods!*

Because Chloe plans to steal from the store on entry, using the principle of R v Jones and Smith, *Chloe is, and knows she is, exceeding the terms of the permission to enter the store and is therefore entering as a trespasser.*

Although they are not usually charged as such, the case of *R v Jones and Smith* suggests that if it can be proved that a shoplifter intended to steal before and on entering the shop (or part of the shop), they could be charged with the offence of burglary. In reality, shoplifters are usually charged with theft.

In summary, for both s 9(1)(a) and s 9(1)(b) burglary, the defendant must enter a building or part of a building as a trespasser. However, there is an additional actus reus requirement that applies under s 9(1)(b), namely that the defendant must also commit the actus reus of theft, attempted theft, grievous bodily harm or attempted grievous bodily harm.

11.2.2 Mens rea

As with the actus reus, there are some elements that are common to both types of burglary, but others that are not.

11.2.2.1 Knowledge or recklessness as to trespass

At civil law, showing that someone did in fact enter premises without permission is sufficient to establish they are a trespasser. However, under the criminal law, just proving that a person was in fact a trespasser is not enough: to establish the trespass element on a charge of burglary, the prosecution must also show that the defendant had a particular state of mind in relation to the fact that they were trespassing. In other words, both the actus reus and the mens rea of trespassing must be proved.

The mens rea of trespass required for a charge of burglary is that the defendant must either know they were entering as a trespasser, or be reckless as to whether they were a trespasser. Recklessness here would require the defendant to foresee the risk that they do not have permission to enter and go on, without justification, to take that risk. If, therefore, the defendant trespasses 'by accident', they will not satisfy this essential element required for a charge of burglary.

When must the defendant have this awareness? The issue was considered in *R v Collins* discussed earlier in this chapter. The Court of Appeal confirmed that the mens rea for entry as a trespasser under s 9(1)(a) burglary was *at the time of entry* into the building or part of a building – a logical conclusion given that the offence is complete at this point. With regard to s 9(1)(b) burglary, as the statute refers to the defendant 'having entered' as a trespasser, they must also have the mens rea on entry. This view is supported by the judgment of Lord Edmund Davies in *R v Collins*, where he states that 'for the purposes of s 9 of the Theft Act 1968, a person entering a building is not guilty of trespass if he enters without knowledge that he is trespassing or at least without acting recklessly as to whether or not he is trespassing'.

11.2.3 Differences between s 9(1)(a) and s 9(1)(b) burglary

Thus far, the elements common to both s 9(1)(a) and s 9(1)(b) burglary have been discussed, namely, entry into a building or part of a building as a trespasser. However, there are also significant differences between the two types, and these are summarised in the table (below).

Summary of actus reus and mens rea for burglary

Type of burglary	s 9(1)(a)	s 9(1)(b)
Actus reus	Enter a building or part of a building as a trespasser	Same
		Commit the actus reus of: • theft; • attempted theft; • grievous bodily harm; or • attempted grievous bodily harm.
Mens rea	Knowledge/recklessness as to being a trespasser	Same
	Intend to commit: • theft; • grievous bodily harm; or • criminal damage	Have the mens rea for: • theft; • attempted theft; • grievous bodily harm; or • attempted grievous bodily harm.

11.2.3.1 Additional mens rea requirements for s 9(1)(a) burglary

In order to establish liability under s 9(1)(a), in addition to proving that the defendant entered a building or part thereof as a trespasser, it is also necessary to show that the defendant, when entering that building or part, intended to steal, cause criminal damage or inflict grievous bodily harm. If the prosecution cannot prove that the defendant intended to commit one of these three relevant offences at the point of entry, the defendant may not be convicted of burglary under s 9(1)(a). However, it is important to remember that there is no need for the defendant actually to commit any of those offences: entering as a trespasser with the *intention* of doing so is sufficient.

Furthermore, from the wording of s 9(2), it is apparent that the defendant must, for s 9(1)(a) burglary, enter a building or part of a building as a trespasser with the intention of either stealing or inflicting grievous bodily harm in *that* building, or in *that part* of the building. In contrast, if the defendant intends to commit criminal damage, it is sufficient that they intend to commit this in *any* part of the building.

11.2.3.2 Conditional intent

It is not unusual for a defendant to have a conditional intent only to commit one of these offences. For example, if they enter a building as a trespasser, thinking 'I will damage any antiques they might have', or if, once inside the building, they think 'I will steal the cash if the safe is open'. In these situations, the defendant is not definitely going to commit an offence: their intent is conditional on certain circumstances existing.

In *Attorney-General's Reference (Nos 1 and 2 of 1979)* [1980] QB 180, the Court of Appeal confirmed that, where the defendants had entered properties looking for money to steal, a conditional intent to steal was sufficient to establish mens rea on a charge of burglary. It was no defence for the defendants to argue that their intent to steal was conditional on there being anything worth stealing in the property.

Although both matters in the *Attorney-General's Reference* related to a conditional intent to steal, the same principle would presumably apply if a defendant was charged under s 9(1)(a) on the basis that they had a conditional intent to cause grievous bodily harm or criminal damage.

11.2.3.3 Additional mens rea requirements for s 9(1)(b) burglary

Although the defendant must satisfy the mens rea for trespass on entry, in contrast to s 9(1)(a) burglary, under s 9(1)(b) the defendant can form the mens rea for the offence of theft or causing grievous bodily harm after they have entered.

The prosecution must prove that the defendant entered a building or part of a building as a trespasser and, once inside, that they stole or attempted to steal, or inflicted grievous bodily harm or attempted to do so. In other words, there is an additional element of both actus reus and mens rea to be proved before a defendant can be convicted of an offence under s 9(1)(b). Note that the offence is satisfied if the defendant had the mens rea for either a s 18 or a s 20 assault under the Offences Against the Person Act 1861.

11.2.4 Summary of burglary

Burglary is an unusual offence as it can be committed in two similar but slightly differing ways, and the main points are summarised below.

(a) For offences under s 9(1)(a) and s 9(1)(b) of the TA 1968, the defendant must enter a building or part thereof as a trespasser.

(b) To satisfy the trespass element of both offences, the defendant must be a trespasser in fact - enter without permission or consent to do so (actus reus); and either know or be reckless as to this on entry (mens rea).

(c) In addition to proving entry into a building (or part) as a trespasser, for s 9(1)(a) burglary it must be proved that, at the time of entering the building (or part), the defendant intended to steal, inflict grievous bodily harm, or cause criminal damage. Provided the intention was present at the time of entry, the fact that the defendant does not go on to commit any of these offences is irrelevant to liability under s 9(1)(a).

(d) In addition to proving entry into a building (or part) as a trespasser, for s 9(1)(b) burglary it must be proved that, having entered, the defendant actually stole or inflicted grievous bodily harm, or attempted to steal or to inflict grievous bodily harm. The mens rea for either theft or the infliction of grievous bodily harm need not be present at the time of entry for s 9(1)(b) – it can be formed once inside the property.

(e) Quite frequently, the defendant will be guilty of offences under both s 9(1)(a) and s 9(1)(b). For example, if a defendant enters a building as a trespasser intending to steal, they are guilty of an offence under s 9(1)(a). If, having entered as a trespasser, they then go on to steal from the building, they will also be criminally liable under s 9(1)(b).

Set out below is a flowchart to assist your understanding of burglary.

Figure 11.2 Burglary

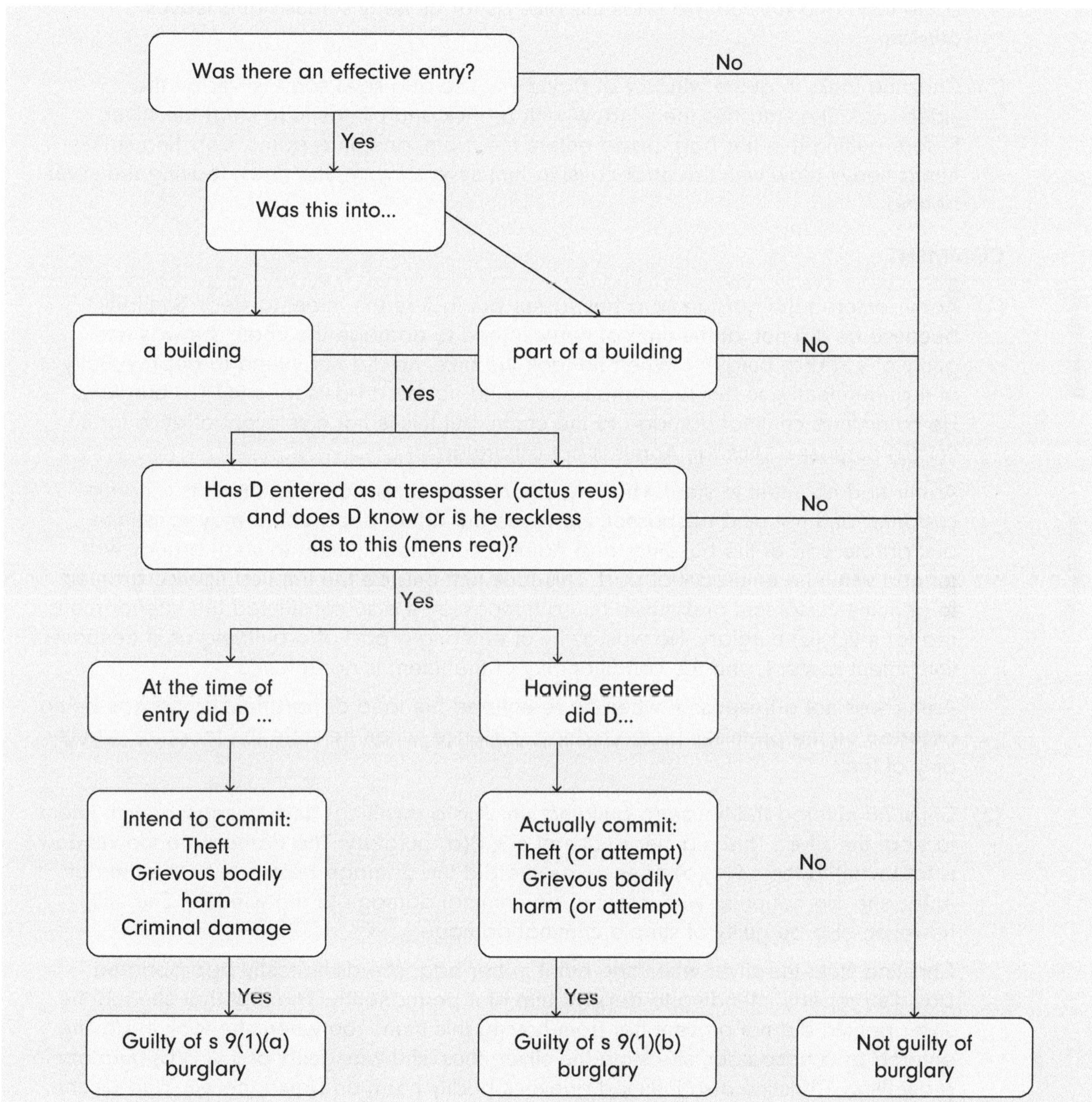

To assist your understanding, you should attempt this activity on burglary.

ACTIVITY

Consider the following scenarios and decide what liability (if any) the defendant might have under s 9(1)(a) and/or s 9(1)(b) of the TA 1968.

(1) Aamir walks into Betty's garage to shelter from the rain. When the rain stops, he notices her bike in the garage. He decides to take it to the local supermarket and return it later in the day but, to take the bike, he has to break a chain which fastens it to the wall. Having entered the supermarket to buy food, Aamir decides to go into the drinks department to see if they have his favourite brandy; if they have any, he intends to steal it. Before he can do so, he is seen by the manager, who thinks Aamir is acting suspiciously. The manager orders him to leave the supermarket and escorts him out, via the food department. Just as he is about to leave the shop, Aamir grabs some food and runs off. He rides the bike as far as Betty's house and leaves it outside.

(2) Christina looks in at the window of David's house and sees some silver on the sideboard. She smashes the window with a brick and climbs in to steal the silver, before putting it in her bag. David enters the room, and, in a panic, Christina strikes him a heavy blow with the brick causing him severe injury. She flees, leaving the silver behind.

COMMENT

(1) Aamir entered the garage as a trespasser but lacked the intent to steal. Similarly, because he did not, at the time of entry, intend to damage the chain, he was not guilty of s 9(1)(a) burglary. When he took the bike, he did not intend to deprive Betty of it permanently, so this is not theft and could not be a basis for s 9(1)(b) burglary. He committed criminal damage to the chain, but this is not a relevant offence for s 9(1)(b) purposes. Thus far, Aamir is not a burglar.

Aamir had no intent to steal when he entered the shop, so he entered as a normal customer and not as a trespasser. However, the drinks department may constitute a separate part of the building, and Aamir's conditional intent to steal brandy was formed when he entered that part. This took him outside the implied licence granted to genuine customers and made him a trespasser; it also constituted the ulterior mens rea for s 9(1)(a) burglary. He was guilty of entering a part of a building as a trespasser with intent to steal, and the conditionality of the intent is no defence.

Aamir was not a trespasser when he re-entered the food department as he was being escorted off the premises by the manager. Hence, when he stole the food, he is guilty only of theft.

(2) Christina entered the house (a building which is a dwelling) as a trespasser with intent to steal the silver. This is a clear case of s 9(1)(a) burglary. The damage to the window is irrelevant to the s 9(1)(a) offence, as she did the damage before or at the time of entry; she did not enter with intent to do criminal damage to the window. She will, however, also be guilty of simple criminal damage.

Christina stole the silver when she put it in her bag; she dishonestly appropriated David's property intending to deprive him of it permanently. The fact that she left the silver behind did not prevent her from having this mens rea when she took it. Having entered as a trespasser, she stole the silver; thus, she was guilty of s 9(1)(b) burglary in a dwelling. Christina also inflicted grievous bodily harm on David therein, and as she had the mens rea of at least an offence under s 20 of the OAPA 1861, this constituted another s 9(1)(b) burglary.

11.3 Aggravated burglary

On occasion, there will be media reports of criminals breaking into people's homes, or into building societies or banks, and tying up the victims or using weapons to threaten or to inflict injury on the occupants of the premises. Criminals who are 'armed' when they commit an offence of burglary can also face liability for an aggravated offence of burglary under s 10 of the TA 1968.

This offence is separate from the 'basic' offence of burglary, and the definition may be found in s 10(1) of the Theft Act 1968 which provides:

> A person is guilty of aggravated burglary if he commits any burglary and at the time has with him any firearm or imitation firearm, any weapon of offence, or any explosive.

Aggravated burglary is an indictable only offence, meaning it can only be tried in the Crown Court, and carries a maximum sentence of life imprisonment to reflect the seriousness of criminals entering premises armed with weapons. The offence requires proof of all the elements of burglary for either s 9(1)(a) or s 9(1)(b) of the TA 1968, but, in addition, the defendant must be in possession of a weapon at the time of the burglary.

11.3.1 Weapons

The items which the law deems to be weapons are listed in the statute under s 10(1). For this purpose:

> (a) 'firearm' includes an airgun or air pistol, and 'imitation firearm' means anything which has the appearance of being a firearm, whether capable of being discharged or not; and
>
> (b) 'weapon of offence' means any article made or adapted for use for causing injury to or incapacitating a person, or intended by the person having it with him for such use; and
>
> (c) 'explosive' means any article manufactured for the purpose of producing a practical effect by explosion, or intended by the person having it with him for that purpose.

A weapon of offence is widely defined and could include a machete as it has been made for use in causing injury; a broken bottle adapted for use in causing injury; a hammer intended for such use; a length of rope as this could be used to incapacitate a person; or handcuffs as these are intended for such use. However, these are just a sample of what could count as a weapon.

11.3.2 Knowledge

The defendant must know they have the item with them, but there is no need to prove that they intended to use the weapon during the burglary. In *R v Stones* [1989] 1 WLR 156, the defendant was in possession of a knife which he said was for the purposes of self-defence. However, he was convicted of aggravated burglary as the court found that any intention not to use the knife was irrelevant.

Furthermore, in the case of *R v Kelly* (1993) 97 Cr App R 245, the defendant used a screwdriver, which he had taken with him in order to break into the property, to assault the occupant who surprised him during the burglary. The Court of Appeal held that the fact the screwdriver was used in the heat of the moment was not a defence to aggravated burglary as the defendant had the intent to use it should the need arise.

11.3.3 'At the time'

The defendant must have the weapon with them 'at the time' of committing the burglary, and this varies depending upon the offence with which they are charged. For s 9(1)(a) burglary, it is at the time of entry; whereas for s 9(1)(b) burglary, the relevant time is when the ulterior offence (theft, grievous bodily harm or attempted theft or grievous bodily harm) is committed.

In *R v Francis* [1982] Crim LR 363, the defendants entered a house armed with sticks but discarded them before committing theft. They were found not guilty of aggravated burglary on appeal as the prosecution could not prove that the accused had the sticks with them at the moment they intended to steal. However, in *R v O'Leary* (1986) 82 Cr App R 341, the defendant armed himself with a knife from within the kitchen of the house before going upstairs and confronting the occupants. Although he had not taken the knife into the property, thus did not have it at the time of entry, he was guilty of aggravated burglary under s 9(1)(b) because he had the weapon with him at the time he committed the theft.

These cases demonstrate the wide interpretation which the courts give to the requirement for a weapon.

11.3.4 Summary of aggravated burglary

Before considering whether the defendant is guilty of an offence under s 10(1) of the Theft Act 1968, the prosecution must first establish that there has been a burglary under s 9. In practice, if the defendant is armed in some way, aggravated burglary is likely to be the relevant offence.

Figure 11.3 Aggravated burglary

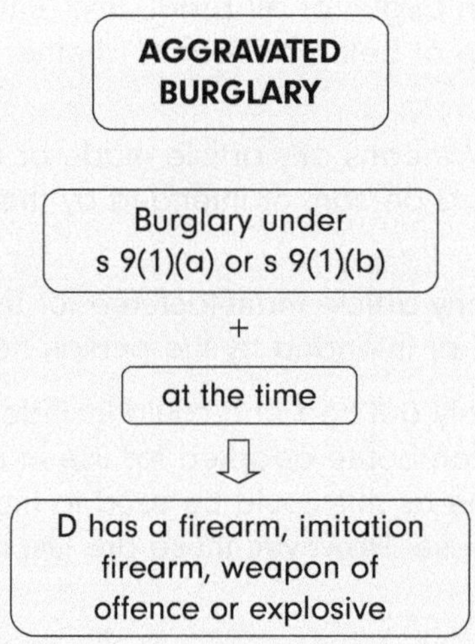

ACTIVITY

Maurice approaches a house intending to break in to steal the cash that he knows the householder, Amelia, keeps in a safe. Suddenly, he remembers that he has a large knife in his rucksack which he always carries for 'self-defence'. He decides to leave this in the bushes to collect on his way out, as he does not think he will need it. Maurice also has a hammer with him which he intends to use to break down the back door. He smashes the lock with the hammer and enters the house. He is shocked to be confronted by Amelia's nephew, Francis, who restrains him and calls the police. When Maurice is arrested, a child's toy pistol is discovered in his pocket.

Is Maurice guilty of aggravated burglary under s 10 of the Theft Act 1968?

COMMENT

Maurice commits burglary under s 9(1)(a) of the TA 1968. He does not commit aggravated burglary in relation to the large knife because he did not have it with him at the time of committing the burglary, this being at the time of entry for burglary with intent. He left it in the bushes to collect on the way out. He is not guilty of aggravated burglary for the hammer as it was intended for use to break in, and not as a 'weapon of offence'. A hammer is not made for use for causing injury to a person, nor was it intended or adapted for such use. However, Maurice is liable for aggravated burglary for the child's toy pistol as the definition of weapons includes 'imitation firearms ... whether capable of being discharged or not'.

12 Criminal Damage

LEARNING OUTCOMES

When you have completed this chapter, you should be able to:

- define simple and aggravated criminal damage and arson, and explain how these are applied in practice;
- explain the concept of lawful excuse and when this will operate as a defence to a charge of criminal damage.

12.1 Introduction

Criminal damage is one of the more common offences committed in society and ranges from the petty, such as the daubing of graffiti on buildings, to the very serious, for example the damage resulting from the full scale riots which occurred in 2011 and cost businesses millions of pounds. The motives of those who commit these crimes are equally varied, from boredom to anger to the political.

Although criminal damage is an either-way offence, most such offences will result in damage valued at less than £5,000, and thus can only be dealt with in the magistrates' court. Criminal damage by fire is known as 'arson' and is triable either way; whereas the aggravated criminal damage offences, where the defendant intended or was reckless as to endangering the life of another, are more serious and are indictable only offences.

12.2 Criminal damage

The relevant offences may be found in the Criminal Damage Act (CDA) 1971 and comprise:

(a) simple criminal damage – s 1(1);

(b) aggravated criminal damage – s 1(2);

(c) simple arson – s 1(3) and s 1(1);

(d) aggravated arson – s 1(3) and s 1(2).

The elements to be proved for simple and aggravated arson are essentially the same, but arson will be charged where the damage is caused by fire.

12.3 Simple criminal damage

The definition of the offence of simple criminal damage under s 1(1) is:

> A person who without lawful excuse destroys or damages any property belonging to another intending to destroy or damage any such property or being reckless as to whether any such property would be destroyed or damaged shall be guilty of an offence.

12.3.1 Actus reus

There are three elements making up the actus reus of the offence, namely:

(a) damage or destruction;

(b) of property;

(c) belonging to another.

These will be considered in turn.

12.3.1.1 Destroy or damage

The first requirement is to 'destroy or damage'. It includes physical harm, whether permanent or temporary, as well as the impairment of the value or usefulness of property - for example, when a part is removed from a machine. Destruction has its normal English language meaning and would cover, for example, the demolition of a building, the burning of a field of crops or where a vase is pushed off a pedestal causing it to smash.

However, what counts as 'damage' is less clear, although it is established that the damage does not have to be extensive. In the case of *Roe v Kingerlee* [1986] Crim LR 735, the court said the issue of whether damage had been caused was a matter of fact and degree to be determined in a common-sense way. Usually if expense is involved in restoring the property to its previous condition, the court is likely to find that damage is caused. Thus, in the case of *Hardman v Chief Constable of Avon and Somerset Constabulary* [1986] Crim LR 330, drawings on a pavement made by using soluble chalks amounted to criminal damage as the local authority incurred expense in cleaning it up. In contrast, the defendant's conviction for criminal damage for spitting on a police officer's raincoat was quashed in *A (a juvenile) v R* [1978] Crim LR 689. The faint mark caused was held not to be sufficient damage as it could have been wiped away with a damp cloth, leaving no mark.

12.3.1.2 Property

The second element of the actus reus of simple criminal damage is that there must be damage or destruction to property. The definition of 'property' for the purposes of the CDA 1971 is contained in s 10(1). The provision is widely drawn and covers property of a tangible nature (so a thing in action such as a bank account cannot be damaged). It includes both real property, for example land and buildings, and personal property including money. With regards to animals and plants, the law takes account of the circumstances, primarily whether the item is wild or not. Animals are included if tamed or ordinarily kept in captivity (pets and zoo animals); or if they have been, or are being, reduced into possession (for example, a rabbit that has been snared).

A similar approach is adopted in relation to plants, so flowers growing in a garden or a local park may be damaged, but wild mushrooms, fruit, flowers, foliage and plants cannot.

12.3.1.3 Belonging to another

Finally, for the actus reus of simple criminal damage, not only must property be damaged or destroyed, the property (for the simple offence) must belong to another. The offence cannot be committed against a person's own property. Usually, this aspect will be straightforward but s 10(2) provides some additional guidance:

(2) Property shall be treated for the purposes of this Act as belonging to any person—

(a) having the custody or control of it;

(b) having in it any proprietary right or interest (not being an equitable interest arising only from an agreement to transfer or grant an interest); or

(c) having a charge on it.

Clearly the legal owner is covered, and the examples below demonstrate who else is.

Examples

(1) Guy kicks in the front door of a house causing damage to the door. If he owns the house, he cannot be liable for criminal damage, unless he owns it subject to a mortgage, in which case the lending company has a charge (and also a proprietary interest). Furthermore, if Guy rents the house then it will belong to another (the landlord); and if he co-owns the house, it also belongs to another (the co-owner).

(2) Nicola scribbles on a textbook that her friend, Ksenia, has borrowed from the library. Ksenia has custody or control, as she is in possession of the book. However, the library owns the textbook and has a proprietary right.

There is one other element of the actus reus of criminal damage to consider, that of lawful excuse, and this is dealt with later in the chapter.

12.3.2 Mens rea

Having considered the elements required to satisfy the actus reus of criminal damage, the prosecution must also prove the necessary mens rea requirements. The defendant must:

(a) intend to damage or destroy property or be reckless as to such damage or destruction; and

(b) know that the property belongs to another or be reckless as to whether the property belongs to another.

In many cases, the criminal damage will be deliberately inflicted, such as the smashing of a bus shelter or the writing of graffiti on a wall, but in other instances the defendant may only be reckless. Since the decision in *R v G* [2004] 1 AC 1034, the test for recklessness in criminal damage has been subjective, and the accused will be judged on the basis of their own state of mind. In this case, the defendants, aged 11 and 12, set fire to newspapers in a yard behind a shop and then threw the newspapers under a wheelie bin, before running away. The fire spread to the shop causing significant damage. The House of Lords amended the law so that the test for recklessness became subjective in this context, and, as it was accepted that neither defendant appreciated the risk of damaging property, they were found not guilty of this offence.

There is a second element to the mens rea, and this is the requirement that the defendant must know or believe the property belongs to another. How does this affect the defendant who believes the property is or may be their own but is mistaken? If the defendant is sure of this, they will lack the mens rea of criminal damage, because they do not know that the property belongs to another nor are they reckless as to this fact (they have not foreseen the risk that the property belongs to another).

In *R v Smith* [1974] QB 354, the defendant, who was a tenant of a property, damaged fixtures at the property wrongly believing that those fixtures belonged to him. His conviction for criminal damage was quashed on appeal. The court held that if a person honestly believed property was their own then they lacked the mens rea. It did not matter whether the belief was reasonably held, as long as it was an honest belief.

Example

Wesley is camping in a tent belonging to Pam. He lights the camping stove to make a cup of tea but, unfortunately, the tent catches fire. The prosecution analyses Wesley's liability for simple arson in view of the following mistakes:

(a) He believes that the tent is fireproof.

(b) He believes that the tent belongs to him.

(c) He believes that the risk of fire is minimal.

In each scenario, Wesley has committed the actus reus of simple arson under s 1(1) and s 1(3) of the CDA 1971 as he has damaged property (the tent) belonging to another (Pam) by fire. With regard to his mens rea:

(a) Wesley is not guilty, as he did not intend to damage the tent nor did he foresee any risk of damaging it, so he lacks the mens rea of intention or recklessness as to damaging property.

(b) Wesley is not guilty. He thinks that the tent belongs to him, so he lacks the mens rea as to whether the property belonged to another.

(c) Wesley is guilty as he has been reckless as to damaging the property. He has foreseen a risk, however slight, and gone on to take it. Taking any risk would be unjustified.

There is one additional phrase within the definition of criminal damage that has not yet been considered. Section 1(1) of the CDA 1971 states that an offence is committed if property is intentionally or recklessly damaged or destroyed without lawful excuse. This will now be considered in more detail.

12.3.3 Lawful excuse

The law sets out two situations where a defendant has a lawful excuse and these can be found in s 5 of the CDA 1971. However, although an accused may rely upon these statutory lawful excuses as a defence to simple criminal damage and arson, they do not apply to aggravated criminal damage.

12.3.3.1 Belief in consent

Under s 5(2)(a), a defendant will have a lawful excuse, and therefore a defence to a charge of criminal damage under s 1(1) of the Act, if they argue that either:

(a) they believed they had the consent of the person who *was* entitled to give permission for the damage to be caused (for example, they thought they had permission from the owner of the property); or

(b) they believed they had the consent of the person whom *they thought* was entitled to give permission for the damage to be caused (for example, they thought they had permission from someone whom they (wrongly) believed to be the owner of the property); or

(c) they believed they *would have had* the consent of the person entitled to give permission if that person had known of the damage and the circumstances; or

(d) they believed they *would have had* the consent of the person whom they thought was entitled to give permission if that person had known of the damage and the circumstances.

Section 5(3) makes it clear that this is a subjective test, and examples of how this would apply in practice are set out below.

Example

Farzana has deliberately smashed the window of her neighbour's car. She satisfies the actus reus and mens rea requirements of simple criminal damage under s 1(1) of the CDA 1971 as she intentionally damaged property belonging to another. However, she can raise a defence of lawful excuse under s 5 of the 1971 Act in the following circumstances:

(1) She had left her purse in the car and she did not think the neighbour would mind her damaging his car in the circumstances. This could be lawful excuse under s 5(2)(a): Farzana honestly believed she would have had the consent of the person entitled to give consent (the neighbour) if the neighbour had known of the damage and the circumstances.

(2) She made a mistake and thought the car belonged to her father. Farzana did not think he would mind her breaking the window to get her purse. This would also fall within s 5(2)(a); she honestly believed she would have had the consent of her father had he known of the situation. Her father, of course, in reality has no right to give her permission to damage the neighbour's car, but Farzana thinks it is her father's car and thus she would have permission from the person she believes is entitled to give consent (her father). The fact that she is wrong in her beliefs and is mistaken as to who can give her permission does not matter, provided she honestly believed she would have had valid permission.

(3) She misheard the instructions shouted to her by her neighbour. He told her to 'check' the car window but she thought he said 'break' the car window, so she did! This scenario would also fall within s 5(2)(a) as Farzana believes she does have the consent of the person entitled to consent. She thinks the neighbour (as the owner of the car) has given her permission to break the window, as he has asked her to do this. Although this appears to be a silly mistake on the part of Farzana, if she honestly thought that is what the neighbour had told her to do, she has lawful excuse.

(4) She saw her pet cat locked in the car. It was a very hot day, so she smashed the window to free the cat. Under s 5(2)(a), Farzana could argue that she honestly thought the neighbour would have consented to the damage if he had known of the circumstances (that the cat was trapped).

In the *Attorney General's Reference on a Point of Law No 1 of 2023* [2024] EWCA Crim 243, the scope and effect of s 5(2)(a) of the Criminal Damage Act 1971 was considered. The defence had become increasingly prominent in the context of the activities of protesters who argued that owners of the property would have consented to the damage had they known of the circumstances of climate change. The Court of Appeal rejected this argument and held that the 'circumstances' of the damage have to be linked directly, so could include, for example, the time, place and extent of the damage, or even that the damage was caused as part of a protest. However, Baroness Carr confirmed that the circumstances 'would not include the political or philosophical beliefs of the person causing the damage' nor the reasoning or wider motivations for the damage. As a consequence, evidence from the defendant about the facts of or effects of climate change would be inadmissible when arguing the defence under s 5(2)(a).

Sometimes a defendant will make a mistake because they were intoxicated. In *Jaggard v Dickinson* [1980] All ER 716, the defendant broke a window to get into a house that she thought belonged to her friend. She (correctly) believed her friend would consent because she had no way of getting home, but, unfortunately, because she was drunk, the defendant mistakenly entered the wrong house. Despite this, the defendant was able to rely on lawful excuse. This is consistent with the test being purely subjective – the requirement that the belief need only be honestly held.

12.3.3.2 Need of protection

There is another form of lawful excuse, and this may be found in s 5(2)(b). Under this provision, the defendant will have lawful excuse if they can argue that:

(a) they believed property (their own or another's) was in immediate need of protection;

and

(b) they believed that the means of protection they adopted (which led to the criminal damage) were reasonable having regard to all the circumstances.

In many cases, the application of s 5(2)(b) is quite straightforward as demonstrated below.

Example

Returning to scenario (4) in the previous example, in which Farzana saw her pet cat locked in the neighbour's car, you will recall that it was a very hot day, so she smashed the window to free the cat. This situation could fall within s 5(2)(a) as stated above but also under s 5(2)(b), as Farzana could claim:

(1) that she honestly believed her property (the cat) was in immediate need of protection; and

(2) that she honestly believed that breaking the window of the car was a reasonable means of protecting the cat in all the circumstances.

However, on occasion, more complex situations arise, and lawful excuse under s 5(2)(b) will be broken down into its different elements.

Purpose?

The first question to be determined is whether the defendant's (real) purpose was the protection of their own or another's property. This is a two-stage process.

(a) The court must be satisfied that the accused honestly believed their action was protecting, or was capable of protecting, property (subjective). In other words, they are not simply using this reason to conceal a different one. In the case of *R v Hunt* (1978) 66 Cr App R 105, a defendant who set fire to a room in a care home to draw attention to the defective fire alarm system failed this test.

(b) Having determined what the defendant's purpose was, the court will rule as a matter of law whether this amounts to a purpose of protecting property. This is an objective test.

In *R v Hunt* (1978) 66 Cr App R 105, the Court of Appeal confirmed that the question of whether a particular act of destruction or damage was done in order to protect property belonging to another must be, on the true construction of the statute, an objective test. This view was followed in the later case of *R v Hill and Hall* (1989) Crim LR 136. The facts were that the defendants, who were members of the Campaign for Nuclear Disarmament, cut the fence surrounding a US naval base. They justified their actions by stating that they wanted to protect properties nearby, which would be damaged or destroyed by the fallout from a nuclear attack if the Russians decided to target the base. Their reasoning was that such action would cause the Americans to leave, so removing that threat. The judge found that this was not something done to protect property as, even if the defendants genuinely believed this, on an objective test, the action was far too remote from the eventual aim of protecting property.

Lawful excuse has been used quite creatively over time. The environmental group, Greenpeace, has successfully argued this defence on more than one occasion: in 2000, when digging up genetically modified crops; and again, in 2007, when scaling a chimney at a power station and painting the word 'Gordon' down the side. At the trial, Greenpeace called experts to support their case that they were trying to protect the world from climate change. However, others have questioned the defendants' motives and suggested that they were simply making a political statement and their real purpose was publicity for the cause. Ultimately, it will be for the judge to decide this question based upon the evidence.

Even if the defendant can overcome this hurdle, the remainder of the legal test must still be satisfied.

Immediate need of protection?

The defendant must also honestly believe that the property was in immediate need of protection. Again, this is a subjective test.

In *Johnson v DPP* [1994] Crim LR 673, the defendant was squatting in a disused house in Leeds. He was charged with simple criminal damage after chiselling off the lock on the front door and replacing it with his own. Johnson admitted changing the lock but submitted that he only did so to secure the property and to prevent his possessions from being stolen. In other words, he was taking steps to protect his property. Unfortunately for Johnson, the argument was not accepted, and he was found guilty of criminal damage. The reason was that there was no evidence the house was in need of immediate protection and the future risk of theft was not sufficient.

Returning to the case of *Hill and Hall* (above), even if the defendants had succeeded in satisfying the objective test that they were protecting property, they would have failed on this subjective test as there was no immediate threat of a nuclear attack.

Reasonable?

Finally, the defendant must satisfy the court that they honestly believed the damage or destruction was reasonable in the circumstances. Again, this is a subjective test so the defendant will be judged on their own beliefs.

> **_Example_**
>
> *Daniel has a right of vehicular access over his neighbour's land and is involved in a court dispute over this. One evening, he returns to find a gate has been built across the track, blocking his way. He needs to feed his horses which are in a field further on and so he removes the gate, causing damage as he does so.*

To rely upon the defence of lawful excuse, Daniel would need to provide evidence that he caused the damage to the gate to protect his property (his horses) and not, for example, to pursue the neighbour dispute. The court must then be satisfied that, in law, his action was capable of doing so - an objective test.

Thereafter, Daniel would have to demonstrate that he honestly believed (a subjective test) that the property (his horses) were in immediate danger and that the means adopted were reasonable. This would depend upon the evidence.

(a) If Daniel's horses needed feeding, he may be able to prove that his property was in immediate danger; but he may fail if it could be established that he could gain access to the horses another way - perhaps by a different route.

(b) Similarly, with the means adopted. If Daniel damaged the hinges as he lifted the gate before setting it down on the side of the track, this would be reasonable; but not if he smashed into the gate with a tractor causing extensive damage.

In summary, although Daniel has intentionally damaged property belonging to another, he may have a lawful excuse for his actions under s 5(2)(b) provided he honestly believed he was protecting his horses and that there was no alternative to removing the gate to do so. Obviously in practice it would depend upon how convincing Daniel's evidence is and whether the prosecution could disprove it.

12.3.3.3 Overview of lawful excuse

Lawful excuse may be summarised as follows:

s 5(2)(a): Honest belief in the owner's consent - subjective

s 5(2)(b): Protection of property

- Was D's (real) purpose the protection of property? - objective
- If yes, did D honestly believe:
    - o the property was in immediate need of protection; and
    - o the means adopted were reasonable? - subjective

12.4 Criminal damage and human rights

One issue that has arisen in recent times is whether defendants may rely upon human rights arguments to escape liability for criminal damage. In the *Attorney General's Reference No 1 of 2022* [2022] EWCA Crim 1259, the Court of Appeal was asked to rule upon the extent to which the European Convention on Human Rights ('the Convention') sanctions the use of violence against property during protest, thereby rendering lawful the causing of damage to property that would otherwise be a crime. The case concerned the acquittal of four defendant protestors for damage to a statue of a merchant, Edward Colston, who had accumulated his substantial fortune from activities which included the trading of slaves. The Court concluded that the Convention does not provide protection to those who cause criminal damage during protest which is violent or not peaceful. Articles 9 (freedom of thought, conscience and religion), 10 (freedom of expression) and 11 (right to freedom of assembly and association) are not engaged in those circumstances and no question of proportionality arises.

12.5 Aggravated criminal damage

Simple criminal damage is usually regarded as a relatively minor offence, but in some cases the defendant may face a much more serious charge of aggravated criminal damage. The definition of this offence is contained in s 1(2) of the CDA 1971. This provides that, in order to be guilty of this offence, the defendant must:

(a) destroy or damage property (actus reus);

(b) intend to destroy or damage any property or be reckless as to whether any property is damaged or destroyed (mens rea);

(c) intend by the destruction or damage to endanger the life of another or be reckless as to whether another's life might be endangered (mens rea).

There are two main differences with the simple offence of criminal damage. First, for the simple offence, the defendant must destroy or damage 'property belonging to another', whereas under s 1(2) the property damaged or destroyed can belong to another person *or* to the defendant. Secondly, there is an additional element of mens rea ('ulterior' mens rea) that needs to be proved to secure a conviction for the aggravated offence. It must be established, not only that the defendant intended or was reckless as to damaging or destroying property, but also that they intended to endanger the life of another or were reckless as to whether the life of another might be endangered. Recklessness for the aggravated offence (as for the simple offence) is a subjective test as confirmed in *R v G*.

Because it is the mens rea of the defendant as to the endangerment of life that is important, if the defendant intended or was reckless as to endangering life, they can be found guilty of the aggravated offence notwithstanding the fact that no-one's life was actually put in danger. This was confirmed by the Court of Appeal in *R v Dudley* [1989] Crim LR 57, where the defendant set fire to a house by throwing a firebomb into the property. The fire was quickly extinguished and only minimal damage was caused. The defendant submitted that he was not guilty of the aggravated offence of criminal damage because the fire did not spread. However, given that it is largely due to luck whether a fire takes hold or not, unsurprisingly, this argument failed and the defendant's conviction under s 1(2) was upheld. The Court of Appeal stated that the mens rea had to be considered at the time the defendant did the act which caused the damage. Thus, if at that moment, the defendant intended to endanger life or was reckless as to that risk, in that they foresaw the risk that life might be endangered and went on to take that risk, they were guilty notwithstanding that no-one's life was actually put in danger.

In the subsequent case of *R v Steer* [1987] 2 All ER 833, it was confirmed that, for aggravated criminal damage, the question to ask is whether the defendant intended or was reckless that *the damage or destruction caused* would endanger life. The facts of the case were that the defendant fired a shot through a window pane, behind which two people were standing. It was accepted by the court at the trial that the defendant did not actually intend to endanger life, but he was convicted nevertheless because he was reckless. However, the House of Lords allowed the defendant's appeal on the basis that it must be shown that the endangering of life arose from the damage and not, as here, from the act that caused the damage. In other words, the endangerment to life must come from the broken glass and not from the firing of the gun.

The justification is that criminal damage is a property offence and not an offence against the person. Indeed, there are many other offences that could be charged if necessary, such as assault or attempted assault.

Note that, if followed through to its logical conclusion, in the context of arson, this would mean that the endangerment of life must arise from (for example) falling ceilings rather than the fire itself. However, the judge in *R v Steer* confirmed that the legal principle could include a victim overcome by smoke or incinerated by flames as it was 'absurd to suggest that this did not result from the damage to the building'.

Examples

(1) Aurelian rips out the copper wires from a signal box on a railway line, leaving live wires exposed. His actions endanger not only the engineers who repair the signals but also passengers on the trains, as the damage to the signals may cause an accident. Aurelian would be guilty of aggravated criminal damage if he is aware of this risk. Even if he did not intend to harm anyone, he is reckless as to the endangering of life.

(2) Ulrika is involved in rioting. She throws bricks at the windscreen of a moving police car and one of the bricks smashes through the window, causing the glass to shatter. Shocked by the impact, the police officer immediately stops the vehicle. Ulrika is guilty of aggravated criminal damage because she intends to damage property (the police car) and she is at least reckless as to endangering life. This is because the broken windscreen could have caused the officer to lose control and crash into pedestrians, particularly if the vehicle was being driven at speed. It is irrelevant that no-one is actually hurt.

Finally, when analysing the offence of simple criminal damage under s 1(1) of the CDA 1971, the defence of lawful excuse within s 5 of the 1971 Act was discussed. 'Without lawful excuse' does not have the same meaning for the aggravated offence of criminal damage. The definition in s 5 does not apply to offences under s 1(2). So even if the defendant has the owner's consent to damage property, if the defendant does so either intending by the damage or destruction to endanger life, or is reckless as to endangering life, they will still be guilty of the s 1(2) offence. This would cover situations where, for example, the defendant set fire to their own factory to secure the insurance monies.

There are circumstances when the defendant may have lawful excuse (outside s 5) to the aggravated offence, such as when the defendant damages property in order to prevent crime or in self-defence. For example, if the defendant is threatened with a knife and picks up a glass and smashes it into the face of their assailant, the defendant has arguably damaged property with the intention or recklessness to endanger life. They will, however, have lawful excuse (provided the force they used was reasonable) as the property was damaged as a result of the defendant's need to defend themselves, and also to prevent crime. (The defence of self-defence/prevention of crime is covered later in this textbook.)

12.6 Summary of criminal damage

There are four distinct offences of criminal damage, ranging in severity up to aggravated arson. One approach to understanding them is to begin with the elements of simple criminal damage and then add in the 'extra' ingredients necessary to form others.

- Criminal damage
  - o AR: destroy or damage property belonging to another.
  - o MR: intention or recklessness as to the damage or destruction and knowledge or belief the property belongs to another.
- Criminal damage + *fire* = arson.
- Criminal damage + 'extra' MR of *intention or recklessness as to endangering life* = *aggravated* criminal damage.
- Criminal damage + 'extra' MR of intention or recklessness as to endangering life by *fire* = aggravated *arson.*
- Note: the s 5 lawful excuses only apply to simple criminal damage or arson.

Set out below are two summary diagrams of the different ways in which criminal damage may be committed.

Figure 12.1 Criminal damage

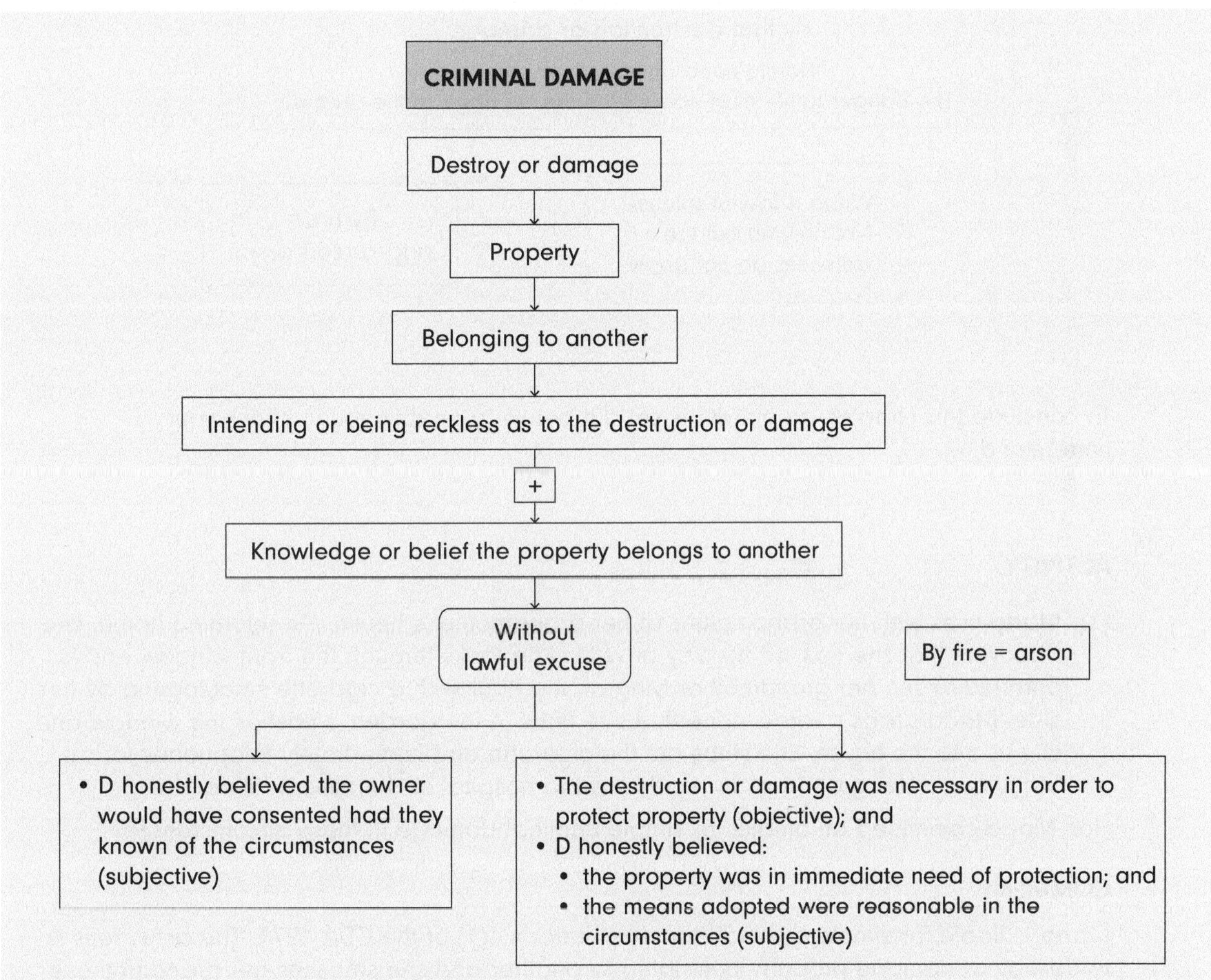

Figure 12.2 Aggravated criminal damage

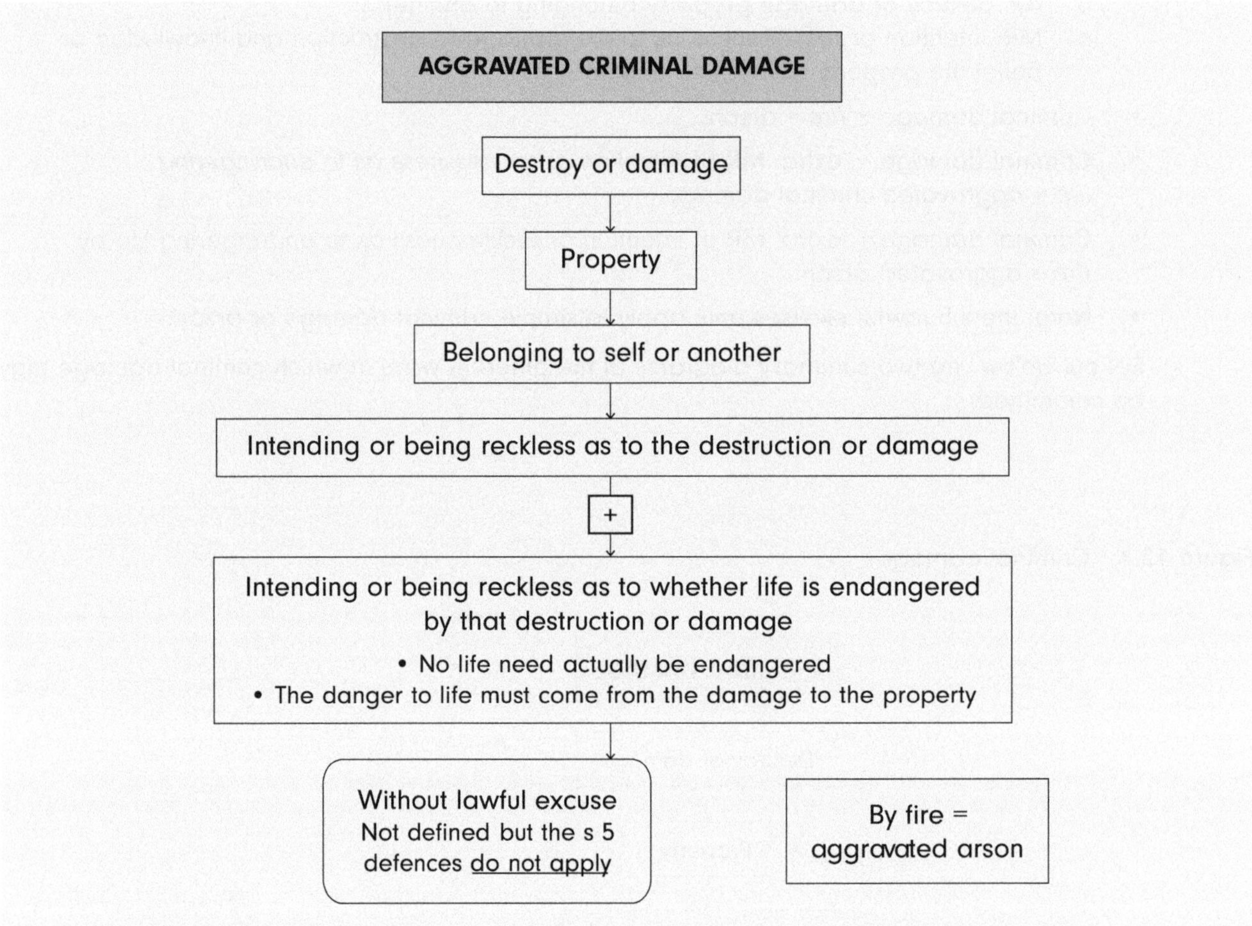

To conclude this chapter, an activity is set out below to enable you to check your understanding.

ACTIVITY

(1) Marta lives with her grandmother at her grandmother's house. On returning home, she discovers that she has left her key at work. She looks through the front window and is horrified to see her grandmother lying on the floor with a cigarette smouldering by her side. Marta grabs a large stone that she finds in the garden, smashes the window and climbs into the house. She stubs out the cigarette and immediately telephones for an ambulance. Her grandmother is admitted to hospital and makes a full recovery.

Has Marta committed an offence of simple criminal damage in these circumstances?

COMMENT

Marta is liable for simple criminal damage under s 1(1) of the CDA 1971. The actus reus is to destroy or damage property belonging to another and she smashes her grandmother's window. The mens rea is satisfied as Marta knew that the property belonged to another; and, in this instance, she intended the damage.

However, Marta will be able to rely on the defence of lawful excuse under s 5(2)(a) of the CDA 1971 as she honestly believed (subjective) that the person entitled to consent to the damage or destruction (her grandmother) would have consented had she known of the circumstances. Lawful excuse under s 5(2)(b) may also apply as the damage to the window was necessary in order to protect property (the house) from burning down, Marta honestly believed the property was in need of immediate protection, as she could see the cigarette smouldering, and smashing the window was reasonable in the circumstances (objective).

(2) Bear, aged 14 years, is at his friend's house. The boys are pretending they are on a survival camp in a forest, and, as part of their play-acting, Bear lights candles around the edge of the bedroom. Although his friend is worried about the risk of fire, Bear reassures him they could easily put out any flames. Unfortunately, one of the candles falls over and sets light to the curtains, which burn fiercely as the material is particularly flammable. The boys are shocked and immediately flee the house. The fire causes considerable damage to the bedroom, and the Fire Service only just manages to prevent the fire from spreading.

Analyse whether Bear is criminally liable for an offence of arson and aggravated arson.

COMMENT

Bear is liable for arson under s 1(1) and s 1(3) of the CDA 1971. The actus reus is to destroy or damage (here, the damage was considerable) property (the bedroom) belonging to another (his friend). With regards to the mens rea, Bear knew that the property belonged to another but did he intend or was he reckless as to the destruction or damage? He did not intend to cause the damage, as evidenced by the fact that he reassured his friend they could put out the flames and was 'shocked' by the fire, but he was reckless. Although Bear is a child, he was aware of his friend's concerns but took the risk regardless.

Bear is unlikely to be liable for aggravated arson under s 1(2) and s 1(3) because he was confident they could put out any flames, was 'shocked' by the fire, and, furthermore, it appears the fire only took hold because the curtains were particularly flammable. Thus, there is no evidence Bear was aware of the risk of endangering life.

13 Defences

LEARNING OUTCOMES

When you have completed this chapter, you should be able to:

- understand and apply the principles relating to voluntary and involuntary intoxication;
- appreciate how the general defence of self-defence and/or the defence of another absolve an accused of criminal liability;
- understand the inter-relationship between the defences of self-defence and intoxication.

13.1 Introduction

Just because someone has committed the actus reus and mens rea of an offence does not necessarily mean they will be found guilty. After all, they may have a defence. At its most straightforward, a defence is simply an assertion as to why the accused should not be convicted; for example, because they are claiming mistaken identity or denying they had the necessary mens rea. There are, however, several formal defences recognised by the law with one of the more common being that of self-defence. These general defences can apply to any criminal offence unless stated otherwise, in contrast to specific defences such as lawful excuse (CDA 1971, s 5(2)) that applies only to simple criminal damage, and consent which relates to the assaults (see earlier in this textbook).

13.2 Intoxication

13.2.1 Intoxication as a defence?

When most people think of intoxication or of someone being intoxicated, it tends to conjure up thoughts of drunkenness. However, when considering the defence of intoxication, remember that it includes drugs as well as alcohol.

Alcohol-related crime has long been a cause for public concern as it leads to a great deal of offending behaviour. Such crimes range from offences of violence to driving offences, criminal damage and public order offences. However, the impact of intoxication on criminal liability is varied.

Example

Set out below are various statements made by defendants charged with a criminal offence to demonstrate the range of scenarios police have to deal with.

(1) 'I don't normally beat people up, but I get aggressive when I'm drunk.'

(2) 'I realised she wasn't consenting to sex, but I couldn't stop because my friend had spiked my lemonade with drugs.'

(3) 'I was so out of it that I didn't have a clue what I was doing.'

(4) 'All I did was take the new pills the doctor gave me – it all became very confused after that.'

(5) 'I drank a whole bottle of whiskey to give myself the courage to kill her.'

Most people would consider that the defendants in scenarios (1) and, particularly, (5) should not be able to rely on intoxication as a defence. They committed serious crimes with the appropriate mens rea for those offences, and any intoxication was their own doing. The same applies to the defendant in scenario (2), although there is a significant difference in that the intoxication is not the defendant's 'fault'. Similarly in scenario (4), for whom there is likely to be the most sympathy, as the defendant did not appear to have any control over their actions. The defendant in scenario (3) also does not know what they are doing, but more information is necessary, such as what did they do and how did they get into that state of intoxication?

It is perhaps controversial to have a defence of voluntary intoxication at all, as a commonly held view is that someone who knowingly and willingly gets so drunk or is so affected by drugs that they cannot control their actions deserves no concessions from the law. To a large extent the courts agree, and this is why limits are placed on the availability of intoxication as a defence.

13.2.2 Absence of mens rea

It is important to appreciate that simply arguing that one was intoxicated is not a defence. It will not assist a defendant if their case is that they only committed the offence because they consumed alcohol or drugs; consequently, it is no defence if an accused has committed a criminal offence (for example, hitting someone) which they would never have done when sober. Nor will it assist the defendant who argues that they acted out of character because they were intoxicated. Alcohol and some drugs have the effect of reducing inhibitions, and it is not uncommon for a person to wake up the next day remembering what they did the night before whilst drunk and cringe with embarrassment!

This is demonstrated by the case of *R v Kingston* [1994] 3 All ER 353 in which the defendant was given coffee which, unknown to him, had been spiked with drugs. Following this, he then indecently assaulted a young boy. The defendant had known paedophile tendencies but claimed that he would not have indecently assaulted the boy if he had not been acting under the effect of the drugs. He argued that he was not guilty of the offence because he was not responsible for taking them. The House of Lords held that the absence of moral fault by Kingston was not in itself sufficient to negate the necessary mental element of the offence. The prosecution had proved that the defendant committed the offence with the necessary mens rea, and therefore the defendant's intoxication could not be relied upon to provide a defence to the charge.

It is clear that intoxication can only ever be a defence if it causes the defendant to lack the relevant mens rea for that offence. Because of this, it is not technically a defence at all as, if successful, the legal outcome is that the prosecution is unable to prove a vital element, namely the mens rea. This is in contrast to, for example, self-defence where the defendant committed the actus reus and possessed the necessary mens rea but submits that their criminal actions are justified. Nevertheless, it is usually treated as such.

Although the first hurdle to overcome when raising intoxication as a defence is to establish that the defendant lacked the necessary mens rea for the offence, this alone is not sufficient.

13.2.3 When intoxication is available as a defence

Having established that the defendant did, or may have, lacked mens rea due to intoxication, there are two further questions to be considered before deciding if the defence may apply:

(a) Was the intoxication voluntary or involuntary?

(b) Is the crime one of basic or specific intent?

To deal with the second question first, classifying a crime is more difficult than it might first appear because the test has developed from a mix of legal principle and public policy on a 'case by case' basis.

13.2.4 Type of offence

The effect of intoxication varies depending upon whether the crime is one of basic or specific intent.

Offences of specific intent

The general view is that crimes of specific intent are those where the mens rea of the offence requires intention and nothing less - recklessness will therefore not suffice. Suggested examples are murder (where the mens rea is an intention to kill or to cause grievous bodily harm), s 18 of the OAPA 1861 (intention to cause grievous bodily harm) and theft under s 1 of the Theft Act 1968 (intention to permanently deprive).

However, the distinction was revisited in *R v Heard* [2007] 3 WLR 475, with confusing results. In this case, the defendant was convicted of sexual assault (s 3 of the SOA 2003). He argued he was not guilty because he was so drunk that he had been incapable of forming the requisite mens rea of an intentional touching. As his intoxication was voluntary, for this defence to work he also had to submit that s 3 was a crime of specific intent. The Court of Appeal disagreed, justifying their judgment on the basis that a significant part of the mens rea for s 3 (the lack of a reasonable belief in consent) is a requirement of mens rea less than intention.

The effect of this ruling is that voluntary intoxication will not provide a defence to any of the sexual offences. This decision is almost certainly based on reasons of public policy, as conceded by Lord Justice Hughes who commented that there was:

> ...no universally logical test for distinguishing between crimes in which voluntary intoxication can be advanced as a defence and those in which it cannot; there is a large element of policy; categorisation is achieved on an offence by offence basis.

Offences of basic intent

In contrast, crimes of basic intent are those where the mens rea can be fulfilled with something less than intent. Most of the assaults come within this category, for example assault occasioning actual bodily harm under s 47 of the OAPA 1861, which merely requires the defendant to intend or be reckless as to the infliction of force. Also, unlawful act manslaughter and criminal damage in its various forms.

Having categorised the offence, the court must also consider whether the accused's intoxication was voluntary or not as the legal principles differ depending upon how the defendant became intoxicated.

13.2.5 Voluntary intoxication

In most cases, it will be clear that the defendant is voluntarily intoxicated, for example, the person who goes out with their friends and drinks cocktails all evening, or takes cocaine to keep them awake during a company deal. However, other situations will be less obvious, including the person whose beer is (unknown to them) 'spiked' with vodka to make it more potent or who drinks alcohol with medication when told not to. What is established is that the defendant who knew they were drinking, but merely underestimated the amount or the effect it was having on them, is voluntarily intoxicated (*R v Allen* [1988] Crim LR 698).

Example

Oti smokes some cannabis that she has recently purchased. It turns out to be much purer (and therefore stronger) than she usually buys, and after smoking three 'joints' she becomes very high. Despite this, Oti is voluntarily intoxicated.

The leading authority on how voluntary intoxication may impact on criminal liability is an appeal case dating back many years.

In the House of Lords decision in *DPP v Majewski* [1976] 2 WLR 623, Lord Elwyn-Jones LC gave the leading judgment.

> ... If a man consciously and deliberately takes alcohol and drugs not on medical prescription, but in order to escape from reality, to go 'on a trip', to become hallucinated, whatever the description may be and thereby disables himself from taking the care he might otherwise take and as a result by his subsequent actions causes injury to another - does our criminal law enable him to say that because he did not know what he was doing he lacked both intention and recklessness and accordingly is entitled to an acquittal?
>
> ... The authority which for the last half century has been relied on in this context has been the speech of the Earl of Birkenhead L.C. in *Director of Public Prosecutions v. Beard* [1920] AC 479, who stated at 494:
>
> 'Under the law of England as it prevailed until early in the 19th century voluntary drunkenness was never an excuse for criminal misconduct; and indeed the classic authorities broadly assert that voluntary drunkenness must be considered rather an aggravation than a defence. This view was in terms based upon the principle that a man who by his own voluntary act debauches and destroys his will power, shall be no better situated in regard to criminal acts than a sober man.'
>
> ... Lord Birkenhead L.C. concluded, at 499, that (except in cases where insanity is pleaded) the decisions he cited
>
> 'establish that where a specific intent is an essential element in the offence, evidence of a state of drunkenness rendering the accused incapable of forming such an intent should be taken into consideration in order to determine whether he had in fact formed the intent necessary to constitute the particular crime. If he was so drunk that he was

> incapable of forming the intent required he could not be convicted of a crime which was committed only if the intent was proved ... In a charge of murder based upon intention to kill or to do grievous bodily harm, if the jury are satisfied that the accused was, by reason of his drunken condition, incapable of forming the intent to kill or to do grievous bodily harm, he cannot be convicted of murder. But nevertheless unlawful homicide has been committed by the accused, and consequently he is guilty of unlawful homicide without malice aforethought, and that is manslaughter: *per* Stephen J. in *Doherty's Case* (1887) 16 Cox CC 306, 307.'
>
> He concludes the passage:
>
> 'the law is plain beyond all question that in cases falling short of insanity a condition of drunkenness at the time of committing an offence causing death can only, when it is available at all, have the effect of reducing the crime from murder to manslaughter.'
>
> From this it seemed clear – and this is the interpretation which the judges placed upon the decision during the ensuing half-century – that it is only in the limited class of cases requiring proof of specific intent that drunkenness can exculpate. Otherwise in no case can it exempt completely from criminal liability.
>
> ... I do not for my part regard that general principle as either unethical or contrary to the principles of natural justice. If a man of his own volition takes a substance which causes him to cast off the restraints of reason and conscience, no wrong is done to him by holding him answerable criminally for any injury he may do while in that condition. His course of conduct in reducing himself by drugs and drink to that condition in my view supplies the evidence of mens rea, of guilty mind certainly sufficient for crimes of basic intent. It is a reckless course of conduct and recklessness is enough to constitute the necessary mens rea in assault cases.

13.2.5.1 Intoxication and crimes of basic intent

The effect of this judgment is that, in cases of voluntary intoxication, the defence will never be available to offences of basic intent whether the defendant lacked mens rea or not. Lord Elwyn-Jones LC's justification for this was that a defendant who reduced themselves by drink or drugs to such a condition that they did not know what they were doing is, by definition, reckless. That recklessness is enough for the mens rea of basic intent crimes and, accordingly, such a defendant should be liable. The judgment demonstrates the impact of public policy in this area of the law.

13.2.5.2 Intoxication and crimes of specific intent

With regard to crimes of specific intent, such as murder, the rules are different.

Here, a defendant may use evidence of their voluntary intoxication to argue that they were so intoxicated at the time of the offence that they lacked the mens rea entirely. The effect was that they were incapable of forming the necessary intent to commit the relevant crime and, thus, are not liable.

In *R v Lipman* [1970] 1 QB 152, the accused had taken the drug, LSD, causing him to hallucinate that he was being attacked by snakes and descending to the centre of the earth. While in this state, he killed the victim by cramming bed sheets into her mouth.

The appeal court held that the defendant's intoxication could be used to establish that he lacked the required mens rea. Murder is a crime of specific intent, and the prosecution must prove that the defendant intended to kill or to cause grievous bodily harm. Because of Lipman's extreme intoxication, they were unable to do so. It does seem somewhat illogical that the most reckless defendants, those who are so intoxicated they have no awareness of what they are doing, can literally 'get away with murder'. However, the reason is that, although the judges have some licence to interpret the law based on public policy, they do not have the power to actually change it. Either the common law (for murder) or Parliament (for s 18 assault and theft) have dictated that intention is the requisite mens rea for these offences.

However, in practice, even if a defendant is successful with their defence of voluntary intoxication to a crime of specific intent, they will usually be guilty of another offence. For example, if the prosecution fails to show that the defendant had the mens rea for murder because of their intoxication, they would still be liable for manslaughter (a crime of basic intent). Equally, if they successfully avoid a conviction under s 18 of the OAPA 1861, they would be guilty of an assault under s 20 of the OAPA 1861 as this can be established by proof of recklessness as to foresight of some harm by the defendant.

This provides another public policy justification for the decision, because virtually all defendants who can argue that they are not guilty of a specific intent offence due to intoxication will be guilty of an alternative, lesser, basic intent offence.

13.2.6 Involuntary intoxication

Before considering the issue of involuntary intoxication, the starting point is to identify what counts as such. Generally speaking, intoxication is only involuntary if either the defendant had no knowledge that they were taking any alcohol or drug, or they take a medically prescribed drug in accordance with the instructions and it has an unusual side effect. If they exceeded the dose or, for example, had alcohol with medication when they had been told not to, they would almost certainly be regarded as voluntarily intoxicated.

A defendant who is involuntarily intoxicated may have a defence to any crime, whether specific or basic intent, if they did not have the mens rea for it. This seems only fair as it is not the defendant's fault they are in such a state. Thus, if the accused's orange juice was spiked with vodka so they became involuntarily intoxicated and they then assaulted the victim, they would have a defence if the prosecution was unable to prove they intended the assault or foresaw the risk of it (recklessness).

It is important to note that the defendant must demonstrate they lacked the mens rea for the offence.

Example

Dorian smashes the glass of a bus shelter on the way home from a night out. He is involuntarily intoxicated as his friends added vodka to his cola. He says: 'I only acted as I did because I had that alcohol forced on me, but I accept that I knew what I was doing when I committed the crime of criminal damage'. In this instance, Dorian's involuntary intoxication will not provide a defence, although it may affect the sentence he receives.

One situation where intoxication may be viewed as involuntary is where someone takes a non-dangerous or prescribed drug which leads to unpredictable and aggressive behaviour that would not normally be expected. This may seem illogical as the drug had been taken voluntarily in the sense that no-one had forcibly pushed it down the defendant's throat. However, the unexpected side effect can render the intoxication involuntary.

In *R v Hardie* [1984] 3 All ER 848 the defendant's girlfriend had left him, and as he was so upset, he took some of his friend's Valium tablets. Later he started a fire and was charged with arson, but he claimed that he did not know what he was doing because of the effect of the drug. The Court of Appeal allowed his appeal against conviction on the basis that his intoxication in this case was involuntary. Although no-one had made him take the tablets, his condition resulted from taking a non-dangerous drug and there was no evidence that Mr Hardie knew, or ought to have known, that the Valium would render him aggressive and incapable of appreciating risks. He had taken the tablets to calm himself down.

The question whether taking drugs in a situation such as this is left to the jury who must be satisfied of two crucial elements: first, that the drug was 'non-dangerous', and second that the defendant's reaction was unpredictable and not one that would normally be associated with that particular drug. Only then will involuntary intoxication absolve the defendant of liability.

To summarise thus far, voluntary intoxication can only be a defence to crimes of specific intent where the defendant was so affected by the drink or drugs that they did not form the necessary intention for the mens rea of the offence. It follows that voluntary intoxication is no defence to any crime that can be committed recklessly (or negligently, or if it is one of strict liability). In contrast, if the defendant is involuntarily intoxicated but still has mens rea, they are guilty; but if not, they may be acquitted.

Figure 13.1 Intoxication

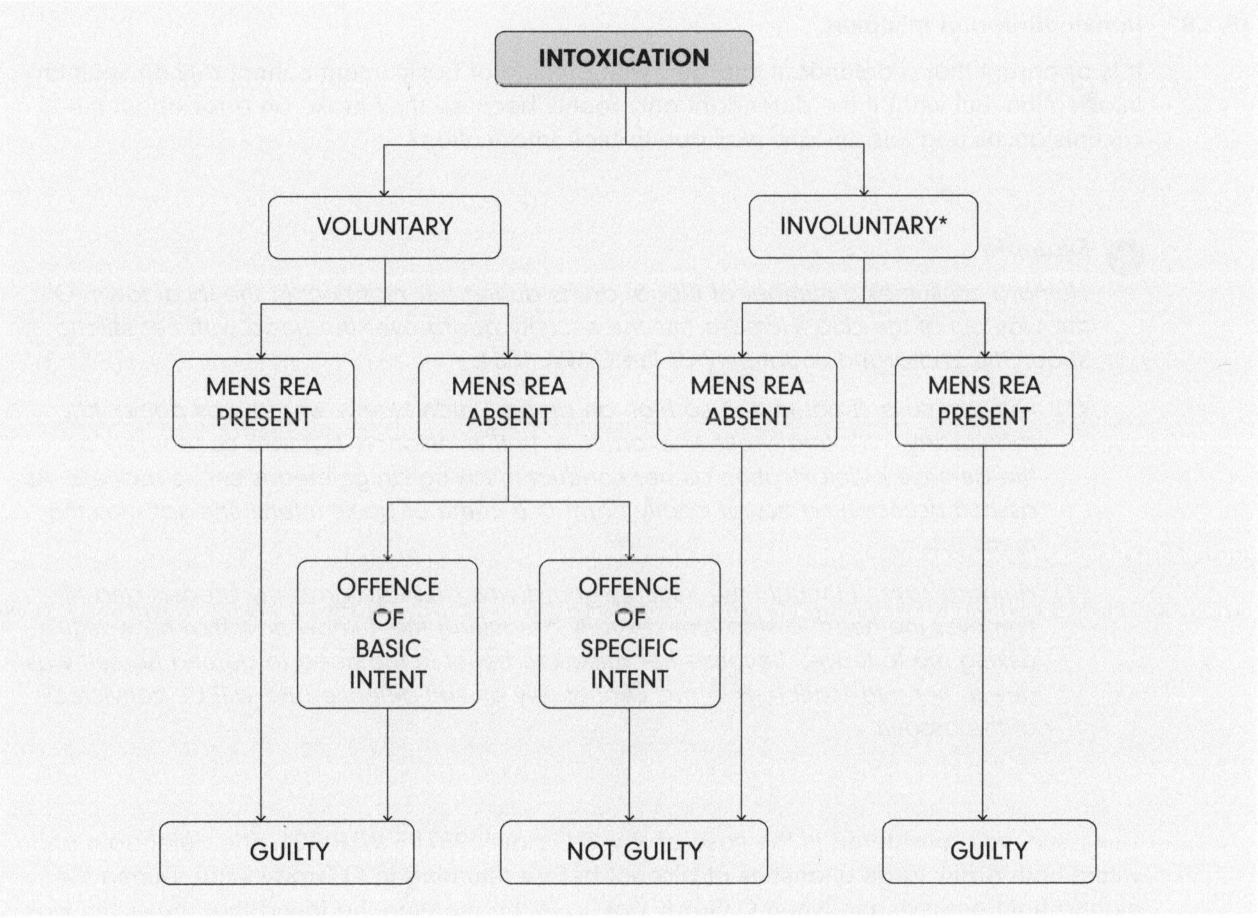

13.2.7 'Dutch courage'

A defendant who deliberately consumes alcohol or drugs in order to gain the confidence to commit a criminal offence may not rely on their intoxication to negate the mens rea.

In *Attorney-General for Northern Ireland v Gallagher* [1963] AC 349, the defendant decided to kill his wife and drank most of a bottle of whiskey to give himself 'Dutch courage'. The House of Lords held that a defendant could not rely on voluntary intoxication if they had the mens rea for the crime before they started to drink. Lord Denning gave the leading judgment and stated:

> My Lords, I think the law on this point should take a clear stand. If a man, whilst sane and sober, forms an intention to kill and makes preparation for it, knowing it is a wrong thing to do, and then gets himself drunk so as to give himself Dutch courage to do the killing, and whilst drunk carries out his intention, he cannot rely on this self-induced drunkenness as a defence to a charge of murder, nor even as reducing it to manslaughter. He cannot say that he got himself into such a stupid state that he was incapable of an intent to kill. ... The wickedness of his mind before he got drunk is enough to condemn him, coupled with the act which he intended to do and did do.

The argument against the decision would appear to be that in these circumstances there is no coincidence of actus reus and mens rea, in other words, when the defendant decides to kill they have not actually killed; and when they do kill, they may not have had the intention to do so. However, the decision was clearly based on public policy reasons. Otherwise, any criminal could go out and deliberately get very drunk before committing their crime in the hope of avoiding liability.

13.2.8 Intoxication and mistakes

It is apparent that a defendant charged with a crime of basic intent cannot rely on voluntary intoxication. But what if the defendant only reacts because they make an error about the circumstances and this mistake was due to their intoxication?

Example

Humara consumes a number of illegal drugs during her night out in the local town. On the way out of the club, Humara hits the security guard over the head with her stiletto shoe. She is charged under s 47 of the OAPA 1861.

(1) Humara says: 'I got myself so high on drugs, I didn't know what I was doing. I'm really sorry – it's totally out of character.' In this instance, Humara cannot rely on the defence of intoxication as her conduct in taking drugs means she is reckless. As assault occasioning actual bodily harm is a crime of basic intent, she satisfies the mens rea.

(2) Humara says: 'I thought the security guard was about to grab my breasts and hit him over the head to stop him sexually assaulting me. I know now that he was just asking me to leave.' Because her mistaken belief in the need to defend herself was due to her intoxication, Humara cannot rely on self-defence and will be convicted of the assault.

This issue was considered in the case of *R v O'Grady* [1987] 3 WLR 321. The defendant and victim both drank large quantities of alcohol before returning to O'Grady's flat. During the night a fight ensued, and when O'Grady got up in the morning, he found that the victim was dead. O'Grady was charged with murder. There was evidence at trial to suggest that O'Grady had attacked the victim and had done so in the belief that he needed to defend himself. The trial judge directed the jury that if the defendant had mistakenly thought he was being attacked and if that belief was due to his intoxication, he could raise the issue of self-defence. Essentially therefore, the judge's direction was that O'Grady could rely on self-defence if his reaction did not exceed that of a sober person in the same situation. O'Grady was convicted of manslaughter and appealed. The Court of Appeal dismissed his appeal, stating that where a defendant was mistaken in their belief that any force, or the force they in fact used, was necessary to defend themselves, and the mistake was caused by their voluntary intoxication, then the defence of self-defence must fail. Lord Lane CJ said (*obiter*) that it did not matter whether the offence was one of specific or basic intent. An intoxicated person whose mistaken belief was induced by drink or drugs has no defence to a charge of manslaughter or murder. This principle was confirmed by the Court of Appeal in *R v Hatton* [2006] 1 Cr App R 16.

If a defendant is facing a charge relating to a crime of basic intent, the decision in *O'Grady* is right in principle as a lack of mens rea due to voluntary intoxication is not a defence to such crimes, with the justification being that the defendant is reckless in getting into such a state in the first place. It follows logically that an accused should not be able to rely on any mistake they make because of that same drunken condition.

However, is it right in principle where the crime is a specific intent crime? In *O'Grady*, the court, in an *obiter* statement, indicated that a drunken mistake would not enable a defendant to rely successfully on a defence of self-defence whether the crime charged was one of basic or specific intent (affirmed in *R v Hatton*).

Example

(1) *Gemma hits her boyfriend Simon and he suffers a fractured skull. She is charged under s 18 of the OAPA 1861 and admits the actus reus of causing him grievous bodily harm. However, her evidence is that she did not intend to cause Simon any injury as she was too drunk at the time to form the relevant mens rea.*

In this instance, Gemma's intoxication appears to have caused her to lack mens rea for the s 18 assault as she did not intend to cause grievous bodily harm. As this is a crime of specific intent, Gemma will have a defence to the charge, despite her lack of mens rea being caused by her voluntary intoxication.

(2) *Gemma causes Simon to suffer serious injuries (as above) and is charged under s 18. She admits intentionally causing him grievous bodily harm but argues that she did so because she honestly, albeit unreasonably, believed Simon was about to attack her. There is evidence that her mistaken belief in the need to defend herself was caused by her voluntary intoxication.*

Here, Gemma accepts that she committed the actus reus and that she possessed the relevant mens rea for a s 18 assault but seeks to rely on the defence of self-defence. However, following O'Grady, *if her mistaken belief in the need to defend herself is due to her intoxication, she will not be able to rely on self-defence and will be convicted.*

If Gemma had been charged instead under s 20, the outcome in scenario (2) would remain unchanged – she could not rely on the defence as, in O'Grady, *the Court of Appeal made it clear that the principle applied whether the crime was one of basic (s 20) or specific (s 18) intent.*

The anomaly produced when considering crimes of specific intent needs consideration. If, on a charge of murder for example, the defendant argues lack of mens rea due to voluntary intoxication, they have a defence to murder and will be acquitted on that charge, although convicted instead of manslaughter. If, instead, they accept that they committed the actus reus and possessed the mens rea of murder but are relying on a belief, induced by voluntary intoxication, in the need to defend themselves, their defence of self-defence will fail (*O'Grady*) and they will be convicted of murder.

It may be contrary to logic and common sense to say that:

(a) an accused who was drunk and therefore did not have the intention to kill or cause grievous bodily harm is not guilty of murder; whereas

(b) an accused who because they were drunk thought they were about to be viciously attacked and so defends themselves is guilty (if *O'Grady* is followed).

Smith and Hogan (*Criminal Law*, 14th edn) criticise the *obiter* comments made in *O'Grady* for the reasons listed above and submit that the better view is that a drunken mistake arising from voluntary intoxication may found a defence to a crime requiring specific intent but not to one of basic intent. However, this approach has not been adopted by the courts.

13.2.9 Intoxication and lawful excuse

There is one further anomaly in this area as a result of the case of *Jaggard v Dickinson* [1980] 3 All ER 716. As this was a case involving criminal damage, the defendant may rely on the defence of 'lawful excuse' under s 5(2) of the CDA 1971 if they honestly believe that the owner had consented or would have consented had they known of the circumstances (s 5(2)(a)). In *Jaggard v Dickinson*, the defendant broke a window to get into a house that she thought belonged to her friend. She (correctly) believed her friend would consent, but, unfortunately, because she was drunk, the defendant mistakenly entered the wrong house. Criminal damage is a crime of basic intent as it can be committed either intentionally or recklessly; thus, if she lacked mens rea for the crime due to her voluntary intoxication, the defence would fail. Despite this, the appeal court decided that the defendant could rely on s 5(2)(a) and her mistaken belief in the owner's consent, even though this was a drunken mistake resulting from her voluntary intoxication.

Although the outcome in *Jaggard v Dickinson* may be appropriate as the belief need only be genuinely held, the law is somewhat inconsistent here. To assist, a comparison of the effect of intoxication on these two areas is set out below.

Figure 13.2 Comparison of the effect of intoxication on self-defence and lawful excuse

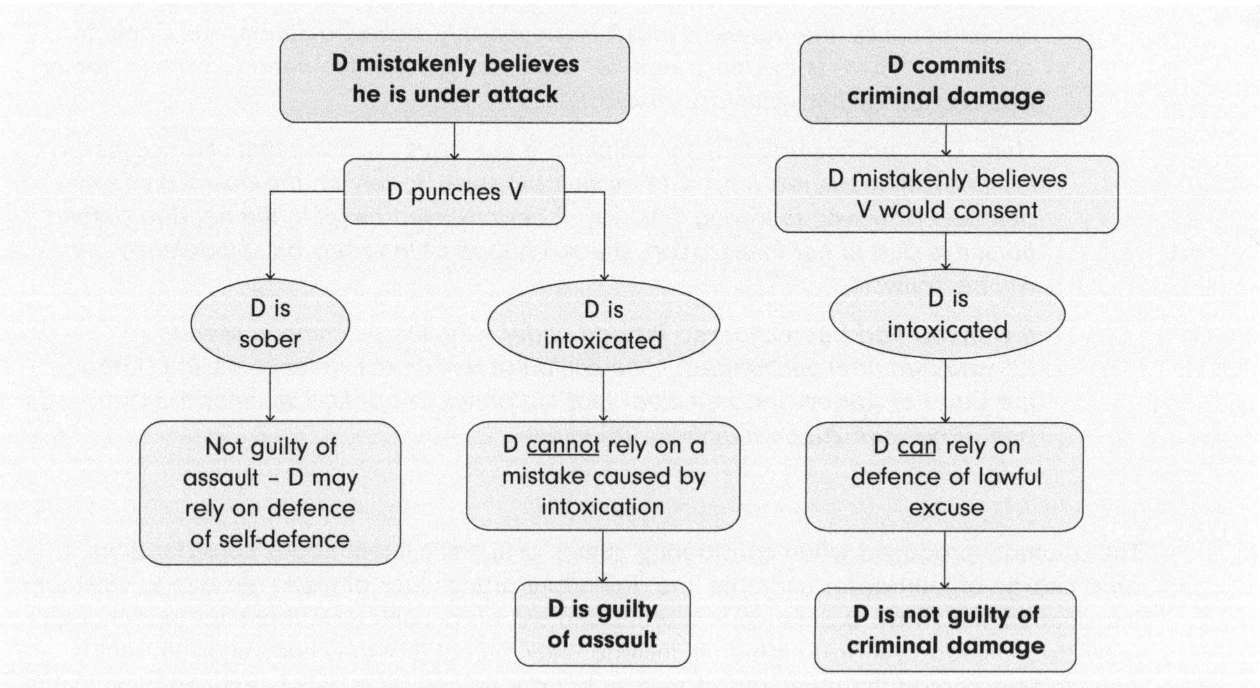

13.2.10 Summary of intoxication

A summary of the law is as follows:

(a) Voluntary intoxication is a defence to a crime of specific intent, where intention is the requisite mens rea, but only if the defendant lacked mens rea. It is not a defence to crimes of basic intent – those that can be committed recklessly.

(b) Intoxication cannot be relied upon by the defendant in 'Dutch courage' cases. It is also not available where the defendant is simply mistaken as to the strength of the alcohol or drugs; or where the effect of the intoxication was that they acted out of character.

(c) Involuntary intoxication may be a defence to a crime of specific or basic intent if the defendant lacked mens rea.

(d) Taking a non-dangerous drug that has unexpected consequences can count as involuntary intoxication, provided the defendant was not reckless as to those possible consequences when they took the drug. In other words, with voluntary intoxication by drink or dangerous drugs, the defendant is deemed reckless; with non-dangerous drugs, the issue is whether the defendant was actually (subjectively) reckless or not.

(e) If the defendant makes a mistake as to the need to defend themselves and that mistake is due to their voluntary intoxication, the defence of self-defence will fail (*O'Grady*). In contrast, if the defendant makes a mistake relating to lawful excuse for criminal damage under s 5(2)(a) of the CDA 1971, they can rely on that defence even if their mistake resulted from their voluntary intoxication (*Jaggard v Dickinson*).

To review your understanding, you should attempt the Activity at the end of this chapter.

13.3 Self-defence and prevention of crime

There are certain circumstances in which the use of force may be justified. An accused may argue they did so to protect themselves, their property or others from attack, or to prevent a crime from being committed. In other words, the defendant is claiming that, although they used force on another person, it was lawful.

> **Example**
>
> *Jack has committed the actus reus of a s 20 assault against Leo with the relevant mens rea. However, there are circumstances where he may have a defence.*
>
> *(1) Self-defence: Jack would be justified in assaulting Leo to prevent Leo from assaulting him.*
>
> *(2) Defence of another: Jack would be justified if he was trying to stop Leo from hitting someone else, for example, Jack's friend, his child or even a complete stranger. In such cases Jack would be trying to prevent a crime (of assault against a third party).*

Self-defence is often highlighted as a defence in the media, leading to discussions on (amongst other aspects) how far a householder may go to protect their own property; indeed, there have been a number of high-profile cases in this regard. In situations where the defendant is held not to be to blame for their conduct, they will be excused from criminal liability altogether and will be acquitted of the charge. However, the law is far from straightforward, and there are also some aspects that overlap, causing confusion at times.

Historically, the common law defence of self-defence applied: 'the accused is entitled to be acquitted [if] the prosecution ... have failed to prove an essential element of the crime namely that the violence used by the accused was unlawful' - as explained by Lord Griffiths in the case of *Beckford v R* [1988] AC 130.

Subsequently, an attempt was made to incorporate the defence into legislation, and s 3(1) of the Criminal Law Act (CLA) 1967 provides that:

> A person may use such force as is reasonable in the circumstances in the prevention of crime, or in effecting or assisting in the lawful arrest of offenders or suspected offenders or of persons unlawfully at large.

Although two defences are being considered here, because of the piecemeal way in which the law developed they often completely overlap. For example, if a defendant was trying to stop a person from hitting them (or someone else), they would raise the common law defence of self-defence and the statutory one of prevention of crime under s 3. Note that, for ease of reference, the defences will collectively be known as 'self-defence'.

Common to these defences is the issue of reasonable force. If such force is used and the defence is successful, they are complete defences and will lead to the acquittal of the defendant. They are also general defences, and as such can operate as a defence to any of the offences including the homicide offences.

13.3.1 Criminal Justice and Immigration Act 2008, s 76

As a result of public pressure to legislate on self-defence, and a perceived lack of transparency in the existing law, the Government codified some of the principles from the various authorities into s 76 of the Criminal Justice and Immigration Act (CJIA) 2008. As s 76(9) makes clear, the aim of the legislation was to clarify the operation of the legal principles that emerged from case law and to place them on a statutory footing. The CJIA 2008 was a consolidating measure, so it brought together the existing law rather than seeking to change it. However, it did set out some important principles which are explored in more detail in this chapter.

13.3.2 Was force necessary?

In determining if the accused can successfully argue self-defence, the first question is whether the use of force was necessary at all. A defendant may not rely on self-defence if they use force on another person out of revenge or in retaliation. Furthermore, the defence will only be available if the defendant's action was necessary to defend themselves or another from attack or to prevent the commission of a criminal offence. This question is subjectively assessed, so the important issue is whether the *defendant* believed that the use of force was necessary.

13.3.3 The effect of mistake

There may be circumstances in which the defendant is mistaken about what the other party is going to do. If an accused believes a person is going to attack them in a bar (whereas in fact the victim is merely walking past to go to the toilet) and so defends themselves by hitting the victim, should the defendant be judged on the facts as they think they are, or as they actually are? Furthermore, should the defendant be judged on their mistaken belief - or should this only be the case if the mistake is a reasonable one?

Case law and statute deal with this issue and confirm that where the defendant acts in self-defence due to a mistaken belief that the use of force is necessary, their mistake will not prevent them from relying upon the defence provided their belief was honestly held.

In the leading case of *R v Williams (Gladstone)* (1984) 78 Cr App R 276, M saw a youth rob a woman. He chased the youth and knocked him to the ground. Only the last part of this incident was seen by the appellant, from his seat on a passing bus. The appellant went and challenged M, who said that he was a policeman and was arresting the youth. M was not, in fact, a policeman, and when he was unable to produce a warrant card, the two men struggled and the appellant ended up punching M in the face. The appellant was charged with assault occasioning actual bodily harm (OAPA 1861, s 47). Lord Lane CJ gave judgment as follows:

> What then is the situation if the defendant is labouring under a mistake of fact as to the circumstances? What if he believes, but believes mistakenly, that the victim is consenting, or that it is necessary to defend himself, or that a crime is being committed which he intends to prevent? He must then be judged against the mistaken facts as he believes them to be. If judged against those facts or circumstances the prosecution fail to establish his guilt, then he is entitled to be acquitted.
>
> The next question is: does it make any difference if the mistake of the defendant was one which, viewed objectively by a reasonable onlooker, was an unreasonable mistake?
>
> ...
>
> The reasonableness or unreasonableness of the defendant's belief is material to the question of whether the belief was held by the defendant at all. If the belief was in fact held, its unreasonableness, so far as guilt or innocence is concerned, is neither here nor there. It is irrelevant ... In other words, the jury should be directed, first of all, that the prosecution have the burden or duty of proving the unlawfulness of the defendant's actions, second, that if the defendant may have been labouring under a mistake as to the facts, he must be judged according to his mistaken view of the facts, and third, that that is so whether the mistake was, on an objective view, a reasonable mistake or not.
>
> In a case of self-defence, where self-defence or the prevention of crime is concerned, if the jury come to the conclusion that the defendant believed, or may have believed, that he was being attacked or that a crime was being committed, and that force was necessary to protect himself or to prevent the crime, then the prosecution have not proved their case. If, however, the defendant's alleged belief was mistaken and if the mistake was an unreasonable one, that may be a powerful reason for coming to the conclusion that the belief was not honestly held and should be rejected.
>
> Even if the jury come to the conclusion that the mistake was an unreasonable one, if the defendant may genuinely have been labouring under it, he is entitled to rely upon it.

The effect of this case is that:

(a) The defendant is judged on the facts as they honestly believe them to be, even if mistaken.

(b) This applies even if that honestly held belief is unreasonable. Hence a defendant can rely on self-defence/prevention of crime if they use reasonable force; and in deciding whether reasonable force was used, they are judged on the facts as they honestly believe them to be.

(c) However, if the defendant's mistake is an unreasonable one to make, this may be a reason for the jury to conclude that the belief was not honestly held.

The principle contained in this case is now enshrined in s 76(4) of the CJIA 2008 which states:

> (4) If D claims to have held a particular belief as regards the existence of any circumstances—
>
> (a) the reasonableness or otherwise of that belief is relevant to the question whether D genuinely held it; but
>
> (b) if it is determined that D did genuinely hold it, D is entitled to rely on it for the purposes of subsection (3), whether or not—
>
> (i) it was mistaken, or
>
> (ii) (if it was mistaken) the mistake was a reasonable one to have made.

Although it is helpful for this principle to be clarified in statute, there are still outstanding issues.

Evidence to be taken into account

When dealing with mistakes and self-defence, what evidence can be taken into account in deciding what the defendant perceived the circumstances to be? A case that considered this issue was *R v Martin (Anthony)* [2002] Crim LR 136 in which a Norfolk farmer, Tony Martin, was convicted of murder when he shot and killed a burglar after discovering him in his house. At his trial, he pleaded self-defence but was unsuccessful. He argued, on appeal, that he suffered from a paranoid personality disorder and so he perceived a greater danger to his physical safety than the average person in his situation. This disorder, he submitted, should be taken into account when assessing whether he used reasonable force in the circumstances as he judged them to be. However, the Court of Appeal held that psychiatric evidence that the defendant would perceive a greater threat is not admissible.

This is interesting because, on the other hand, evidence of the physical characteristics of the defendant are admissible, for example, a threat will seem greater perhaps to a frail elderly lady than to a robust healthy young person. The decision in *Martin* seems at odds with the Privy Council in *Shaw (Norman) v R* [2002] Crim LR 140. Here, the court said the jury should look at the circumstances and the danger as the defendant honestly believed them to be in deciding if the force was reasonable. Professor Smith suggests that if *Shaw* is correct, evidence of the kind raised in *Martin* (psychiatric evidence) would be directly relevant and should be admissible.

Mistaken belief due to voluntary intoxication

There is a further point to consider on the issue of mistaken belief in the need for force; what if the defendant made their mistake because they were intoxicated? The cases of *R v O'Grady* [1987] QB 995 and *R v Hatton* [2005] All ER (D) 308 were discussed earlier in this chapter. The Court of Appeal held that a mistaken belief in the need for force is no defence if that mistake is based on voluntary intoxication where the defendant has chosen to take drink or drugs. This is an exception to the usual rule seen in *Williams (Gladstone)* - no doubt because of the public policy issues that lie behind these cases.

Again, this is confirmed in statute, and s 76(3) and (5) of the CJIA 2008 state:

> (3) The question whether the degree of force used by D was reasonable in the circumstances is to be decided by reference to the circumstances as D believed them to be, and subsections (4) to (8) also apply in connection with deciding that question.
>
> (5) But subsection (4)(b) does not enable D to rely on any mistaken belief attributable to intoxication that was voluntarily induced.

The effect of these legal principles is demonstrated by the next examples.

Examples

(1) *Lawrence is drunk, having been out for the evening and consumed a significant quantity of alcohol. This causes him to mistakenly believe that Justin is about to attack him. In response, Lawrence grasps a nearby empty bottle and strikes Justin on the head. Because Lawrence's belief was induced by alcohol, he cannot argue self-defence.*

(2) *Ayo is drunk, having had his drinks spiked by an associate. He mistakenly and unreasonably believes that he is being attacked by Tom, whereas Tom has simply lost his balance and fallen onto him. Ayo lashes out to get Tom away from him, causing him a wound. In this situation, s 76(5) does not apply as Ayo's intoxication is involuntary and so he can rely upon his mistaken belief.*

13.3.4 Was the amount of force used reasonable?

Where a defendant claims to have acted in self-defence or prevention of crime, they will be able to rely on the defence only if they used reasonable force. This will depend on all the circumstances and is ultimately a question of fact for the jury to decide. The defence can be applied to all crimes, not just assaults, including to protect property from a burglar or from criminal damage. However, only reasonable force may be used. What this is and what factors are taken into account is considered next.

Example

Ying sees a youth in his garden pick up some stones and start throwing them at his windows. One of the windows breaks. Ying chases after the youth and:

(a) *grabs hold of him until the police arrive.*

(b) *gives him numerous slaps around the face.*

(c) *gives him a severe beating.*

(d) *threatens to give him a beating until the youth promises to pay for the damage.*

Whether the court considers that Ying acted reasonably in each situation will depend on a number of factors, including the seriousness of the offence threatened which Ying was trying to prevent (here, criminal damage) and the degree of force used to defend his property. Grabbing hold of the youth until the police arrive would be reasonable, whereas giving him a severe beating would not. With regard to the other two outcomes, people may have differing opinions.

The defendant is judged on the basis of the facts as they honestly and genuinely believed them to be, and this is confirmed by s 76(3) of the CJIA 2008 which is set out earlier in this chapter. Essentially, to plead self-defence successfully, the defendant must argue that they used (objectively) reasonable force in the circumstances (subjectively) as they believed them to be. Remember also that the reasonableness or otherwise of that belief is relevant to the question whether the defendant genuinely held it (CJIA 2008, s 76(4)).

Example

Ichika, a maths teacher, is passing Lucy on her way to her next class, when she trips and loses her balance. Lucy claims that she thought that Ichika was lunging at her to push her against the wall and so she shoves Ichika away forcefully. In this situation, the court may question whether Lucy genuinely believed that the teacher was about to push her. They were just passing each other in a school corridor and there is no reason to suggest that Ichika would behave in this way. Thus, the court may conclude that Lucy's belief is so unreasonable that, in fact, she did not honestly hold it.

The statute provides further guidance on what is meant by the word 'reasonable'. Householders are dealt with differently and more generously than other defendants and will be considered later in this chapter.

> The degree of force used by the defendant is not to be regarded as having been reasonable in the circumstances as they believed them to be if it was disproportionate in those circumstances (s 76(6)).

The Crown Prosecution Service's website states that when dealing with cases of self-defence, account should be taken of the balance that needs to be struck between the public interest in promoting a responsible contribution on the part of citizens in preserving law and order, and in discouraging vigilantism and the use of violence.

In general, the greater the danger to the defendant, the more force they may use to repel an attack. However, if the jury or magistrates determine that the level of force is excessive, the defence will fail.

Evaluating this issue may prove difficult as much will depend upon the facts, and some decisions of the courts have proved controversial. In *R v Clegg* [1995] 1 AC 482, the defendant, a young soldier, was convicted of murder after shooting at a car being driven towards him while he was on duty during the conflict in Northern Ireland. It was held that the first three shots were legitimately fired in self-defence as the car approached Clegg and his colleagues at high speed. However, Clegg's final shot, which was fired at the car after it had broken through the checkpoint and after the danger had passed, amounted to excessive force.

In summary, although the reasonableness of the force used is assessed objectively, the question is whether the defendant used reasonable force in the circumstances as they believed them to be. The test is therefore not wholly objective. If the jury conclude that the force used was excessive, the defence fails and the defendant will be found guilty; thus, it is an 'all or nothing' defence. Given that the outcome is so reliant upon the specific facts, whether a defendant is convicted may lead to inconsistent outcomes depending upon the particular magistrates or jury who decide the case.

13.3.5 Householder cases

After the CJIA 2008 had been implemented, concerns remained primarily in respect of those who were caught by the criminal justice system as a result of protecting their homes. As a consequence, an important amendment was made to s 76 in relation to 'householder' cases, where a defendant uses force on someone they find in their dwelling. The provision is designed to safeguard those who use self-defence or in defence of another while in or partly in:

(1) a building or part of a building that is a dwelling;

(2) forces accommodation; or

(3) a vehicle or vessel that is a dwelling.

Further guidance may be found in subsections (8A), (8B) and (8F) which state that where:

(a) a part of a building is a dwelling where D dwells,

(b) another part of the building is a place of work for D or another person who dwells in the first part, and

(c) that other part is internally accessible from the first part,

that other part, and any internal means of access between the two parts, are each treated for the purposes of subsection (8A) as a part of a building that is a dwelling.

To assist in understanding what places are covered by the householder defence, a list of examples is provided below.

Examples

In each case, Diana disturbs a burglar (Polly) during the night and reacts by hitting her with a hockey stick. Diana may be able to rely on the 'householder' defence if she assaults Polly:

(1) In the bedroom of her detached property that she owns.

(2) In her houseboat moored on the River Severn.

(3) In the army barracks where she is living on a temporary basis.

(4) In a campervan where she is staying on holiday.

(5) While halfway out of the door of her rented house.

(6) In her grocery shop, which is on the floor below the flat where she lives (because Diana's dwelling would be accessible from her place of work).

She could not rely on the defence if she assaults Polly:

(7) Outside her home on the driveway.

(8) At the factory premises where she works.

(9) When she is trespassing in her neighbour's apartment.

The accused need not be a homeowner, but to benefit from this provision they cannot be a trespasser. Furthermore, they must, at the time, believe that the victim was in, or entering, the building or part as a trespasser.

The additional protection for householders was achieved by inserting a new subsection into the 2008 Act, which provides:

> (5A) In a householder case, the degree of force used by D is not to be regarded as having been reasonable in the circumstances as D believed them to be if it was grossly disproportionate in those circumstances.

This is in contrast to the use of reasonable force in all other types of cases, as stated in s 76(6) referred to above.

Thus, it is now possible for force to be used that is both reasonable and disproportionate in a 'householder' case, providing of course it is not grossly disproportionate.

Example

This example appeared in the Ministry of Justice Circular No 2013/02:

A householder is woken during the night by the sound of breaking glass downstairs. His wife and children have also woken up and are very frightened. The householder goes downstairs to investigate and meets an intruder armed with a knife in the hallway. The intruder had broken a glass panel in the door to enter the property. A scuffle ensues and the householder wrestles the knife from the intruder's hand and it drops to the floor. Having dropped his weapon and with the mother and children screaming upstairs, the intruder realises he has met his match and turns to flee through the open door. With adrenaline pumping and heart pounding, the householder instinctively punches the intruder on the back of the head as he leaves. He falls awkwardly and is knocked unconscious.

The jury would need to consider whether the householder used disproportionate but not grossly disproportionate force. In other words, in light of s 76(5A), would such force be regarded as reasonable? Would it make any difference if the intruder had died as a result of the blow to the head; or if the householder had used the knife on the fleeing intruder?

There is clearly no right or wrong answer here as ultimately it will be a question of fact for the particular jury to determine, although punching a burglar as he is leaving is unlikely to be regarded as 'grossly disproportionate'. In contrast, if the householder had picked up the burglar's knife and stabbed him repeatedly, this would be.

The important point to appreciate is that what may otherwise be described as unreasonable force may now amount to reasonable force in a 'householder' case. This in turn may appear incompatible with Article 2 of the European Convention on Human Rights which provides that everyone's life shall be protected by law. Whilst this is not an absolute right, there was some debate as to whether the UK would have difficulty in arguing that the use of disproportionate force resulting in the death of even a burglar was compatible with Article 2.

In *R (Collins) v Secretary of State for Justice* [2016] EWHC 33 (Admin), such a challenge was indeed made. On 15 December 2013, Denby Collins, aged 39, was found in a house where he was restrained by a householder by means of a headlock. As a result of the restraint, he suffered personal injuries from which he never fully recovered. After a police investigation, the CPS decided not to prosecute the householder. Mr Collins (acting through his father as his litigation friend) sought to challenge this decision on the basis that the householder defence was incompatible with Article 2. This application for judicial review of the decision not to prosecute was dismissed by the court on the basis that the householder defence was not incompatible with Article 2. The court stated:

> The effect of section 76(5A) is not to give householders *carte blanche* in the degree of force they use against intruders in self-defence. A jury must ultimately determine whether the householder's action was reasonable in the circumstances as he believed them to be.
>
> There may be instances when a jury may consider the actions of a householder in self-defence to be more than what might objectively be described as the minimum proportionate response but nevertheless reasonable given the particular and extenuating circumstances of the case. This does not weaken the capacity of the criminal law of England and Wales to deter offences against the person in

> householder cases. The headline message is and remains clear: a householder will only be able to avail himself of the defence if the degree of force he used was reasonable in the circumstances as he believed them to be. In that context, it is not irrelevant that Article 2 and Article 8 rights of the householder are also engaged.

This interpretation of the effect of s 76(5A) was followed by the Court of Appeal in *R v Ray* [2018] 2 WLR 1148.

The consequence of these decisions is that, whereas in non-householder cases, the focus is exclusively on the reasonableness of the force used by the defendant; in householder cases, the focus is on the issue of proportionality.

In summary, for a householder case:

(a) The use of proportionate force is reasonable.

(b) Disproportionate force may be reasonable or unreasonable and this will be a matter for the jury to decide taking account of all the circumstances.

(c) Grossly disproportionate force will be unreasonable.

Figure 13.3 Householder cases

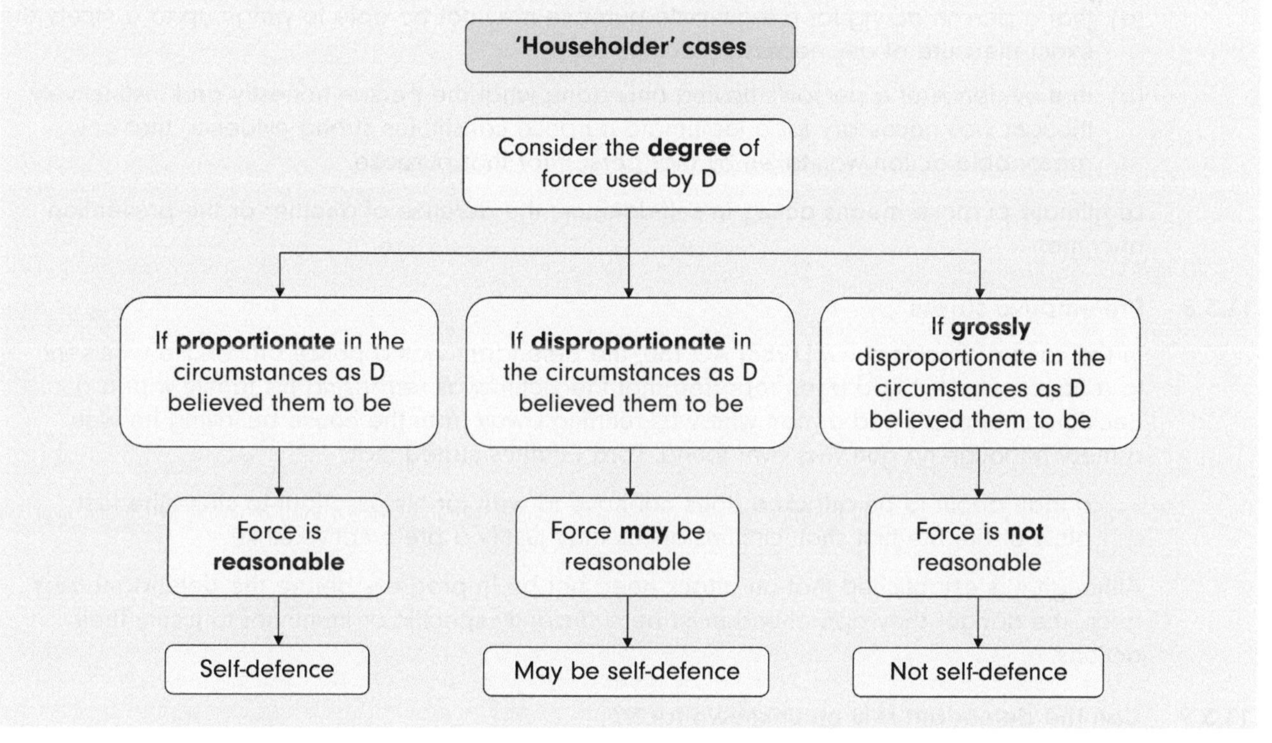

The effect of this provision is that where a householder is involved, they may use more than proportionate force provided they have not 'gone totally over the top'.

13.3.6 No duty to retreat

There is no rule of law which states that the defendant must retreat before resorting to self-defence, nor do they have to wait for their assailant to hit them first (*R v Bird* [1985] 2 All ER 513). This is confirmed by s 76(6A) which provides that, in deciding whether the force used was reasonable:

> a possibility that D could have retreated is to be considered (so far as relevant) as a factor to be taken into account, rather than as giving rise to a duty to retreat.

Thus, the possibility of the defendant retreating is a factor that the jury would consider in determining if the defence applies, but it is not definitive.

13.3.7 The 'heat of the moment'

When analysing whether the force used was reasonable, the jury or magistrates must take into account that the defendant will have had very little time to consider their response when deciding if force is necessary and, if so, to what degree. Furthermore, that the defendant may have acted very differently with the benefit of hindsight. Indeed, the courts have recognised that such defendants will have been under significant pressure. For example, in *Palmer v R* [1971] AC 814, Lord Morris acknowledged that a defendant acting in self-defence may not always have time to make a rational decision and would be acting 'in a moment of unexpected anguish'.

This view is now enshrined in statute under s 76(7) of the CJIA 2008. In deciding whether a defendant acted reasonably, the jury must take into account:

(a) that a person acting for a legitimate purpose may not be able to weigh up to a nicety the exact measure of any necessary action; and

(b) that evidence of a person's having only done what the person honestly and instinctively thought was necessary for a legitimate purpose constitutes strong evidence that only reasonable action was taken by that person for that purpose.

Legitimate purpose means acting in self-defence, the defence of another or the prevention of crime.

13.3.8 Pre-emptive strikes

In the case of *Beckford v R* [1988] AC 130, the defendant was a police officer. He was sent to a house where it had been reported that the victim was terrorising his family with a gun. Beckford shot and killed a man who was running away from the house believing he was armed, although no gun was ever found. Lord Griffiths stated that:

> a man about to be attacked does not have to wait for his assailant to strike the first blow or fire the first shot: circumstances may justify a pre-emptive strike.

Although it is established that an attack need not be in progress before the defendant uses force, the danger they apprehend must be sufficiently specific or imminent to justify their actions.

13.3.9 Can the defendant rely on unknown facts?

In deciding whether a defendant used reasonable force, a defendant who is pleading self-defence cannot rely on facts of which they were unaware when they committed the offence (*R v Dadson* (1850) 4 Cox CC 358).

Example

Warren pushes in front of Olga at a bus stop and Olga slaps him hard in the face. In fact, unknown to Olga, Warren was about to attack the bus driver and steal the fares.

Olga cannot rely on facts of which she was unaware in deciding whether she used reasonable force. Therefore, the question the court would have to answer is - did Olga use reasonable force in preventing Warren from queue jumping? It seems likely that the force she used was excessive. As Olga was unaware of the imminent robbery, that factor cannot be taken into account.

This seems correct in principle as a defendant should not be able to evade criminal liability when using excessive violence based on facts of which they were unaware.

13.3.10 The legal and evidential burden

Where an accused wishes to rely upon self-defence, they have what is described as an evidential burden to discharge. In other words, although they do not need to prove the defence, they are required to raise it to make it a live issue at trial. Generally, this will be done by cross-examining prosecution witnesses, usually the alleged victim, and by the defendant themselves giving evidence that they acted in self-defence. Once the defence has discharged its evidential burden, the prosecution must disprove the defence beyond a reasonable doubt. If it fails to do so, the accused must be acquitted and will walk away from the court a free person.

13.3.11 Summary - reasonable use of force in self-defence or prevention of crime

Here is a brief summary of the main points you have studied:

(a) There is a common law defence of reasonable force in self-defence, and a statutory defence under s 3(1) of the Criminal Law Act 1967 of reasonable use of force in the prevention of crime. These are general defences so they can apply to any crime and, if successful, lead to a complete acquittal. Many of the points from case law on these defences have now been included in s 76 of the Criminal Justice and Immigration Act 2008.

(b) The court must first consider whether the use of force was necessary at all, and this will be subjectively assessed based on the defendant's own beliefs.

(c) Whether or not the force used was reasonable in the circumstances is assessed objectively by the jury. Force will not be reasonable where it is disproportionate (s 76(6)), unless it is a 'householder' case where it will be unreasonable force if it is grossly disproportionate (s 76(5A)).

(d) If the defendant has made a mistake about the circumstances, the reasonableness of the force used will be assessed on the basis of the facts as they honestly, even if unreasonably, believed them to be (*R v Williams (Gladstone)* (1984) 78 Cr App R 276). There is an exception to this; if the defendant's mistake was due to their voluntary intoxication, they cannot rely on their mistaken view of the facts as a basis for self-defence (*R v O'Grady* [1987] QB 995).

(e) There is no duty to retreat (s 76(6)(A)); and a defendant may act pre-emptively (*Beckford v R* [1988] AC 130). Account will also be taken of the fact that the defendant acted in the 'heat of the moment' (*Palmer v R* [1971] AC 814 and s 76(7)(a) and (b)).

Figure 13.4 Self-defence

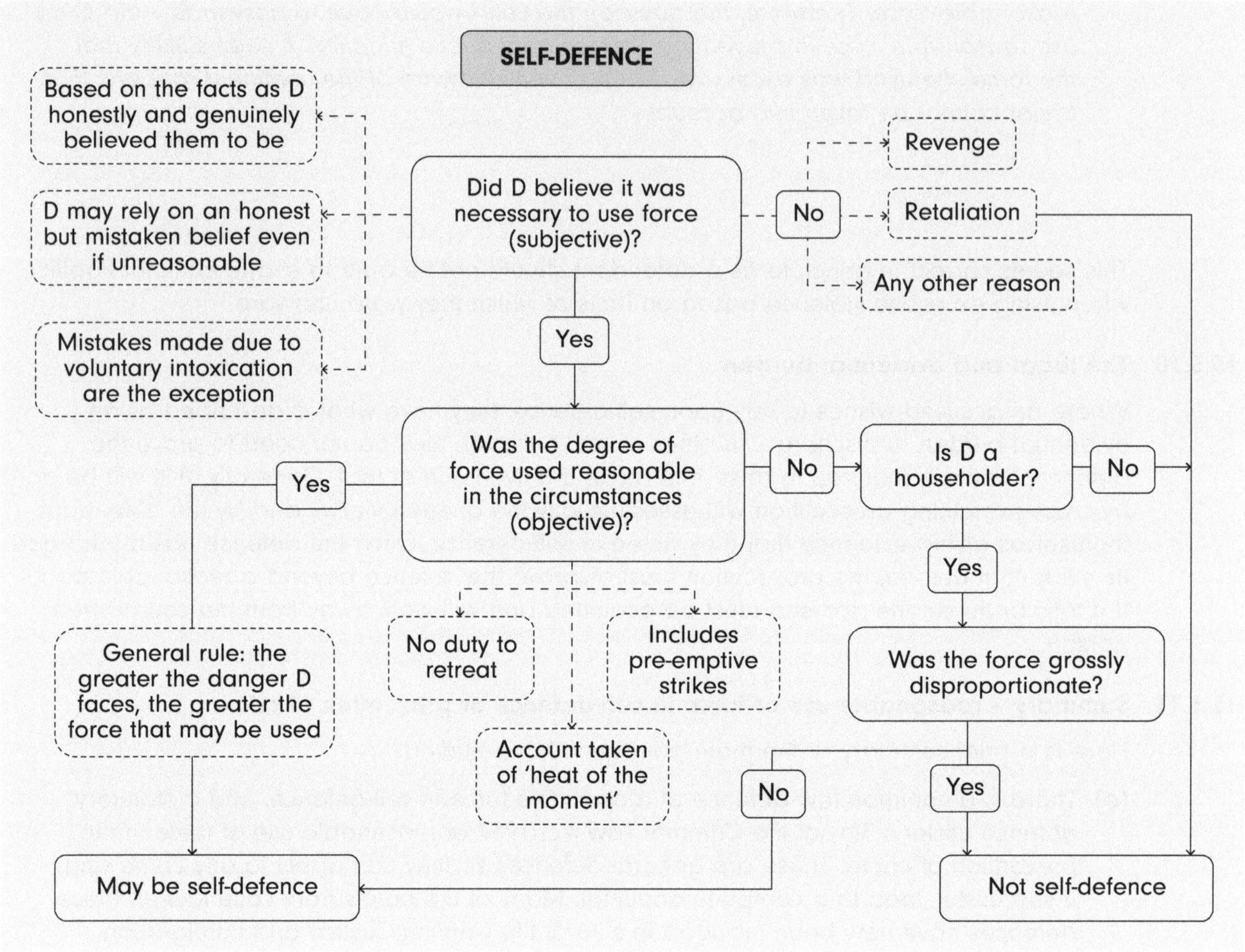

13.4 Review of the defences

To enable you to check your understanding of the two general defences studied in this chapter, you should attempt the Activity below.

ACTIVITY

PART 1

(1) Alistair drinks a bottle of brandy. When his wife expresses annoyance at this, he pushes her off the balcony of their third floor flat. She breaks both legs and is left with a permanent limp. Is Alistair guilty of an offence under s 18 of the OAPA 1861 in the following situations?

(a) He intended to cause her serious harm but formed that intention only because he was drunk.

(b) He was so drunk that he forgot they were not on the ground floor and just wanted to push her over into the flower-bed.

(c) He was so drunk that he lost control of his limbs and pushed her off the balcony without intending to do anything at all.

(2) In each of the above circumstances, is Alistair guilty of an offence under s 20 of the OAPA 1861?

(3) Brenda and Clarrie take the hallucinatory drug LSD and lie in the grass in a park. They are approached by a park attendant who is carrying a spike for picking up litter. He asks them if they are unwell. Brenda thinks he is a monster from the centre of the earth, and Clarrie believes he is a criminal who is about to stab her to death. The women struggle with him and deliberately stab him to death with his own spike. Are they guilty of either murder or manslaughter?

(4) Would the answer to Question (3) be different if the LSD had been added to the women's lemonade without their knowledge?

COMMENT

(1) (a) Yes: Alistair committed the actus reus of s 18 by causing grievous bodily harm to his wife. He intended to do her grievous bodily harm, so had the mens rea for this offence. The fact that he would not have formed this mens rea had he been sober is no excuse.

(b) No because, although Alistair has committed the actus reus, this time, there is no intent to cause grievous bodily harm. Because s 18 is an offence of specific intent, he is entitled to rely on his lack of mens rea.

(c) No: as above, he lacks mens rea and s 18 is an offence of specific intent.

(2) (a) Yes, because he is guilty under s 18, he will also be guilty under s 20. The actus reus of both offences is the same, and if Alistair intended grievous bodily harm, he must inevitably also intend or be reckless as to some bodily harm.

(b) Yes: despite his intoxication, Alistair did intend or was at least reckless as to some bodily harm (he was 'malicious'); this is sufficient mens rea for s 20.

(c) Yes: Alistair lacked the mens rea for s 20 but this is attributable to his voluntary intoxication and s 20 is an offence of basic intent. Thus, Alistair cannot rely on his intoxication: if he attempts to do so, he is simply deemed to have the necessary mens rea.

(3) Brenda is not guilty of murder as she thought the attendant was a monster and so she lacked the required intent to kill or cause grievous bodily harm to a human being. Her belief that he was a monster from the centre of the earth was presumably attributable to her voluntary intoxication with LSD. However, this does not prevent her relying upon her lack of mens rea because murder is an offence of specific intent.

Nevertheless, Brenda will not escape liability entirely as she will be guilty of manslaughter. This is because she cannot assert her lack of mens rea caused by her voluntary intoxication for an offence of basic intent, such as manslaughter - see the case of *R v Lipman*.

Clarrie committed the actus reus of homicide with intent to kill or cause grievous bodily harm to a human being. Thus, she is guilty of murder unless she can assert a genuine (although not necessarily reasonable) belief that she was being attacked. However, she is not permitted to rely on voluntary intoxication to do this even if the charge is for a specific intent crime such as murder; still less for manslaughter - see the case of *R v O'Grady*.

(4) The answer would be different if the defendants' drinks had been spiked. Brenda would be free to assert her lack of the appropriate mens rea for both murder and manslaughter due to involuntary intoxication. Clarrie could similarly rely on her genuine belief that she was being attacked.

PART 2

(1) Ruth is out with some friends having a drink at a local bar. Jonah, who is sitting on a stool next to her, keeps touching her knee inappropriately. Ruth reacts by slapping Jonah across the face.

(2) Albert is annoyed at Tanisha who has parked in a disabled space when she has no legal right to do so. He kicks her car and causes a small dent. Tanisha is furious and drives her car at Albert to prevent him from doing so again. Albert is hit by the vehicle and breaks his leg.

Will Ruth and Tanisha succeed in their defence under s 76 of the CJIA 2008?

COMMENT

(1) Ruth believed (subjective) that it was necessary to use force against Jonah. Furthermore, slapping him is a reasonable response (objective) to the sexual assault and so Ruth would successfully argue self-defence – s 76(3).

(2) Tanisha will argue that she believed it was necessary to use force to prevent the crime of criminal damage (subjective); although there may be an issue as to whether her act was in retaliation to Albert's action. Even if Tanisha satisfies this aspect, her reaction is not a reasonable use of force. Albert has caused a small dent to her car and, in response, she has broken his leg. This is a disproportionate use of force in the circumstances – s 76(6).

14 Attempts

LEARNING OUTCOMES

When you have completed this chapter, you should be able to:

- understand and apply the law in relation to attempted offences;
- appreciate how impossibility impacts upon criminal liability for attempts.

14.1 Introduction

Although most defendants are convicted of a substantive offence such as assault, murder, theft or criminal damage, the scope of criminal liability is wider than this. The law punishes not only those who commit a crime, but also those who take steps towards this but fail to complete the offence ('attempts'). Even though nothing criminal has actually happened, the defendant may still be liable. This is for public policy reasons because, otherwise, unsuccessful defendants would evade responsibility. Furthermore, it would be absurd for the police to have to wait until the full offence was completed before being able to take action.

An attempt to commit a crime is an offence in itself and is known as an 'inchoate' offence – one that is incomplete in some way. There are several inchoate offences but this chapter only deals with attempts. There are two types of scenario where a person could be liable for attempting to commit an offence. The first is an incomplete attempt, where the defendant has not done all the acts necessary to bring about the offence, for example, if they are arrested before they kill the proposed victim. The second is a complete attempt, where the defendant has done all the acts necessary to commit the offence, but the desired result has not followed.

Example

The defendant laces their victim's drink with poison planning to kill them, but the victim accidentally spills the contents of the glass on the floor and so survives because they do not drink the poison.

The justification for criminalising attempts is that the defendant has carried out all the necessary acts for the offence and intended to commit it, and therefore is no less blameworthy than a person who successfully completes the offence. Only an unexpected event or chance prevented the crime being committed. This is correct on the basis of subjective principles, but also, on a practical level, society needs to allow official intervention before harm is done.

14.2 Definition of attempt

To attempt to commit a crime is an offence contrary to s 1(1) of the Criminal Attempts Act (CAA) 1981 which provides:

> (1) If, with intent to commit an offence to which this section applies, a person does an act which is more than merely preparatory to the commission of the offence, he is guilty of attempting to commit the offence.

Almost all indictable offences (those capable of being tried in the Crown Court) can be the subject of an attempt charge, but s 1(4) of the CAA 1981 specifies certain offences which cannot. For our purposes, the most important exception is that a defendant may not be charged with attempting to be an accomplice (secondary participant) to a crime (see **Chapter 15**).

Summary only offences - those that must be dealt with in the magistrates' court - are excluded by the Act. The effect is that although a person may be convicted of attempted murder, they cannot be charged with, for example, an attempted simple assault. There are, however, some offences (outside the scope of this textbook) where the statute creating the summary only offence specifically created an attempt, with one such example being attempting to drive a motor vehicle while over the prescribed limit for alcohol.

14.3 Actus reus

The definition under s 1 of the CAA1981 requires that the defendant does an act which is more than merely preparatory to the commission of the offence. What, then, is the position if they fail to do something?

Example

Matthew and Daria neglect their 8-year-old daughter, Annie. They refuse to feed her as they want her to die. If Annie does die, the actus reus of murder is established because, by their omission, Matthew and Daria have caused her death. Usually, there is no criminal liability for failing to act, but Annie's parents would come within an exception to that general principle as they have both a special relationship and a statutory duty towards their daughter. Consequently, they would be liable for their omission.

However, if Annie survives, the actus reus of attempted murder cannot be established. This is because the actus reus of an attempt requires an act, and there is no reference to an omission in the definition of the offence. Hence, Matthew and Daria would not meet the required elements of the actus reus of attempted murder, although they would no doubt face other charges which are outside the scope of this textbook.

14.3.1 More than merely preparatory

Assuming the defendant has done an act, the actus reus of attempt is not complete unless this is *more than merely preparatory* to the commission of the offence. Quite when an act satisfies this test (and therefore potentially incurs liability for attempt) is the subject of much debate. However, although it is a question of fact to be decided by the jury based upon the evidence in each particular case, guidance has been provided by the judges in determining this issue.

In *R v Gullefer* [1987] Crim LR 195, the defendant placed a bet on a dog at a greyhound racing track. During the race, when it became clear that the dog was not going to win, the defendant jumped onto the track hoping that the stewards would declare the race void so he would be entitled to a refund of his bet. The defendant's conviction for attempted theft of the money was quashed on appeal on the basis that his act was merely preparatory. In this instance, the court ruled that the defendant had not done enough to be criminally liable for an attempt. Lord Lane indicated that to satisfy the test, the accused needed to be 'on the job', and this 'begins when the merely preparatory acts have come to an end and the defendant embarks on the crime proper'.

Whilst this provides some assistance, given that the facts will vary in every case, there is clearly scope for inconsistency. Gullefer's appeal was allowed because the Court of Appeal took the view that he was still only in the preparatory stages of stealing the money from the bookmaker. Although the judges did not list what the defendant needed to do to be liable for attempted theft, there were a number of steps outstanding before he was in a position to complete the full offence; in particular, climb back over the fence, go to the bookmakers, present his ticket and ask for a refund.

The law distinguishes mere acts of preparation (where there will be no liability for attempt) from those acts which effectively indicate that the defendant is engaged 'on the job'. When this occurs may be surprisingly late.

Example

Michael intends to kill Ganesh and does the following:

(1) Buys a shotgun and ammunition.

(2) Shortens the barrel of the shotgun and loads it.

(3) Puts on a disguise.

(4) Waits for Ganesh at the school gates, knowing that Ganesh will shortly be arriving by car to drop off his daughter.

(5) Jumps into the rear seat of the car when the daughter gets out.

(6) Points the loaded gun at Ganesh, releases the trigger and says: 'You're not going to like this.'

The point at which Michael goes beyond mere preparation is a matter of opinion, but most people would probably opt for somewhere between stages (4) and (5). Stages (1), (2) and (3) are merely preparatory and stage (6) is definitely more than this, as Michael only has to pull the trigger in order to commit the offence.

The facts of this scenario are based on the case of *R v Jones* [1990] 3 All ER 886. Here, the jury had to decide at what stage the actus reus for attempted murder was complete; in other words, when did Jones cross what is known as 'the line in the sand' from preparatory steps to 'embarking on the crime proper'. The Court of Appeal held that there was sufficient evidence for the jury to determine whether there was an act that was more than merely preparatory to the commission of the offence when Jones climbed into the victim's car; indeed, at this point, the only reason the victim survived at all was because he managed to grab the gun from Jones and escape.

It is apparent that the stage at which the defendant is liable for attempt may be somewhat late in the process, and this can cause difficulties for the law enforcement agencies. If they act too quickly, the defendant will be acquitted, but, if too late, the crime will be completed, and the public may be put at risk. Essentially, in each case, the court must look at what the defendant has actually done, then consider what else they need to do in order to commit the offence. In particular, is what the defendant did *more than* merely preparatory, or only merely preparatory to the commission of that offence?

In summary, there are three main points to determine for the actus reus of attempt:

(a) The test is set out in statute - an act (not an omission) is needed which is more than merely preparatory to the commission of the full offence.

(b) Case law seems to suggest that significant steps need to be taken towards the commission of the full offence, but, as a matter of law, it is not necessary to establish that the defendant has done all they intend to do (*R v Jones*).

(c) Whether an act is more than merely preparatory will be a question of fact in each case, provided the judge feels there is some evidence that the defendant has 'embarked upon the crime' (*R v Gullefer*) so that the matter can be left to the jury.

14.4 Mens rea

Having established the actus reus, the prosecution must also prove the mens rea, and this is usually straightforward because the defendant must intend to commit the specific offence attempted. For example, if charged with attempting to cause grievous bodily harm, it must be proved that they intended to cause grievous bodily harm. As a consequence, the charge would always be attempted s 18 - the prosecution would rarely charge someone with an attempted s 20 assault, as for this offence there is no need to prove an intention to cause grievous bodily harm.

If the offence is a result crime (see **Chapter 2**), the defendant must intend the prohibited result even if a 'lesser' mens rea would satisfy the full offence. In *R v Whybrow* (1951) 35 Cr App R 141, the defendant wired up a soap dish to the electricity supply in order to electrocute and kill his wife. At his trial the judge directed the jury that an intention to kill or cause grievous bodily harm would suffice on a charge of attempted murder. However, on appeal, the Court of Appeal said that this was a misdirection and only an intention to kill will do.

So far as intent is concerned, this can include both direct and indirect intent, so the test in *R v Woollin* (considered in **Chapter 3**) applies. In other words, foresight (of death) as a virtual certainty is evidence from which the jury may find an intention.

Another case which illustrates the point that only an intention to commit the offence will suffice is *R v Millard and Vernon* [1987] Crim LR 393, where the defendant was charged with attempted criminal damage. The judge had directed the jury at the trial that they could convict if the defendant was reckless as to whether the property would be damaged. Again, the Court of Appeal confirmed that an intention to commit attempted criminal damage must be proved even though recklessness is an adequate mens rea for the full offence.

Example

Larry lives with his partner, Janice. He has been told that Janice is having an affair, and when Janice returns home, he confronts her with the accusation. Janice denies it, and the two have a heated argument during which Larry grabs a carving knife from the kitchen sideboard. In anger, he waves the knife at Janice and then launches himself at her causing a small cut to her face.

(1) Larry could be charged with an attempt to kill Janice. However, if Larry denies this was his intention, direct intent may be difficult to establish in the circumstances. The prosecution could try to argue that death is virtually certain to occur if a defendant launches themselves at the victim with a knife, and that Larry was aware of this which would satisfy the test for indirect intent. Again, this may prove problematic on the evidence provided.

(2) Alternatively, Larry could be charged with attempting to cause grievous bodily harm under s 18 of the OAPA 1861. His use of a weapon to cut Janice is evidence of his intent to cause really serious harm.

(3) If the prosecution decides to pursue Larry for the lesser s 20 assault, they still have to establish an intent to inflict grievous bodily harm, despite the fact that the full offence only requires an intent or recklessness as to causing some harm. As a consequence, there is no advantage in charging a defendant with an attempted s 20 assault.

14.4.1 The role of recklessness in attempt

As intention to commit the full offence is needed, what part (if any) does recklessness play in attempts? As stated above, the defendant must intend all consequences which form part of the actus reus of the full offence even if recklessness would have sufficed for the full offence. However, some crimes involve an element of ulterior mens rea, for example, aggravated criminal damage. Although the actus reus of this offence is simply causing damage or destruction to property, the mens rea is intention or recklessness as to the damage or destruction, and intention or recklessness as to whether life is endangered by the damage or destruction.

In *Attorney-General's Reference (No 3 of 1992)* [1994] 2 All ER 121, it was held that on a charge of attempted aggravated criminal damage, the defendant must intend to damage property so they must intend the consequence forming the actus reus of the offence, but they can be reckless as to whether life is endangered because this is an issue of ulterior mens rea. There is no need for life to be endangered to establish the actus reus of the full offence, and so recklessness will suffice as to this element of mens rea in an attempted offence.

Example

The police receive a tip off that Junaid is planning to start a fire at a house where his ex-partner, Sunita and her two children are now living. The police covertly survey the property and see a car pull up outside the house at 6pm. Junaid is seen to go to the boot of his car, take out a can of petrol and walk towards the house. He is arrested halfway down the garden path. When searched, the police find a cigarette lighter and a cloth rag in his pocket.

Junaid admits driving to Sunita's house intending to cause a fire. However, he denies intending to endanger anyone's life as he believed his ex-partner and the children were out. In fact, they were inside the house having their evening meal. Junaid accepts that he did consider the risk that they may have been at home but thought it very unlikely as Sunita takes the children to a swimming class at that time.

Junaid is charged with two offences (note that he is charged under the Criminal Attempts Act 1981 and not under the Criminal Damage Act 1971):

(1) Attempted criminal damage by arson, contrary to s 1(1) of the CAA 1981

The actus reus is doing an act that is more than merely preparatory. In this instance, it is likely the jury would find that Junaid had moved from the preparation stage to the commission stage and that he had 'embarked on the crime proper'. The mens rea is satisfied as Junaid admits that he intended to damage the house by fire – the offence of arson.

(2) Attempted aggravated criminal damage by arson, contrary to s 1(1) of the CAA 1981

The actus reus is the same as for attempted arson (above). Turning to the mens rea, in addition to the intention to cause damage by fire, the prosecution must prove that Junaid intended or was reckless as to endangering life. This is because aggravated arson is a crime of ulterior intent. Here, because Junaid admits to foreseeing a risk that Sunita and the children could be in the house and therefore presumably that their lives might be endangered, he is reckless as to this aspect.

What about the mens rea required with regard to certain material circumstances of the offence? For example, if the defendant is charged with attempted rape, does he have to intend to have non-consensual sexual intercourse?

In *R v Millard and Vernon* [1987] Crim LR 393 (above), Mustill LJ set out the difficulties that recklessness can produce in presenting argument to juries. He distinguished, on the one hand, those more straightforward cases where the substantive offence consists simply of the act that constitutes the actus reus – what he called 'the result'. Here, he said, when looking at the defendant's mens rea, 'for an attempt, nothing but conscious volition will do'. He then contrasted that, on the other hand, with situations or cases where the substantive offence goes beyond one result and one mens rea, and requires another state of mind directed to some circumstances or act which the prosecution must prove in addition to proving the result. Mustill LJ used attempted rape as an example, even though *Millard and Vernon* was a case about criminal damage. He said:

> The problem may be illustrated by reference to the offence of attempted rape. As regards the substantive offence the 'result' takes the shape of sexual intercourse with a woman. But the offence is not established without proof of an additional circumstance (namely that the woman did not consent), and a state of mind relative to that circumstance (namely that the defendant knew she did not consent, or was reckless as to whether she consented).
>
> When one turns to the offence of attempted rape, one thing is obvious, that the result, namely the act of sexual intercourse, must be intended in the full sense. Also obvious

> is the fact that proof of an intention to have intercourse with a woman, together with an act done towards that end, is not enough: the offence must involve proof of something about the woman's consent, and something about the defendant's state of mind in relation to that consent.

This raises the question: can the 'something' (about the defendant's state of mind in relation to that consent) be recklessness?

The Court of Appeal made a further attempt to deal with this matter when a case involving attempted rape arose: *R v Khan* [1990] 2 All ER 783. Referring to Mustill LJ's analysis above, it was held that the defendant must intend sexual intercourse either knowing of the lack of consent, or being reckless as to the other's consent.

14.4.2 Conditional intent

The final point in this section is that a conditional intent is adequate. For example, if someone puts their hand into the victim's pocket intending to take anything 'if it is worth stealing', that is an adequate mens rea for attempted theft.

14.4.3 Summary of mens rea for attempts

(a) Usually, the prosecution must establish that the defendant intended the consequences which form the actus reus of the full offence. For example, on a charge of attempted murder, the defendant must intend to kill, and an intention to cause grievous bodily harm is not enough.

(b) If the full offence involves an element of ulterior mens rea, recklessness in relation to that ulterior mens rea will suffice for an attempt charge. This would apply to aggravated criminal damage, for example.

14.5 Impossibility

In some situations, the crime 'attempted' may be impossible to commit successfully. However, this will not prevent the establishment of the actus reus of attempt because s 1(2) of the CAA 1981 provides:

> A person may be guilty of attempting to commit an offence to which this section applies even though the facts are such that the commission of the offence is impossible.

Example

Assume in each case the defendant does an act that is more than merely preparatory.

(1) José is a pickpocket. He puts his hand into Lesley's pocket hoping to steal her purse, but her pocket is empty.

(2) Selena tries to break into a safe using a teaspoon.

(3) Mahathir thinks that it is a crime to commit adultery. He tries to have sexual intercourse with Siobhan (with her consent) whom he knows to be married.

In Example (1), José would be liable for attempted theft under s 1(1) of the CAA 1981. The fact that Lesley's pocket was empty, and therefore theft of the purse is impossible, is deemed to be irrelevant due to the provisions of s 1(2). Similarly, Selena would be liable for attempted theft in Example (2), even though her use of a teaspoon to try and open the safe means her goal is impossible. Impossibility as to ends (Example (1)) and impossibility of means (Example (2)) are no defence to a charge of attempting to commit an offence.

However, the law says that Example (3) cannot be an attempt. Even if Mahathir had succeeded in having sexual intercourse with Siobhan, no crime has been committed as adultery is not an offence and he cannot attempt a crime that does not exist.

The mens rea is covered by s 1(3) of the CAA 1981 which states:

> (3) In any case where–
>
> (a) apart from this subsection a person's intention would not be regarded as having amounted to an intent to commit an offence; but
>
> (b) if the facts of the case had been as he believed them to be, his intention would be so regarded,
>
> then, for the purposes of subsection (1) above, he shall be regarded as having had an intent to commit that offence.

In effect, this means that the defendant will be deemed to have the intent to commit a crime if, on the facts which they believed to be true, they would have had such intent. Essentially, impossibility does not prevent the establishment of the mens rea of attempt.

Example

Katrina intends to kill Roya by shooting her. She points the gun at the victim and only fails in her objective because there is no bullet in the gun. Katrina has satisfied the actus reus of attempted murder as her actions go beyond the merely preparatory and it is irrelevant that it was impossible for her to kill Roya with the gun.

With regards to the mens rea, Katrina is judged on the facts as she believed them to be, and she thought the gun was loaded. Thus, she is deemed to have the relevant intent to commit murder.

In the case of *R v Shivpuri* [1987] AC 1, the defendant was arrested carrying a package from India which he believed to contain either heroin or cannabis. In fact, the substance was harmless and not an illegal drug at all. It was held by the House of Lords that he was guilty of attempting to be knowingly concerned in dealing with or harbouring a controlled drug, even though that was impossible on the facts as the substance was harmless. The defendant committed the actus reus as he did an act - bringing the parcel into the country - which was more than merely preparatory to the commission of the offence. Under s 1(2) of the CAA 1981, the fact that the commission of the offence was impossible did not prevent the actus reus of attempt being satisfied.

Furthermore, Mr Shivpuri had the necessary intent required to establish the charge of attempt. If the facts had been as he believed, with the parcel containing illegal drugs, the requisite intent (to deal with or harbour a controlled drug) would have been present. Under s 1(3), impossibility does not prevent the establishment of the mens rea of attempt.

14.6 Summary of attempts

To assist your understanding of attempts, the law is summarised in the flowchart below.

Figure 14.1 Attempts

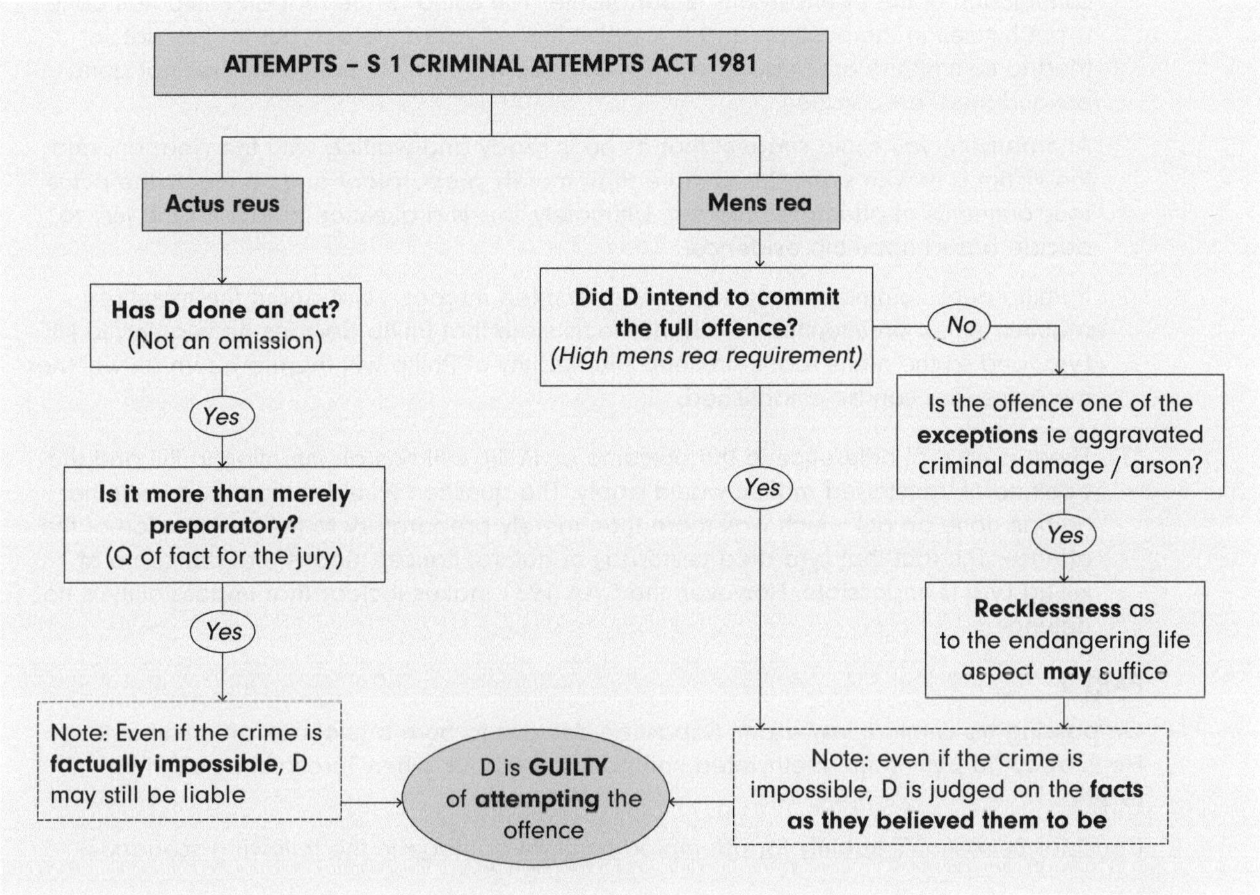

Finally, to enable you to apply your understanding of the legal principles, complete the activity below.

ACTIVITY

PART 1

Analyse the scenarios and consider whether the defendant in each case could be liable for an attempted offence. Look at the comment to each scenario before moving on to the next.

(1) Philip decides he is going to kill Lyra. He gets a kitchen knife out of the drawer and walks to a dark alley that he knows Lyra uses as a shortcut. Philip is arrested by a police officer just as Lyra starts to walk down the alley.

Is Philip liable for attempted murder?

(2) Does your answer differ if Lyra had died of natural causes yesterday and the person walking down the alley was Rosie?

COMMENT

(1) Philip's liability would depend first on whether the actus reus of attempted murder is established – has he done an act that is more than merely preparatory to the commission of the offence? This is debatable. You could argue that all Philip has done is put himself in the position and equipped himself to do the act, but he has not yet tried to commit the act in question (*R v Geddes* 160 JP 697); hence, he has not gone beyond mere preparation.

Alternatively, you could suggest that as he is ready and waiting with the weapon, and the victim is now in sight, this is more than merely preparatory and so meets the actus reus elements of attempted murder. Ultimately, this is a question of fact for the jury to decide based upon the evidence.

If Philip does commit the actus reus of attempted murder, what about the mens rea requirement of an intention to kill? The facts state that Philip decides he is going to kill Lyra, and so the mens rea is present. The liability of Philip will therefore turn on whether the actus reus can be established.

(2) There is no real difference to the outcome as Philip still has an intention to kill and the doctrine of transferred malice would apply. The question would remain as to whether he has done an act which was more than merely preparatory to the commission of the offence. The fact that Lyra died yesterday of natural causes means that the crime of killing Lyra is impossible. However, the CAA 1981 makes it clear that impossibility is no defence.

PART 2

On passing his criminal law exam, Sebastian decides to burn a textbook on criminal law. He is about to pour some methylated spirit on to the book when Teresa shouts at him to stop.

Consider Sebastian's liability for attempted criminal damage in the following scenarios:

(1) The book is Teresa's; Sebastian believes the book certainly belongs to him.

(2) The book is Teresa's; Sebastian believes the book probably belongs to him.

(3) The book is Sebastian's; Sebastian believes the book belongs to Teresa.

COMMENT

In each scenario, Sebastian has done an act that is more than merely preparatory to the commission of the full offence even though there are further steps for him to take – pouring on the fuel and setting light to the book. The question of his liability turns on mens rea issues. In all cases Sebastian intends to damage the book, but are all elements of mens rea present?

(1) The book belongs to Teresa but Sebastian does not realise this. Applying, by analogy, the decision as to existing circumstances in *Khan* regarding attempted rape, Sebastian must know or be reckless as to the fact that the property belongs to another. Here he does not know or foresee such a risk, and so he lacks the mens rea required for the charge to stand.

(2) This time Sebastian is aware that the book might belong to another. He therefore does have the mens rea for attempt, as he intends to damage the property and is reckless as to whether the property belongs to another.

(3) The book belongs to Sebastian, but he believes it belongs to Teresa. He therefore has the mens rea of attempted criminal damage as he intends to destroy the book and he believes it belongs to another. The fact that he is wrong in his belief is irrelevant, as impossibility is no defence to a charge of attempted criminal damage.

15 The Scope of Criminal Liability - Secondary Participation

LEARNING OUTCOMES

When you have completed this chapter, you should be able to:

- appreciate how the net of criminal liability is widened to include those who help or encourage others to commit crimes, and the social and practical reasons for this;
- explain in detail the law relating to secondary participation;
- understand the controversial mens rea requirements of secondary participation.

15.1 Introduction

Thus far, the focus has been on the criminal liability of the individual who actually commits a substantive offence such as murder, theft, robbery or criminal damage, whether that be the full offence or an attempt. However, the law casts its net wider than this to catch those who do not commit a crime but who simply encourage or assist by, for example, providing a gun with which to shoot a victim, or holding the victim while another person punches them. Effectively, they are involved but on the fringes. Such a person can incur criminal liability even though they did not commit the criminal act and, to reflect the responsibility of all those involved, the law allows for several people to be charged with the same offence, even though they may have played very different roles at the time. Such 'helpers' are referred to as accomplices, accessories or secondary parties to a crime. In this textbook, they are referred to as accomplices.

15.2 The parties to a crime

The terminology used to describe the different parties to an offence and their roles can be quite confusing. When analysing a scenario that involves more than one defendant, the first step is to identify the principal offender and to consider their criminal liability. Only then should those with lesser involvement (secondary offenders) be discussed.

A principal offender is the person who commits the actus reus elements of a substantive criminal offence. Where two or more people commit an offence together, they will be labelled co-principals. A person can also be charged as a principal offender where they have used an innocent agent to commit the actus reus of an offence: and this is covered later in the chapter.

Those who assist in the commission of an offence in some way, whilst not committing the actus reus of the offence themselves, are known as accomplices. The distinction between principals and accomplices is illustrated here.

Example

Farah and Samina attack Tariq, intending to cause him grievous bodily harm. They both strike him with wooden poles. Tariq suffers a fractured skull as a result of the blows and subsequently dies from his injuries. Before the attack, Farah and Samina had told Nadim of their plans. Nadim supplied the wooden poles used in the attack.

In this case, Farah and Samina have both committed the actus reus of the offence of murder: their joint attack on Tariq has caused his death and they would therefore be charged as co-principals to the offence of murder. Nadim is not a principal offender: he has not committed the actus reus of the offence of murder in that his actions are not the cause of death. He has, however, helped Farah and Samina to commit the offence by supplying them with their weapons (the poles), and he would therefore be charged as an accomplice to murder.

The criminal liability of accomplices is laid down in statute. Under s 8 of the Accessories and Abettors Act (AAA) 1861, it is provided that:

> whosoever shall aid, abet, counsel or procure the commission of any indictable offence ... shall be tried, indicted and punished as a principal offender.

Unsurprisingly, given that the statute is over 160 years old, the language is rather archaic. In particular, the reference to being indicted is misleading as it is possible to be an accomplice to both either-way and indictable only offences. There is a similar provision dealing with accomplice liability for summary offences under s 44 of the Magistrates' Courts Act 1980.

The effect of both statutory provisions is to emphasise that the law regards a person who assists in the commission of an offence to be as culpable as the person who commits the crime. As a consequence, conviction as an accomplice will attract the same powers of punishment as the principal offender. If, therefore, a defendant is convicted as an accomplice to murder, they will be subject to a mandatory sentence of life imprisonment in the same way as the person who actually caused the death.

15.3 Actus reus

Both actus reus and mens rea must be established against a defendant before they can be convicted as an accomplice to a crime. It will become apparent that, although it is usually straightforward to prove the actus reus elements, the mens rea is more complex.

According to the statute, an accomplice may satisfy the actus reus of accomplice liability in four different ways, namely by aiding, abetting, counselling or procuring the commission of the offence. The meaning of these words has been considered in case law. In *Attorney-General's Reference (No 1 of 1975)* [1975] QB 773 (considered in detail below), the Court of Appeal confirmed that the words – aid, abet, counsel and procure – were to be given their ordinary meaning. The judges were of the view that each of the four words must mean something different to the other three, otherwise there was little point in using the four different terms. However, in reality, a criminal charge will usually allege that the defendant aided, abetted, counselled or procured, and no one term will be singled out.

15.3.1 Aiding

The word 'aiding' suggests physically helping, assisting or supporting the principal offender in some way, to enable them to commit the crime. Generally, aid will be given at the time of the offence, although it can also be earlier. However, it does not include those whose only involvement is after the offence, for example disposing of evidence, or deleting incriminating emails (there are separate offences that covers such scenarios).

Aiding before the offence would include providing the principal offender with the weapon or giving specific information to allow the crime to succeed, such as the code to a security gate to facilitate a burglary, or teaching a person the technology skills to commit internet fraud. Acting as a lookout or holding the victim down while the principal assaults the victim would be aiding at the time of the offence.

15.3.2 Abetting

The second word listed in s 8 of the AAA 1861 is 'abet', and this requires the accomplice to encourage the principal in some way to commit the crime at the time of the offence. This can be by words or actions, such as shouting specific words of encouragement, for example 'Kick him!' while a victim is being assaulted, or using gestures, such as miming the action of a punch or even giving a thumbs up.

15.3.3 Counselling

An accomplice can also counsel the offence. This involves instigating, soliciting or encouraging, or even threatening, the principal to commit the offence. Counselling occurs at some stage before the offence. This is how it differs from abetting, which requires the prosecution to prove that the defendant wilfully encouraged the offence at the scene, thus when the offence is in the process of being committed. Encouraging an assault by 'winding up' the principal offender, for example stating (in response to the principal's comment that he would 'punch his son's teacher') that the teacher deserved it and should show respect to the child would be counselling. Alternatively, a defendant who suggested it would be a 'brilliant idea' for the principal to scrawl graffiti on a bus shelter.

The amount of encouragement offered does not need to be particularly great for liability to arise. In *R v Gianetto* [1997] 1 Cr App R 1, the principal offender stated, 'I am going to kill your wife', to which the accomplice responded, 'Oh goody'. This was found to be enough to convict the husband as an accomplice on the basis that he had counselled the offence of murder.

15.3.4 Procuring

Procuring is a different concept entirely to the other three types of behaviour. According to Lord Widgery in the *Attorney General's Reference (No 1 of 1975)* (see above) this means 'to produce by endeavour'. The accused sets out to achieve a particular state of affairs and takes appropriate steps to bring about that offence. Because procuring usually requires the accomplice to actually cause the crime, this will occur at an earlier time to the offence. A defendant who secretly adds alcohol to their friend's drink, knowing that the friend would shortly be driving home, procures the offence of driving with excess alcohol contrary to s 5 of the RTA 1988. By 'spiking' the drink, the defendant puts the principal offender in a position whereby they commit an offence that they would not otherwise have done.

15.3.5 Overview

It is possible, therefore, to be an accomplice before or at the time of the offence, and this aspect of the law is summarised below:

	What must the accomplice do for the principal offender?	Before the offence?	During the offence?
Aid	Help or assist	✓	✓
Abet	Encourage	X	✓
Counsel	Instigate, solicit or encourage	✓	X
Procure	Produce by endeavour	✓	X

To assist with the practical aspect, the following examples analyse the actus reus of accomplice liability in context.

Examples

(1) Tunji gives Kola a key to his house so that Kola can go there to assault Tunji's wife, Constance (assistance).

(2) He tells Kola that there is a spare key to the house under the plant pot outside the front door (advice). Kola uses this key to access the house and assaults Constance.

(3) He helps Kola to climb through a window to the house by letting Kola stand on his shoulders to get in so that Kola can assault Constance (physical assistance).

(4) He says to Kola that he thinks it would be an excellent idea for Kola to assault Constance (verbal encouragement).

In all these scenarios, Tunji has acted or spoken before the crime occurs and could therefore be an accomplice to the assault committed by Kola.

(5) Tunji is unaware of Kola's attack on Constance until Kola telephones him immediately afterwards to confess. Tunji dislikes his wife and so he allows Kola to use his bathroom to clean up and his garden shed to hide from the police.

In this instance, Tunji cannot be an accomplice to the assault as his only involvement is after the offence has been committed. Accomplice liability depends on the defendant's involvement before or at the time of the offence.

15.3.6 Presence at the scene

According to the decision in *R v Allen* [1965] 1 QB 130, mere presence at the scene of a crime is not, in itself, sufficient to amount to the actus reus of being an accomplice. In this case, the defendant was at the scene of a fight. He was entirely passive and did nothing to encourage either party, but he did admit to harbouring a secret desire to become involved if needed. The Court of Appeal held that mere presence alone was insufficient because: 'To hold otherwise would be in effect ... to convict a man on his thoughts, unaccompanied by any physical act other than the fact of mere presence.'

It would appear, therefore, that to be liable as an accomplice in this situation, it must be established that the accomplice was present by prior arrangement with the principal, or actually encouraged or assisted the principal (by words and/or actions) at the scene of the crime.

In some cases, however, presence at the scene of the crime, without any obvious evidence of encouragement, has been found to be sufficient. This applies where the defendant is present at an illegal event. In *Wilcox v Jeffrey* [1951] 1 All ER 464, the defendant was found guilty of being an accomplice simply by being a spectator at a jazz concert. A famous American musician was allowed entry into the country provided he did not work, so his performance was illegal. The defendant was found to have encouraged the commission of the offence as he met the musician at the airport, bought a ticket for the concert and attended the performance. It would appear, therefore, that paying to attend an illegal event could amount to encouragement of the crime and so establish the actus reus of accomplice liability. The justification for this decision is that there would not have been a performance without the audience, so the presence of each spectator was an encouragement to the principal offender to perform. In determining guilt, the particular facts will be relevant.

In a more recent case, *R v Trenton* [2024] EWCA Crim 1580, the extent to which presence at the scene on the part of an accomplice can be sufficient to assist or encourage the principal in their crime was considered. The facts were that a group of men chased the victim into a car park where they stabbed and killed him. The defendant was with the group initially and joined in the chase, albeit 15 seconds behind the others, before peeling off and hiding behind a garage. He therefore was not present in the car park at the time of the stabbing, although he later met up again with the some of the group of men. The Court of Appeal held that, despite being slightly behind during the chase and stopping prior to entering the car park, there was sufficient evidence upon which a jury *could* have concluded that the defendant could both see and be seen and had therefore encouraged the principals.

Example

Penrhyn owns a Ferrari motor car. He and his brother Clwyd are apprehended by the police who allege that the car was being driven at a dangerous speed. Penrhyn denies liability as an accomplice to the charge of dangerous driving, arguing that he did nothing – he simply sat in the passenger seat while Clwyd drove the car at high speed. Penrhyn submits that he did not encourage Clwyd in his driving.

Penrhyn's mere presence in the car at the time of the speeding may, according to the decision in Allan above, enable him to avoid accomplice liability. This is because he did not do or say anything to encourage Clwyd. Alternatively, by not saying anything, he was implying that he consented to the speeding; it was his car, and thus his silence could amount to encouragement.

Remaining silent, or failing to intervene at the scene of a crime where there is a right or a duty to act to control the actions of the principal offender, can therefore amount to encouragement of the offence and lead to accomplice liability. This was confirmed in the case of *Tuck v Robson* [1970] 1 WLR 741. The licensee of a public house, who allowed his customers to drink after hours, was held to be an accomplice to the offence of drinking after hours as he had the right (or a duty) to stop them, and his failure to do so, by his inactivity, amounted to encouragement.

In the case of *R v Russell and Russell* (1987) 85 Cr App R 388, the failure of one parent to intervene to protect their child from ill-treatment by the other parent amounted to encouragement of the offence and led to accomplice liability. The passive parent was under a duty to act and their failure to do so encouraged the crime. Thus, the principle that defendants are not liable for their omissions, unless an exception applies, applies as much to accomplice liability as to that of a principal offender.

In summary, a person will satisfy the actus reus requirements of accomplice liability if either:

(a) they help to bring about the crime by acting, advising, assisting or encouraging *before* the crime occurs; or

(b) they are *present at the scene* of the crime *in order* to assist or encourage; or

(c) they are *present at the scene* of the crime and *do* assist or encourage (by words and/or actions).

Furthermore, because accomplices are treated in the same way as principal offenders as far as trial and sentence are concerned, the fact that the court could not determine whether the defendant was a principal offender or an accomplice does not matter if it can be proved that they were one or the other.

15.3.7 Link between the principal and accomplice

In most situations, the prosecution will have no difficulty in establishing that the parties met or liaised in some way to arrange the details of the crime, but is it a requirement for there to be a link between them? In other words, must the principal be aware of the assistance, advice or encouragement given by the accomplice, and does it matter that they would have committed the offence without this?

In the case of *Attorney-General's Reference (No 1 of 1975)* [1975] QB 773, Lord Widgery CJ expressed his opinion that there would usually be a mental link – a meeting of minds – between principal and accomplice in cases where it was alleged that the accomplice had aided, abetted or counselled the principal in the commission of the offence. He said that such cases 'almost inevitably' involved contact between principal and accomplice. However, the judge confirmed that there was no need for a mental link, indeed any contact, between principal and accomplice where it was alleged that the accomplice had procured the commission of the offence. This was because procuring meant 'producing by endeavour' or setting out to ensure that something (in this case a crime) happens and taking the appropriate steps to achieve this. Lord Widgery CJ said that, in the view of the Court of Appeal, there were 'plenty of instances in which a person may be said to procure the commission of a crime ... even though there is no attempt at agreement or discussion'.

It is clear from this judgment that contact is not required between the principal and the accomplice in cases of procurement. With regards to aiding, abetting and counselling, there usually will be contact between the parties, but is this necessary to establish accomplice liability? There are situations where the accomplice has assisted the principal in the commission of an offence without the latter being aware of that help.

Example

Padraig is in the middle of causing criminal damage to a shop. Dearbhla is passing by and deliberately trips up a police officer who is about to apprehend Padraig. Dearbhla has assisted (aided) in the commission of the crime by enabling Padraig to complete the act of criminal damage, but Padraig may be totally unaware of that assistance. In scenarios involving aiding, no contact is required between the alleged principal and accomplice.

In cases of counselling and abetting, however, there does need to be a meeting of minds at some stage between accomplice and principal, as it is difficult to argue that the accomplice advised or encouraged the principal in the commission of the offence if the principal is not aware of this.

This was confirmed in the case of *R v Calhaem* [1985] QB 808. Here, the defendant hired a hit man (the principal offender) to kill her love rival. The 'hit man' claimed he had no intention of killing the woman but went to the house to give this impression. When the intended victim saw him, she screamed, causing the principal offender to go berserk and kill her. The defendant argued that she was not an accomplice to the murder as her counselling had not caused the 'hit man' to commit the offence. Unsurprisingly, her appeal was rejected by the Court of Appeal, which said there was no need to establish that the defendant's acts or words had been a substantial cause of the crime. She was an accomplice to murder, and the fact that the killer might have carried out the offence regardless of her encouragement was irrelevant.

The need for a causal link between the accomplice and the principal, so it can be demonstrated that the behaviour of the accomplice caused the crime to be committed, appears, therefore, to be restricted to cases where the alleged accomplice has acted in order to bring about the crime, namely, where they have procured it.

Note that a meeting of minds, as discussed by Lord Widgery CJ, does not mean the parties must have discussed the matter before the crime occurs. If the principal becomes aware of the accomplice's encouragement or advice *during* the commission of the crime, that will suffice to establish the actus reus of accomplice liability.

What happens where there is a meeting of minds as to the harm the parties might do to one another, but an entirely innocent person unexpectedly falls victim? This was the situation in *R v Gnango* [2012] 1 AC 827. B pulled out a gun and began firing at the defendant (D), who returned fire. A passer-by was hit in the head by a bullet from B's gun and was killed. D was charged with murder on the basis that he had been engaged in a joint enterprise with B. The Supreme Court restored D's conviction, reasoning that a person who aided, abetted, counselled or procured another to shoot at them was guilty of the attempted murder of themselves. As there was a common plan or agreement to shoot one another, this was a proper basis for a finding of murder, either by a combination of the principles relating to aiding and abetting and transferred malice, or, in the alternative, D could be regarded as a principal to a joint enterprise to engage in unlawful violence specifically designed to cause death or serious injury, from which death had resulted.

The interpretation of existing case law can be summarised as follows:

(a) In cases of aiding (acts of assistance), neither a mental nor a causal link between the principal offender and the accomplice is required; indeed, the principal may not even know of the assistance. Furthermore, there is no need to establish that this help influenced or impacted their decision to commit the crime.

(b) Where the accomplice is accused of abetting and counselling, a mental link is required so the principal must be aware of the encouragement or advice, but there need not be a causal link. Thus, it is irrelevant that the principal would have committed the crime regardless.

(c) In cases where the accomplice is said to have procured the offence, there is no necessity for a mental link with the principal but there must be a causal link.

An overview of these requirements is set out below.

	Mental link required?	**Causal link required?**
Aid	✗	✗
Abet	✓	✗
Counsel	✓	✗
Procure	✗	✓

15.4 Effect of principal liability

In most instances, the principal offender will be convicted of the same offence as the accomplice. However, on occasion, the liability of the principal is less than straightforward, and this may raise issues such as whether an individual can be charged as an accomplice to a crime where the principal is found not guilty.

15.4.1 Commission of the principal offence

It is established law that a person cannot be convicted as an accomplice unless the actus reus (at least) of the principal offence is committed.

Example

Hank suggests to Neil that he should kill his wife, but Neil laughs off the suggestion and nothing further happens. Hank cannot be charged as an accomplice to murder because no crime has taken place, and it would make no sense to say Hank is an accomplice to murder when one of the key elements of the actus reus of that crime (a dead body) is missing.

The need for the actus reus of a crime to be committed by a principal offender was confirmed in *R v Dias* [2002] Crim LR 490. Here, the defendant was charged as an accomplice to a charge of unlawful act manslaughter. The victim had injected himself with drugs supplied by the defendant and died. The Court of Appeal held that the defendant could not be an accomplice as the victim had committed no unlawful act by injecting himself with drugs.

15.4.2 Principal has a defence

On occasion, the principal offender may commit the actus reus of a crime but have a specific defence, such as reasonable use of force, that leads to their acquittal. In this situation, the accomplice may still be convicted.

In *R v Cogan and Leak* [1976] 1 QB 217, the Court of Appeal upheld L's conviction as an accomplice to rape, on the basis that he had procured the commission of the offence by acting to ensure that C had sexual intercourse with L's wife without her consent. In the judges' view, the fact that C was acquitted of the principal offence (due to his belief in L's wife's consent) did not prevent L being convicted as an accomplice. The actus reus of rape had been committed by C – he had had sexual intercourse with L's wife without her consent – and there was therefore no bar to upholding the conviction of L as an accomplice to that offence.

15.4.3 Principal not prosecuted

Another situation where only the accomplice may be convicted is where the principal is not prosecuted for some reason; perhaps they cannot be traced.

In *R v Gnango* (referred to above), the defendant was engaged in a shoot-out with a second unidentified male, referred to in court as 'Bandana Man' as he was wearing a red bandana, when Bandana Man accidentally shot a passer-by. Despite the principal offender never being arrested, the defendant was found guilty as an accomplice to murder.

15.4.4 Innocent agency

An innocent agent is someone who commits the actus reus of a crime but who is not guilty of the offence either because they lack mens rea, or because they have a specific defence available to them. In cases where an individual has used an innocent agent to commit the actus reus, the law will usually charge the instigator of the crime as the principal offender rather than as an accomplice.

> **_Example_**
>
> *Celia tells Eric that she wants some of her property destroyed. She asks him to collect it from her office and burn it. Eric gets the property and burns it, believing Celia's story, but in fact it belongs to Sumeena who reports the matter to the police.*
>
> *Eric successfully argues that he is not guilty of criminal damage by pleading lawful excuse under s 5(2)(a) of the Criminal Damage Act 1971. Although he has damaged property belonging to Sumeena and intended the damage, he has a defence because he believed he had the consent of the owner. Despite this, Celia could be charged as an accomplice to the crime committed by Eric. This is because Celia procured the offence of criminal damage (by acting to bring it about), as she instigated it.*
>
> *Alternatively, Celia could be charged with criminal damage as the principal offender. The allegation would be that she acted through an innocent agent, and she would be tried and sentenced as if she had damaged the property belonging to Sumeena herself.*

In the case of *R v Cogan and Leak*, L could be said to have used an innocent party to commit the offence of rape for him. It seems that L wanted to ensure that his wife would be subjected to non-consensual sexual intercourse, and, rather than commit the sexual act himself, he used C to do it for him. Lawton LJ said that there was no reason, in the view of the Court, why L could not have been charged as a principal offender acting through an innocent agent. However, this part of the decision has been criticised because the very nature of sexual offences seems to require personal involvement by the offender.

In summary, in situations where the defendant has used an innocent party to commit the actus reus of a crime, the defendant would usually be charged as the principal offender acting through an innocent agent. However, in cases involving sexual offences, the appropriate charge is that of acting as an accomplice having procured the commission of the offence.

15.5 Mens rea

There is a particular phrase that is associated with accomplice liability, namely 'joint enterprise' or 'joint venture'. Where there is more than one party committing an offence, it will be described as a joint venture if they commit the crime with a common purpose or plan. This may be because there are a number of principal offenders, such as four defendants who all work in a greenhouse producing and cultivating cannabis. However, in more recent times, the term has come to be associated with those defendants who are on the periphery of the offence, but who are nevertheless caught up by the criminal justice system. In particular, those individuals who are involved in gangs, and who were at the scene but did not fire the gun or stab the victim with a knife.

The mens rea of accomplice liability is a complex area of the law that has caused difficulties for even the most senior judges. There are two elements for the prosecution to prove, with the first concerning the mens rea in relation to the act or words that establish the actus reus of accomplice liability. The second part of the mens rea involves a consideration of the alleged accomplice's knowledge or awareness of the circumstances of the principal offence.

15.5.1 Intention to do the act

The first requirement is proof that the defendant intentionally (or deliberately) did the act that assisted, encouraged or procured the commission of the offence, or intentionally spoke the words that advised, procured or encouraged the crime. Once established, this element of mens rea is made out, even if the defendant does not wish the crime to be committed.

The case of *National Coal Board v Gamble* [1959] 1 QB 11 involved a defendant accused of being an accomplice to an offence of driving an overloaded vehicle on a public road. A lorry filled with coal was driven onto a weigh-bridge, where the operator (an employee of the National Coal Board) weighed the lorry and told the driver that the load was nearly four tons overweight. The driver said that he would risk taking the overload, so the operator gave him a ticket which allowed him to leave the colliery. The driver was later stopped by the police, and his firm was convicted of contravening the Motor Vehicles (Construction and Use) Regulations 1955. The National Coal Board was charged with aiding and abetting the firm in the commission of the offence. The defendant claimed that he had not wanted this offence to happen, but Devlin J stated that there were two elements to the mens rea of an accomplice:

(a) an intention to aid (proved by a positive act of assistance voluntarily done); and

(b) knowledge of the circumstances (considered later in this chapter).

Devlin J confirmed that the fact the defendant may not have wanted or intended the offence to occur, or that they may not have intended to assist in the commission of the offence, was immaterial to their liability: '... an indifference to the result of a crime does not of itself negative abetting'. The majority view of the court therefore was that the mens rea of accomplice liability is established if the defendant, with knowledge of the circumstances, deliberately (rather than accidentally) does an act or speaks words that amounted to encouragement and so on.

What if the defendant argues that they had to do the act of assistance, for example in order to fulfil a contractual obligation? This point was considered in *Garrett v Arthur Churchill (Glass) Ltd and Another* [1969] 2 All ER 1141. The defendant purchased an antique glass goblet on behalf of a client. The client paid the defendant for the goblet and the defendant handed it over, knowing that the client was going to attempt to export it without the required licence (an offence at that time under the Customs and Excise Act 1952). The defendant argued that he should not be liable as an accomplice to this offence, as in giving the goblet he was merely fulfilling a binding contractual obligation and a refusal to comply would render him in breach of contract.

Lord Parker CJ found that:

> albeit there was a legal duty in ordinary circumstances to hand over the goblet to the owners once the agency was determined, I do not think that an action would lie for breach of that duty if the handing over would constitute the offence of being knowingly concerned in its exportation.

In other words, the criminal law will take precedence over the civil law, and a defendant should refuse to comply with their contractual obligation if they know that, in doing so, they would be assisting a crime. The civil obligation could not be enforced against them in these circumstances.

This part of the test rarely presents any issues for the prosecution; indeed, if the conduct is deliberate, it is difficult to imagine situations where this element of the mens rea will not be established.

15.5.2 Knowledge of the circumstances

In *National Coal Board v Gamble*, Devlin J stated that the accomplice must 'have knowledge of the circumstances' in addition to an intention to encourage and so forth. This is the second element of accomplice mens rea. Its meaning was explained in *Johnson v Youden* [1950] 1 KB 544, where Lord Goddard CJ stated that for a person to be convicted of aiding and abetting a crime, it must be shown that they knew 'the essential matters which constitute that offence'. He went on to say that the defendant did not have to know that a crime had been committed 'because he may not know that the facts constitute an offence and ignorance of the law is not a defence'.

It is clear from the decision in *Johnson v Youden* that, to be guilty of an offence as an accomplice, it must be shown that:

(a) the defendant intended to do the act which assisted and so on; and

(b) the defendant had within their contemplation all the circumstances of the principal offence.

This means they must have known that certain things were going to happen, or at least contemplated that those things might happen which *in fact* constitute an offence.

In the case of *R v Craig and Bentley* (1952) The Times, 10 December, it was argued that Derek Bentley, aged 19, did not intend to assist an offence. Bentley was hanged in 1953 for the murder of Police Constable Sidney Miles, committed in the course of an attempted burglary. The murder of the police officer was actually carried out by a friend of Bentley's, Christopher Craig, who was only aged 16 at the time and therefore too young to receive the death penalty. Bentley was convicted as an accomplice to the murder on the basis that the killing amounted to a joint enterprise. The crucial evidence against Bentley was his alleged instruction to Craig to 'Let him have it!'. Lord Chief Justice Goddard, who was the trial judge, sentenced Bentley to death describing him as 'mentally aiding the murder'. In fact, Bentley could equally have meant 'hand over the gun', in which case the mens rea for accomplice liability would not have been satisfied. The outcome for Bentley was dire and the case led to a 45-year-long campaign to win him a posthumous pardon. This was granted in 1993 and his murder conviction was also subsequently quashed - far too late for Bentley himself.

Fortunately, such cases are rare, with the next example being more representative of how the law usually applies.

Example

Farah suggests to Colin that he should scratch the side of Ayesha's car, which he then does. To convict Farah as an accomplice to the offence of criminal damage, the prosecution must prove:

(1) That she aided, abetted, counselled or procured Colin in the commission of the offence. Farah has clearly done so as she made the suggestion to him in the first place: she has encouraged (counselled) the commission of the offence. The actus reus of accomplice liability is therefore satisfied.

(2) That she intended to do the act which encouraged Colin - she intended to speak the words. In this case Farah clearly did, as she deliberately made the suggestion to Colin.

(3) That she knew all the circumstances of the offence, namely either that:

(a) Farah knew Colin would destroy or damage property, that the property belonged to another, and that Colin would intend or foresee the risk of damage and would know or foresee the risk that the property belonged to another; or

(b) Farah contemplated that damage might occur, that the property might belong to another, and that Colin might intend or foresee the risk of damage and might know or foresee the risk that it belonged to another.

In other words, all the elements of the crime committed by the principal must be intended or contemplated as possibly happening by the alleged accomplice before liability as an accomplice can be established.

In order to incur liability as an accomplice, the defendant must always have within their contemplation the circumstances that make the principal's conduct criminal. This is so even if the principal offence is one involving negligence or strict liability.

Crimes of strict liability are those where a defendant may be convicted even though they lacked mens rea for one or more of the elements of the offence. However, as far as the accomplice is concerned, it is necessary to establish mens rea even in these cases.

An example of this is the authority of *Callow v Tillstone* (1900) 83 LT 411. Here, a shopkeeper was convicted of a strict liability offence of selling meat unfit for human consumption despite having had the meat checked by a vet, who gave him a certificate allowing him to sell it. The vet, however, was acquitted of the charge of aiding and abetting this offence, as he did not know and had not contemplated that the meat was unfit to eat. He had been negligent in his job: he should have realised it but did not. He did not therefore have within his contemplation all the circumstances of the offence, and thus lacked the mens rea of accomplice liability.

This appears somewhat unjust as the shopkeeper (the principal offender) was guilty of the principal offence on the basis of strict liability despite being diligent, whereas the veterinary surgeon, although negligent and so perhaps more blameworthy than the shopkeeper, escapes liability.

15.5.3 Extent of accomplice's knowledge

As the mens rea requirements of accomplice liability specify that the defendant must have within their contemplation all the essential elements of the offence, the question arises as to how specific their knowledge or awareness must be.

Accomplice has full knowledge

If the accomplice is aware of the crime that the principal intends to commit, the second limb of the mens rea will be established quite easily.

Example

Mitchell accompanies Alfie to act as a lookout while Alfie breaks into an office building to steal a number of computers. Mitchell satisfies the actus reus of accomplice liability as he aids Alfie at the time of the offence by acting as a lookout. With regard to the mens rea, not only does Mitchell act intentionally, he also has knowledge of the circumstances that make this a crime. He knows that Alfie intends to enter the building as a trespasser and steal property from inside.

Accomplice has knowledge of an offence

In most instances, the accomplice will be fully involved and entirely aware of the facts that lead to the commission of a crime. However, the circumstances may not be as clear cut, and determining what level of knowledge the defendant has becomes key to establishing whether they are guilty as an accomplice. Does the accused merely need to suspect that a particular type of crime may be committed, or must they have precise details of the offence? The question of how specific the accomplice's knowledge must be has been considered in two important cases, which provide some helpful guidance.

In *R v Bainbridge* [1960] 1 QB 129, the defendant was convicted of being an accomplice to breaking into a bank, having supplied oxygen cutting equipment that was used by the principal offenders. Although he did not know the exact details of the crime to be committed, the defendant was aware that the equipment was to be used for breaking into some sort of premises. The Court of Appeal said that the accomplice must know a 'crime of the type in question was intended'. As long as the type of crime is known, for example that a burglary is to occur, the defendant need not know the exact details such as the time and location of the planned offence. However, an awareness only that the principal was going to commit some form of illegal act was insufficient to establish the mens rea of accomplice liability.

In *Maxwell v DPP for Northern Ireland* [1978] 1 WLR 1350, the defendant acted as a guide for other members of the Ulster Volunteer Force ('UVF'), showing them the way to a particular pub where the principal offenders threw in a pipe bomb. He was charged with aiding and abetting this offence. He argued that he did not know exactly what the principal offenders were going to do, and thus did not have the mens rea necessary to be convicted as an accomplice. His appeal was dismissed on the basis that the defendant, being a member of the illegal organisation that carried out armed attacks on persons or property, knew when he acted as a guide that he was taking part in an attack either on the pub or on the people therein, and that the weapon or weapons to be used must have been in the car he was guiding. As Lord Parker said: 'He knew that a "military" operation was to take place. With his knowledge of the UVF's activities, he must have known that it would involve the use of a bomb or shooting or the use of incendiary devices. Knowing that, he led them there and so he aided and abetted whichever of these forms the attack took. It took the form of placing a bomb.'

Therefore, the defendant knew the essential matters constituting the offences, and he had been rightly convicted of being an accomplice to both unlawfully and maliciously doing an act with intent to cause an explosion and being in possession of a bomb.

In *Maxwell* the House of Lords went further than the Court of Appeal in *Bainbridge* and found that if a defendant, charged as an accomplice, had a range of offences within their contemplation, they were liable for whichever of those offences the principal chose to commit.

15.5.4 Accomplice liability for a different offence to the principal offender

As confirmed above, there can be no liability as an accomplice unless the actus reus of the principal offence is committed. If, therefore, a person suggests that their enemy should be killed, but the suggestion is ignored and the enemy remains alive and well, clearly there can be no liability as an accomplice to murder as the actus reus of murder is not made out. However, some offences share the same actus reus, for example, murder and manslaughter, and ss 18 and 20 of the OAPA 1861. The only difference is what is going on in the defendant's mind at the time they carry out the attack, and this determines the offence for which they are criminally liable. So, what is the position if the principal commits the actus reus with a lower or higher mens rea than that held by the accomplice? Can an accomplice be convicted of a different offence to that of the principal? As will become apparent, the accomplice's liability will be based on their own level of mens rea, whether that be higher or lower than the principal's.

Remember that if the accomplice has the same plan in mind as the defendant, they have the mens rea for the offence committed. An alternative scenario is being considered here – where the parties do the agreed act but with a different mens rea. From the outside, it would appear that both defendants have a common goal, but in fact their thought processes are not the same.

Accomplice has higher mens rea than the principal offender

In *R v Howe* [1987] 1 417, the victim was driven to an isolated area where he was killed. To assist in determining the appropriate offence to which the accused was an accomplice, Lord Mackay gave the following example. Names have been added for clarity.

> The accomplice, Ben, hands a gun to Alex but reassures him that it is loaded with blank ammunition. He then tells Alex to go and scare the victim, Connor, by firing the gun at him. In fact, the gun is loaded with live ammunition. Alex shoots Connor and kills him.

Alex is the principal offender because he is the person who killed Connor. However, he had no idea the gun contained real ammunition, so he is only guilty of unlawful act manslaughter. The reason is that he intentionally committed an unlawful and dangerous act, specifically an assault because his aim was to scare the victim, and this caused Connor's death.

In contrast, Ben is guilty as an accomplice to murder. This is because Ben knew the gun was loaded with real ammunition and intended to kill Connor. Effectively, Ben becomes liable as an accomplice to the crime that, if he himself had committed it, he would have been guilty of.

Thus, following *Howe*, the accomplice may be guilty of murder if they intended death or grievous bodily harm, or had death or grievous bodily harm within their contemplation, even if the principal is only guilty of manslaughter (the actus reus being the same). The same principle would apply to the assaults.

Examples

(1) Abu (the accomplice) has paid Presley (the principal offender) £5,000 to inflict serious injury on Tunde. Presley attacks Tunde but does not want to hurt him badly (lower mens rea). He trips him up, and as a result Tunde suffers a badly sprained right ankle. Presley pleads guilty to an offence under s 47 of the OAPA 1861.

There can be no accomplice liability unless the actus reus of the relevant offence is committed. No matter what Abu's intentions or wishes were, he cannot be liable as an accomplice to an offence under s 18 of the OAPA 1861 as the actus reus of that offence has not occurred: there has been no grievous bodily harm caused and Tunde has not suffered a wound.

Abu can only be liable as an accomplice to an offence under s 47 of the OAPA 1861. He is guilty as an accomplice here because he has encouraged the commission of the offence, by paying Presley to commit it, and had knowledge of the circumstances (the facts) which made Presley's conduct criminal. If Abu believed that Presley was going to cause really serious harm to Tunde, as per his instructions, he must necessarily have had it within his contemplation that some injury might occur and that Presley might intend or be reckless as to an assault on Tunde.

(2) Presley pushes Tunde with such force that Tunde falls and fractures his skull on the pavement. Presley has the same mens rea as above (he intends some harm). Presley pleads guilty to an offence under s 20 of the OAPA 1861, as he has caused grievous bodily harm and admits that he foresaw the risk that some harm might occur.

Abu can be convicted of liability as an accomplice under s 18 of the OAPA 1861 even though the principal has only been convicted of the less serious s 20 offence.

In this scenario, the principal offender, Presley, carried out the agreed act (of causing grievous bodily harm) but with a different mens rea to that intended by the accomplice, Abu. Presley only foresaw that some harm might occur, thus he is guilty of the lesser s 20 offence. However, there is no reason why Abu should not be liable as an accomplice to a s 18 assault. This is because the actus reus of that offence is present (grievous bodily harm has occurred), Abu has encouraged it (by paying Presley) and he has knowledge of the circumstances – not only that grievous bodily harm might occur, but also that Presley may intend to cause this.

The effect is that the Abu is an accomplice to the offence which matches his own mens rea – a s 18 assault.

Accomplice has lower mens rea than the principal offender

In *R v Gilmour* [2000] 2 Cr App R 407, the defendant drove the two principals to a house where they threw a petrol bomb. Sadly, three children died from the resulting house fire. Gilmour remained in the car throughout. Although the principals intended to cause death or grievous bodily harm and so were guilty of murder, Gilmour only believed they were going to cause criminal damage. Because of this, his conviction as an accomplice was overturned and replaced with one for manslaughter.

Example (continued)

The facts are now slightly different, and in this (revised) scenario Abu (the accomplice) now has a lower mens rea than the principal. Abu has paid Presley £5,000 to inflict some bodily harm on Tunde, unaware that Presley has a grudge against Tunde and that he intends to cause serious injury to his victim. Presley attacks Tunde so ferociously that he dies of his injuries.

Presley, the principal offender, is guilty of murder. However, although he carried out the agreed act (the assault), Presley did so with a different, higher, mens rea to Abu. Abu is an accomplice but to what? Consider this: if Abu himself had intended Tunde some bodily harm and caused death, he would be guilty of unlawful act manslaughter; thus, he becomes liable as an accomplice to the offence which matches his own mens rea, namely, manslaughter.

To conclude, the accomplice may be guilty of a more or less serious offence than the principal based on their own level of mens rea where different offences share the same actus reus. Such offences are relatively uncommon, with murder/manslaughter and ss 18/20 assaults being the most likely.

15.5.5 Liability of the accomplice where the principal goes beyond the plan

Although many crimes will proceed as planned by the participants, the situation may develop, unexpectedly or otherwise, so there is a departure by the principal offender from the original plan or joint venture. In other words, two or more people set out to commit one offence, and in the course of that joint venture the principal offender commits a different crime. Whether the accomplice remains liable for the principal's acts and what mens rea is required for them to be guilty as an accomplice to this new offence is considered below.

This question was revisited by the Supreme Court and the Privy Council in the case of *R v Jogee; Ruddock v The Queen* [2016] UKSC 8, with the judges concluding unanimously that the previously established law on accomplice liability was wrong. In this case, the principal offender (H) stabbed the victim (F) to death in the hallway of a house, using a knife which he took from the kitchen. Jogee remained outside with a bottle during the altercation but shouted to H to do something to F and, at one stage, came to the door and threatened to smash the bottle over F's head. H was convicted of murder and Jogee as an accomplice to the same offence. Jogee appealed and the Supreme Court took the opportunity to review previous authorities on this area of the law. The judges concluded that a wrong turn had been made over 30 years previously which should be corrected. Specifically, an error was made in equating foresight of the 'new' offence with intent to assist. The Court held that 'the correct approach is to treat [foresight] as evidence of intent' from which the jury can infer intention, but it clarified that foresight and intention are not synonymous.

Thus, to determine liability, the court must evaluate what was going on in the accomplice's mind at the time of the crime and whether they intended that the 'new' offence would be committed. However, just because the accomplice foresees that the 'new' offence *might* occur does not mean they intended it to; and such foresight is only evidence of intent but no more.

How does this work in practice? If the jury are satisfied that there was an agreed common purpose to commit Crime A but also that the accomplice foresaw that, in the course of committing Crime A, the principal may well commit Crime B, it may be appropriate for them to conclude that the accomplice had the necessary intent that Crime B would be committed if the occasion arose. In other words, it was within the scope of the plan to which the accomplice consented and gave their support. The judges gave two examples to illustrate this:

(a) If the defendants attack a bank where one or more of them are armed, whilst they may hope it is unnecessary to use their weapons, the jury could properly infer that the accused were intending to use the guns should they be met with resistance. Thus, if a bank employee is shot dead, the principal is liable for murder; and the accomplice is liable for the same offence.

(b) Similarly, if a group of young men face down a rival group, they may hope that the other gang will slink away, but it is a perfectly proper inference to draw that all were prepared to inflict grievous bodily harm should a fight ensue. As a consequence, the gang members may all be liable as accomplices to assault causing grievous bodily harm if this occurs.

But what if the accomplice envisages that an assault will take place, but the violence escalates and results in the victim's death? In this instance, whether the secondary party is liable as an accomplice to murder, or indeed to the death at all, will depend upon the circumstances. If the accomplice was aware that the principal carried a knife and that they had a history of violence, including for wounding, this would provide evidence of intent from which the jury could infer that the accomplice had the relevant foresight of the death. Whether they are liable as an accomplice for murder or manslaughter will depend upon their own mens rea.

Example

Delilah and Andrea decide to steal Val's wallet. Andrea distracts the victim whilst Delilah removes the wallet from Val's pocket. Both defendants are guilty of theft as it was their common purpose to steal, one as principal and the other as accomplice.

However, during the theft, Delilah departs from the scope of the plan, producing a knife and cutting the victim. Delilah is clearly the principal to the offence of robbery, but the issue is whether Andrea is liable for the consequences of the unauthorised act. Andrea's evidence is that she knew Delilah carried a knife, but that this was only for the purposes of 'self-defence' as the estate on which they live is notoriously violent; further, that despite committing numerous similar thefts, Delilah had never previously used the knife. Nevertheless, in cross-examination, Andrea accepts that carrying a knife makes it more likely such a weapon will be used. Despite this, the jury may conclude that Andrea is not guilty as an accomplice to the robbery as her foresight of what Delilah may do is evidence of intent only, and the overall weight of the evidence favours Andrea.

In *R v Jogee*, the judges did acknowledge that 'it is possible for death to be caused by some overwhelming supervening act by the perpetrator which nobody in the defendant's shoes could have contemplated might happen and is of such a character as to relegate his acts to history'. For example, A and B are football fans and are punching each other on the ground after a match when a police horse, spooked by a loud noise, steps back and tramples on B's head, killing them. In this instance, A will not be criminally responsible for B's death at all.

Set out below is an illustration of the law in practice.

Example

Gary and Patrick decide to burgle premises they believe to be empty. They break into the premises and are in the process of stealing items when they are disturbed by a security guard, Dean. A struggle ensues between the three of them when Gary produces a gun and shoots Dean dead.

Gary: Murder

The actus reus is complete as Gary produces a gun and shoots Dean, who dies from the bullet. The mens rea is also satisfied as, presumably, Gary intends to kill or at least cause Dean really serious harm. There are no defences available, so Gary is guilty of the murder of Dean.

Patrick: Accomplice liability for murder

Patrick appears to be engaged in a joint venture with Gary, as both are struggling with Dean. This is sufficient to constitute the actus reus of aiding and abetting. The mens rea is established as Patrick intends to assist as he is deliberately struggling with Dean. However, does he intend to assist or encourage the commission of the actual crime Gary commits (NCB v Gamble), *namely for Gary to murder or cause really serious harm to Dean?*

- *If Patrick did in fact intend to help Gary to kill or cause serious harm to Dean, then he will have the requisite mens rea.*
- *If Patrick knew that Gary had a gun with him and realised there was a risk that Gary might use the gun, whether or not Patrick wanted Gary to do this, then he has foresight/contemplation that Gary might intend to kill or cause serious harm. Under* R v Jogee, *although this does not equate to an intent to assist or encourage, it is something that a jury could regard as evidence of intent. In other words, the jury might infer the necessary intent to assist from their common criminal purpose which includes the subsequent killing of Dean, if the occasion for it were to arise.*
- *If Patrick had no idea that Gary had a gun and did not give any thought to the possibility of Gary killing or causing serious harm to Dean, then he will not be guilty as an accomplice to murder. However, he is still likely to be found guilty of manslaughter, because he will be liable to the extent of his own mens rea. Here he intends to assist Gary in assaulting Dean, as they both struggle with Dean, so he is will be liable for unlawful act manslaughter -* R v Gilmour.

15.5.6 Summary of the mens rea of accomplice liability

This is a complex area of the law, but the overview flowchart (below) should assist your understanding.

Figure 15.1 Mens rea of accomplice liability

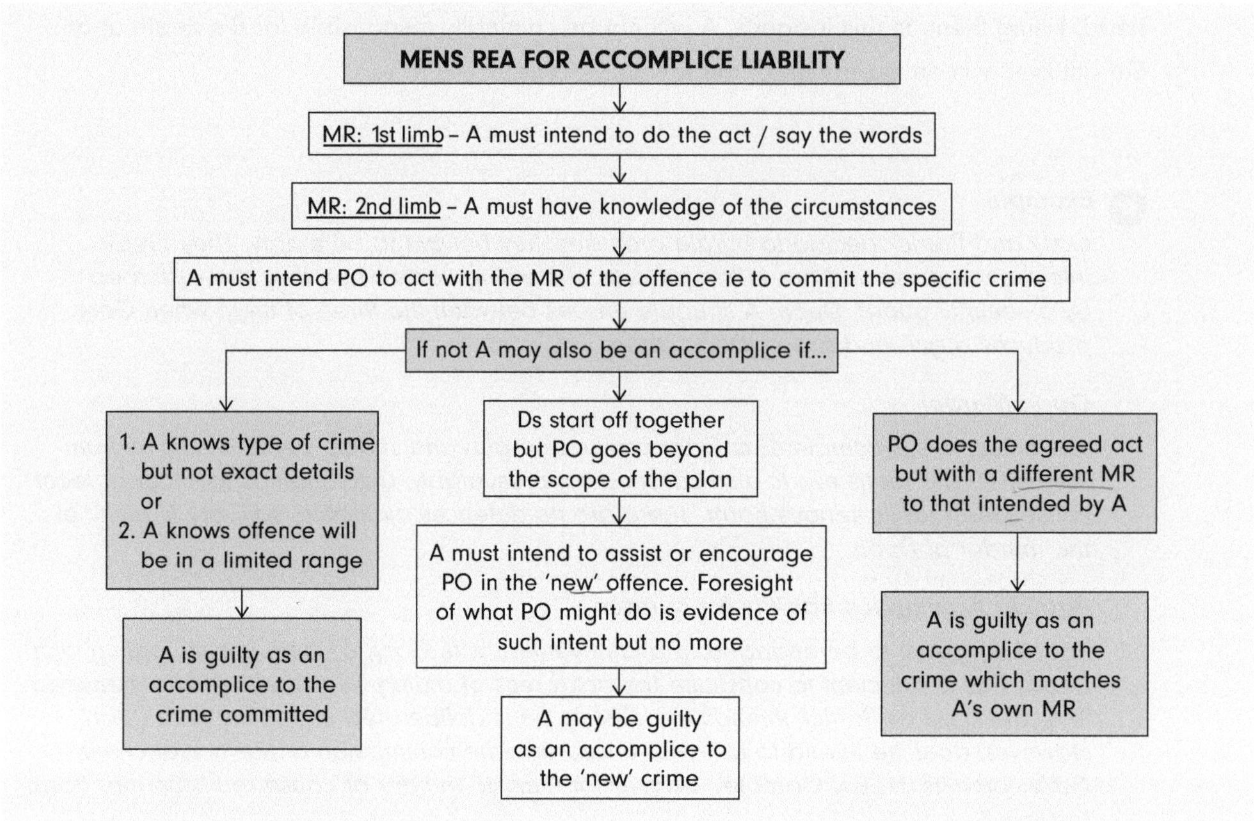

15.6 Withdrawal from the plan

Many alleged accomplices are not present at the scene of the crime. They may, for example, have given encouragement, or advice or physical assistance to the principal offender before the offence was committed. Whether such accomplices can avoid liability by claiming that, afterwards, they had a change of heart about the commission of the offence was considered in the case of *R v Becerra* (1975) 62 Cr App R 212.

In his judgment, Roskill LJ approved of and adopted the views expressed in the Canadian case of *R v Whitehouse* [1941] 1 WWR 112. The judge commented that the action necessary to 'break the chain of causation and responsibility', to ensure that the accomplice had effectively withdrawn from the plan so as to avoid liability, depended 'upon the circumstances of each case'. However, he went on to say that there was one essential element to an effective withdrawal:

> Where practicable and reasonable there must be timely communication of the intention to abandon the common purpose ... What is 'timely communication' must be determined by the facts of each case but where practicable and reasonable it ought to be such communication, verbal or otherwise, that will serve unequivocal notice upon the other party to the common unlawful cause that if he proceeds upon it he does so without the further aid and assistance of those who withdraw.

In *R v Becerra*, the words 'come on, let's go', followed by the accomplice's act of going through the window, were not sufficient to amount to an effective withdrawal. Although the court was of the opinion that more was needed, the judges did not clarify what. Roskill LJ stated there would be a stage at which nothing less than physical intervention to prevent the crime would suffice but declined to say when that was necessary.

It is apparent from this case that effective communication of the decision to withdraw is 'one essential element' but not the only element. Indeed, from the decision reached in *Becerra* it would appear that, at the scene of the crime, such communication on its own is not enough. To escape liability at this point, the defendant would need to demonstrate more than simply words and leaving the scene, and it is likely that physical intervention such as the defendant taking the knife away from the principal offender may be required.

Words alone may suffice, however, where the withdrawal takes place *before* the crime occurs. In *R v Grundy* [1977] Crim LR 543, an alleged accomplice who provided information to a principal and then spent two weeks trying to persuade him not to commit the crime was ruled by the trial judge not to have effectively withdrawn from the plan. On appeal, the Court of Appeal said that his defence of withdrawal should have been left to the jury.

To summarise, whether there has been an effective withdrawal from the plan will depend on the circumstances of the case, but, in simple terms, the more the accused has done to set up the crime, the more they are expected to do to withdraw from it. Exactly what they need to do will depend upon the stage at which the defendant attempts to withdraw and the method by which they do so.

(a) Withdrawal before the crime is committed may be established by proof that the accomplice communicated the fact of their withdrawal to the principal. However, if physical (rather than verbal) assistance has been given, communication of the fact of withdrawal may not suffice. There is no authority on the point although it appears that some physical intervention, such as warning the intended victim or notifying the police, would be needed here.

(b) Withdrawal at the scene of the crime requires something more than communication of the fact of withdrawal, although it could, however, be satisfied by physical intervention to prevent the crime being committed.

Ultimately this will be a question of fact for a jury to decide, although case law suggests that the accomplice will need to try and negate whatever they originally did to assist the principal.

Figure 15.2 Withdrawal from the plan

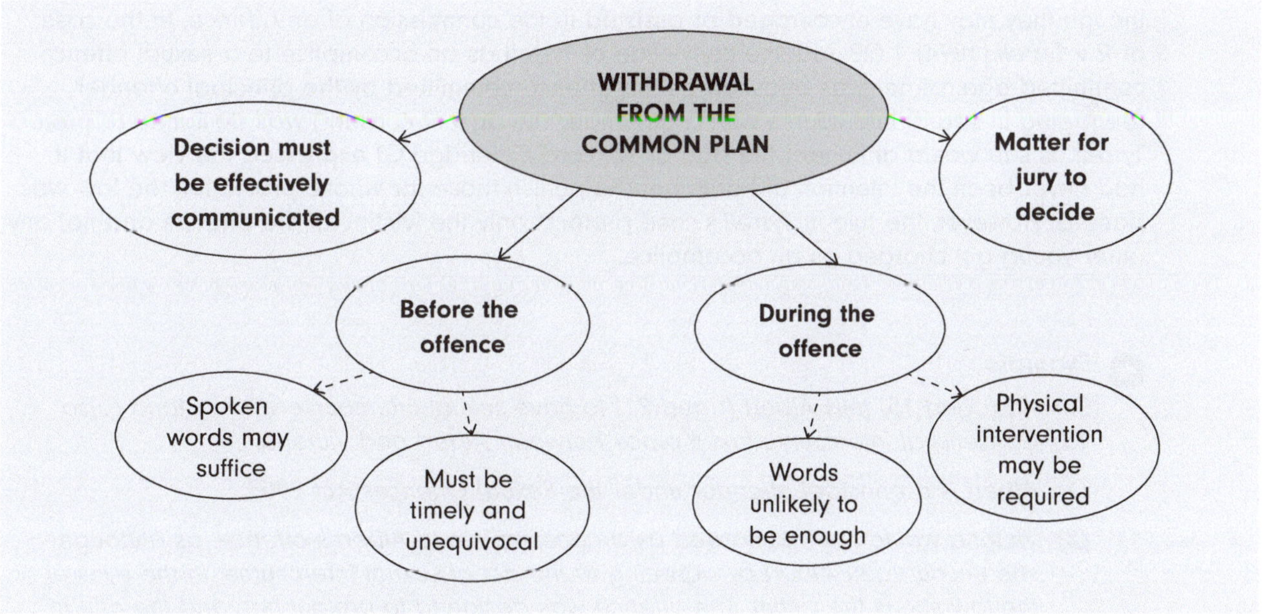

Set out below is an illustration of how the concept of effective withdrawal from the plan may apply in a practical setting.

Example

Bella is a manager at a local supermarket. She agrees with her friend, Quentin, to carry out a robbery of the premises after hours. She provides Quentin with details of when the cash will be collected and her key to give him access to the yard at the rear where the security van will be parked. She also agrees to act as look out. Bella subsequently changes her mind and tries to persuade Quentin not to go ahead, but he commits the robbery anyway. Has Bella done enough to withdraw from their joint venture?

Bella is clearly an accomplice to Quentin's robbery as she aided the offence by providing him with information and giving him a key; she would also have abetted at the time of the crime if she had acted as a lookout.

Whether Bella can argue she has successfully withdrawn is a question of fact for the jury, but they would need to know exactly what she did once she changed her mind. For it to be an effective withdrawal, Bella would at least have to try and persuade Quentin not to commit the robbery, which she did. Although this may have been enough had Bella only agreed to act as a lookout, because she gave Quentin a key and 'inside' information, it is likely that she would have to do more in this situation. This could include getting the key back from him, possibly also warning her employer (particularly as she is a manager at the supermarket) and informing the police.

15.7 Who can be an accomplice?

Anyone may face liability as an accomplice provided they are above the age of criminal responsibility, which is 10 years old or more, and fit to stand trial. Accomplices have the same general defences available to them as do principal offenders, so all the defences covered in this textbook are equally applicable to an individual charged with being an accomplice to a crime.

There are, however, some people who are unlikely to face liability as an accomplice even though they may have encouraged or assisted in the commission of an offence. In the case of *R v Tyrrell* [1894] 1 QB 710, the conviction of Tyrrell as an accomplice to a sexual offence committed against her was quashed as the offence committed by the principal offender (engaging in sexual intercourse with a girl under the age of consent) was designed to protect Tyrrell as she was a girl under the age of 16. Lord Coleridge CJ expressed the view that it had never been the intention of Parliament to punish those for whose protection the law was passed. However, the rule in *Tyrrell's* case protects only the 'victim' of the offence and not any other young girl charged as an accomplice.

Example

Serena (aged 15) tells Albert (aged 21) to have sexual intercourse with Victoria (also 15). Consensual intercourse takes place between Albert and Victoria.

(1) Albert is a principal offender under the Sexual Offences Act 2003.

(2) Victoria would not be charged as an accomplice to Albert's offence, as although she encouraged Albert by agreeing to the act of sexual intercourse, in the eyes of the law she is the victim. The offence was designed to protect her, and the rule in Tyrrell's case operates so that she is not liable as an accomplice.

(3) Serena is an accomplice to Albert's offence and is not protected by the rule in Tyrrell's case because, although she falls within the group of people for whose protection the offence was introduced (girls under 16), she is not the victim.

15.8 Summary of accomplice liability

Accomplice liability is traditionally an area that causes difficulties to those studying criminal law, and the summary below may assist in identifying the key areas.

(a) When assessing criminal liability, the starting point is to distinguish between principal offender(s), namely those who commit the substantive offence with the appropriate mens rea, and any accomplices.

(b) The actus reus of accomplice liability is established by proof that the defendant aided, abetted, counselled or procured the commission of the offence. This usually involves physical or verbal advice or assistance before or at the time of the offence. Any situation where an individual becomes involved only after the principal offence has been committed will not attract accomplice liability.

(c) To convict someone as an accomplice, mens rea must also be proved, specifically that the defendant:

  (i) intended to do the act or say the words that assisted or encouraged; and

  (ii) had all the circumstances of the principal offence within their contemplation.

(d) The accomplice need not know or intend the specific type of crime that the principal commits. It is enough if the offence is within the range of possible offences that the accomplice intentionally assisted or encouraged them to commit – *DPP for Northern Ireland v Maxwell* [1978]. Nor does the accomplice need to know the exact details of the crime – *R v Bainbridge* [1960].

(e) Depending upon the level of mens rea of the parties, the principal may be convicted of a different offence to that of the accomplice – *R v Howe* [1987] and *R v Gilmour* [2000].

(f) If the principal goes beyond the scope of the plan, the accomplice must intend to assist or encourage the principal in the commission of the 'new' offence. Foresight of what the principal might do is evidence of such intent but no more – *R v Jogee* [2016].

(g) A person can be convicted as an accomplice notwithstanding the fact that the principal is acquitted or is not charged.

(h) A person may avoid accomplice liability if they have withdrawn from the joint plan but only if this is effective. This will depend on the participation of the defendant and the stage at which they seek to withdraw.

Set out below is an activity for you to complete to check your understanding.

ACTIVITY

Consider the scenario below and discuss the liability of the defendants. Ensure that you consider principal liability first (who committed the main offences) before moving on to analyse any accomplice liability in relation to each offence.

Andrew, Benny and Cathy agree to go to the grounds of a stately home and damage a statue. Andrew, with Benny's knowledge, takes a gun with him. Cathy drives Andrew and Benny in her car and waits outside the grounds while the other two enter to damage the statue. As they are in the process of destroying it, Andrew and Benny are surprised by the gamekeeper. Andrew shoots the gamekeeper with the gun, badly wounding him. They all escape in Cathy's car.

Consider the criminal liability of Andrew, Benny and Cathy for criminal damage, assault and injuries caused by the shooting.

COMMENT

In this case, it is sensible to start with the first crime committed.

Criminal damage: Criminal Damage Act 1971, s 1(1)

Andrew and Benny are principal offenders and can be charged with the offence of criminal damage. Acting as co-principals, they damaged property belonging to another when they destroyed the statue. They clearly intended to damage property and knew it belonged to another.

Accomplice liability: Accessories and Abettors Act 1861, s 8

Cathy is an accomplice to criminal damage. She commits the actus reus of accomplice liability as she encouraged Andrew and Benny by agreeing to the crime (counselled) and assisted them by driving them to the scene of the offence (aided). With regards to the mens rea, Cathy intended to do the act or speak the words that assisted and encouraged as she deliberately (or intentionally) agreed to the commission of the crime and drove Andrew and Benny in her car. She also had all the essential elements of the offence within her contemplation because Cathy knew they were going to damage the statue.

Assault: Offences Against the Person Act 1861, ss 18 and 20

In addition to the property damage, there is a serious attack on the gamekeeper. Andrew will face liability as a principal offender in relation to this attack as he is the person who fired the gun and shot the gamekeeper. Because Andrew has seriously injured the victim, he has committed the actus reus of an offence under ss 18 or 20 as he caused grievous bodily harm.

Andrew will be guilty of an offence under s 18 if he intended to cause grievous bodily harm. There is insufficient evidence as to his state of mind, but, arguably, by firing a gun at the gamekeeper, he did intend to cause really serious harm. If Andrew lacks the mens rea for the more serious assault, he will almost certainly be guilty of an offence under s 20. The actus reus is established by the infliction of grievous bodily harm. As far as the mens rea is concerned, by shooting at the gamekeeper, Andrew must have foreseen the risk of causing some harm.

In the unlikely event that Andrew can persuade the court that he lacked the mens rea for a s 20 offence, for example that he fired the gun only to frighten the gamekeeper, he is definitely guilty of an offence under s 47 of the OAPA 1861. This is because he has assaulted the gamekeeper causing actual bodily harm and he intended to commit a simple or physical assault against him. For s 47 liability, the defendant need not have intended or foreseen the risk of any harm occurring.

Accomplice liability: Accessories and Abettors Act 1861, s 8

Benny may be an accomplice to the assault committed by Andrew as he was with Andrew when he attacked the gamekeeper. Furthermore, Benny was there by prior arrangement and could be said to have encouraged Andrew by his presence (aiding and abetting). He intended to be there and knew Andrew had a gun, so if Benny knew or foresaw the risk that Andrew might use the gun to attack anyone who interrupted their plan, he is liable as an accomplice to the assault. The only way Benny could avoid liability would be if it had been agreed, for example, that under no circumstances would the gun be used to do more than frighten anyone who interrupted, and Benny had not thought Andrew would breach that agreement. In such a case, if Andrew deliberately used it to inflict injury, it could be argued that he had gone beyond the scope of the plan and Benny would have no liability for the attack.

With regards to Cathy, she is not an accomplice to the assault as this does not appear to have been within her contemplation. There is no evidence that she knew Andrew had a gun (or indeed any weapon) with him and so she does not have the required mens rea to be an accomplice to the shooting. As Andrew (and possibly Benny) have gone beyond the scope of the plan to which Cathy was a party, she has no liability as an accomplice to the attack at all.

Index

A

J

L

M